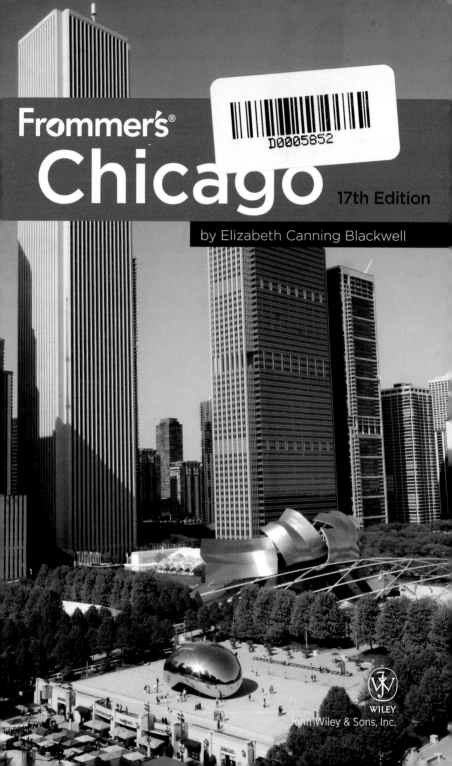

Frommer's®
Chicago

17th Edition

by Elizabeth Canning Blackwell

WILEY

John Wiley & Sons, Inc.

Published by:
John Wiley & Sons, Inc.
111 River St.
Hoboken, NJ 07030-5774

ISBN 978-1-118-01720-3 (paper); ISBN 978-1-118-16240-8 (ebk); ISBN 978-1-118-16239-2 (ebk); ISBN 978-1-118-16241-5 (ebk)

Editor: Jessica Langan-Peck and Linda Barth
Production Editor: Heather Wilcox
Cartographer: Tim Lohnes
Photo Editor: Alden Gewirtz
Cover Photo Editor: Richard Fox
Design and Layout by Vertigo Design
Graphics and Prepress by Wiley Indianapolis Composition Services
Front cover photo: The Crown Fountain, by Jaume Plensa, in Millenium Park © Richard Ellis/Alamy Images
Back cover photo: LEFT: Volleyball at North Avenue Beach © Kim Karpeles/Alamy Images MIDDLE: The Cloud Gate sculpture, in Millennium Park © JLImages/Alamy Images RIGHT: Chicago Cubs at bat © Chuck Eckert/Alamy Images

For information on our other products and services or to obtain technical support, please contact our Customer Care Department within the U.S. at 877/762-2974, outside the U.S. at 317/572-3993 or fax 317/572-4002.

Wiley also publishes its books in a variety of electronic formats. Some content that appears in print may not be available in electronic formats.

Manufactured in China

5 4 3 2 1

CONTENTS

LIST OF MAPS

ABOUT THE AUTHOR

Elizabeth Canning Blackwell began life on the East Coast, but 4 years at Northwestern University transformed her into a Midwesterner. She has worked as a writer and editor at *Encyclopedia Britannica*, Northwestern University Medical School, the *Chicago Tribune*, and *North Shore*, a lifestyle magazine for the Chicago suburbs. She has also written for national magazines on everything from planning the perfect wedding to fighting a duel. She lives just outside the city with her husband, three kids, and an extensive collection of long underwear.

HOW TO CONTACT US

In researching this book, we discovered many wonderful places—hotels, restaurants, shops, and more. We're sure you'll find others. Please tell us about them, so we can share the information with your fellow travelers in upcoming editions. If you were disappointed with a recommendation, we'd love to know that, too. Please write to:

Frommer's Chicago, 17th Edition
John Wiley & Sons, Inc. • 111 River St. • Hoboken, NJ 07030-5774
frommersfeedback@wiley.com

ADVISORY & DISCLAIMER

Travel information can change quickly and unexpectedly, and we strongly advise you to confirm important details locally before traveling, including information on visas, health and safety, traffic and transport, accommodations, shopping, and eating out. We also encourage you to stay alert while traveling and to remain aware of your surroundings. Avoid civil disturbances, and keep a close eye on cameras, purses, wallets, and other valuables.

While we have endeavored to ensure that the information contained within this guide is accurate and up-to-date at the time of publication, we make no representations or warranties with respect to the accuracy or completeness of the contents of this work and specifically disclaim all warranties, including without limitation warranties of fitness for a particular purpose. We accept no responsibility or liability for any inaccuracy or errors or omissions, or for any inconvenience, loss, damage, costs, or expenses of any nature whatsoever incurred or suffered by anyone as a result of any advice or information contained in this guide.

The inclusion of a company, organization, or website in this guide as a service provider and/or potential source of further information does not mean that we endorse them or the information they provide. Be aware that information provided through some websites may be unreliable and can change without notice. Neither the publisher nor author shall be liable for any damages arising herefrom.

FROMMER'S STAR RATINGS, ICONS & ABBREVIATIONS

Every hotel, restaurant, and attraction listing in this guide has been ranked for quality, value, service, amenities, and special features using a **star-rating system**. In country, state, and regional guides, we also rate towns and regions to help you narrow down your choices and budget your time accordingly. Hotels and restaurants are rated on a scale of zero (recommended) to three stars (exceptional). Attractions, shopping, nightlife, towns, and regions are rated according to the following scale: zero stars (recommended), one star (highly recommended), two stars (very highly recommended), and three stars (must-see).

In addition to the star-rating system, we also use seven feature icons that point you to the great deals, in-the-know advice, and unique experiences that separate travelers from tourists. Throughout the book, look for:

special finds—those places only insiders know about

fun facts—details that make travelers more informed and their trips more fun

kids—best bets for kids and advice for the whole family

special moments—those experiences that memories are made of

overrated—places or experiences not worth your time or money

insider tips—great ways to save time and money

great values—where to get the best deals

The following abbreviations are used for credit cards:

AE American Express	**DISC** Discover	**V** Visa
DC Diners Club	**MC** MasterCard	

TRAVEL RESOURCES AT FROMMERS.COM

Frommer's travel resources don't end with this guide. Frommer's website, www.frommers.com, has travel information on more than 4,000 destinations. We update features regularly, giving you access to the most current trip-planning information and the best airfare, lodging, and car-rental bargains. You can also listen to podcasts, connect with other Frommers.com members through our active-reader forums, share your travel photos, read blogs from guidebook editors and fellow travelers, and much more.

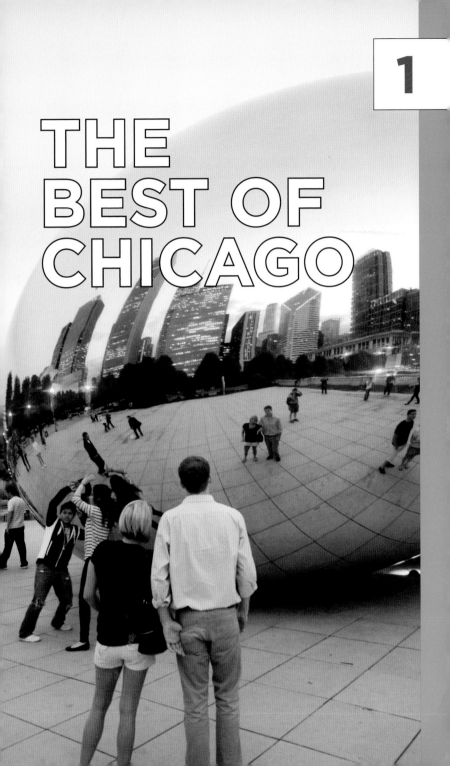

THE BEST OF CHICAGO

The quintessential American city, Chicago offers world-class culture with zero attitude. From Grant Park, the skyline is awe-inspiring, while the attractions of the nearby Museum Campus draw visitors and locals alike. Serious shoppers head for the high-fashion boutiques and multilevel malls along the Magnificent Mile, but the tree-lined streets of the Gold Coast and walking trails along the Lake Michigan shoreline offer a respite from the crowds. A rattling El ride through the heart of the Loop brings the city's booming business district up close and personal.

Things to Do For an overview of Chicago's iconic cityscape, head for the top of the **Willis (Sears) Tower** or the **John Hancock Center.** Admire *American Gothic* and other masterpieces at the **Art Institute,** then get a waterfront view of the city's past and present on a **Chicago Architecture Foundation** boat tour. Traveling with kids? Stroll **Lincoln Park Zoo** (for free!) or spend a day exploring the U505 submarine and other wonders of the **Museum of Science and Industry.**

Active Pursuits Explore the miles-long path that hugs the **Lake Michigan** coastline, then rent a bike or join a pickup volleyball game at sprawling **North Avenue Beach.** Culturally minded? Take a sculpture-spotting stroll through the **Loop** to admire works by Picasso and Miró, and walk through the wildly popular bean-shaped **"Cloud Gate."** Baseball fans can pay homage to one of the last of

ABOVE: **Chicago's iconic skyline;** PREVIOUS PAGE: **Visitors check out their reflections in Millennium Park's beanlike sculpture,** *Cloud Gate.*

the old-time ballparks, **Wrigley Field;** cheer on the Cubbies from the raucous bleachers, or check out the view from the field on a behind-the-scenes tour.

Restaurants & Dining From haute to down-home, Chicago has restaurants to suit all tastes. Chef Grant Achatz redefined fine dining at **Alinea,** while his fellow superstar chefs at **Charlie Trotter's, Moto,** and **Spiaggia** get global raves. Explore the city's ethnic diversity in **Greektown** and at Mexican mainstay **Frontera Grill.** For gut-busting satisfaction, chow down on Chicago-style deep-dish pizza at **Gino's East** or the original **Pizzeria Uno.**

Nightlife & Entertainment The **Goodman Theatre** and **Chicago Shakespeare Theatre** are the heavy-hitters of Chicago's vibrant theater scene. Classical superstars take the stage at the **Lyric Opera** and **Chicago Symphony Orchestra,** while **Second City** and **iO** continue the city's legacy of improv comedy. Catch top pop acts at venues such as the **Chicago Theatre,** or head to grungy-cool **Wicker Park** to hear up-and-coming bands.

THE most UNFORGETTABLE TRAVEL EXPERIENCES

o **Studying the Skyline:** The birthplace of the modern skyscraper, Chicago is the perfect place to learn about—and appreciate—these dramatic buildings. If you're in town for only a short time, get a quick skyscraper fix by strolling through the heart of downtown, known as the Loop, where you'll be surrounded by canyons of stone, concrete, and glass. (To get the full urban experience, visit on a weekday, when the streets are bustling.) If you have more time, take an architectural tour by foot, bus, bike, or boat. See "Sightseeing Tours," p. 224.

o **Chilling Out on the Lakefront:** It really is cooler by the lake (both meteo-rologically and metaphorically), and we Chicagoans treat the Lake Michigan

Lake Michigan is Chicagoans' personal playground during the warm months.

waterfront as our personal playground. Miles of parkland hug the shoreline; walk to Monroe Harbor for picture-perfect views of the city or join active Lincoln Park singles for biking or jogging farther north. For an even better look at the city, get out on the water. At Navy Pier, you can board a vessel that's just your speed, from a powerboat to a tall-masted schooner. See "Staying Active," p. 231.

Ride the El for a unique perspective on Chicago's high-rises.

○ **Riding the Rails:** Find out why the Loop is so named by hopping a Brown Line elevated train (or "the El," for short). Watch the city unfold as the train crosses the Chicago River and screeches past downtown high-rises. Half the fun is peeping into the windows of offices and homes as you speed by. (Don't feel guilty—we all do it!) See "Getting Around," p. 343, and "Sightseeing Tours," p. 224.

○ **Escaping Downtown:** Local politicians like to refer to Chicago as "a city of neighborhoods"—and, in this case, they're telling the truth. You won't really experience Chicago unless you leave downtown and explore some residential areas, whether it's the historic wood-framed homes in Old Town or the eclectic boutiques of Wicker Park. See "Neighborhoods in Brief," p. 48.

THE best SPLURGE HOTELS

○ **The Elysian** (11 E. Walton St.; www.elysianhotels.com; ✆ 800/500-8511): The Parisian-style exterior exudes Old World glamour, but inside, the Elysian is all about sleek, streamlined luxury. The guest rooms are some of the biggest in town, and include bonuses such as fireplaces and furnished terraces. The Gold Coast location—removed from the traffic of downtown—adds to the feeling of an urban retreat. See p. 85.

○ **Park Hyatt** (800 N. Michigan Ave.; www.parkchicago.hyatt.com; ✆ 800/233-1234): If the thought of overstuffed couches and thick brocade curtains makes you wince, this is the hotel for you. With its focus on modern design and clean lines, the Park Hyatt feels like one of those cool urban spaces featured in *Architectural Digest*. The coolest feature? Moveable bathroom walls that allow you to soak in the view while you lounge in the tub. See p. 74.

○ **Peninsula** (108 E. Superior St.; www.chicago.peninsula.com; ✆ 866/288-8889): Inspired by the elegance of 1920s Shanghai and Hong Kong, the Chicago outpost of this Asian chain is a seamless blend of classic and modern. The grand public spaces may be a throwback to the past, but the hotel's amenities are ultramodern. The top-notch gym, spa, and indoor swimming pool (filled with natural light) make the Peninsula a must for fitness fanatics. See p. 74.

o **The Ritz-Carlton Chicago** (160 E. Pearson St.; www.fourseasons. com/chicagorc; ✆800/621-6906): Appropriately enough in this skyscraper-packed city, some of the best hotels perch far above the sidewalk. Located above the Water Tower Place shopping center, the Ritz has one of the most welcoming lobbies in town, with light streaming through the windows, masses of fresh flowers, and bird's-eye views of the city. The elegant guest rooms are decorated in Art Deco–inspired shades of silver, black, and gold, and the staff prides itself on granting every wish. See p. 74.

The Park Hyatt.

o **Trump International Hotel & Tower** (401 N. Wabash Ave.; www.trump chicagohotel.com; ✆877/458-7867): Want to make-believe you've got your own *pied-à-terre* in the heart of downtown? This is the place to live out your fantasy—the contemporary-cool rooms are actually studio apartments with full kitchens, plenty of space to lounge, and killer views of the skyline. See p. 81.

THE best MODERATELY PRICED HOTELS

o **Hotel Allegro Chicago** (171 W. Randolph St.; www.allegrochicago.com; ✆800/643-1500): Its prime Loop location and stylish decor make the Allegro an appealing home base for visitors in search of an urban getaway. Rooms are compact but cheerful, and you can mingle with other guests at the complimentary evening wine reception in the lobby. See p. 72.

o **Hampton Inn & Suites Chicago Downtown** (33 W. Illinois St.; www.hampton inn.com; ✆800/HAMPTON [426-7866]): Located in a busy neighborhood full of restaurants and nightlife, the Hampton Inn feels more expensive than it is. The rooms have an upscale urban look, and the indoor pool is a draw for families. The hotel's hot breakfast buffet, included in the room rates and served in an attractive second-floor lounge, puts the standard coffee-and-doughnut spread at other motels to shame. See p. 85.

o **Red Roof Inn** (162 E. Ontario St.; www.redroof-chicago-downtown.com; ✆800/733-7663): This high-rise version of the roadside motel is your best bet for the cheapest rates downtown. The rooms don't have much in the way of style (or natural light), and the bathrooms, though spotless, are a little cramped, but it fits the bill if you want a central location and plan on using your hotel as a place to sleep rather than hang out. See p. 80.

o **Majestic Hotel** (528 W. Brompton St.; www.cityinns.com; ℂ 800/727-5108): A bit off the beaten path, this neighborhood hotel is tucked away on a residential street just a short walk from Wrigley Field and the lakefront. You won't find lots of fancy amenities, but the atmosphere here has the personal touch of a B&B. Rates include continental breakfast and afternoon tea in the lobby. See p. 88.

> ### Impressions
>
> *We were on one of the most glamorous corners of Chicago. I dwelt on the setting. The lakeshore view was stupendous. I couldn't see it but I knew it well and felt its effect—the shining road beside the shining gold vacancy of Lake Michigan. Man had overcome the emptiness of this land. But the emptiness had given him a few good licks in return.*
> —**Saul Bellow, *Humboldt's Gift*, 1975**

THE most UNFORGETTABLE DINING EXPERIENCES

o **Charlie Trotter's** (816 W. Armitage Ave.; ℂ 773/248-6228): Charlie Trotter is the city's original celebrity chef, and his intimate restaurant, inside a town house, is a must for foodie visitors. The formula may be rigid (tasting menus only), but the food is anything but: fresh-as-can-be ingredients in dazzling combinations. The service lives up to Trotter's legendary perfectionism; the chef himself has been known to come out of the kitchen and ask diners why they didn't finish a certain dish. See p. 131.

o **Alinea** (1723 N. Halsted St.; ℂ 312/867-0110): Chef Grant Achatz has been at the forefront of the molecular gastronomy movement, and foodies make pilgrimages from around the world to eat at his serene Chicago restaurant. Each course of the ever-changing prix-fixe menu showcases Achatz's creativity, whether it's duck served on a scented "pillow" of juniper or a complete reinvention of wine and cheese (frozen grape juice rolled in grated bleu cheese

Globe artichoke soup at Charlie Trotter's.

Live large at Gibsons Bar & Steakhouse.

Georges Seurat's *A Sunday on the Grande Jatte* is one of the Art Institute's most notable works.

and served with red wine gelée). An added bonus: Service that's friendly, not snobby. See p. 131.

o **Gibsons Bar & Steakhouse** (1028 N. Rush St.; ℭ **312/266-8999**): Chicago has no shortage of great steakhouses, but Gibsons has a great scene, too—a mix of moneyed Gold Coast singles, expense-account-fueled business travelers, and the occasional celebrity. This is the kind of place to live large (literally). The portions are enormous, so you're encouraged to share, which only adds to the party atmosphere. See p. 109.

o **foodlife** (Water Tower Place, 835 N. Michigan Ave.; ℭ **312/335-3663**): Leaps and bounds beyond the standard mall food court, foodlife offers a wide range of nonchain food stations at affordable prices, making it a top pick for an affordable, family-friendly meal downtown. Get everything from Asian noodles and vegetarian fare to more standard options such as pizza and burgers. See p. 118.

o **The Italian Village** (71 W. Monroe St.; ℭ **312/332-7005**): The old-school fettuccine alfredo won't win any culinary awards, but eating at this Chicago landmark is like taking a trip back in time, from the so-tacky-they're-cool twinkling stars on the ceiling to the vintage waiters (some of whom look like they've been working here since the place opened in 1927). See p. 100.

THE best MUSEUMS

o **Art Institute of Chicago** (111 S. Michigan Ave.; ℭ **312/443-3600**): A must-see for art lovers, the Art Institute manages to combine blockbuster exhibits with smaller, uncrowded spaces for private meditation. Internationally known for its French Impressionist collection, the Art Institute can also transport you to Renaissance Italy, ancient China, or the world of the Old Masters. The dazzling, light-filled Modern Wing, added in 2009, has also given the museum's 20th-century modern art collection the setting it deserves. See p. 154.

○ **Field Museum of Natural History** (Roosevelt Rd. and Lake Shore Dr.; ✆312/922-9410): The grand neoclassical entrance hall will make you feel as if you've entered somewhere important, a sense of drama only enhanced by the towering figure of Sue, the largest *Tyrannosaurus rex* skeleton ever uncovered. The Field can easily entertain for an entire day. Exhibits include ancient Egyptian mummies, a full-size Maori Meeting House, and stuffed figures of the notorious man-eating lions of Tsavo. See p. 173.

○ **John G. Shedd Aquarium** (1200 S. Lake Shore Dr.; ✆312/939-2438): Sure, you'll find plenty of tanks filled with exotic fish, but the Shedd is also home to some wonderful large-scale re-creations of natural habitats. Stroll through Wild Reef, and you'll see sharks swim overhead. The lovely Oceanarium, where you can watch a dolphin show, features floor-to-ceiling windows; you'll feel as if you're sitting outdoors, even on the chilliest Chicago day. See p. 175.

○ **Museum of Science and Industry** (57th St. and Lake Shore Dr.; ✆800/468-6674): Families can easily spend an entire day at this sprawling museum and still not see everything. Although the exhibits promote scientific knowledge, most have an interactive element that keeps kids engaged. But it's not all computers and technology. Some of the classic exhibits—the underground re-creation of the coal mine and the World War II German U-boat—have been drawing visitors for generations. See p. 193.

○ **Frank Lloyd Wright Home and Studio** (951 Chicago Ave., Oak Park; ✆708/848-1976): The Midwest's greatest architect started out in the Chicago suburb of Oak Park, and his house—now a museum with guided tours—gives a firsthand look at how his ideas developed and influenced American architecture. The surrounding neighborhood, where Wright's Prairie-style homes sit side by side with rambling Victorian villas, is an eye-opening lesson in architectural history. See p. 210.

Kid will be fascinated by the marine life at the John G. Shedd Aquarium.

THE best NIGHTLIFE EXPERIENCES

o **Getting the Blues:** Here, in the world capital of the blues, you've got your pick of places to feel them, from the touristy but lively atmosphere of Kingston Mines in Lincoln Park, where musicians perform continuously on two stages, to the roadhouse feel of Buddy Guy's Legends, where musicians in town while on tour have been known to play impromptu sets. See "The Music Scene," p. 308.

o **Taking in a Show:** The stage lights rarely go dark on one of the country's busiest theater scenes. Chicago is home to a downtown Broadway-style district anchored

The Green Mill.

by beautifully restored historic theaters, the nationally known Goodman Theatre, and the city's resident Shakespeare troupe. Beyond downtown, you'll find a number of innovative independent companies, where future stars get their big breaks and the pure love of theater makes up for the low budgets. See "The Performing Arts," p. 291.

o **Experiencing Cool Jazz at the Green Mill:** This atmospheric Uptown jazz club is the place to go to soak up smooth sounds from some of the hottest up-and-coming performers on the jazz scene, while the club itself is a living museum of 1930s Chicago. The Sunday night "Poetry Slam" is a big crowd-pleaser. See p. 309.

o **Watching Improv Come Alive:** Chicago is a comedy breeding ground, having launched the careers of John Belushi, Bill Murray, Mike Myers, and Tina Fey, through improv hot spots such as Second City and iO. The shows may soar or crash, but you just might catch one of comedy's newest stars. See p. 305.

THE best PLACES TO HANG WITH THE LOCALS

o **Shopping the Town:** Michigan Avenue is often touted as a shopper's paradise, thanks to its lineup of big-name designer boutiques and multilevel high-end shopping malls. But that's all stuff you can find in any other big city. For more distinctive items, head to Chicago's residential districts, where trendy independent clothing boutiques sit next to eclectic home design stores filled with one-of-a-kind treasures. The home decor shops along Armitage Avenue

Shopping at Clever Alice, one of Wicker Park's many unique shops.

It's a Chicago tradition to play hooky and catch a game at Wrigley Field.

cater to stylish young families with plenty of spending money, while Wicker Park and Bucktown attract edgy fashionistas with a range of funky clothing shops. Southport Avenue (near Wrigley Field) and West Division Street (south of Wicker Park) are the newest cool shopping meccas—with no nametag-wearing conventioneers in sight. See chapter 8.

o **Soaking Up Sun at Wrigley Field:** It's a Chicago tradition to play hooky for an afternoon, sit in the bleachers at this historic baseball park, and watch the Cubbies try to hit 'em onto Waveland Avenue. Despite being perennial losers, the Cubs sell out almost every game; your best bet is to buy tickets for a weekday afternoon (although you'll often find season ticket holders selling seats at face value in front of Wrigley right before a game). Even if you can't get in, you can still soak in the atmosphere at one of the neighborhood's many watering holes. See "In the Grandstand: Watching Chicago's Athletic Events," p. 236.

o **Playing in the Sand:** If you're staying at a downtown hotel, you can hit the sands of Chicago's urban beaches almost as quickly as your elevator gets you to the lobby. Oak Street Beach (at Michigan Ave. and Lake Shore Dr.) is mostly for posing. North Avenue Beach, a little farther north along the lakefront path, is home to weekend volleyball games, family beach outings, and a whole lot of eye candy. You probably won't do any swimming (even in the middle of summer, the water's frigid), but either beach makes a great place to hang out with a picnic and a book on a warm afternoon. See "Beaches," p. 231.

o **Raising a Glass (or a Coffee Cup):** Chicago has its share of trendy lounges that serve overpriced specialty martinis, but the heart of the city's nightlife remains the neighborhood taverns. These are the places you can soak in a convivial atmosphere without attitude or self-consciously flashy decor, but also have a conversation without being drowned out by the hoots and hollers of drunken frat boys (although there are plenty of bars catering to that particular demographic). Favorite local hangouts include **Celtic Crossings** (751 N. Clark St.; ℂ 312/337-1005) in River North, **Miller's Pub** (134 S. Wabash Ave.; ℂ 312/645-5377) in the Loop, and the **Map Room** (1949 N. Hoyne Ave.; ℂ 773/252-7636) in Bucktown. If you prefer to keep things nonalcoholic, grab coffee and dessert at **Third Coast** (1260 N. Dearborn St.; ℂ 312/649-0730), on the Gold Coast, or **Uncommon Ground** (1214 W. Grace St.; ℂ 773/929-3680) in Wrigleyville. See chapter 9.

Soak in the convivial atmosphere at Celtic Crossings, a favorite local hangout.

THE best FREE (OR ALMOST FREE) THINGS TO DO

○ **Exploring Millennium Park:** This downtown park, carved out of the northwest corner of Grant Park, is one of the city's best spots for strolling, hanging out, and people-watching. (**Bonus:** It's an easy walk from downtown hotels.) While the Pritzker Music Pavilion, designed by Frank Gehry, is the highest-profile attraction, the park's two main sculptures have quickly become local favorites. *Cloud Gate,* by British sculptor Anish Kapoor, looks like a giant silver kidney bean; watch your reflection bend and distort as you walk around and underneath. The *Crown Fountain,* designed by Spanish sculptor Jaume Plensa, is framed by two giant video screens that project faces of ordinary Chicagoans. It looks a little creepy at first, but watch the kids splashing in the shallow water and you'll soon realize that this is public art at its best. See p. 158.

○ **Bonding with the Animals at Lincoln Park Zoo:** You have no excuse not to visit: Lincoln Park Zoo is open 365 days a year and—astonishingly—remains completely free, despite many recent upgrades. Occupying a prime spot in Lincoln Park close to the lakefront, the zoo is small enough to explore in an afternoon and varied enough to make you feel as though you've traveled around the world. For families, this is a don't-miss stop. See p. 186.

○ **Listening to Music Under the Stars:** Summer is prime time for live music—and often you won't have to pay a dime. The Grant Park Music Festival presents free classical concerts from June through August in Millennium Park. A few blocks south, you'll find the outdoor dance floor that's home to Chicago SummerDance, where you can learn new dance moves and swing to a variety of live acts on Thursday through Sunday nights. The summer also brings a range of large-scale music festivals—from Blues Fest to a

Blues Fest in Grant Park.

rock-'n'-roll-themed Fourth of July concert—but the Grant Park classical concerts are considerably less crowded (and far more civilized). See "Classical Music," p. 294.

o **Discovering Future Masterpieces:** Chicago's vibrant contemporary art scene is divided between two different neighborhoods. The original, River North, is still home to many of the city's best-known galleries and is within walking distance from downtown hotels. The West Loop houses newer galleries—with, overall, a younger perspective—in freshly renovated lofts. You don't need to be a serious collector to browse; just bring an open mind. See "Art Galleries," p. 270.

Millennium Park's *Crown Fountain.*

THE best ONE-OF-A-KIND SHOPS

o **ArchiCenter Shop** (224 S. Michigan Ave.; ☏ **312/922-3432**): Looking for unique, well-designed souvenirs? This store, run by the Chicago Architecture Foundation, should be your first stop. You'll find Frank Lloyd Wright bookmarks, puzzles of the Chicago skyline, picture frames with patterns designed by famed local architect Louis Sullivan, and a great selection of Chicago history books. See p. 286.

Uncle Fun is chock-full of retro dime-store gadgets.

o **Uncle Fun** (1338 W. Belmont Ave.; ☎ 773/477-8223): No other place lives up to its name like Uncle Fun, one of the quirkiest shops in town. This old-fashioned storefront is crammed with a random assortment of classic dime-store gadgets (hand buzzers, Pez dispensers, rubber chickens), along with an equally eclectic selection of retro bargain-bin items. (Where else can you pick up a Mr. T keychain?) See p. 278.

o **The T-Shirt Deli** (1739 N. Damen Ave.; ☎ 773/276-6266): Got a soft spot for those cheesy 1970s "Foxy Lady" T-shirts? Head to the T-Shirt Deli, where the staff will customize shirts while you wait. Come up with your own message, or browse the hundreds of in-stock iron-on decals (everything from Gary Coleman to Hello Kitty). And just like at a real deli, your purchase is wrapped in white paper and served with a bag of potato chips. See p. 278.

o **Architectural Artifacts, Inc.** (4325 N. Ravenswood Ave.; ☎ 773/348-0622): This vast warehouse of material salvaged from historic buildings is a home renovator's dream. Although it's far off the usual tourist route, design buffs will find it well worth the trip—the enormous inventory includes fireplace mantels, stained glass windows, and

> **Impressions**
>
> *He glances at the new Civic Center, a tower of russet steel and glass, fronted by a gracious plaza with a fountain and a genuine Picasso-designed metalwork sculpture almost fifty feet high. He put it all there, the Civic Center, the plaza, the Picasso. And the judges and county officials who work in the Civic Center, he put most of them there, too.*
>
> *Wherever he looks as he marches, there are new skyscrapers up or going up. The city has become an architect's delight, except when the architects see the great Louis Sullivan's landmark buildings being ripped down for parking garages or allowed to degenerate into slums.*
>
> —Mike Royko, *Boss: Richard J. Daley of Chicago,* 1971

garden sculptures. The owners display pieces of particular historic value in an attached museum. See p. 269.

THE best CHICAGO WEBSITES

Picasso's *Untitled*, in Daley Plaza.

- **Metromix** (www.chicago.metromix.com): Operated by the *Chicago Tribune,* this site features expanded versions of the newspaper's entertainment and restaurant coverage. It's a good place to check reviews and get an early look at new bars and nightclubs.

- **The Chicago Reader** (www.chicagoreader.com): The site of the city's alternative weekly paper is the place to find extensive coverage of the local music scene and reviews of smaller theater productions.

- **Time Out Chicago** (http://chicago.timeout.com): The online version of the city's weekly entertainment magazine covers food, music, the art scene, and shopping with a slightly irreverent attitude. Scroll through the site's extensive event listings, and you'll find more than enough cool happenings to keep you busy while you're here.

- **Chicago Office of Tourism** (www.explorechicago.org): This local government site gives a good overview of festivals, parades, and other upcoming events in town.

- **Chicagoist** (www.chicagoist.com): Want to see what issues have Chicagoans riled up? Check out this sounding board for local news (an offshoot of the New York–centric site Gothamist.com), which covers everything from government corruption scandals to the latest celebrity sightings. You'll find a similar roundup of news, local gossip, and opinion pieces at the online magazine ***Gapers Block*** (www.gapersblock.com).

- **LTH Forum** (www.lthforum.com/bb/index.php): Local foodies come to this bulletin board to get the scoop on hot new restaurant openings. The site also keeps a running list of "Great Neighborhood Restaurants," if you're looking for places with character rather than buzz.

- **League of Chicago Theatres** (www.chicagoplays.com): If you're planning to catch a show while in town, visit this comprehensive theater site, where you can search specific dates to see what's playing.

CHICAGO
IN DEPTH

Chicago has spent the last few years in the national media spotlight, for reasons both inspiring and embarrassing. On the one hand, it's the adopted hometown of President Barack Obama, the place he got his start in politics and where he still maintains his Hyde Park home. His victory rally in downtown's Grant Park signaled Chicago's vitality and influence to the whole world (many of his top presidential advisors were local business and philanthropic leaders before they moved to Washington).

Unfortunately, Chicago must also lay claim to politicians such as former Illinois state governor Rod Blagojevich. "Blago," a product of the city's shady Democratic political machine, stunned even cynical Chicagoans with his blatant moneygrubbing and attempts to sell Obama's former Senate seat to the highest bidder. Obama's talk about a new era of hope in politics turned out to be short-lived, with his ties to Chicago wheeler-dealers a liability. Blagojevich proved that the old ways of doing business aren't so easily erased.

It's easy to be cynical about Chicago politics—the miracle is that such cynicism doesn't pervade the way Chicagoans feel about their city. We're proud of our gorgeous skyline and love nothing better than hearing visitors compare our hometown favorably to New York. (You'll make friends for life if you tell us you'd rather live here than the Big Apple.) As the retail, financial, and legal center of the Midwest, Chicago has a thriving, diverse business community and an active arts scene, attracting everyone from thrifty wannabe hipsters to ambitious future CEOs. The one thing they've got in common? A certain humility that comes with living in the Second City. Being down-to-earth is a highly rated local virtue.

In this chapter, you'll get an overview of the issues facing the city today, as well as a quick primer on Chicago's history. Because architecture plays such an important role in the look of the city—and so many influential architects have worked here—you'll also find a guide to the major styles of buildings you'll pass by during your visit. But you won't get a full sense of the city's spirit unless you understand the city's role in popular culture, too. Chicago

President Obama tossing the first pitch at a Cubs game.

PREVIOUS PAGE: **The Chicago River has played a major role in the history of the city.**

has been home to many great writers and has served as a setting for dozens of films, so this chapter includes a section on recommended books and movies. Check out a few before your trip to put you in a Chicago state of mind.

CHICAGO TODAY

Like other major American cities, Chicago has benefited from a renewed interest in urban living over the past 2 decades, as former suburbanites flock to luxury high-rise condos downtown. Where the Loop used to shut down after dark and on weekends, it's now buzzing all week long, with a busy theater district and lively restaurants. Massive new condo buildings have sprung up along the lakefront south of the Loop, while the West Loop—once a no-man's-land of industrial buildings—has become another hot residential neighborhood.

In many ways, this building boom has erased the physical legacy of Chicago's past. The stockyards that built the city's fortune have disappeared; the industrial factories that pumped smoke into the sky south of the city now sit vacant. While no one misses the stench of the stockyards or the pollution that came with being an industrial center, the city's character has become muted along the way. Living here no longer requires the toughness that was once a hallmark of the native Chicagoan.

And yet a certain brashness remains. While some people may still have a "Second City" chip on their shoulders, we've gotten more confident about our ability to compete with New York or Los Angeles. We know our museums, restaurants, and entertainment options are as good as any other city's in the country; we just wish everyone else knew it, too.

Relatively affordable compared to New York, Chicago is a popular post-college destination for ambitious young people from throughout the Midwest. The city also draws immigrants from other countries (as it has for more than 100 years). Hispanics (mostly of Mexican origin) now make up about one-third of the city's population. Immigration from Eastern Europe is also common, especially from countries such as Poland, Russia, and Romania. This constant influx of new blood keeps the city vibrant.

This is not to say the city doesn't have problems. With roughly 2.8 million people total, Chicago has nearly equal numbers of black and white residents—a rarity among today's urban areas—but the residential districts continue to be some of the most segregated in the country. The South Side is overwhelmingly black; the North Side remains mostly white. As in other major cities, the public school system seems to constantly teeter on the edge of disaster. While fine schools are scattered throughout the city, many families are forced to send their children to substandard local schools with high dropout rates.

However, the waves of gentrification sweeping the city have transformed many neighborhoods for the better. For years, the city's public housing was a particular disgrace, epitomized by decrepit 1960s high-rises that had degenerated into isolated bastions of violence and hopelessness. The largest and worst complexes have been torn down during the last decade, replaced with low-rise, mixed-income housing. Some streets I used to avoid after dark are now lined with brand-new supermarkets, parks, and—inevitably—a Starbucks or two.

The city's crime problem has been more intractable. Despite a murder rate that's one of the highest in the country, Chicago doesn't strike visitors as a dangerous place, because most of the violence is contained within neighborhoods where gangs congregate and tourists rarely go. But gang-instigated shootings are still shockingly common on the South Side, and children are often innocent victims caught in the crossfire. It's something we've gotten far too blasé about, and it continues to be a blot on Chicago's reputation.

Another continuing embarrassment is our local politics. Time and again, our aldermen and other city officials reward our cynicism with yet another scandal involving insider payoffs and corrupt city contracts. For more than 20 years under Mayor Richard M. Daley (himself the son of another longtime mayor, Richard J. Daley), Chicagoans accepted a certain level of shady behavior—after all, there was no denying that the city blossomed under the Daleys' leadership.

Rahm Emanuel, Chicago's mayor.

When the younger Daley stepped aside in the spring of 2011, his potential successors were quick to serve up the usual campaign promises about wiping out corruption. Now we're left wondering: Is it possible? Our newest mayor, Rahm Emanuel, is no stranger to political fights: He worked in the Clinton White House, served as a member of the U.S. House of Representatives, and survived 2 years as President Obama's chief of staff. It will be interesting to see how his take-no-prisoners style goes down with the complacent, business-as-usual Chicago City Council. Another test of his leadership will come as he attempts to reform the city's struggling public-school system. Emanuel, a dance- and theater-lover, has also pledged his strong support to the city's sometimes cash-strapped cultural institutions, which is good news for residents and visitors alike. In spite of the local politicians, we Chicagoans passionately defend and boast about our city. Ever since the stockyards were our main source of wealth, we've become masters of overlooking the unsavory. As long as Chicago thrives, we don't seem to really care how it happens.

LOOKING BACK: CHICAGO HISTORY

First Settlement

Chicago owes its existence to its strategic position: The patch of land where it stands straddles a key point along an inland water route linking Canada to the Gulf of Mexico.

In 1673, Jacques Marquette, a French Jesuit missionary, and Louis Joliet, an explorer, found a short portage between two critically placed rivers, one connected to the Mississippi, and the other (via the Chicago River) to Lake Michigan. Although Native Americans had blazed this trail centuries beforehand, its discovery by the French was the first step in Chicago's founding—although no permanent settlement was built there for another 100 years.

> Speaking of Chicago . . .
>
> *Chicago is a facade of skyscrapers facing a lake, and behind the facade every type of dubiousness.*
>
> **–E. M. Forster, British author**

By then, the British controlled the territory, having defeated the French over 70 years of intermittent warfare. After the Revolutionary War, the land around the mouth of the Chicago River passed to the United States. The Native American inhabitants, however, wouldn't give up their land without a fight, which is why the first building erected here—between 1803 and 1808—was the military outpost Fort Dearborn. (It sat on the south side of what is now the Michigan Avenue Bridge, on the site of the current McCormick Tribune Bridgehouse & Chicago River Museum; p. 164.) Skirmishes with local Native American tribes continued until 1832. A year later, the settlement of 300-plus inhabitants was officially incorporated under the name "Chicago." (A French version of a Native American word believed to mean "wild onion," it may also have referred to the equally non-aromatic local skunks.)

Gateway to the West

Land speculation began immediately, and Chicago was carved piecemeal and sold off to finance the Illinois and Michigan Canal, which eliminated the narrow land portage and fulfilled the long-standing vision of connecting the two great waterways. Commercial activity quickly followed. Chicago grew in size and wealth, shipping grain and livestock to the Eastern markets and lumber to the prairies of the West. Ironically, by the time the Illinois and Michigan Canal was completed in 1848, the railroad had arrived, and the water route that gave Chicago its raison d'être was rapidly becoming obsolete. Boxcars, not boats, became the principal mode of transportation throughout the region. The combination of the railroad, the emergence of local manufacturing, and, later, the Civil War, caused Chicago to grow wildly.

The most revolutionary product of the era sprang from the mind of Chicago inventor Cyrus McCormick, whose reaper filled in for the farmhands who had been sent off to the nation's battlefields. Local merchants not only thrived on the contraband trade in cotton during the war, but also secured lucrative contracts from the federal government to provide the army with tents, uniforms, saddles, harnesses, lumber, bread, and meat. By 1870, Chicago's population had grown to 300,000, a thousand times greater than its original population, in just 37 years since incorporation.

The Great Fire

A year later, the city lay in ashes. The Great Chicago Fire of 1871 began on the southwest side of the city on October 8. Legend places its exact origin in the O'Leary shed on DeKoven Street, although most historians have exonerated the poor cow that supposedly started the blaze by kicking over a lantern. The fire jumped the river and continued north through the night and the following day, fizzling out only when it started to rain. The fire took 300 lives—a relatively low number, considering its size—but destroyed 18,000 buildings and left 90,000 people homeless.

The city began to rebuild as soon as the rubble was cleared. By 1873, the city's downtown business and financial district was up and running again, and 2 decades later Chicago had sufficiently recovered to stage the 1893 World's Columbian Exposition commemorating the 400th anniversary of the discovery of America. The Exposition was, in effect, Chicago's grand coming-out party, a chance to show millions of visitors that this was a modern, progressive city. Chicago already had a reputation as a brash business center; now it proved it could also be beautiful. *Harper's Magazine* described the "White City," the collection of formal buildings constructed for the Exposition, as "a Venus that arose from Lake Michigan."

Looking Back at Chicago

6 **The Great Chicago Fire** of 1871 starts in the barn behind the O'Leary house—although Mrs. O'Leary's cow was never proven as the culprit. What's on the site today? The Chicago Fire Depart- ment's training academy.

7 Demonstrators and Chicago police clash in front of the Chicago Hilton during the **1968 Democratic Convention**. Reflecting on the events a few days later, Mayor Richard J. Daley utters the unfortunate malapropism: "The policeman isn't there to create disorder, the policeman is there to preserve disorder."

1 Seven men are shot in a garage on North Clark Street in what becomes known as the **St. Valentine's Day Massacre**, in 1929. Al Capone—suspected of masterminding the killings—becomes an international celebrity, much to the dismay of embarrassed Chicagoans.

2 **1959** was a big year for Chicago: the improv-comedy troupe **Second City** sets up on Wells Street, and a few blocks away, Hugh Hefner establishes the original **Playboy Mansion** in the swanky Gold Coast neigh- borhood (a sign over the doorbell reads: "If You Don't Swing, Don't Ring"). Hef moves to California in the 1970s, and Chicago—unfortunately—becomes considerably less swingin'.

3 **Fort Dearborn**, the first permanent settlement in what would become Chicago, is completed in 1803. Although the site occupies prime real estate today, at the time it over-looked swampy marshland and was filled with the not-so-fragrant scent of wild onions.

Lake Michigan

Olive Park

LINCOLN PARK

Lincoln Park Zoo

1929

1959

OLD TOWN

GOLD COAST

Oak Street Beach

John Hancock Center

Newberry Library

Washington Square Park

Stanton Park

Seward Park

Chicago River

N. Branch Chicago River

1/4 mi
0.25 km

M Subway/El stop

N. Lake Shore Dr.
N. Astor St.
N. State Pkwy.
N. Dearborn St.
N. Clark St.
N. LaSalle St.
N. Wells St.
N. Park Ave.
N. Sedgwick St.
N. Hudson Ave.
N. Cleveland Ave.
N. Mohawk St.
N. Larrabee St.
Lincoln Ave.
N. Clark St.
W. Armitage Ave.
W. Wisconsin St.
W. Menomonee St.
W. Eugenie St.
W. Schiller St.
W. Goethe St.
W. Scott St.
W. Blackhawk St.
W. Division St.
North Blvd.
LaSalle Dr.
Sedgwick
Clark/Division
N. Franklin St.
N. Orleans St.
Locust St.
N. Sedgwick St.
N. Hudson Ave.
N. Larrabee St.
Oak St.
N. Crosby St.
N. Clybourn Ave.
N. North Ave.
North/Clybourn
N. Halsted St.
N. Dayton St.
N. Kingsbury St.
Hooker St.
Hickory Ave.
North Branch St.
N. Branch St.
W. Chicago Ave.
N. Halsted St.
N. Milwaukee Ave.
E. Superior St.
E. Huron St.
E. Erie St.
E. Ontario St.
E. Chestnut St.
E. Pearson St.
E. Chicago Ave.
N. Fairbanks Ct.
N. St. Clair St.
N. Michigan Ave.
N. Rush St.
N. Wabash Ave.
N. State St.
E. Delaware Pl.
E. Walton Pl.
Bellevue Pl.
E. Cedar St.
E. Elm St.
E. Oak St.
W. Superior St.
W. Huron St.
W. Erie St.
W. Ontario St.
Chicago
MCA

4 Throughout the 1990s, at the **United Center** stadium, Michael Jordan makes the Chicago Bulls an international sports powerhouse. Finally—a Chicagoan more famous than Al Capone!

5 The **Sears Tower** is completed in 1973, giving Chicago bragging rights to the world's tallest building. The bragging comes to an abrupt halt in 1998, when Malaysia's Petronas Towers snags the title.

An artist's rendering of the aftermath of the Great Chicago Fire.

The Great Fire gave an unprecedented boost to the professional and artistic development of the nation's architects. Drawn by the unlimited opportunities to build, they gravitated to the city in droves, and the city raised a homegrown crop of architects. Chicago's reputation as an American Athens, packed with monumental and decorative buildings, is a direct byproduct of the disastrous fire that nearly brought the city to ruin.

In the meantime, the city's labor pool continued to grow, as many immigrants decided to stay rather than head for the prairie. Chicago still shipped meat and agricultural commodities around the nation and the world, and the city was rapidly becoming a mighty industrial center, creating finished goods, particularly for the markets of the ever-expanding Western settlements.

The Cradle of Organized Labor

Chicago never seemed to outgrow its frontier rawness. Greed, profiteering, exploitation, and corruption were as critical to its growth as hard work, ingenuity, and civic pride. The spirit of reform arose most powerfully from the working classes, people whose lives were plagued by poverty and disease despite the city's prosperity. When the labor movement awoke in Chicago, it did so with a militancy and commitment that would inspire unions throughout the nation.

The fear and mistrust between workers and the local captains of industry came to a head during the Haymarket Riot in 1886. On May 1, tens of thousands of workers went on strike to demand an 8-hour workday. (Eventually, that date would be immortalized as a national workers' holiday around the world—although never, ironically, in the United States.) A few days later, toward the end of a rally held by a group of anarchist labor activists in Haymarket Square, a bomb exploded near the line of policemen standing guard. The police fired into the crowd, and seven policemen and four workers were killed.

Although the 5-minute incident was in no sense a riot, it

> Speaking of Chicago . . .
>
> *Chicago is not the most corrupt American city, it's the most theatrically corrupt.*
> **–Studs Terkel, Chicago writer**

seemed to justify fears about the radicalism of the labor movement, and eight rally leaders were soon arrested. After a speedy and by no means impartial trial, five of the men—none of whom were ever proven to have a connection to the bombing—were sentenced to death. The bomber was never found. Haymarket Square itself no longer exists, but a plaque commemorates the spot, on a fairly desolate stretch of Des Plaines Street, just north of Randolph Street.

The city's labor movement fought on. By the 1890s, many of Chicago's workers were organized into the American Federation of Labor. The Pullman Strike of 1894 united black and white railway workers for the first time in a common struggle for higher wages and workplace rights. The Industrial Workers of the World, or the Wobblies, which embraced for a time so many great voices of American labor—Eugene V. Debs, Big Bill Haywood, and Helen Gurley Flynn—was founded in Chicago in 1905.

The Gangster Era

During the 1920s, the combination of Prohibition and a corrupt city administration happy to accept kickbacks from mobsters allowed organized crime to thrive. The most notorious local gangster of the era was a New York transplant named Al Capone, who muscled his way into control of the so-called Chicago Outfit. During his heyday, in the mid-1920s, Capone's operations included bootlegging, speakeasies, gambling joints, brothels, and pretty much every other unsavory-but-profitable business; the Outfit's take was reportedly $100 million a year.

Capone liked to promote himself as a humble, selfless business man—and he did set up soup kitchens at the start of the Great Depression—but he was also a ruthless thug who orchestrated gangland killings while always giving himself an alibi. The most notorious of these hits was the Valentine's Day Massacre of 1929, when four of Capone's men killed seven members of a rival gang in a North Side garage. To gain access to the building, two of Capone's gang dressed as policemen. Thinking it was a raid, the intended victims dropped their guns and put their hands up against the wall, only to be gunned down. The execution-style murder became national news, reinforcing Chicago's already bloody reputation.

In the end, Capone and the Outfit were brought down by a combination of growing public outrage and federal government intervention. With the repeal of Prohibition, the gangsters' main source of income was erased. At around the same time, an agent of the Internal Revenue Service put together evidence that Capone—who had never filed a tax return and claimed to have no income—was, in fact, earning plenty of cash. He was found guilty of tax evasion and served 7 years in prison, including a stint at Alcatraz in San

Notorious mobster Al Capone.

Francisco. After his release, he retired to Florida and died of a heart attack in 1947, at the age of 48. Although the Chicago Outfit continued its shady dealings after Capone's fall—using Las Vegas casinos for massive money-laundering operations—the city was no longer the site of vicious turf battles.

> Speaking of Chicago . . .
>
> *Loving Chicago is like loving a woman with a broken nose. You may find lovelier lovelies, but never a lovely so real.*
> **—Nelson Algren, Chicago novelist**

The Chicago Machine

While Chicago was becoming a center of industry, transportation, and finance, and a beacon of labor reform, it was also becoming a powerhouse in national politics. Between 1860 and 1968, Chicago was the site of 14 Republican and 10 Democratic presidential nominating conventions. (Some even point to the conventions as the source of Chicago's "Windy City" nickname, laying the blame on politicians who were full of hot air.) The first of the conventions gave the country Abraham Lincoln; the 1968 convention saw the so-called Days of Rage, a series of increasingly violent confrontations between demonstrators protesting the Vietnam War and Chicago police officers. The simmering tension culminated in a riot in Grant Park, outside what's now the Chicago Hilton; as police began beating protestors and bystanders with clubs and fists, TV cameras rolled, and demonstrators chanted, "The whole world is watching."

And it was. The strong-arm tactics of Mayor Richard J. Daley—a supporter of eventual nominee Hubert Humphrey—made Humphrey look bad by association and may have contributed to Humphrey's defeat in the general election. (Maybe it was a wash; some also say that Daley stole the 1960 election for Kennedy.) A national inquiry later declared the event a police-instigated riot, while the city's own mayor-approved investigation blamed out-of-town extremists and provocateurs.

Crowds protesting the 1968 Democratic National Convention, in defiance of Mayor Daley.

chicago stories: **THE GREAT MIGRATION**

From 1915 to 1960, hundreds of thousands of black Southerners poured into Chicago, trying to escape segregation and seeking economic freedom and opportunity. The "Great Migration" radically transformed Chicago, both politically and culturally, from an Irish-run city of recent European immigrants into one in which no group had a majority and no politician—white or black—could ever take the black vote for granted. Unfortunately, the sudden change gave rise to many of the disparities that still plague the city, but it also promoted an environment in which many black men and women could rise from poverty to prominence.

The supposed ringleaders of the uprising included Black Panther leader Bobby Seale; Tom Hayden, co-founder of Students for a Democratic Society; and Abbie Hoffman and Jerry Rubin, founders of the Youth International Party, or Yippies. They were charged with conspiracy and incitement to riot in the trial of the so-called Chicago 8 (later the Chicago 7, after charges in one case were dropped). Five were sentenced to prison terms, but their sentences were soon reversed after it was revealed that the FBI had bugged the offices of the defense lawyers.

The reversal was a setback for Mayor Daley, but his local power base held firm. The Democratic machine that he put in place during his years in office, from 1955 to 1976, was based on a practical sharing of the spoils: As long as the leaders of every ethnic and special interest group in town were guaranteed a certain number of government jobs, their leaders would bring in the votes.

His reach extended well beyond Chicago's borders; he controlled members of Congress, and every 4 years he delivered a solid Democratic vote in the November elections. But he also helped build Chicago into a modern business powerhouse, promoting the construction of O'Hare Airport, the McCormick Place Convention Center, and the Sears Tower, as well as expanding the city's highway and subway systems. Since his death in 1976, the machine has never wielded such national power, but it still remains almost impossible for a Republican to be voted into local office.

While jobs in the factories, steel mills, and stockyards paid much better than those in the cotton fields, Chicago was not the paradise that many blacks envisioned. Segregation was almost as bad here as it was down South, and most blacks were confined to a narrow "Black Belt" of overcrowded apartment buildings on the South Side. But the new migrants made the best of their situation, and for a time in the 1930s and '40s, the Black Belt—dubbed "Bronzeville" or the "Black Metropolis" by the community's boosters—thrived as a cultural, musical, religious, and educational mecca. As journalist Nicholas Lemann writes in The Promised Land: The Great Black Migration and How It Changed America, "Chicago was a city where a black person could be somebody."

Some of the Southern migrants who made names for themselves in Chicago included black separatist and Nation of Islam founder Elijah Muhammed; Robert S. Abbott, publisher of the powerful Chicago Defender newspaper, who launched a "Great Northern Drive" to bring blacks to the city in 1917; Ida B. Wells, the crusading journalist who headed an antilynching campaign; William Dawson, for many years the only black congressman; New Orleans–born jazz pioneers "Jelly Roll" Morton, King Oliver, and Louis Armstrong; Native Son author Richard Wright; John H. Johnson, publisher of Ebony and Jet magazines and one of Chicago's wealthiest residents; blues musicians Willie Dixon, Muddy Waters, and Howlin' Wolf; Thomas A. Dorsey, the "father of gospel music," and his greatest disciple, singer Mahalia Jackson; and Ralph Metcalfe, the Olympic gold medalist sprinter who turned to politics once he got to Chicago, eventually succeeding Dawson in Congress.

> Speaking of Chicago . . .
>
> *Come and show me another city with lifted head singing, so proud to be alive and coarse and strong and cunning.*
> **–From the poem "Chicago,"**
> **by Carl Sandburg**

When a 1948 Supreme Court decision declared it unconstitutional to restrict blacks to certain neighborhoods, the flight of many Bronzeville residents to less crowded areas took a toll on the community. Through the 1950s, almost a third of the housing became vacant, and by the 1960s, the great social experiment of urban renewal through wholesale land clearance and the creation of large tracts of public housing gutted the once-thriving neighborhood.

Community and civic leaders now appear committed to restoring the neighborhood to a semblance of its former glory. Landmark status has been secured for several historic buildings in Bronzeville, including the Liberty Life/Supreme Insurance Company, 3501 S. King Dr., the first African-American–owned insurance company in the northern United States; and the Eighth Regiment Armory, which, when completed in 1915, was the only armory in the U.S. controlled by an African-American regiment. The former home of the legendary Chess Records at 2120 S. Michigan Ave.—where Howlin' Wolf, Chuck Berry, and Bo Diddley gave birth to the blues and helped define rock 'n' roll—now houses a museum and music education center. Willie Dixon's widow, Marie Dixon, set up the Blues Heaven Foundation (✆ 312/808-1286; www.bluesheaven.com) with financial assistance from rock musician John Mellencamp. Along Dr. Martin Luther King, Jr., Drive, between 24th and 35th streets, several public art installations celebrate Bronzeville's heritage. The most poignant is sculptor Alison Saar's Monument to the Great Northern Migration, at King Drive and 26th Street, depicting a suitcase-toting African-American traveler standing atop a mound of worn shoe soles.

For information about tours of Bronzeville, see "Neighborhood Tours" in chapter 6 (p. 230).

CHICAGO'S ARCHITECTURE

Although the Great Chicago Fire leveled almost 3 square miles of the downtown area in 1871, it did clear the stage for Chicago's emergence as a breeding ground for innovative architecture. Some of the field's biggest names—Frank Lloyd Wright, Louis Sullivan, and Ludwig van der Rohe—made their mark on the city. And today Chicago's skyline is home to iconic buildings, including the John Hancock Center and the (former) Sears Tower.

Early Skyscrapers (1880–1920)

In the late 19th century, important technical innovations—including safety elevators, fireproofing, and telecommunications—combined with advances in skeletal construction to create a new building type: the skyscraper. These buildings were spacious, cost-effective, efficient, and quick to build—in short, the perfect architectural solution for Chicago's growing downtown. Architect Louis Sullivan (1865–1924) was the first to formalize a vision of a tall building based on the parts of a classical column. His theories inspired the Chicago school of

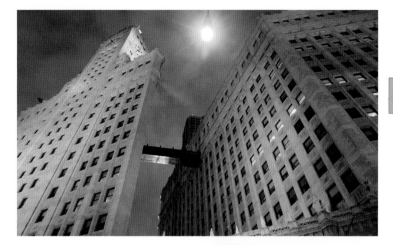

architecture, examples of which still fill the city's downtown. Features of Chicago school buildings include a rectangular shape with a flat roof; large windows (made possible by the development of load-bearing interior skeletons); and the use of terra cotta, a light, fireproof material that could be cast in any shape and attached to the exterior, often for decoration.

A good example of the development of the skyscraper is the Monadnock Building, 53 W. Jackson Blvd. (Holabird & Root, 1889–91; Holabird & Roche, 1893). The northern section has 6-foot-thick walls at its base to support the building's 17 stories; the newer, southern half has a steel frame clad in terra cotta (allowing the walls to be much thinner). The Reliance Building, now the Hotel Burnham (p. 69), 1 W. Washington St.

TOP: The gleaming white Wrigley Building; ABOVE: The Monadnock building, an early skyscraper.

(Burnham & Root and Burnham & Co., 1891–95), was influential for its use of large glass windows and decorative spandrels (the horizontal panel below a window).

Second Renaissance Revival (1890–1920)

The grand buildings of the Second Renaissance Revival, with their textural richness, suited the tastes of the wealthy Gilded Age. Typical features include a cubelike structure with a massive, imposing look; a symmetrical facade, including distinct horizontal divisions; and a different stylistic treatment for each floor, with different column capitals, finishes, and window treatments on each level. A fine example of this style is the **Chicago Cultural Center,** 78 E. Washington

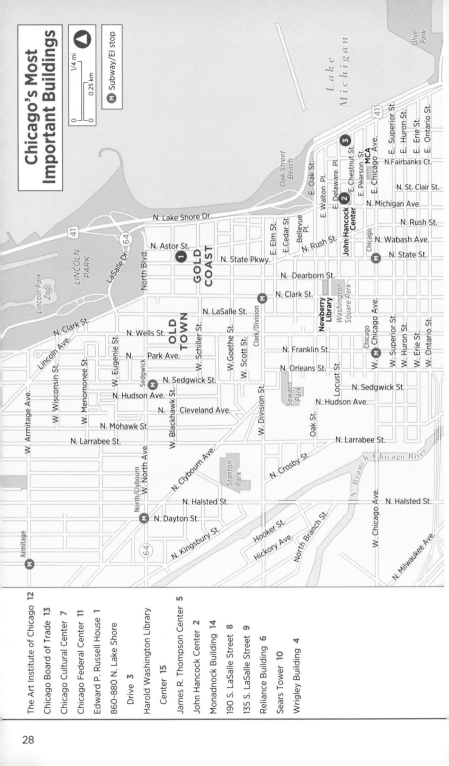

Chicago's Most Important Buildings

M Subway/El stop

STREETER-
VILLE

RIVER
NORTH

THE LOOP

SOUTH
LOOP

GREEK-
TOWN

UNIVERSITY
OF ILLINOIS
AT CHICAGO

Chicago River

Monroe
Harbor

GRANT   PARK

Shedd
Aquarium

Field Museum
of Natural History

E. Ohio St.
E. Grand Ave.
E. Illinois St.
E. North Water St.
E. Wacker Dr.
Harbor Dr.
Field Blvd.
E. Randolph Dr.

Columbus Dr.

S. Lake Shore Dr.

Columbus Dr.

E. Monroe Dr.
E. Jackson Dr.
E. Balbo   Dr.

Art Institute
of Chicago

MILLENNIUM PARK

N. Stetson Ave.
Randolph
Madison
Adams
Jackson
Library
E. Congress Pkwy.
E. Harrison St.
E. Harrison

S. Michigan Ave.
S. Michigan Ave.
E. 8th St.
Wabash Ave.

Roosevelt Rd.
Station

Roosevelt/
Wabash

S. State St.
S. Plymouth Ct.
Dearborn St.
S. Dearborn St.
S. Federal St.
S. Clark St.
S. LaSalle St.
S. Sherman St.
S. Wells St.

N. Wabash   Ave.
N. State St.
N. Dearborn St.
N. Clark St.
N. LaSalle St.
N. Wells St.
N. Franklin St.

State
Clark/Lake
Lake St.
Madison St.
Monroe St.
Washington
S. Franklin St.

W. Lake St.
W. Wacker Dr.
Merch Mart

W. Ohio St.
W. Grand Ave.
W. Illinois St.
W. Hubbard St.

Grand

N. Kingsbury

Sears
Tower
Quincy
N. Wacker Dr.   S. Wacker Dr.

Lasalle
LaSalle
W. Congress Pkwy.

S. Branch Chicago River

N. Canal St.
N. Clinton St.
N. Jefferson St.
N. Des Plaines St.

Clinton
Union
Station
W. Adams St.
W. Jackson Blvd.
W. Van Buren St.

Eisenhower Expwy.

Clinton
W. Polk St.
S. Jefferson St.
S. Des Plaines St.

S. Canal St.
S. Clinton St.

W. Roosevelt Rd.

W. Grand Ave.
N. Milwaukee Ave.
W. Hubbard St.
W. Kinzie St.
N. Sangamon St.
N. Peoria St.
N. Green St.
N. Fulton St.
W. Lake St.
W. Randolph St.
W. Washington Blvd.
W. Madison St.
W. Monroe St.
N. Morgan St.

S. Green St.
S. Peoria St.
S. Morgan St.

Halsted/U of I
W. Harrison St.

290

S. Halsted St.
S. Canal St.
W. Taylor St.
W. Roosevelt Rd.

90   94

90   94

4

7

12

5

6

11

14

9

8

13

15

10

Lake Michigan
3 mi
3 km
0
CHICAGO
Wrigley
Field
Map area
U.S. Cellular
Field
Midway
41
90   94
290
94
90
55
41

St. (Shepley, Rutan & Coolidge, 1897), originally built as a public library. This tasteful edifice, with its sumptuous decor, was constructed in part to help secure Chicago's reputation as a culture-conscious city.

Beaux Arts (1890–1920)

This style takes its name from the Ecole des Beaux-Arts in Paris, where a number of prominent American architects received their training, beginning around

A fine example of Second Renaissance Revival, the Chicago Cultural Center was originally built as a public library.

the mid–19th century. In 1893, Chicago played host to the World's Columbian Exposition, attended by 21 million people at a time when Chicago's population was just over 1 million. Overseen by Chicagoan Daniel H. Burnham (1846–1912), the fairgrounds in Hyde Park were laid out in Beaux Arts style, with broad boulevards, fountains, and temporary ornate white buildings, mostly by New York–based architects. (One of the few permanent structures is now the Museum of Science and Industry, p. 193.)

Grandiose compositions, exuberance of detail, and a variety of stone finishes typify most Beaux Arts structures. Chicago has several Beaux Arts buildings that exhibit the style's main features. The oldest part of the Art Institute of Chicago, Michigan Avenue at Adams Street (Shepley, Rutan & Coolidge, 1893), was built for the World's Columbian Exposition. A later example of yet another skyscraper is the gleaming white Wrigley Building, 400–410 N. Michigan Ave. (Graham, Anderson, Probst & White, 1919–24), which serves as a gateway to North Michigan Avenue.

Art Deco (1925–33)

Art Deco buildings are characterized by a linear, hard edge or angular composition, often with a vertical emphasis and highlighted with stylized decoration. The Chicago Board of Trade, 141 W. Jackson Blvd. (Holabird & Root, 1930), punctuates LaSalle Street with its dramatic Art Deco facade. High atop the pyramidal roof, an aluminum statue of Ceres, the Roman goddess of agriculture, gazes down over the building. The last major construction project in Chicago before the Great Depression, 135 S. LaSalle St. (originally the Field Building; Graham, Anderson, Probst & White, 1934), has a magnificent Art Deco lobby. A fine example of an Art Deco town house is the Edward P. Russell House, 1444 N. Astor St. (Holabird & Root, 1929), in the city's Gold Coast.

International Style (1932–45)

The International Style was popularized in the United States through the teachings and designs of **Ludwig Mies van der Rohe** (1886–1969), a German émigré who taught and practiced architecture in Chicago after leaving Germany's influential Bauhaus school of design. In the 1950s, erecting a "Miesian" office building made companies appear progressive. Features of the style include a rectangular shape; the frequent use of glass; an absence of ornamentation; and a

ONLY IN CHICAGO: the master builders

Visitors from around the world flock to Chicago to see the groundbreaking work of three major architects: Sullivan, Wright, and Mies. They all lived and worked in the Windy City, leaving behind a legacy of innovative structures that still inspire architects today. Here's the rundown on each of them:

Louis Sullivan (1865–1924)

o **Quote:** "Form ever follows function."

o **Iconic Chicago building:** Auditorium Building, 430 S. Michigan Ave. (1887–89).

o **Innovations:** Father of the Chicago school, Sullivan was perhaps at his most original in the creation of his intricate, nature-inspired ornamentation.

Frank Lloyd Wright (1867–1959)

o **Quote:** "Nature is my manifestation of God."

o **Iconic Chicago building:** Frederick C. Robie House, 5757 S. Woodlawn Ave., Hyde Park (1909).

o **Innovations:** While in Chicago, Wright developed the architecture of the Prairie School, a largely residential style combining natural materials, communication between interior and exterior spaces, and the sweeping horizontals of the Midwestern landscape. (For tours of Wright's home and studio, see "Exploring the 'Burbs," p. 208.)

Ludwig Mies van der Rohe (1886–1969)

o **Quote:** "Less is more."

o **Iconic Chicago building:** Chicago Federal Center, Dearborn Street between Adams Street and Jackson Boulevard (1959–74).

o **Innovations:** Mies van der Rohe brought the office tower of steel and glass to the United States. His stark facades don't immediately reveal his careful attention to details and materials.

clear expression of the building's form and function. (The interior structure of stacked office floors is clearly visible, as are the locations of mechanical systems, such as elevator shafts and air-conditioning units.)

Some famous Mies van der Rohe designs are the **Chicago Federal Center,** Dearborn Street between Adams Street and Jackson Boulevard (1959–74), and 860–880 N. Lake Shore Dr. (1949–51). Interesting interpretations of the style by **Skidmore, Owings & Merrill,** a Chicago firm that helped make the International Style a corporate staple, are the **Sears Tower** (1968–74) and the **John Hancock Center** (1969)—impressive engineering feats that rise 110 and 100 stories, respectively.

Postmodern (1975–90)

As a reaction against the stark International Style, postmodernists began to incorporate classical details and recognizable forms into their designs—often applied in outrageous proportions. One example, **190 S. LaSalle St.** (John Burgee Architects with Philip Johnson, 1987), brings the shape of a famous Chicago building back to the skyline. The overall design is that of the 1892 Masonic Temple (now razed), complete with the tripartite divisions of the Chicago school. Another amalgam of historical precedents is the **Harold Washington Library Center,**

400 S. State St. (Hammond, Beeby & Babka, 1991). An extremely modern interpretation of a three-part skyscraper—but you have to look for the divisions to find them—is **333 Wacker Dr.** (Kohn Pedersen Fox, 1979–83), an elegant green-glass structure that curves along a bend in the Chicago River. Unlike this harmonious juxtaposition, the **James R. Thompson Center,** 100 W. Randolph St. (Murphy/Jahn, 1979–85), inventively clashes with everything around it.

CHICAGO IN POPULAR CULTURE
Books

So many great American writers have come from Chicago, lived here, or set their work in the city that it's impossible to recommend a single book that says all there is to say about the city. But here are a few to get you started.

Upton Sinclair's enormously influential *The Jungle* tells the tale of a young immigrant encountering the brutal, filthy city (see box, "Jungle Fever," below). James T. Farrell's trilogy *Studs Lonigan,* published in the 1930s, explores the power of ethnic and neighborhood identity in Chicago. Other novels set in Chicago include Saul Bellow's *The Adventures of Augie March* and *Humboldt's Gift,* and Richard Wright's *Native Son. The Time Traveler's Wife,* by local author Audrey Niffenegger, unfolds amid recognizable Chicago backdrops such as the Newberry Library. (The movie version, alas, filmed only a few scenes here.)

For an entertaining overview of the city's history, read *City of the Century,* by Donald Miller (an excellent PBS special based on the book is also available on DVD). Erik Larson's **Devil in the White City,** a history book that reads like a thriller, tells the engrossing story of the 1893 World's Columbian Exposition and the serial killer who preyed on young women who visited from out of town. For another look at the seamy underside of Chicago's history, try *Sin in the Second City,* by Karen Abbott, which focuses on the city's most notorious—and expensive—brothel.

Two books give a human face to the city's shameful public housing history: Daniel Coyle's *Hardball: A Season in the Projects,* the true story of youngsters on a Little League baseball team; and Alex Kotlowitz's *There Are No Children Here,* a portrait of children growing up in one of the city's most dangerous projects. Kotlowitz also wrote *Never a City So Real: A Walk in Chicago,* which tells the stories of everyday Chicagoans, from a retired steelworker to a public defender, to the owner of a soul-food restaurant.

But no one has given a voice to the people of Chicago like Studs Terkel, whose books **Division Street: America, Working,** and **Chicago** are based on interviews with Chicagoans from every neighborhood and income level; and the late newspaper columnist **Mike Royko,** author of perhaps the definitive account of Chicago machine politics, *Boss.* His columns have been collected in *One More Time: The Best of Mike Royko* and *For the Love of Mike: More of the Best of Mike Royko.*

Upton Sinclair's enormously influential *The Jungle.*

jungle **FEVER**

It's hard to get a man to understand something if his salary depends on him not understanding it.

—Upton Sinclair

The most influential work of Chicago-based literature may also be the most disturbing. Upton Sinclair's *The Jungle,* an exposé of the city's meatpacking industry, caused a sensation when it was published in 1906. Although the book is a novel, following the tragic life of a poorly paid Lithuanian immigrant, it was based on Sinclair's firsthand observations at the Union Stockyards; many of its most gruesome scenes, such as when a man falls into a processing tank and is ground up along with the rest of the meat, were based on fact. After *The Jungle* became an international bestseller, U.S. meat exports plummeted and panicked meat-packing companies practically begged for government inspections to prove their products were safe. A Food and Drug Act was passed soon after, which made it a crime to sell food that had been adulterated or produced using "decomposed or putrid" substances; eventually, that led to the founding of the Food and Drug Administration (FDA).

Film

Chicago became a popular setting for feature films in the 1980s and '90s. For a look at Chicago on the silver screen, check out *Ferris Bueller's Day Off* (1985), the ultimate teenage wish-fulfillment fantasy, which includes scenes filmed at Wrigley Field and the city's annual St. Patrick's Day Parade; *The Fugitive* (1993), which used the city's El trains as an effective backdrop; and *My Best Friend's Wedding* (1996). For many Chicagoans, the quintessential hometown movie scene is the finale of *The Blues Brothers* (1979), which features a multicar pileup in the center of downtown Daley Plaza.

Sometimes locally born actors choose to shoot movies in their hometown. A film that fueled a thousand paparazzi photographs was *The Break-Up* (2006), starring local-boy-made-good Vince Vaughn and Jennifer Aniston, and filmed on location throughout the city. Another hometown actor, John Cusack, starred in *High Fidelity* (2000), where hip Wicker Park makes an appropriate backdrop for the tale of a music-obsessed record store owner. Director Michael Mann, a Chicago native, filmed part of the gangster movie *Public Enemies* (2009) in town—appropriately enough, since this was the place where bank robber John Dillinger (played by Johnny Depp in the movie) was caught and killed by federal agents.

Though it technically takes place in Gotham City, the setting of the Batman blockbuster *The Dark Knight* is clearly recognizable as Chicago—although, rest assured, the real city isn't nearly as dark as the movie version! Swaths of downtown were also overrun by rampaging robots in *Transformers 3* (2011).

Music

If Chicagoans were asked to pick one musical style to represent their city, most of us would start singing the blues. Thanks in part to the presence of the influential **Chess Records,** Chicago became a hub of blues activity after World War II, with musicians such as Muddy Waters, Howlin' Wolf, and Buddy Guy recording

A CHICAGO playlist

The classic swingin' anthem of the city is Frank Sinatra's rendition of **"Chicago"** ("That toddlin' town . . . free and easy town, brassy, breezy town"), overblown versions of which show up regularly at local karaoke bars. Sinatra also sang his praises to the city in **"My Kind of Town (Chicago Is),"** which mentions the Wrigley Building and the Union Stockyards. But an even better pick for official city theme song is Robert Johnson's **"Sweet Home Chicago,"** with its appropriately bluesy riff ("Come on, baby don't you want to go, to the same old place, Sweet Home Chicago").

The 1970s pop-lite group Chicago didn't sing specifically about the city (probably because they moved to L.A. as soon as they hit it big), but their cheery **"Saturday in the Park"** captures the spirit of Grant Park and Lincoln Park in the summertime. Fast-forwarding a few decades, the blistering **"Cherub Rock"** by Smashing Pumpkins is a harsh take on the city's 1990s-era music scene (opening with the line: "Freak out, give in, doesn't matter what you believe in . . ."); more mellow is the elegiac **"Via Chicago"** by indie darlings Wilco. And no survey of Chicago music would be complete without mentioning the maestros of hip-hop, Common and Kanye West, who name-check their hometown in the songs **"Southside"** and **"Homecoming,"** respectively.

and performing here. (For a glimpse of what the music studio was like in its glory days, rent the 2008 movie *Cadillac Records,* starring Jeffrey Wright as Muddy Waters and Beyoncé Knowles as Etta James.) Buddy Guy is still active on the local scene, making regular appearances at his eponymous downtown blues club, one of the best live music venues in the city (p. 312).

Blues legend Muddy Waters.

Don't miss the annual, free Blues Fest in Grant Park.

In the '60s and '70s, Chicago helped usher in the era of "electric blues"—low-tech, soulful singing melded with the rock sensibility of electric guitars. Blues-influenced rock musicians, including the Rolling Stones, Led Zeppelin, and Eric Clapton, made Chicago a regular pilgrimage spot.

Today the blues has become yet another tourist attraction, especially for international visitors, but the quality and variety of blues acts is still impressive. Hard-core blues fans shouldn't miss the annual (free) **Blues Fest,** held along the lakefront in Grant Park in early June. For a listing of the city's best blues clubs, see chapter 9.

EATING & DRINKING

Joke all you want about bratwurst and deep-dish pizza; Chicago is a genuine culinary hot spot. One of the city's most creative dining spots, **Alinea,** was even named the top restaurant in the United States by *Gourmet* magazine in 2007 (take that, New York and San Francisco!). What makes eating out in Chicago fun is the variety. We've got it all: stylish see-and-be-seen spots, an amazing array of steakhouses, chef-owned temples to fine dining, and every kind of ethnic cuisine you could possibly crave—plus, yes, some not-to-be-missed deep-dish pizza places.

Fueled in part by expense-account-wielding business travelers, high-end dining is a growth industry here. What makes Chicago's top restaurants unique, however, is their inclusive, low-key attitude. This isn't the kind of city where snooty waiters show off their foodie expertise or stare in horror if you have no idea what wine to order. By and large, hospitality is more than just a buzzword here, and as long as you can afford the eye-popping bill, the city's top chefs will welcome you. If you want to splurge on a one-of-a-kind meal—the kind you'll be describing to friends weeks later—Chicago is the place to do it. (See chapter 5, "Where to Eat.")

That said, ever-increasing restaurant prices are one of my pet peeves; eating out downtown has become more and more of a luxury. While finding bargains in the Loop or around the Magnificent Mile isn't easy, you can still fill up without going broke by stopping at one of the food courts inside the malls along Michigan Avenue (as many locals on their lunch break do). Ethnic restaurants also tend to be less expensive, whether you're sampling *spanakopita* in Greektown (p. 107) or a noodle dish at a Thai restaurant (see the box "A Taste of Thai," on p. 138).

And about that pizza: Yes, Chicagoans hate to be stereotyped as cheese-and-sausage-devouring slobs, but we really do eat deep-dish pizza, which was created in the 1940s at the original **Pizzeria Uno** restaurant (p. 130). If you've never had this decadent, cholesterol-raising delicacy, you should definitely try it while you're here (especially on a chilly day—it's not as appealing during a summer heat wave). You'll find a rundown of the best pizza spots on p. 116.

Deep dish pizza is a Chicago tradition.

35

WHEN TO GO

You'll see Chicago at its best if you visit during the summer or fall. Summer offers a nonstop selection of special events and outdoor activities; the downside is that you'll be dealing with the biggest crowds and periods of hot, muggy weather. Autumn days are generally sunny, and the crowds at major tourist attractions grow thinner—you don't have to worry about snow until late November at the earliest. Spring is extremely unpredictable, with dramatic fluctuations of cold and warm weather, and usually fair amounts of rain. If your top priority is indoor cultural sights, winter's not such a bad time to visit: no lines at museums, the cheapest rates at hotels, and the pride that comes with slogging through the slush with the natives.

When planning your trip, book a hotel as early as possible, especially if you're coming during the busy summer tourist season. The more affordable a hotel, the more likely it is to be sold out in June, July, and August, especially on weekends. It's also worth checking if a major convention will be in town during the dates you hope to travel (see the "Major Convention Dates" box, later). It's not unusual for every major downtown hotel to be sold out during the Housewares Show in late March or the Restaurant Show in mid-May.

Weather

Chicagoans like to joke that if you don't like the weather, just wait an hour—it will change. In spring and autumn, be prepared for a wide range of temperatures; you may be shivering in a coat and gloves in the morning, only to be fine in a T-shirt by mid-afternoon. While Chicago winters get a bad rap, they're no worse than in other northern American cities. January isn't exactly prime tourist season, but the city doesn't shut down; as long as you've got the proper cold-weather gear and sturdy boots, you should be fine. Summers are generally warm and sunny, with temperatures that range from pleasant to steamy. The closer you are to the lake, the more you'll benefit from the cool breezes that float off the water.

As close to your departure as possible, check the local weather forecast at the websites of the **Chicago Tribune** newspaper (www.chicagotribune.com) or the **Weather Channel** (www.weather.com). You'll find packing a lot easier if you know whether to expect snow, rain, or sweltering heat. (That said, bring a range of clothes and an umbrella if you're going to be in town for awhile—you should be prepared for anything!)

Chicago's Average Temperatures & Precipitation

	JAN	FEB	MAR	APR	MAY	JUNE	JULY	AUG	SEPT	OCT	NOV	DEC
HIGH °F	29	34	45	58	70	80	84	82	75	63	48	35
LOW °F	13	18	28	39	48	57	63	62	54	42	31	20
HIGH °C	−1	1	7	14	21	26	28	27	23	17	9	2
LOW °C	−10	−7	−2	3	8	13	17	16	12	5	−1	−7
RAINFALL (IN.)	1.7	1.4	2.7	3.6	3.2	3.8	3.6	4.1	3.5	2.6	2.9	2.2

Holidays

Banks, government offices, post offices, and many stores, restaurants, and museums are closed on the following legal national holidays: January 1 (New

Year's Day), the third Monday in January (Martin Luther King, Jr., Day), the third Monday in February (Presidents' Day), the last Monday in May (Memorial Day), July 4 (Independence Day), the first Monday in September (Labor Day), the second Monday in October (Columbus Day), November 11 (Veterans' Day/Armistice Day), the fourth Thursday in November (Thanksgiving Day), and December 25 (Christmas). The Tuesday after the first Monday in November is Election Day, a federal government holiday in presidential-election years (held every 4 years, and next in 2012).

Chicago Calendar of Events

The best way to stay on top of the city's current crop of special events is to check in with the **Chicago Convention & Tourism Bureau** (© 877/CHICAGO [244-2246]; www.choosechicago.com). Visit their website to browse the *Chicago Destination Guide,* which surveys special events, including parades, street festivals, concerts, theatrical productions, and museum exhibitions (you can also get a copy mailed to you). The **Mayor's Office of Special Events** (© 312/744-3315) lets you search for upcoming festivals, parades, and concerts on its website, www.explorechicago.org.

For an exhaustive list of events beyond those listed here, check http://events.frommers.com, where you'll find a searchable, up-to-the-minute roster of what's happening in cities all over the world.

JANUARY

Chicago Boat, RV & Outdoor Show, McCormick Place, 23rd Street and Lake Shore Drive (© 312/946-6200; www.chicagoboatshow.com). All the latest boats and recreational vehicles are on display, plus trout fishing, a climbing wall, boating safety seminars, and big-time entertainment. January 11 to 15, 2012.

Winter Delights. Throughout January and February, the city's Office of Tourism (© 877/CHICAGO [244-2246]; www.choosechicago.com) offers special travel deals to lure visitors during tourism's low season. Incentives include bargain-priced hotel packages, affordable prix-fixe dinners at downtown restaurants, and special music and theater performances. Early January through February.

Chinese New Year Parade, Wentworth and Cermak streets (© 312/326-5320; www.chicagochinatown.org). Join in as the sacred dragon whirls down the boulevard and restaurateurs pass out small envelopes of money to their regular customers. In 2012, Chinese New Year

begins on January 23; call to verify the date of the parade.

FEBRUARY

Chicago Auto Show, McCormick Place, 23rd Street and Lake Shore Drive (© 630/495-2282; www.chicagoautoshow.com). More than 1,000 cars and trucks, domestic and foreign, current and futuristic, are on display. The event draws nearly a million visitors, so try to visit on a weekday rather than Saturday or Sunday. Many area hotels offer special packages that include show tickets. February 10 to 19, 2012.

MARCH

St. Patrick's Day Parade. In a city with a strong Irish heritage, this holiday is a big deal. The Chicago River is even dyed green for the occasion. The parade route is along Columbus Drive from Balbo Drive to Monroe Street. A second, more neighborhood-like parade is held on the South Side the day after the Dearborn Street parade, on Western Avenue from 103rd to 115th streets. Visit www.chicagostpatsparade.com for information. The Saturday before March 17.

APRIL

Opening Day. For the **Cubs,** call ☎ 773/404-CUBS [2827] or visit **www. cubs.mlb.com**; for the **White Sox,** call ☎ 312/674-1000 or go to **www.white sox.mlb.com**. Make your plans early to get tickets for this eagerly awaited day. The calendar may say spring, but be warned: Opening Day is usually freezing in Chi-town. (The first Cubs and Sox home games have occasionally been postponed because of snow.) Early April.

Chicago Improv Festival. Chicago's improv comedy scene is known as a training ground for performers who have gone on to shows such as *Saturday Night Live* or *MADtv.* Big names and lesser-known (but talented) comedians converge for a celebration of silliness, with large main-stage shows and smaller, more experimental pieces. Most performances are at the Lakeshore Theater on the North Side (3175 N. Broadway; ☎ 773/472-3492; www.chicagoimprov festival.org). Late April.

MAY

Buckingham Fountain Color Light Show, Congress Parkway and Lake Shore Drive. This massive, landmark fountain in Grant Park operates daily from May 1 to October 1. From sundown to 11pm, a colored light show adds to the drama.

The Ferris Wheel and Carousel begin spinning again at Navy Pier, 600 E. Grand Ave. (☎ 312/595-PIER [7437]; www.navypier.com). The rides operate through October. From Memorial Day through Labor Day, Navy Pier also hosts twice-weekly fireworks shows Wednesday nights at 9:30pm and Saturday nights at 10:15pm.

Art Chicago, the Merchandise Mart, at the intersection of Kinzie and Wells streets (☎ 312/527-3701; www.art chicago.com). The city's biggest contemporary art show brings together collectors, art lovers, and gallery owners from throughout the Midwest. You don't have to be an expert to check out the show:

Tours and educational programs are offered to make the work accessible to art novices. The **Next** show, which runs concurrently, focuses on work by emerging international artists. First week in May.

Celtic Fest Chicago, Pritzker Music Pavilion, Randolph Street and Columbus Drive, in Millennium Park (☎ 312/744-3315; www.explorechicago.org). This festival celebrates the music and dance of global Celtic traditions. But the mood is far from reverential: There's a limerick contest and a "best legs" contest exclusively for men wearing kilts. First weekend in May.

Wright Plus Tour, Frank Lloyd Wright Home and Studio, Oak Park (☎ 708/848-1976; www.wrightplus.org). This annual tour of 10 buildings, including Frank Lloyd Wright's home and studio, the Unity Temple, and several other notable buildings in both Prairie and Victorian styles, is very popular, so plan on buying tickets in advance (they go on sale March 1). Third Saturday in May.

JUNE

Chicago Gospel Festival, Pritzker Music Pavilion, Randolph Street and Columbus Drive, Millennium Park (☎ 312/744-3315; www.explorechicago.org). Blues may be the city's most famous musical export, but Chicago is also the birthplace of gospel music: Thomas Dorsey, the "father of gospel," and the greatest gospel singer, Mahalia Jackson, were from the city's South Side. This 3-day festival—the largest outdoor, free-admission event of its kind—offers music on three stages with more than 40 performances. First weekend in June.

Printers Row Lit Fest, Dearborn Street from Congress Parkway to Polk Street (☎ 312/222-3986; http://printersrowlit fest.org). One of the largest free outdoor book fairs in the country, this weekend event celebrates the written word with everything from readings and signings by big-name authors to panel discussions on penning your first novel.

Located within walking distance of the Loop, the fair also features more than 150 booksellers with new, used, and antiquarian books; a poetry tent; and special activities for children. First weekend in June.

Chicago Blues Festival, Petrillo Music Shell, Randolph Street and Columbus Drive, Grant Park (© **312/744-3315;** www.explorechicago.org). Muddy Waters would scratch his noggin over the sea of suburbanites who flood into Grant Park every summer to quaff Budweisers and accompany local legends Buddy Guy and Lonnie Brooks on air guitar. Truth be told, you can hear the same great jams and wails virtually any night of the week in one of the city's many blues clubs. Still, a thousand-voice chorus of "Sweet Home Chicago" under the stars has a rousing appeal. All concerts at the Blues Fest are free, with dozens of acts performing over 3 days, but get there in the afternoon to get a good spot on the lawn for the evening show. Second weekend in June.

Ravinia Festival, Ravinia Park, Highland Park (© **847/266-5100;** www.ravinia. com). This suburban location is the open-air summer home of the Chicago Symphony Orchestra and the venue of many first-rate visiting orchestras, chamber ensembles, pop artists, and dance companies. See also "Exploring the 'Burbs," in chapter 6. June through September.

Puerto Rican Fest, Humboldt Park, Division Street and Sacramento Boulevard (© **773/292-1414;** http:// prparadechicago.org). One of the city's largest festivals, this celebration includes 5 days of live music, theater, games, food, and beverages. It peaks with a parade that winds its way from Wacker Drive and Dearborn Street to the West Side Puerto Rican enclave of Humboldt Park. Mid-June.

Old Town Art Fair, Lincoln Park West and Wisconsin Street, Old Town

(© **312/337-1938;** www.oldtowntriangle. com). This juried fine arts fair has drawn browsers to this historic neighborhood for more than 50 years with the work of more than 250 painters, sculptors, and jewelry designers from the Midwest and around the country on display. It also features an art auction, garden walk, concessions, and children's art activities. It tends to get crowded, but the overall vibe is low-key festive rather than rowdy. Second weekend in June.

Wells Street Art Festival, Wells Street from North Avenue to Division Street (© **312/951-6106;** www.oldtownchicago. org). Held on the same weekend as the more prestigious Old Town Art Fair, this event is lots of fun, with 200 arts and crafts vendors, food, music, and carnival rides. Second weekend in June.

Grant Park Music Festival, Pritzker Music Pavilion, Randolph Street and Columbus Drive, in Millennium Park (© **312/742-7638;** www.grantparkmusicfestival.com). One of the city's greatest bargains, this classical music series presents free concerts in picture-perfect Millennium Park. Many of the musicians are members of the Chicago Symphony Orchestra, and the shows often feature internationally known singers and performers. Bring a picnic and enjoy dinner beforehand with a view of the skyline. Concerts begin the last week in June and continue through August.

Taste of Chicago, Grant Park (© **312/744-3315;** www.explorechicago. org). The city claims that this is the largest free outdoor food fest in the nation. Three and a half million rib and pizza lovers feeding at this colossal alfresco trough say they're right. Over 10 days of feasting in the streets, scores of Chicago restaurants cart their fare to food stands set up throughout the park. To avoid the heaviest crowds, try going on weekdays earlier in the day. **Claustrophobes, take note:** If you're here the evening of July 3 for the Independence Day fireworks, pick out a vantage point farther north on the lakefront—unless dodging sweaty limbs, spilled beer, and the occasional bottle rocket sounds fun. Admission is free; you pay for the sampling. June 27 through July 6, 2012.

Gay and Lesbian Pride Parade, Halsted Street, from Belmont Avenue to Broadway, south to Diversey Parkway, and east to Lincoln Park, where a rally and music festival are held (✆ **773/348-8243;** www.chicagopridecalendar.org). This parade is the colorful culmination of a month of activities by Chicago's gay and lesbian communities. Halsted Street is usually mobbed; pick a spot on Broadway for a better view. Last Sunday in June.

JULY

Independence Day Celebration (✆ **312/744-3315;** www.explorechicago. org). Chicago celebrates the holiday on July 3 with a free classical music concert in Grant Park in the evening, followed by fireworks over the lake. Expect huge crowds. July 3.

Old St. Patrick's World's Largest Block Party, 700 W. Adams St., at Des Plaines Avenue (✆ **312/648-1021;** www.oldst pats.org). This hugely popular blowout is hosted by the city's oldest church, an Irish Catholic landmark in the West Loop area. It can get pretty crowded, but Old St. Pat's always lands some major acts. Six bands perform over 2 nights on two stages and attract a young, lively crowd. Second weekend in July.

Chicago Yacht Club's Race to Mackinac Island, starting line at the Monroe Street Harbor (✆ **312/861-7777;** www.chicago yachtclub.org). This 3-day competition is the grandest of the inland water races. The public is welcome at a Friday night party. On Saturday, jockey for a good place to watch the boats set sail toward northern Michigan. Mid-July.

Sheffield Garden Walk, starting at Sheffield and Webster avenues (✆ **773/929-9255;** www.

sheffieldfestivals.org). More than 50 Lincoln Park homeowners open their back yards to visitors at this annual event, giving you a chance to snoop around these normally hidden retreats. The walk isn't just for garden nuts; it has also grown into a lively street festival, with live bands, children's activities, and food and drink tents. It's a popular destination for a wide cross-section of Chicagoans, from singles to young families to retirees. Third weekend in July.

Dearborn Garden Walk & Heritage Festival, North Dearborn and Astor streets (✆ **312/632-1241;** www.dearborn gardenwalk.com). A more upscale affair than the Sheffield Garden Walk, this event allows regular folks to peer into private gardens on the Gold Coast, one of the most expensive and exclusive neighborhoods in the city. As you'd expect, many yards are the work of the best landscape architects, designers, and art world luminaries that old money can buy. There's also live music, a marketplace, and a few architectural tours. Third Sunday in July.

Chicago SummerDance, east side of South Michigan Avenue between Balbo and Harrison streets (✆ **312/742-4007;** www.explorechicago.org). From July through late August, the city's Department of Cultural Affairs transforms a patch of Grant Park into a lighted outdoor dance venue on Thursday, Friday, and Saturday from 6 to 9:30pm, and Sunday from 4 to 7pm. The 4,600-square-foot dance floor provides ample room for throwing down moves while live bands play music—from ballroom and klezmer to samba and zydeco. One-hour lessons are offered from 6 to 7pm. Free admission.

Taste of Lincoln Avenue, Lincoln Park, between Fullerton Avenue and Wellington Street (✆ **773/868-3010;** www.wrightwoodneighbors.org). This is one of the largest and most popular of Chicago's many neighborhood street fairs; it features 50 bands performing music on five stages. Neighborhood restaurants staff the food stands, and there's also a kids' carnival. Last weekend in July.

Newberry Library Book Fair & Bughouse Square Debates, 69 W. Walton St. and Washington Square Park (℡ **312/255-3501;** www.newberry.org). Over 4 days, the esteemed Newberry Library invites the masses to rifle through bins stuffed with tens of thousands of used books, most of which go for a few dollars. Better than the book fair is what happens across the street in Washington Square Park: soapbox orators re-creating the days when left-wing agitators came here to make their case. Late July.

AUGUST

Northalsted Market Days, Halsted Street between Belmont Avenue and Addison Street (℡ **773/883-0500;** www.northalsted.com). The largest of the city's street festivals, held in the heart of the North Side's gay-friendly neighborhood, Northalsted Market Days offers music on three stages, lots of food and offbeat merchandise, and some of the best people-watching of the summer. First weekend in August.

Bud Billiken Parade and Picnic, starting at 39th Street and King Drive and ending at 55th Street and Washington Park (℡ **773/536-3710;** www.budbillikenparade.com). This annual African-American celebration, which has been held for more than 80 years, is one of the oldest parades of its kind in the nation. It's named for the mythical figure Bud Billiken, reputedly the patron saint of "the little guy," and features the standard floats, bands, marching and military units, drill teams, and glad-handing politicians. Second Saturday in August.

Chicago Air & Water Show, North Avenue Beach (℡ **312/744-3315;** www.explorechicago.org). The U.S. Air Force Thunderbirds and Navy Seals usually make an appearance at this hugely popular aquatic and aerial spectacular. (Even if you don't plan to watch it, you can't help but experience it with jets screaming overhead all weekend.) Expect huge crowds, so arrive early if you want a spot along the water, or park yourself on the grass along the east edge of Lincoln Park Zoo, where you'll get good views (and some elbow room). Free admission. Third weekend in August.

SEPTEMBER

Chicago Jazz Festival, Petrillo Music Shell, Jackson and Columbus drives, Grant Park (℡ **312/744-3315;** www.explorechicago.org). Several national headliners are always on hand at this steamy gathering, which provides a swell end-of-summer bookend opposite to the gospel and blues fests in June. The event is free; come early and stay late. First weekend in September.

The art season, in conjunction with the annual Visions series of art gallery programs for the general public, begins with galleries holding their season openers in the Loop, River North, River West, and Wicker Park/Bucktown gallery districts. Contact the **Chicago Art Dealers Association** (℡ **312/649-0065;** www.chicagoartdealers.org) for details. First Friday after Labor Day.

Boulevard Lakefront Bike Tour (Active Transit Alliance; ℡ **312/427-3325;** www.activetrans.org). This 35-mile leisurely bicycle excursion is a great way to explore the city, from the neighborhoods to the historic link of parks and boulevards. There's also a 10-mile tour for children and families. The Sunday morning event starts and ends at the University of Chicago in Hyde Park, which plays host to vendors and entertainment at the annual Bike Expo. Mid-September.

Mexican Independence Day Parade, Dearborn Street between Wacker Drive and Van Buren Street (℡ **312/744-3315**). This parade is on Saturday; another takes place the next day on 26th Street in the

Little Village neighborhood (📞 **773/521-5387**). Second Saturday in September.

Viva! Chicago Latin Music Festival, Pritzker Music Pavilion, Randolph Street and Columbus Drive, in Millennium Park (📞 **312/744-3315;** www.explorechicago. org). This free musical celebration features salsa, mambo, and performances by the hottest Latin rock acts. Free admission. Third weekend in September.

OCTOBER

Chicago International Film Festival (📞 **312/683-0121;** www.chicagofilm festival.org). The oldest U.S. festival of its kind screens films from around the world, as well as a few high-profile American independent films. It's a great way to catch foreign movies that may never be released in the U.S. Screenings take place over 2 weeks, with most held at downtown movie theaters that are easily accessible to visitors. First 2 weeks of October.

Chicago Country Music Festival, Pritzker Music Pavilion, Randolph Street and Columbus Drive, in Millennium Park (📞 **312/744-3315;** www.explorechicago. org). Chicago may be a long way from Dixie, but country music still has a loyal Midwest fan base. This popular event features free concerts from big-name entertainers. First weekend in October.

Chicago Marathon (📞 **312/904-9800;** www.chicagomarathon.com). Sponsored by Bank of America, Chicago's marathon is a major event on the international

---

MAJOR convention DATES

Listed below are Chicago's major (20,000 visitors or more) conventions for 2012, with projected attendance figures. Plan ahead, because hotel rooms and restaurant reservations can be hard to come by when the big shows are in town—and even if you snag a room, you'll be paying top price. Contact the **Chicago Convention and Tourism Bureau** (📞 **877/CHICAGO** [244-2246]; www.choosechicago.com) to double-check the latest info before you commit to your travel dates, as convention schedules can change.

EVENT	2012 DATES	PROJECTED ATTENDANCE
International Heating and Air Expo	Jan 23–25	60,000
Chicago Dental Society	Feb 23–25	30,000
America's Beauty Show	Mar 3–5	48,000
International Home and Housewares Show	Mar 11–13	60,000
Kitchen & Bath Industry Show	April 27–29	60,000
National Restaurant Association Show	May 19–22	55,000
American Society of Clinical Oncology	June 1–5	35,000
Neo-Con—World's Trade Fair	June 11–13	40,000
International Manufacturing Tech Show	Sept 10–15	80,000
Graph Expo	Oct 7–10	30,000
Pack Expo	Oct 28–Nov 1	45,000
Process Expo	Oct 29–31	90,000
Radiological Society of North America	Nov 25–30	55,000

long-distance running circuit. It begins and ends in Grant Park but can be viewed from any number of vantage points along the route. Second Sunday in October.

NOVEMBER

The **Chicago Humanities Festival** takes over locations throughout downtown, from libraries to concert halls (✆ 312/661-1028; www.chfestival. org). Over a 2-week period, the festival presents cultural performances, readings, and symposiums tied to an annual theme (recent themes included "Brains & Beauty" and "Crime & Punishment"). Expect appearances by major authors, scholars, and policymakers, all at a very reasonable cost (usually $5–$10 per event). Early November.

Dance Chicago (✆ 773/989-0698; www.dancechicago.com). All of the city's best-known dance troupes (including Hubbard Street and Joffrey Ballet) and many smaller companies participate in this month-long celebration of dance, with performances and workshops at the **Athenaeum Theatre,** 2936 N. Southport Ave., on the city's North Side. It's a great chance to check out the range of local dance talent.

Magnificent Mile Lights Festival (✆ 312/642-3570; www.magnificent milelightsfestival.com). Beginning at dusk, a colorful parade of Disney characters makes its way south along Michigan Avenue, from Oak Street to the Chicago River. Thousands of lights are entwined around trees, and street lights switch on as the procession passes. Carolers, elves, and minstrels appear with Santa along the avenue throughout the day and into the evening, and many retailers offer hot chocolate and other treats. It's a great,

family-friendly event, but get to the parade route early if you want your little ones to see the procession. Saturday before Thanksgiving.

Christmas Tree Lighting, Daley Plaza, in the Loop (✆ 312/744-3315). The arrival of the city's official tree signals the beginning of the Christmas season. The mayor flips the switch the day after Thanksgiving, around dusk.

DECEMBER

Christkindlmarket, Daley Plaza, in the Loop (✆ 312/644-2662; www. christkindlmarket.com). This annual holiday event is inspired by traditional German Christmas festivals. A mini–European village springs up in downtown's Daley Plaza, where German-speaking vendors showcase handcrafted ornaments and other seasonal decorations. Of course, it wouldn't be a German celebration without beer, sausages, and hot spiced wine, too. The fair is open from Thanksgiving Day until Christmas Eve but is usually packed Thanksgiving weekend; visit on a December weekday for a more enjoyable visit.

A Christmas Carol, Goodman Theatre, 170 N. Dearborn St. (✆ 312/443-3800; www.goodman-theatre.org). This seasonal favorite, performed for more than 2 decades, runs from Thanksgiving to the end of December.

The Nutcracker ballet, Joffrey Ballet of Chicago, Auditorium Theatre, 50 E. Congress Pkwy. For tickets, call ✆ 312/559-1212 (Ticketmaster) or contact the Joffrey office (✆ 312/739-0120; www.joffrey.com). The esteemed company performs its Victorian-American twist on the holiday classic. Late November to mid-December.

RESPONSIBLE TRAVEL

Chicago has become a breeding ground for urban environmental initiatives, starting with the green roof that was installed on the top of City Hall and the appointment of a Chief Environmental Officer on the mayor's staff. Throughout the city, architects and contractors are building according to environmentally responsible principles, and an addition to the already massive McCormick Place Convention Center was the largest new construction building in the country to receive LEED (Leadership in Energy and Environmental Design) certification from the U.S. Green Building Council. An active pro-cycling community has pushed for more bike lanes in the city's streets, and Millennium Park provides secured bike parking and showers for two-wheeled commuters. (See p. 348 for bike rental information.)

A city-wide Green Hotels Initiative has encouraged hotels to become more energy-efficient and change back-room operations to minimize their impact on the environment. The nonprofit organization Green Seal has certified many local hotels for their role in minimizing waste, conserving water, and promoting energy

obama's **CHICAGO**

For years, Chicago's biggest hometown celebrity was Oprah Winfrey (despite the fact that she's rarely seen out and about, preferring to spend her free time at her sprawling California estate). These days, she's been replaced by another big O—President Barack Obama. Though his primary residence is now a certain White House in Washington, D.C., the First Couple still own a home here and maintain strong local ties.

Tourists from around the world make pilgrimages to the Obamas' house at 5046 S. Greenwood Ave. on the city's South Side. You can get a glimpse of the home from a distance, but you won't see much; the whole block is closed to passersby for security reasons. However, the surrounding neighborhood of Kenwood—with its lovingly restored historic mansions—as well as adjacent Hyde Park, are well worth a stroll (see "Exploring Hyde Park," p. 189). After visiting the campus of the University of Chicago—where President Obama once taught constitutional law—you can browse the stacks at the **Seminary Co-op Bookstore** (pictured at right; p. 274), where he was a regular.

Chicago-based fashion maven Ikram Goldman helped cultivate Michelle Obama's sense of style. For a first-lady-worthy makeover, head to her boutique, **Ikram** (p. 277), which stocks pieces by up-and-coming and off-the-radar designers.

For dinners out, the Obamas have often eaten at the upscale Mexican restaurant **Topolobampo** (p. 121). Another favorite for special occasions is savings; among those getting the highest marks are the **Hotel Allegro** (p. 72), **Hotel Burnham** (p. 69), **Hotel Felix** (p. 82), **InterContinental Chicago** (p. 77), **Hotel Monaco** (p. 69), and **Talbott Hotel** (p. 77).

A focus on locally produced, organic ingredients has become a hallmark of the city's top chefs. Following the lead of well-known chefs such as **Charlie Trotter** (p. 131), Bruce Sherman of **North Pond** (p. 134), and Paul Kahan of **Blackbird** (p. 102), more and more local restaurateurs are highlighting seasonal ingredients on their menus, and the **Green City Market** (p. 113) has become a popular shopping destination for both culinary professionals and local foodies.

In addition to the resources for Chicago listed above, see frommers.com/planning for more tips on responsible travel.

Spiaggia (p. 110), one of the best Italian restaurants in the country—and among the most expensive. To celebrate their first Valentine's Day as first couple, the Obamas chose **Table Fifty-Two** (p. 113), an unassuming spot that gives classic Southern dishes an upscale twist. Not only is the restaurant's owner, Art Smith, a friend and former South Side neighbor, but he also happens to be Oprah's former personal chef.

For more casual meals in Hyde Park, the Obamas were regulars at **Italian Fiesta Pizzeria,** 1400 E. 47th St. (© 773/684-2222; italianfiestapizzeria. com), a family-owned restaurant that was also a favorite of Michelle and her parents when she was growing up. Barack has also mentioned the **Valois Cafeteria,** 1518 E. 53rd St. (© 773/667-0647; www.valoisrestaurant.com), a no-frills, old-school neighborhood landmark, as his top breakfast spot in the city. For family outings on the North Side, the Obamas liked to stop in at **R. J. Grunts,** 2056 N. Lincoln Park West (© 773/929-5363; www.rjgrunts chicago.com), known for its all-American lineup of burgers and Tex-Mex specialties, as well as its enormous salad bar. An added bonus for kids: It's right across the street from Lincoln Park Zoo.

3

SUGGESTED CHICAGO ITINERARIES

D owntown Chicago is relatively compact, so it's possible to get a general sense of the city in 1 day (although, of course, you really should spend more than 24 hours here). How you spend your time depends in part on your interests and the weather; you could easily spend 3 days exploring Chicago's museums, and if you're here in the winter, that's probably a lot more appealing than a daylong walking tour. On a sunny summer day, though, you might be tempted to spend an afternoon wandering along the lakefront without any particular destination. In this spirit, I've composed the following itineraries, which contain a mix of cultural institutions and scenic walks.

ORIENTATION

Chicago proper has about three million inhabitants living in an area about two-thirds the size of New York City; another five million make the suburbs their home. The **Chicago River** forms a Y that divides the city into its three geographic zones: North Side, South Side, and West Side. (Lake Michigan is where the East Side would be.) The downtown financial district is called **the Loop.** The city's key shopping street is **North Michigan Avenue,** also known as the **Magnificent Mile.** In addition to department stores and vertical malls, this stretch of property north of the river houses many of the city's most elegant

ABOVE: **"The Loop" refers to a core of high-rises surrounded by elevated train tracks;** FACING PAGE: **Chicago's Pilsen neighborhood.**

47

hotels. North and south of this downtown zone, Chicago stretches along 29 miles of Lake Michigan shoreline that is, by and large, free of commercial development, reserved for public use as green space and parkland from one end of town to the other.

Finding an Address

Chicago is laid out in a **grid system,** with the streets neatly lined up as if on a giant piece of graph paper. Because the city itself isn't rectangular (it's rather elongated), the shape is a bit irregular, but the perpendicular pattern remains. A half-dozen or so major diagonal thoroughfares make moving through the city relatively easy.

Point zero is located at the downtown intersection of State and Madison streets. **State Street** divides east and west addresses, and **Madison Street** divides north and south addresses. From here, Chicago's highly predictable addressing system begins. Making use of this grid, it's easy to plot the distance in miles between any two points in the city.

Virtually all of Chicago's principal north–south and east–west arteries are spaced by increments of 400 in the addressing system—regardless of the number of smaller streets nestled between them—and each addition or subtraction of the number 400 to an address is equivalent to a half-mile. Thus, starting at point zero on Madison Street and traveling north along State Street for 1 mile, you will come to 800 N. State St., which intersects Chicago Avenue. Continue uptown for another half-mile and you arrive at the 1200 block of North State Street at Division Street. And so it goes, right to the city line, with suburban Evanston located at the 7600 block north, 9½ miles from point zero.

The same rule applies when you're traveling south, or east to west. Thus, starting at point zero and heading west from State Street along Madison and Halsted streets, the address of 800 W. Madison St. would be the distance of 1 mile, while Racine Avenue, at the intersection of the 1200 block of West Madison Street, is 1½ miles from point zero. Madison Street then continues westward to Chicago's boundary with the nearby suburb of Oak Park along Austin Avenue, which, at 6000 W. Madison, is approximately 7½ miles from point zero.

Once you've got the grid figured out, you can look at a map and estimate about how long it will take to walk around any given neighborhood. The other convenient aspect of the grid is that every major road uses the same numerical system. In other words, the cross street (Division St.) at 1200 N. Lake Shore Dr. is the same as at 1200 N. Clark St. and 1200 N. LaSalle St.

Street Maps

Free maps are available at the city's official visitor information centers at the **Chicago Cultural Center** and the **Chicago Water Works Visitor Center** (see "Visitor Information," p. ###). You can also print out maps before your trip by visiting the Chicago Convention and Tourism Bureau's website, **www.choose chicago.com**.

Neighborhoods in Brief

DOWNTOWN

THE LOOP The Loop refers literally to a core of high-rises surrounded by a rectangular "loop" of elevated train tracks. But when Chicagoans use the term,

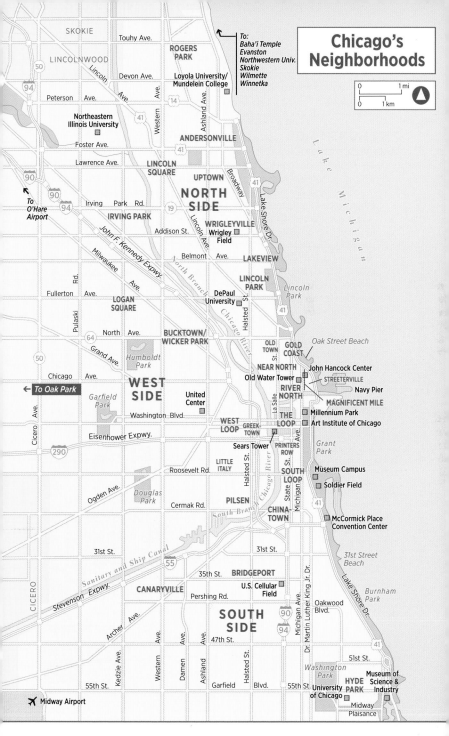

Chicago's Neighborhoods

To:
Baha'i Temple
Evanston
Northwestern Univ.
Skokie
Wilmette
Winnetka

0   1 mi
0   1 km

SKOKIE
LINCOLNWOOD
ROGERS PARK
Touhy Ave.
Devon Ave.
Loyola University/ Mundelein College
Peterson Ave.
Northeastern Illinois University
Foster Ave.
Lawrence Ave.
LINCOLN SQUARE
ANDERSONVILLE
UPTOWN
NORTH SIDE
IRVING PARK
Irving Park Rd.
To O'Hare Airport
John F. Kennedy Expwy.
Milwaukee Ave.
Addison St.
WRIGLEYVILLE
Wrigley Field
Belmont Ave.
LAKEVIEW
Fullerton Ave.
LOGAN SQUARE
LINCOLN PARK
DePaul University
Lincoln Park
North Ave.
BUCKTOWN/ WICKER PARK
Humboldt Park
Chicago Ave.
OLD TOWN
GOLD COAST
Oak Street Beach
NEAR NORTH
John Hancock Center
WEST SIDE
To Oak Park
Garfield Park
United Center
Old Water Tower
STREETERVILLE
RIVER NORTH
Navy Pier
Washington Blvd.
MAGNIFICENT MILE
Eisenhower Expwy.
WEST LOOP
GREEK-TOWN
THE LOOP
Millennium Park
Art Institute of Chicago
Sears Tower
PRINTERS ROW
Grant Park
Roosevelt Rd.
LITTLE ITALY
SOUTH LOOP
Museum Campus
Soldier Field
Cermak Rd.
PILSEN
CHINA-TOWN
McCormick Place Convention Center
Douglas Park
31st St.
31st St.
31st Street Beach
BRIDGEPORT
35th St.
U.S. Cellular Field
CANARYVILLE
Pershing Rd.
Burnham Park
Oakwood Blvd.
CICERO
Stevenson Expwy.
SOUTH SIDE
47th St.
51st St.
Washington Park
55th St.
Garfield Blvd.
HYDE PARK
Museum of Science & Industry
University of Chicago
Midway Plaisance
Midway Airport

Lake Michigan
Lincoln Ave.
Broadway
Lake Shore Dr.
Ashland Ave.
Western Ave.
Halsted St.
North Branch Chicago River
South Branch Chicago River
Sanitary and Ship Canal
Chicago River
Archer Ave.
Ashland Ave.
Damen Ave.
Western Ave.
Kedzie Ave.
Cicero Ave.
Pulaski Rd.
Grand Ave.
Ogden Ave.
Dr. Martin Luther King Jr. Dr.
Michigan Ave.
State St.
La Salle
Lake Shore Dr.

they're referring to the city's downtown, bounded by the Chicago River to the north and west, by Michigan Avenue to the east, and by Roosevelt Avenue to the south. For the most part, the Loop is strictly business, filled with office buildings rather than residential developments. For a suggested walking tour of the Loop, see p. 241.

THE NORTH SIDE

MAGNIFICENT MILE North Michigan Avenue from the bridge spanning the Chicago River to its northern tip at Oak Street is known as the Magnificent Mile (or, simply, "Michigan Avenue," although the street itself stretches much farther). Many of the city's best hotels and most concentrated shopping can be found here. The area stretching east of Michigan Avenue to the lake is sometimes referred to as "Streeterville"—the legacy of George Wellington "Cap" Streeter. Streeter was an eccentric, bankrupt showman who lived in Chicago in the mid-1880s. Looking for a new way to make money, Streeter bought a steamship with a plan to become a gun runner in Honduras. The steamship ran aground during a test cruise in Lake Michigan, and Streeter left the ship where it was, staking out 200 acres of self-created landfill. He then declared himself "governor" of the "District of Lake Michigan." True story.

RIVER NORTH Just to the west of the Mag Mile is an old warehouse district called River North. These formerly industrial buildings have been transformed into one of the city's most vital commercial districts, with many of the city's hottest restaurants and nightspots; you'll also find the city's highest concentration of art galleries here. Large-scale residential loft developments have sprouted on its western and southwestern fringes.

THE GOLD COAST Some of Chicago's most desirable real estate and historic architecture is found along Lake Shore Drive, between Oak Street and North Avenue and along the adjacent side streets. Despite trendy pockets of real estate that have popped up elsewhere, the moneyed class still prefers to live by the lake. On the neighborhood's southwestern edge, around Division and Rush streets, a string of raucous bars and late-night eateries contrasts sharply with the rest of the area's sedate mood. For a suggested walking tour of the neighborhood, see p. 246.

You'll find many of the city's hottest nightspots in River North.

OLD TOWN West of LaSalle Street, principally on North Wells Street between Division Street and North Avenue, is the residential district of Old Town, which boasts some of the city's best-preserved historic homes (a few even survived the Great Chicago

Fire of 1871). This area was a hippie haven in the 1960s and '70s; now the neighborhood is one of the most expensive residential areas in the city. Old Town's biggest claim to fame, the legendary Second City comedy club, has served up the lighter side of life to Chicagoans for more than 30 years.

LINCOLN PARK Chicago's most popular residential neighborhood for young singles and urban-minded families is Lincoln Park. Stretching from North Avenue to Diversey Parkway, it's bordered on the east by the huge park of the same name, which is home to one of the nation's oldest zoos (established in 1868). The trapezoid formed by Clark Street, Armitage Avenue, Halsted Street, and Diversey Parkway also contains many of Chicago's liveliest bars, restaurants, retail stores, music clubs, and off-Loop theaters—including the nationally acclaimed Steppenwolf Theatre Company.

LAKEVIEW & WRIGLEYVILLE Midway up the city's North Side is a one-time blue-collar, now mainstream middle-class quarter called Lakeview. It has become the neighborhood of choice for many gays and lesbians, recent college graduates, and residents priced out of Lincoln Park. The main thoroughfare is Belmont Avenue, between Broadway and Sheffield Avenue. Wrigleyville is the name given to the neighborhood in the vicinity of Wrigley Field—home of the Chicago Cubs—at Sheffield Avenue and Addison Street. Not surprisingly, the ball field is surrounded by sports bars and memorabilia shops.

UPTOWN & ANDERSONVILLE Uptown, which runs along the lakefront as far north as Foster Avenue, has traditionally attracted waves of immigrants. While crime was a major problem for decades, the area has stabilized, with formerly decrepit buildings being converted into—you guessed it—condominiums. Vietnamese and Chinese immigrants have transformed Argyle Street between Broadway and Sheridan Road into a teeming market for fresh meat, fish, and all kinds of exotic vegetables. Slightly to the north and west is the old Scandinavian neighborhood of Andersonville, whose main drag is Clark Street, between Foster and Bryn Mawr avenues. The area has an eclectic mix of Middle Eastern restaurants, a distinct cluster of women-owned businesses, and a burgeoning colony of gays and lesbians.

LINCOLN SQUARE West of Andersonville and slightly to the south, where Lincoln, Western, and Lawrence avenues intersect, is Lincoln Square, a neighborhood that still retains traces of Chicago's once-vast German-American community. The surrounding leafy residential streets have attracted many families, who flock to the Old Town School of Folk Music's theater and education center, a beautiful restoration of a former library building.

ROGERS PARK Rogers Park, which begins at Devon Avenue, is located on the northern fringes of the city bordering suburban Evanston. Its western half has been a Jewish neighborhood for decades. The eastern half, dominated by Loyola University's lakefront campus, has become the most cosmopolitan enclave in the entire city: African Americans, Asians, East Indians, and Russian Jews live side by side with the ethnically mixed student population drawn to the Catholic university. The western stretch of Devon Avenue is a Midwestern slice of Calcutta, colonized by Indians who've transformed the street into a veritable restaurant row serving tandoori chicken and curry-flavored dishes.

THE WEST SIDE

WEST LOOP Also known as the Near West Side, the neighborhood just across the Chicago River from the Loop is the city's newest gentrification target, as old warehouses and once-vacant lots have been transformed into trendy condos and stylish restaurants. Chicago's old Greektown, still the Greek culinary center of the city, runs along Halsted Street between Adams and Monroe streets. Much of the old Italian neighborhood in this vicinity was the victim of urban renewal, but remnants still survive on Taylor Street. The same is true for a few old delis and shops on Maxwell Street, dating from the turn of the 20th century when a large Jewish community lived in the area.

BUCKTOWN/WICKER PARK Centered near the intersection of North, Damen, and Milwaukee avenues, this resurgent area has hosted waves of German-, Polish-, and, most recently, Spanish-speaking immigrants (not to mention writer Nelson Algren). In recent years, it has morphed into a bastion of hot new restaurants, alternative culture, and loft-dwelling yuppies, although the neighborhood still feels somewhat gritty. The terms Bucktown and Wicker Park are often used interchangeably, but Bucktown is technically the neighborhood north of North Avenue, while Wicker Park is to the south. For a walking tour of the area, see p. 253.

THE SOUTH SIDE

SOUTH LOOP The generically rechristened South Loop area was Chicago's original "Gold Coast" in the late 19th century, with Prairie Avenue (now a historic district) as its most exclusive address. But in the wake of the 1893 World's Columbian Exposition in Hyde Park, and continuing through the Prohibition era of the 1920s, the area was infamous for its Levee vice district, home to gambling and prostitution, some of the most corrupt politicians in Chicago history, and Al Capone's headquarters at the old Lexington Hotel. However, in recent years, its prospects have turned around. The South Loop—stretching from Harrison Street's historic Printers Row south to Cermak Road (where Chinatown begins), and from Lake Shore Drive west to the south branch of the Chicago River—is now one of the fastest-growing residential neighborhoods in the city.

PILSEN Originally home to the nation's largest settlement of Bohemian-Americans, Pilsen (named for a city in what's now the Czech Republic) was for decades the principal entry point in Chicago for immigrants of every ethnic background. Centered at Halsted and 18th streets just southwest of the Loop, Pilsen now contains one of the largest Mexican-American communities in the U.S. This vibrant and colorful neighborhood, which was happily invaded by the outdoor mural movement launched years earlier in Mexico, boasts a profusion of authentic taquerías and bakeries. The artistic spirit that permeates the community isn't confined to Latin American art. In recent years, artists of every stripe, drawn partly by the availability of loft space in Pilsen, have nurtured a small but thriving artists' colony here.

HYDE PARK Hyde Park is like an independent village within the confines of Chicago, right off Lake Michigan and roughly a 30-minute train ride from the Loop. Fifty-seventh Street is the main drag, and the University of Chicago—with all its attendant shops and restaurants—is the neighborhood's principal tenant. The most successful racially integrated community in the city, Hyde Park is an oasis of furious intellectual activity and liberalism that, ironically, is hemmed in on all sides by neighborhoods suffering some of the highest crime rates in Chicago. Its main attraction is the world-famous Museum of Science and Industry.

THE BEST OF CHICAGO IN 1 DAY

The day begins with a walking tour of the Loop, which is the best way to get your bearings (and understand why Chicago's architecture is world famous). Then you can squeeze in a quick visit to one of the city's preeminent museums before strolling along Michigan Avenue, Chicago's most famous thoroughfare, which takes you to the ritzy Gold Coast neighborhood. If possible, follow this itinerary on a weekday, when downtown offices are open and the sidewalks buzz with energy. This route works fine on weekends as well, but you won't experience quite the same big-city rush. **Start:** *Green, Orange, Brown, or Purple lines to Adams, or Red Line to Jackson.*

1 Chicago Architecture Foundation

Start your day with the Chicago Architecture Foundation's "Historic Downtown: Rise of the Skyscraper" tour, which begins daily at 10am year-round. The 2-hour walking tour takes you to the oldest high-rises in the Loop, and the docents explain why these early office buildings were revolutionary. Sure, you'll get a basic architecture education, but this is also a great way to get a sense of the Loop's layout and dramatic canyonlike vistas. (Another popular tour, "Modern Skyscrapers," starts daily at 1pm.) See p. 229.

2 The Art Institute ★★★

Across the street from the Chicago Architecture Foundation stands one of the city's most prestigious cultural institutions; if you have time for only one

Edward Hopper's *Nighthawks* at the Art Institute of Chicago.

Suggested Chicago Itineraries

M Subway/El stop

DAY ONE

1 Chicago Architecture Foundation
2 The Art Institute
3 Millennium Park
4 Park Grill
5 Michigan Avenue Bridge
6 The Magnificent Mile
7 Hancock Observatory
8 Oak Street Beach
9 Third Coast
10 The Gold Coast

DAY TWO

1 Field Museum of Natural History
2 Buckingham Fountain
3 Lake Michigan or Chicago River cruise/ Shoreline Sightseeing
4 Navy Pier/Chicago Children's Museum
5 Charlie's Ale House
6 Wrigley Field
7 Southport Avenue
8 Julius Meinl
9 Buddy Guy's Legends
9A Kingston Mines
9B Blue Chicago
9C B.L.U.E.S.

The Pritzker Pavilion features Frank Gehry's signature ribbons of steel.

museum while you're here, this is the one to visit. Since you've got limited time, head right for the two must-see exhibits: first, the world-famous Impressionist collection, followed by the 20th-century American modern art gallery, which houses masterpieces such as Edward Hopper's *Nighthawks*. See p. 154.

Skaters on Millennium Park's rink.

3 Millennium Park ★★★

Just north of the Art Institute is one of the city's most popular gathering spots. Check out the massive video-screen faces on the Crown Fountain, then take a walk around (and under) Anish Kapoor's bean-shaped sculpture, **Cloud Gate.** The Pritzker Music Pavilion, designed by Frank Gehry, features the architect's signature ribbons of silver steel; Gehry also designed the adjoining serpentine bridge. See p. 158.

4 Park Grill 🍽 ★★

In the winter, this restaurant overlooks Millennium Park's ice-skating rink; come summer, the rink transforms into an outdoor cafe, perfect for sipping a drink and admiring the skyline. Stay for a full meal or grab a sandwich to go. 11 N. Michigan Ave. ✆ **312/521-PARK** (521-7275). See p. 97.

5 Michigan Avenue Bridge

Walk north along Michigan Avenue and you'll come to this bridge, which spans the Chicago River. Stop here for a great photo op—on a nice day, you'll be joined by plenty of other visitors doing the exact same thing.

6 The Magnificent Mile

The 14-block stretch of Michigan Avenue from the river to Oak Street, known as the "Magnificent Mile," is shopping central, a dense concentration of high-rise malls, designer boutiques, and practically every mass-market clothing brand. Even if you're not a shopper, it's worth a stroll; busy at almost all hours, it's great for people-watching. Some Chicagoans dismiss the Mag Mile as too touristy, but I think walking here makes you feel like you're part of a vibrant metropolis. See p. 73.

7 Hancock Observatory ★★

This may only be Chicago's third-tallest building, but the view from the top is spectacular: In the right weather conditions, you can see all the way to three other states (Wisconsin, Indiana, and Michigan). The "talking telescopes" help you get your bearings by pointing out landmarks in each direction. See p. 179.

8 Oak Street Beach

Where Michigan Avenue merges into Lake Shore Drive at Oak Street, head down the underpass to get to Oak Street Beach, a curved stretch of sand that's a summertime hot spot and a great background for photos. Bikers, skaters, and joggers fill the paths, while kids play in the sand. Think of it as Chicago's own miniresort getaway—just don't plan on swimming in the frigid water. See p. 231.

9 Third Coast ☕ ★

If you're tired of generic chain coffeehouses (of which Chicago has plenty), stop by this somewhat shabby lower-level cafe that welcomes both well-heeled locals and the occasional starving artist. In addition to the usual lattes and muffins, there's a full lunch and dinner menu, and wine and beer are available. 1260 N. Dearborn St. © **312/649-0730.** See p. 336.

10 The Gold Coast

To get an idea of how Chicago's wealthiest live, take a stroll through this neighborhood of historic town homes (including the original Playboy Mansion, at 1340 N. State Pkwy.). The

tranquil, tree-lined streets are only a few blocks away from Michigan Avenue, but they feel like a different city. (For a suggested walking tour, see p. 246.) Finish up the night with dinner at one of the many restaurants in River North, or catch a show and discover Chicago's vibrant theater scene. See p. 291.

The original Playboy Mansion.

The Best of Chicago in 1 Day

THE BEST OF CHICAGO IN 2 DAYS

After Day 1, you should be familiar with downtown Chicago. Now it's time to explore at least part of the Museum Campus, home to three major museums. Although I recommend the Field Museum for this itinerary, you could certainly substitute the nearby **Shedd Aquarium** (p. 175) or **Adler Planetarium** (p. 172), depending on your interests. The first part of this day keeps you firmly in tourist territory, but you'll journey off the beaten track later in the day when you wander through Wrigleyville and get a sense of how real Chicagoans live. ***Start:*** *Bus no. 6, 10, 12, 130, or 146 to Roosevelt Road and Lake Shore Drive.*

1 Field Museum of Natural History ★★★

You'll feel as though you've entered a truly grand place when you walk into the museum's massive Stanley Field Hall and come face to face with Sue, the largest *Tyrannosaurus rex* fossil ever discovered. The Field Museum is one of those classic something-for-everyone institutions where you can wander for hours. The ***Inside Ancient Egypt*** exhibit is more than just mummies: It's a complete re-creation of ancient daily life, including a marketplace, royal barge, and religious shrines (with lots of hands-on activities for kids). The second-floor African and South Pacific exhibits are also worth a stop, with beautifully designed interactive displays. But the Fields also has a certain timeless quality: The old-fashioned animals-of-the-world dioramas, for example, have remained unchanged for decades. See p. 173.

2 Buckingham Fountain ★

This grand stone fountain is one of the city's iconic structures. (If you're a sitcom fan, you might recognize it from the opening credits of *Married with*

A hands-on exhibit at the Field Museum of Natural History.

Buckingham Fountain blazes with colored lights at night.

Children.) Try to get here on the hour, when jets of water spurt dramatically into the sky. The fountain blazes with colored lights at night, so if you're staying downtown, it's also worth a stop after dark. (**Note:** The fountain is closed Nov–Mar.) See p. 162.

3 Lake Michigan or Chicago River cruise

Departing from a dock at the nearby Shedd Aquarium, **Shoreline Sightseeing ★** runs water taxis that cruise north to Navy Pier (daily from Memorial Day to Labor Day). From the pier, you can also catch boats that cruise along the Chicago River all the way to the Sears Tower. See p. 226.

4 Navy Pier ★

Yes, it's touristy and crowded, but Navy Pier is also full of energy—and if you stroll all the way to the end, you'll be rewarded with great views of downtown. If you're traveling with kids, stopping at Navy Pier is pretty much mandatory; it has a carousel and other carnival-type rides, lots of boats to admire, and the **Chicago Children's Museum.** See p. 180.

5 Charlie's Ale House ☕

Head to the outdoor patio of this casual saloon for a front-row look at Navy Pier's busy waterfront. Cool off with a drink, or fill up on comfort food classics like burgers or chicken pot pie. 700 E. Grand Ave. ✆ **312/595-1440.** See p. 128.

From Navy Pier, take the free Navy Pier shuttle to the Grand El station (Red Line), and ride north to the Addison Street stop.

6 Wrigley Field ★★

If you're a baseball fan, Wrigley is hallowed ground: the second-oldest stadium in the major leagues, home to the perennially jinxed **Chicago Cubs.** The surrounding blocks are a good place to stock up on Cubs souvenirs. If you want to catch a game, tickets can be tough to come by (the entire season tends to be sold out by Opening Day). Show up an hour or so before a game, and you can sometimes find a season ticket holder trying to sell unused seats (and ticket brokers always have seats available—for a price). See p. 236.

If you're not staying for a game and would rather explore a residential neighborhood, walk west on Addison Street for 5 blocks until you get to:

7 Southport Avenue

This area is well into the gentrified stage (witness the number of trendy clothing boutiques), but it's still very much a neighborhood. Wander Southport between Belmont Avenue and Grace Street, and you'll see young moms pushing designer strollers, singles walking their dogs, and hardly any other tourists. If you're here in the early evening, you'll find plenty of low-key, affordable restaurants for dinner. When you're ready to head back downtown, you can hop on the Brown Line at the Southport stop. See p. 268.

European pastries and coffee at Julius Meinl.

8 Julius Meinl 🍽 ★

Run by an Austrian coffee company, this cafe is a mix of Old World and New. Large picture windows make it feel bright and inviting, while the European pastries and coffee (served elegantly on silver trays) are a welcome change from standard chain coffeehouses. 3601 N. Southport Ave. ℭ **773/868-1857.** See p. 335.

9 Buddy Guy's Legends ★★

Chicago is the birthplace of "electric blues," that rocking blend of soulful singing and wailing electric guitars. To experience the city's most famous form of music, head for Buddy Guy's Legends in the South Loop, which has the honky-tonk feel of a Southern roadhouse. The owner, blues guitarist and Rock and Roll Hall of Famer Buddy Guy, makes regular appearances; even if he's not on the bill, the talent level is always top-notch. (If you're staying on the North Side of the city and would rather stick close to home, try **Kingston Mines, Blue Chicago,** or **B.L.U.E.S.**) See p. 312.

THE BEST OF CHICAGO IN 3 DAYS

For this itinerary, it's time to escape downtown completely and spend the day on the North Side of the city. You'll start out in Lincoln Park, which is both an actual park and the name of a popular residential neighborhood, where singles and young families can be seen strolling or jogging along the lakefront paths during nice weather. You'll also visit two major cultural institutions, both suitable for kids, and then head into a residential neighborhood for some shopping. **Start:** *Bus no. 151 or 156 to North Cannon Drive and Fullerton Parkway.*

Farm-in-the-Zoo's main attraction, the giant John Deere Tractor.

1 Lincoln Park Zoo ★★★

A beloved local institution, this zoo won't dazzle you a la San Diego, but it does a good job of covering all the bases, with a mix of indoor habitats and naturalistic outdoor environments (plus, did I mention it's *free?*). Don't miss the *Regenstein African Journey* exhibit (which re-creates both a tropical jungle and a dusty African savanna) and the internationally renowned Great Ape House. If you have kids, stop at the **Children's Zoo,** where a unique climbing structure gives little ones 2 and older a chance to release some energy. See p. 186.

2 Farm-in-the-Zoo ★

Just south of the zoo, this re-creation of a working farm gets children in touch (literally) with animals. The highlight for many little ones is the giant John Deere tractor; you'll usually find a line of kids waiting for their turn to sit behind the massive steering wheel (along with parents waiting to snap a picture). See p. 222.

3 Big Cats Café ☕

This cafe, located on the roof of the zoo's gift shop, has outdoor seating and panoramic views over the zoo. You can order the usual hot dogs and fries, but there's also a selection of more health-conscious wraps. 2200 N. Cannon Dr. ✆ **312/742-2000.**

4 North Avenue Beach

Come summer, this is Lincoln Park's prime playground—a place to jog, play volleyball, build sandcastles, or simply pose. Even in August, the water is usually icy, but if you want to at least dip your feet in Lake Michigan, this wide stretch of sand is the place to do it. Just south of the beach, a grassy stretch of park offers picture-perfect views of downtown. See p. 231.

Take a taxi to the corner of Halsted Street and Armitage Avenue.

5 Armitage Avenue

To call this the city's chicest shopping strip isn't meant as a put-down to Michigan Avenue; while

Armitage Avenue's chic shops tend to be small and personal.

the Mag Mile goes for big and showy, the boutiques along Armitage tend to be smaller and more personal (most are independently owned rather than chain stores). You'll find an especially appealing selection of home decor stores and gift shops with eclectic selections of well-designed merchandise. Wander the surrounding side streets to see the neighborhood's eclectic mix of historic homes and modern mansions. See p. 266.

If you're ready to wind down, you'll find plenty of restaurants nearby or in adjacent Old Town. But if you'd like to explore one more neighborhood, take a taxi to the corner of North Avenue and Damen Avenue, then walk north along Damen.

6 Bucktown

If you're not shopped out yet, finish up the day with a walk through Bucktown, home to the city's highest concentration of edgy clothing boutiques. It feels grittier than Armitage Avenue, and that's part of the appeal for the cool kids who live here. See p. 268.

7 Northside Café 🍺

Bucktown's unofficial neighborhood hangout, this low-key cafe is a sandwich spot by day and a bustling bar by night. When the weather's nice, grab a seat on the outdoor patio and people-watch with everyone else. 1635 N. Damen Ave. ✆ **773/384-3555.** See p. 144.

8 Improv Comedy

Although it's best known for **Second City,** Chicago is home to a number of excellent improv comedy troupes. You can catch rising stars before they land their own sitcom deals. Second City is the big man on campus, while **iO** is the slightly scrappier and more creative bunch. If you're here with older kids or teens, catch the family-friendly **ComedySportz.** See p. 305.

4

WHERE TO STAY

D owntown Chicago is packed with hotels, thanks to the city's position as the business center of the Midwest. The majority are tucked amid the high-rises of the Loop and North Michigan Avenue, so staying here offers the pros and cons of any urban destination: Your room may look out onto a stunning cityscape, or no farther than the building next door. Lake Michigan views are highly prized—and therefore command the highest prices. Although every hotel caters to business travelers, this is not a city where luxury hotels have dibs on all the prime real estate; casual, family-friendly properties are scattered throughout downtown. Affordable rooms, unfortunately, aren't so easy to find: Chicago hotels are among the most expensive in the country.

BEST BETS

- **Best Splurge:** The **Elysian,** steps from Barneys New York and Prada on the Gold Coast, fits right in with its swanky neighborhood. King rooms come with fireplaces, Italian luxury linens, and extra-large soaking tubs; guests can lounge at the spa, or take advantage of the hotel's fleet of Lexus automobiles to head beyond downtown. For a more contemporary take on luxury living, the sleek rooms at the **Trump International Hotel & Tower** feel like spacious urban apartments and include modern kitchens stocked with Sub-Zero appliances. Spa Suites allow easy access to a dizzying array of specialty treatments. See p. 85 and 81, respectively.

- **Best Bang for Your Buck:** The **Hampton Inn & Suites** not only offers consistently lower rates than other hotels in centrally located River North, it's also more stylish than the name implies, with Deco-style touches in the lobby and common rooms. What really sets it apart, though, are the amenities that come with those reasonable rates: an indoor pool with hot tub, rooftop deck, and a free hot breakfast buffet. See p. 85.

- **Best Historic Hotels:** The **Drake Hotel** is Chicago's original luxury hotel, and walking into its grand, formal lobby is like stepping back into the 19th century, especially if you settle down for afternoon tea in the elegant Palm Court. The comfortable rooms don't have quite as much character, but those facing north offer only-in-Chicago views of Lake Michigan and Lake Shore Drive. To experience Chicago architectural history first-hand, book a room at the **Hotel Burnham,** a complete rehab of the revered Reliance Building, one of the world's first glass-walled skyscrapers. See p. 76 and p. 69, respectively.

- **Best for Business Travelers:** Virtually every hotel in Chicago qualifies, but the **Swissôtel Chicago** combines extensive business services with stunning views from all rooms. Traveler-friendly amenities include generously sized desks and ergonomic chairs in each room, and the light-filled penthouse fitness center allows you to admire the city while working out. See p. 71.

○ **Best Service:** The attention to detail, regal pampering, and well-connected concierges at both the **Ritz-Carlton,** 160 E. Pearson St. (✆ **800/621-6906**), and the **Four Seasons,** 120 E. Delaware Place (✆ **800/332-3442**), make them the hotels of choice for travelers who want to feel like royalty. See p. 74 and 73, respectively.

○ **Most Romantic:** For a splurge, the **Peninsula** pampers couples with luxurious rooms and top-notch amenities, including massages in the on-site spa and an outdoor terrace for lounging; the dimly lit, sexy lobby bar makes a good spot for a nightcap, especially if you snag a spot by the fireplace. For a cozier getaway, try the **Talbott Hotel,** which is centrally located but tucked away from the crowds. Book the hotel's Romance Package, and you'll get a set of monogrammed bathrobes, as well as a late-afternoon checkout. See p. 74 and p. 77, respectively.

○ **Best Views:** Almost every hotel in town has rooms with great views—and others that look straight into neighboring offices. The **Swissôtel** and the **Park Hyatt Chicago** are both set apart from surrounding buildings, giving their rooms unobstructed views across the city (the higher the room, the more you'll see). For a distinctly urban vista, **The Wit Hotel** looks out over the Loop's busy El tracks; its rooftop lounge is the perfect place to admire the city lights by night. See p. 71, 74, and 71, respectively.

○ **Best for Families:** With every room a suite, the **Embassy Suites** and **Homewood Suites** are ideal for families looking for a little more than the typical hotel room provides (Homewood Suites also include a full kitchen, so parents can save money by preparing their own meals). Both have indoor pools, so the kids can splash around no matter what the weather, and offer a free hot breakfast buffet. See p. 84 and 79, respectively.

○ **Best Hotel Pool:** With its floor-to-ceiling windows overlooking Michigan Avenue, the pool at the **Peninsula Chicago** is a bright, stylish oasis flooded with natural light. But for historic charm, it's hard to beat the Spanish-styled junior Olympic-size pool at the **InterContinental Chicago.** Considered an engineering marvel when it was constructed in 1929, it was a favorite training spot for Olympic gold-medal swimmer (and later *Tarzan* star) Johnny Weissmuller. See p. 74 and 77, respectively.

○ **Best Off-the-Beaten-Path Hotels:** The **City Suites Hotel,** 933 W. Belmont Ave. (✆ **800/248-9108**); the **Majestic Hotel,** 528 W. Brompton St. (✆ **800/727-5108**); and the **Best Western Hawthorne Terrace,** 3434 N. Broadway Ave. (✆ **888/401-8781**), located in residential North Side neighborhoods, have a more personal feel than many downtown hotels. They're also convenient to public transportation. See p. 87, 88, and 87, respectively.

Price Categories	
Very Expensive	$300 and up
Expensive	$200–$350
Moderate	$125–$200
Inexpensive	Under $150

WHAT YOU'LL really PAY

Chicago hotel rates vary widely throughout the year, making it difficult to pin down the average price for any given property. For each hotel listed, I've provided a range of rates that reflect the city's seasonal price fluctuations (cheaper in the winter, more expensive in the summer). The highest rate, known as the rack rate, is the maximum a hotel charges.

You can typically find discounts of up to 20% for rooms when booking through websites such as hotels.com or expedia.com (see "Getting the Best Deal" on p. 89 for more tips). The hotels' own websites are also a good place to check for specials. During slow times, it's not impossible to obtain a room at an expensive property for the same rate as a more moderate one. Rack rates at the W Chicago City Center start at $279 but in March 2011, just a cursory search of the usual Web discount sites revealed that the going rate was actually closer to $179. *Note:* Quoted rates do not include Chicago's hefty hotel tax; at 14.9%, it can add significantly to the cost of your stay.

THE LOOP

Strictly speaking, "downtown" in Chicago means the Loop—the central business district, a 6 × 8-block rectangle enveloped by elevated tracks on all four sides. Here's where you'll find the city's major financial institutions, trading markets, and government buildings, making for a lot of weekday hustle and bustle.

BEST FOR Visitors who want a real "city" experience, with dramatic skyscraper vistas. Loop hotels are also within walking distance of Chicago's major museums, as well as Grant Park and the lake.

DRAWBACKS Except for a few theaters and restaurants, the Loop shuts down at night. If nightlife is a priority, you won't find many options here.

Expensive

The Blackstone, A Renaissance Hotel ★★ The Blackstone was once one of Chicago's top hotels; in 1920, when Republican leaders gathered there to pick Warren G. Harding as their presidential candidate, the term "smoke-filled room" was born. Reopened in 2008, it may no longer be the height of luxury, but you'll get a glimpse of the hotel's original glamour in the wood-lined lobby. (The multicolored carpeting and dance-tune soundtrack, unfortunately, detract a bit from the vintage experience.) The rooms, decorated in understated cream, red, and wood tones, are quite spacious compared to other vintage hotels in town, and the large modern bathrooms have marble vanities and glass-enclosed shower stalls. For a great view, book a (more expensive) lakefront room; the well-stocked fitness room also looks out over Lake Michigan. When you've worked up an appetite, grab dinner at **Mercat a la Planxa** (p. 97), a stylish, airy tapas restaurant.

636 S. Michigan Ave. (at Balbo St.), Chicago, IL 60605. www.blackstonerenaissance.com. © **800/468-3571** or 312/447-0955. Fax 312/765-0545. 332 units. $185–$389 double; $3,000 suite. AE, DC, DISC, MC, V. Valet parking $47 with in-out privileges. Subway/El: Red Line to Harrison. **Amenities:** Restaurant; concierge; executive rooms; exercise room; room service. *In room:* TV, hair dryer, minibar, Wi-Fi ($13/day).

Hotels in the Loop & West Loop

Subway/El stop M

The Blackstone, A Renaissance Hotel 13
Fairmont Chicago Millennium Park 5
Hard Rock Hotel Chicago 4
Hilton Chicago 14
Hotel Allegro Chicago 7
Hotel Burnham 8
Hotel Monaco 3
Hyatt Regency McCormick Place 15

J.W. Marriott 12
Palmer House Hilton 10
Renaissance Chicago Hotel 1
The Silversmith Hotel & Suites 9
Swissôtel Chicago 6
W Chicago City Center 11
Wheeler Mansion 15
The Wit Hotel 2

Fairmont Chicago Millennium Park ★★ The grand circular lobby sets the Fairmont's tone: upscale and lavish rather than cozy and personal (you might wander awhile before finding the elevators). Although it's within easy walking distance of Michigan Avenue and the Art Institute, the Fairmont's tucked-away location among anonymous office towers makes it feel somewhat cut off from the life of the city. Still, all the rooms are large and bright, with contemporary wood furniture and plush bedding. Befitting its name, the hotel does boast picture-perfect views of Millennium Park—but only from some south-facing rooms, so call the hotel when you book if you're set on admiring that only-in-Chicago vista. For in-house pampering, visit the tranquil spa, adjacent to a good-sized fitness center. Visiting in winter? The Fairmont is connected to the city's underground "pedway" system, through which you can walk all the way to Macy's on State Street.

200 N. Columbus Dr. (at Lake St.), Chicago, IL 60601. www.fairmont.com/chicago. ✆ **800/526-2008** or 312/565-8000. Fax 312/856-1032. 692 units. $229–$349 double; suites from $319. AE, DC, DISC, MC, V. Valet parking $51 with in-out privileges. Subway/El: Red, Green, Orange, Brown, or Blue line to State/Lake. Small pets accepted for a $25 fee. **Amenities:** Restaurant; lounge; babysitting; concierge; executive-level rooms; health club and spa; room service; free Wi-Fi in lobby. *In room:* TV, hair dryer, high-speed Internet access ($15/day), minibar, MP3 docking station.

Hard Rock Hotel Chicago ★ Despite the name, you'll pass more business travelers than rock stars in the hallways, but the Hard Rock's eclectic decor gives it an edgier vibe than other Loop hotels. The overall theme here is music: Rock tunes echo throughout the lobby, glass cases display pop-star memorabilia, and guests are offered free Gibson guitar rentals during their stay. But the mix of old and new can be somewhat jarring—the black-and-gray lobby feels like a nightclub, while the marble-and-gold-trimmed elevator bank still feels like the office building this once was. Guest rooms go for a neutral, modern look, with larger-than-average windows that let in plenty of natural light. "Platinum" rooms on the corners of each floor are larger than the standard double rooms and feature chaise lounges for stretching out. The lobby bar, Base, hosts live music and DJs most nights till 4am.

230 N. Michigan Ave. (at Lake St.), Chicago, IL 60601. www.hardrockhotelchicago.com. ✆ **866/966-5166** or 312/345-1000. Fax 312/345-1012. 387 units. $199–$249 double; suites from $299. AE, DC, DISC, MC, V. Valet parking $36 with in-out privileges. Subway/El: Red or Blue line to State/Lake. Pets accepted for a $25 fee. **Amenities:** Restaurant; bar; concierge; exercise room; room service. *In room:* TV w/DVD player, CD player, hair dryer, minibar, Wi-Fi ($9.95/day).

Hilton Chicago ★★ ☺ The sprawling Hilton is one of the Loop's best choices for families, thanks to its indoor pool, proximity to major museums and Grant Park (where kids can run around). The hotel's colorful history includes visits by every president since FDR, as well as riots outside its front door during the 1968 Democratic Convention. The classical-rococo public spaces—such as the Versailles-inspired Grand Ballroom and Grand Stair Lobby—are magnificent, but the rest of the hotel falls into the chain-hotel mold: comfortable and well run, but fairly impersonal. Some rooms are on the small side, but all feel homey, thanks to the warm cherry furniture, and many have two bathrooms. Rooms facing Michigan Avenue offer sweeping views of Grant Park and the lake (and, no surprise, you'll pay more for them).

720 S. Michigan Ave. (at Balbo Dr.), Chicago, IL 60605. http://chicagohilton.com. ✆ **800/HILTONS** [445-8667] or 312/922-4400. Fax 312/922-5240. 1,544 units. $199–$399 double; suites from $299. AE, DC, DISC, MC, V. Valet parking $55; self-parking $43. Subway/El: Red Line to

Harrison. **Amenities:** 2 restaurants; 2 lounges; concierge; executive-level rooms; health club w/ indoor track, hot tubs, sauna, and indoor pool; room service. *In room:* TV, hair dryer, minibar, MP3 docking station, Wi-Fi ($20/day).

Hotel Burnham ★★★ If you're looking to commune with Chicago history, this sophisticated small hotel delivers a one-of-a-kind experience. Formerly known as the Reliance Building (and named for its architect, Daniel Burnham), this was one of the first skyscrapers ever built. The building retains a number of vintage elements, but the rooms have gotten a luxurious modern makeover, with plush gold-and-blue upholstery, mahogany writing desks, and chaise lounges. For views of both the city and lakefront, ask for a room on a high floor in the northeast corner. Don't come to the Burnham if you're looking for extensive amenities—the lobby is tiny, as is the exercise room—but the on-site **Atwood Café** (p. 94) serves creative comfort food against a Gilded Age backdrop. There's also complimentary Starbucks coffee in the lobby every morning and a wine reception each afternoon from 5 to 6pm.

1 W. Washington St. (at State St.), Chicago, IL 60602. www.burnhamhotel.com. © **866/690-1986** or 312/782-1111. Fax 312/782-0899. 122 units. $195–$380 double; $259–$479 suite. AE, DC, DISC, MC, V. Valet parking $45 with in-out privileges. Subway/El: Red or Blue line to Washington. Pets allowed. **Amenities:** Restaurant; concierge; exercise room and access to nearby health club; room service. *In room:* TV, hair dryer, minibar, Wi-Fi ($10/day, free for hotel loyalty program members).

Hotel Monaco ★★ This boutique hotel deftly manages to straddle the line between fun and conservative. Unlike many other Loop hotels, views at the Monaco are relatively unobstructed by surrounding buildings, especially if you request a room overlooking the Chicago River. Guest rooms feature an eclectic mix of colors and patterns, including dramatic mirrored headboards and red graphic carpeting, but also a business-friendly work desk and adjustable task chair. All rooms include "meditation stations"—comfy seats tucked into the larger-than-average windows, which are perfect for taking in the cityscape outside. Suites come with a two-person whirlpool spa and pull-out queen-size sofa bed. (If you're taller than average, you can request a Tall Room, with longer beds.) Given the hotel's playful spirit, it attracts a younger clientele, with an overall vibe that is laid-back and friendly rather than so-hip-it-hurts (this is Chicago, not New York).

225 N. Wabash Ave. (at Wacker Dr.), Chicago, IL 60601. www.monaco-chicago.com. © **800/397-7661** or 312/960-8500. Fax 312/960-1883. 192 units. $189–$379 double; $279–$509 suite. AE, DC, DISC, MC, V. Valet parking $40 with in-out privileges. Subway/El: Brown, Green, or Orange line to Randolph, or Red Line to Washington. Small pets allowed. **Amenities:** Restaurant; concierge; small exercise room and access to nearby health club; room service. *In room:* TV, CD player, hair dryer, minibar, Wi-Fi ($10/day, free for hotel loyalty program members).

J.W. Marriott Chicago ★★ Although it's a relatively new property (open since 2011), the J.W. Marriott feels like a vestige of 19th century Chicago, updated for the modern age. The building was designed as a bank by noted architect Daniel Burnham, and the grand but somewhat impersonal lobby sets the tone for this business-focused hotel. The J.W. Marriott exudes a sense of restrained elegance, from the marble-walled bathrooms to the rich gold carpeting and plush terry robes in the guest rooms. Overall, given its central Loop location, rooms are relatively dark, though ones on the west end of the hotel look directly out at the Willis (Sears) Tower. If you're up for a splurge, the corner suites have massive, spa-style bathrooms, complete with mosaic-tile tubs and mini-TVs set into the mirrors—so you can channel-surf while soaking. The executive floor has oversized rooms and a lounge stocked with gourmet treats (for an extra $60/day).

151 W. Adams St. (at LaSalle St.), Chicago, IL 60603. www.jwmarriottchicago.com. ✆ **877/458-7867** or 312/660-8200. Fax 312/660-8201. 610 units. $219–$309 double; suites from $500. AE, DC, DISC, MC, V. Valet parking $52 with in-out privileges. Subway/El: Red Line to Monroe. **Amenities:** Restaurant; lounge; concierge; fitness center w/spa and indoor pool; room service. *In room:* TV, hair dryer, minibar, Wi-Fi ($15/day).

Palmer House Hilton ★ The longest continually operating hotel in North America—open since 1871—the Palmer House retains a Gilded Age aura in its grand lobby and opulently decorated guest rooms. (The gorgeous lobby is worth a look even if you're not staying here.) But, given its popularity with groups, the place sometimes feels like an extension of the McCormick Place Convention Center. Room sizes vary from cramped to fairly spacious (to the Hilton's credit, the former are billed as "smaller rooms" and come at a discount). No matter where your room is located, don't expect grand views; most windows look out into offices across the street. Executive Level rooms on the top two floors come with DVD players, a dedicated concierge, and complimentary breakfast and afternoon hors d'oeuvres. The Palmer House caters overwhelmingly to business travelers, but because it's so big, you can snag good deals here when there are no conventions in town.

17 E. Monroe St. (at State St.), Chicago, IL 60603. www.palmerhousehiltonhotel.com. ✆ **800/HILTONS** (445-8667) or 312/726-7500. Fax 312/917-1797. 1,639 units. $159–$309 double; suites from $349. AE, DC, DISC, MC, V. Valet parking $51 with in-out privileges. Subway/El: Red Line to Monroe. **Amenities:** Restaurant; lounge; concierge; executive-level rooms; health club and spa w/indoor pool and Jacuzzi for $10/day or $20/entire stay; room service. *In room:* A/C, TV, hair dryer, high-speed Internet access ($9.95/night), minibar, MP3 docking station.

Renaissance Chicago Hotel ★ A hotel without much of a personality, the Renaissance Chicago is tasteful and understated—perfectly suited to the business travelers who are the hotel's bread and butter. Standard rooms include a small sitting area with an armchair and desk. Club-level rooms, located on the top four floors, are half a room larger and have their own concierge and private lounge, where complimentary continental breakfast and evening hors d'oeuvres are served. Request a river view for the best cityscape (corner suites also have excellent views of both the Chicago River and Lake Michigan). This large operation offers standard high-end amenities but is indistinguishable from executive-style hotels elsewhere in the country.

1 W. Wacker Dr. (at State St.), Chicago, IL 60601. www.marriott.com. ✆ **800/HOTELS-1** (468-3577) or 312/372-7200. Fax 312/372-0093. 553 units. $199–$399 double; $249–$399 club-level double; suites from $500. AE, DC, DISC, MC, V. Valet parking $49 with in-out privileges, self parking $33. Subway/El: Brown Line to State/Lake, or Red Line to Washington. Small pets accepted for a $45 fee. **Amenities:** Restaurant; lounge; concierge; executive-level rooms; health club and spa; indoor pool; room service. *In room:* TV, CD player, hair dryer, minibar, Wi-Fi ($15/day).

The Silversmith Hotel & Suites ★★ 🛅 The Silversmith is a hidden gem that eschews the usual chain-hotel conformity for a Frank Lloyd Wright–inspired look. The downside is that this very urban hotel is surrounded by other buildings, so natural light is limited; rooms on the main corridor tend to be quite dark. For a quintessentially Chicago view, request a room at the front on the fifth floor or higher, overlooking the El tracks along Wabash Avenue. Yes, the windows are extra thick to muffle the noise of the rumbling trains, but you'll want to avoid the lower-level floors if you like things quiet. Rooms have a residential feel, with 12-foot-high ceilings, wrought-iron fixtures, and armoires. Because of the Silversmith's relatively low profile, rooms don't book up here as quickly as other hotels and can sometimes be booked at a significant discount.

10 S. Wabash Ave. (at Madison St.), Chicago, IL 60603. www.silversmithchicagohotel.com. ✆ **800/979-0084** or 312/372-7696. Fax 312/372-7320. 143 units. $159–$259 double; from $229 suite. AE, DC, DISC, MC, V. Valet parking $46 with in-out privileges. Subway/El: Brown, Green, or Orange line to Madison, or Red Line to Washington. **Amenities:** Restaurant (deli); lounge; concierge; executive-level rooms; exercise room; room service; free Wi-Fi in lobby. *In room:* TV, CD player, fridge, hair dryer, free high-speed Internet access, minibar.

Swissôtel Chicago ★★★ ☺ This sleek, modern hotel may look a bit icy, but its no-nonsense aura makes it especially attractive to business travelers in search of tranquillity. The hotel's triangular design gives every room a panoramic vista of Lake Michigan, Grant Park, and/or the Chicago River. The bright, spacious rooms have separate sitting areas and contemporary wood furnishings. Active guests will want to break a sweat in the lofty environs of the Penthouse Health Club, perched on the 42nd floor—just make sure the views don't distract you from your workout. In a bid to attract more families, the hotel has also introduced Kids' Suites, separate but adjoining rooms complete with junior-sized furniture and age-appropriate toys.

323 E. Wacker Dr., Chicago, IL 60601. www.swissotelchicago.com. ✆ **888/737-9477** or 312/565-0565. Fax 312/565-0540. 632 units. $199–$359 double; from $395 suite. AE, DC, DISC, MC, V. Valet parking $52 with in-out privileges. Subway/El: Red, Brown, Orange, or Green line to Randolph. **Amenities:** 2 restaurants; lounge; concierge; executive-level rooms; health club; indoor pool; room service; sauna. *In room:* High-definition TV, hair dryer, minibar, MP3 docking station, Wi-Fi ($9.95/day).

W Chicago City Center ★ One of two Chicago properties in the hip W hotel chain (the other is the **W Chicago Lakeshore,** p. 78), this is an oasis of cool in the buttoned-down Loop. The rooms tend toward the small and dark (most look out into a central courtyard), and the W color scheme—deep purple and gray—doesn't do much to brighten the spaces. But if you're the loll-around-in-bed type, this is a great place to do it; the super-comfy beds feature cushiony pillow-top mattresses, soft duvets, and mounds of pillows. The lobby bar is a stylish spot to sit and pose amid dance music and cocktail waitresses who look like models. Given its location, this W is foremost a business hotel—although one that's definitely geared toward younger workers rather than crusty old executives.

172 W. Adams St. (at LaSalle St.), Chicago, IL 60603. www.whotels.com. ✆ **877/W-HOTELS** (946-8357) or 312/332-1200. Fax 312/332-5909. 368 units. $219–$329 double; $399–$1,500 suite. AE, DC, DISC, MC, V. Valet parking $51 with in-out privileges. Subway/El: Brown Line to Quincy. Pets allowed for a $25 fee. **Amenities:** Restaurant; lounge; concierge; exercise room; room service. *In room:* TV/DVD w/movie library, CD player, hair dryer, high-speed Internet access ($9.95/day), minibar.

The Wit Hotel ★★ This vibrant, fun hotel immerses guests in its urban setting: Two-story-high lobby windows look directly onto a bustling El station. Although it belongs to the Doubletree chain, the Wit has a boutique sensibility: The rooms mix dark wood furniture with orange and blue decorative fabrics, and the popular top-floor bar, **Roof,** brings a dash of South Beach style to the conservative Loop.

(It's definitely worth stopping by for a drink or weekend brunch; if you dare, you can sit at a table suspended beyond the edge of the building, complete with see-through floor.) King rooms come with a comfy chaise lounge for hanging out and enjoying the city views; rooms with two queen beds have only an armchair. While the standard rooms have shower stalls rather than bathtubs, "spa suites" come with oversize tubs where you can soak while staring at the skyline.

201 N. State St. (at Lake St.), Chicago, IL 60601. www.thewithotel.com. © **866/318-1514** or 312/467-0200. Fax 312/467-0202. 298 units. $179–$329 double; suites from $299. AE, DC, DISC, MC, V. Valet parking $46 with in-out privileges. Subway/El: Red, Green, Orange, Brown, or Blue line to State/Lake. **Amenities:** Restaurant; lounge; concierge; exercise room and spa; room service. *In room:* TV, hair dryer, minibar, MP3 docking station, Wi-Fi ($9.95/day).

Moderate

Hotel Allegro Chicago ★ ✦ The Allegro's laid-back vibe makes it a better bet for families and couples than other, more business-focused Loop hotels. The only downside is that you won't have room to spread out: The compact guest rooms don't have much space beyond the bed, an armoire, and an armchair. Still, the bright white-and-blue color scheme is cheery, and the compact bathrooms have

☺ family-friendly HOTELS

Chicago has plenty of options for families on the go. At the south end of the Loop, the **Hilton Chicago** (p. 68) has lots of public space for wandering, and many of the rooms come with two bathrooms. Another bonus: Both the Field Museum and the Shedd Aquarium are within walking distance. At the north end of the Loop near the intersection of Lake Michigan and the Chicago River, the **Swissôtel Chicago** offers Kids' Suites filled with kid-sized furniture, DVDs, stuffed animals, and coloring books (p. 71).

In River North, the **Hampton Inn & Suites** (p. 85) keeps the kids in a good mood with a pool, Nintendo, free breakfast, and proximity to the Hard Rock Cafe and the Rainforest Cafe. The **Best Western River North Hotel** (p. 84) won't win any prizes for its no-frills decor, but it's close to both Michigan Avenue and a dozen family-friendly restaurants. The indoor pool and outdoor deck—with great city views—are other big draws.

When you want a little extra room to spread out, both **Homewood Suites** (p. 79) and **Embassy Suites** (p. 84) make traveling en masse a little easier with separate bedrooms and kitchenettes (so you can save money on food).

Both offer free breakfast buffets and have indoor pools.

Of course, luxury hotels can afford to be friendly to all of their guests. At the **Four Seasons Hotel** (p. 73), kids are indulged with little robes, balloon animals, Nintendo, and milk and cookies; the hotel also has a wonderful pool. The concierge at the **Ritz-Carlton Chicago** (p. 74) keeps a stash of toys and games for younger guests to borrow, and kids' menu items are available 24 hours; the hotel even provides a special gift pack just for teenage guests. The upscale **Westin Chicago River North** (p. 84) also caters to families with baby accessories and programs for older kids, respectively.

built-in marble shelves for ample storage. The Allegro appeals to younger travelers, many of whom can be found at the complimentary evening wine hour. The hotel's restaurant, **312 Chicago** (p. 99), attracts nonguests in search of seasonal Italian cuisine. *A note to theater fans:* The Allegro has access to exclusive seats for many high-profile downtown shows and often promotes special theater packages.

171 W. Randolph St. (at LaSalle St.), Chicago, IL 60601. www.allegrochicago.com. © **800/643-1500** or 312/236-0123. Fax 312/236-0917. 483 units. $139–$279 double; $239–$479 suite. AE, DC, DISC, MC, V. Valet parking $49 with in-out privileges; self-parking $45. Subway/El: All lines to Washington. Pets allowed. **Amenities:** Restaurant; lounge; concierge; exercise room; room service. *In room:* High-definition TV, hair dryer, minibar, MP3 docking station, Wi-Fi ($10/day, free for hotel loyalty program members).

THE MAGNIFICENT MILE

The stretch of North Michigan Avenue that runs from the Chicago River to Oak Street is known as the "Magnificent Mile," and it's home to some of Chicago's most luxurious hotels. (You'll note from the addresses below, however, that most entrances are actually on side streets a block or two off the avenue.) Despite the high price of real estate here, a few moderate properties thrive among the glitz. The Magnificent Mile attracts visitors year-round, but is especially packed during the summer and Christmas vacation season.

BEST FOR Serious shoppers, who can take advantage of everything from designer boutiques to large department stores. Travelers who like to be in the center of the action will enjoy the busy pace, as well as the easy access to bustling Oak Street Beach.

DRAWBACKS The crowds. If you're looking for a peaceful getaway, head further north to the Gold Coast (see p. 85, below).

Very Expensive

Four Seasons Hotel ★★★ ☺ Consistently voted one of the top hotels in the world by frequent travelers, the Four Seasons offers an understated luxury that appeals to publicity-shy Hollywood stars and wealthy families. The hotel's location—hidden between the 30th and 46th floors of the 900 N. Michigan Ave. mall—epitomizes the hotel's discretion. The elegant rooms feature contemporary furnishings, subdued colors, and modern artworks. The largest rooms overlook the lake (and, therefore, cost more), but because the hotel is so high up, even city-facing rooms have relatively unobstructed views. Despite the sophisticated setting, families are positively welcomed here; kid-friendly services include child-size robes and bathtub amenities, board and video games, a special room service menu, and even a dedicated "Teen Concierge" during the summer. The hotel's elegant fitness center exudes upscale exclusivity. (The pool, surrounded by Roman columns, looks like it could be part of an aristocratic private club.)

120 E. Delaware Place (at Michigan Ave.), Chicago, IL 60611. www.fourseasons.com/chicagofs. © **800/332-3442** or 312/280-8800. Fax 312/280-1748. 343 units. $395–$495 double; suites from $695. AE, DC, DISC, MC, V. Valet parking $49 with in-out privileges; self-parking $34. Subway/El: Red Line to Chicago. Pets accepted. **Amenities:** 2 restaurants; lounge; concierge; health club and spa w/indoor pool; room service. *In room:* TV/DVD player, CD player, hair dryer, minibar, free Wi-Fi.

Park Hyatt Chicago ★★★ Searching for chic modern luxury and money's no object? Then the Park Hyatt is the coolest hotel in town. The building occupies one of the most desirable spots on Michigan Avenue, and the best rooms are those that face east, overlooking the bustling Mag Mile and the lake. The lobby looks like a sleek modern art gallery, with German painter Gerhard Richter's *Piazza del Duomo Milan* as the centerpiece. Rooms feature Eames and Mies van der Rohe reproduction furniture and window banquettes with city views. (*Another plus:* The windows actually open.) The comfortable beds are well appointed with masses of plush pillows. The spalike bathrooms are especially wonderful: Slide back the cherrywood wall for views of the city while you soak in the oversize tub. When you're ready to explore the city, borrow one of the hotel's complimentary bikes and hit the lakefront trail, only a few blocks away.

800 N. Michigan Ave., Chicago, IL 60611. www.parkchicago.hyatt.com. ✆ **800/233-1234** or 312/335-1234. Fax 312/239-4000. 198 units. $385–$495 double; suites from $695. AE, DC, DISC, MC, V. Valet parking $49 with in-out privileges. Subway/El: Red Line to Chicago. **Amenities:** Restaurant; lounge; concierge; health club and spa w/Jacuzzi and indoor pool; room service. *In room:* A/C, TV/DVD player w/movie library, CD player, hair dryer, minibar, MP3 docking station, free Wi-Fi.

Peninsula Chicago ★★★ The Peninsula Chicago mixes an Art Deco sensibility with modern tech conveniences, but it's the public spaces that set it apart. The fitness center is my pick as the best hotel health club in the city; the sleek, light-filled workout rooms and indoor pool have views overlooking Michigan Avenue, and the outdoor deck is a great place to relax after a spa treatment; the stylish bar is also a cool late-night hangout. Rooms are understated, but come with all the high-tech amenities: A small "command station" by every bed allows guests to control all the lights, the TV, heating, or air-conditioning without getting out from under the covers. (You can also check the temperature outside, which is particularly useful during our unpredictable spring months.) Add the flatscreen TVs in the marble-filled bathrooms and you have a classic hotel that's very much attuned to the present.

108 E. Superior St. (at Michigan Ave.), Chicago, IL 60611. www.chicago.peninsula.com. ✆ **866/288-8889** or 312/337-2888. Fax 312/751-2888. 339 units. $475–$650 double; suites from $725. AE, DC, DISC, MC, V. Valet parking $49 with in-out privileges. Subway/El: Red Line to Chicago. Pets accepted. **Amenities:** 3 restaurants; bar; concierge; health club and spa w/indoor pool; room service. *In room:* A/C, TV/DVD player, CD player, fax, hair dryer, minibar, free Wi-Fi.

The Ritz-Carlton Chicago ★★★ ☺ Top-notch service and a bright, airy setting make this one of Chicago's most welcoming hotels. Perched high atop the Water Tower Place mall, the Ritz-Carlton's lobby is on the 12th floor, with a large bank of windows to admire the city below. Standard rooms are fairly compact; lake views cost but are well worth the splurge (although in all the rooms, you're up high enough that you're not staring into surrounding apartment buildings). Families will find this luxury crash pad quite welcoming: Kids can borrow toys and games from a stash kept by the concierge, and the room service menu includes family-friendly food. (You can even arrange for delivery of fresh-baked cookies and milk to your door!) The hotel's excellent Sunday brunch includes a special buffet for children replete with M&Ms, macaroni and cheese, and pizza.

160 E. Pearson St., Chicago, IL 60611. www.fourseasons.com/chicagorc. ✆ **800/621-6906** or 312/266-1000. Fax 312/266-1194. 435 units. $350–$495 double; suites from $695. AE, DC, DISC,

Affinia Chicago **16**

The Allerton Hotel **15**

Amalfi Hotel Chicago **31**

Ambassador East **1**

Best Western River North Hotel **25**

Conrad Chicago **28**

Dana Hotel and Spa **18**

Doubletree Hotel Chicago
   Magnificent Mile **24**

The Drake Hotel **5**

The Elysian **4**

Embassy Suites Chicago–
   Downtown **19**

Flemish House of Chicago **3**

Four Seasons Hotel **7**

Hampton Inn &
   Suites Downtown **30**

Homewood Suites **26**

Hotel Cass **20**

Hotel Felix **17**

Hotel Indigo **2**

Hotel Palomar **27**

Hotel Sax Chicago **33**

InterContinental Chicago **29**

The James Chicago **21**

Millennium Knickerbocker
   Hotel **6**

Park Hyatt Chicago **13**

Peninsula Chicago **14**

Red Roof Inn **22**

The Ritz-Carlton Chicago **12**

Sofitel Chicago
   Water Tower **9**

Talbott Hotel **8**

Tremont Hotel **11**

Trump International Hotel &
   Tower **34**

W Chicago Lakeshore **23**

Westin Chicago
   River North **32**

Whitehall Hotel **10**

MC, V. Valet parking $45 with in-out privileges; self-parking $35 with no in-out privileges. Subway/El: Red Line to Chicago. Pets accepted. **Amenities:** 2 restaurants; lounge; concierge; health club w/spa and indoor pool; room service. *In room:* TV, CD player, hair dryer, minibar, free Wi-Fi.

Expensive

Affinia Chicago ★ The Affinia has the requisite contemporary-cool boutique hotel look, but its personal touches and low-key attitude gives it the feel of a small, neighborhood find. Before arriving, guests can choose from a menu of preferences via e-mail: Pick your favorite from six different pillow types, request a complimentary walking tour kit (complete with iPod, map, and pedometer), even order up a golf club or guitar to be waiting in the room upon arrival. Overall, the Affinia's casual vibe attracts younger travelers; the bright, fairly spacious rooms mix neutral-toned bedding and dark wood furniture with bright splashes of color. The rooftop lounge C-View (with both indoor and outdoor seating) is a cozy spot for after-dinner drinks year-round.

166 E. Superior St. (at St. Clair St.), Chicago, IL 60611. www.affinia.com. ✆ **866/246-2203** or 312/787-6000. Fax 312/787-6133. 215 units. $199–$299 double; suites from $259. AE, DC, DISC, MC, V. Valet parking $48 with in-out privileges. Subway/El: Red Line to Chicago. **Amenities:** Restaurant; lounge; concierge; exercise room; room service. *In room:* TV, CD player, hair dryer, high-speed Internet access ($9.95/day), MP3 docking station.

Conrad Chicago ★ Tucked toward the back of The Shops at North Bridge mall, the Conrad Chicago—part of the Hilton hotel group's upscale "boutique" brand—maintains a low profile, making it a good fit for those who prefer an atmosphere of subdued elegance. From the dark wood furniture in the lobby to the deep brown curtains in the tranquil guest rooms, the Conrad exudes a sense of calm—and the older clientele to match. Rooms tend to be small (especially the least expensive ones on the north side), but the in-room amenities are top-of-the-line, including Bose sound systems and ergonomic leather work chairs. High rollers can book one of the Terrace Suites, with views of Michigan Avenue.

521 N. Rush St. (at Grand St.), Chicago, IL 60611. http://conradhotels1.hilton.com. ✆ **800/ HILTONS** [445-8667] or 312/645-1500. Fax 312/645-1550. 311 units. $195–$355 double; from $270 suite. AE, DC, DISC, MC, V. Valet parking $51 with in-out privileges. Subway/El: Red Line to Chicago. **Amenities:** Restaurant; bar; concierge; large exercise room; room service. *In room:* TV, CD player, fridge, hair dryer, MP3 docking station, free Wi-Fi.

The Drake Hotel ★★★ Chicago's version of New York's Plaza or Paris's Ritz may no longer be the most luxurious hotel in town, but its public spaces still maintain the regal grandeur of days gone by. Guest rooms have been modernized with upscale-but-homey furniture, and most rooms include a small sitting area with couch and chairs, making them good places to relax after a day of sightseeing (Family Rooms come with two bathrooms). The Drake is the only hotel in town that directly faces Lake Shore Drive, and north-facing rooms have spectacular views of the lakefront (of course, they also cost more). Be forewarned that "city view" rooms on the lower floors look out onto another building, so you'll probably be keeping your drapes shut. The hotel's retro-style restaurants include the **Cape Cod Room** (p. 109), an old-timey seafood spot; and the **Coq d'Or** (p. 318), one of Chicago's most atmospheric piano bars.

140 E. Walton Place (at Michigan Ave.), Chicago, IL 60611. www.thedrakehotel.com. ✆ **800/55-DRAKE** [553-7253] or 312/787-2200. Fax 312/787-1431. 535 units. $179–$439 double; from $549 suite. AE, DC, DISC, MC, V. Valet parking $49 with in-out privileges. Subway/El: Red

Line to Chicago. **Amenities:** 2 restaurants; 2 lounges; concierge; executive-level rooms; large exercise room; room service; free Wi-Fi in lobby. *In room:* TV, hair dryer, high-speed Internet access ($13/day), minibar.

InterContinental Chicago ★★ Another of Chicago's original luxury hotels, the InterContinental is now more comfortable than swanky, though traces of its original opulence remain. Built as the Medinah Athletic Club in 1929, the building features grand details in its public areas: marble columns, hand-stenciled ceilings, and historic tapestries. (Architecture buffs can pick up a free audio tour from the concierge.) Rooms in the Main Building (a 1960s addition) have an elegant, urban look, with dark wood and red velvet banquettes. The original Historic Tower has a more old-world feel, thanks to the elaborately carved headboards and deep-red-and-cream bedding; the bathrooms are also significantly larger. (You'll pay about $50 more for those rooms.) The InterContinental's main claim to fame is its junior Olympic-size pool on the top floor, a beautiful 1920s gem. Despite its historic pedigree, the InterContinental has been on the cutting edge of environmental awareness and has won awards for its eco-friendly practices.

505 N. Michigan Ave. (at Grand Ave.), Chicago, IL 60611. www.chicago.intercontinental.com. ✆ **800/327-0200** or 312/944-4100. Fax 312/944-1320. 790 units. $175–$350 double; from $350 suite. AE, DC, DISC, MC, V. Valet parking $53 with in-out privileges. Subway/El: Red Line to Grand. **Amenities:** Restaurant; 2 lounges; concierge; executive-level rooms; health club w/sauna and indoor pool; room service. *In room:* High-definition TV, hair dryer, high-speed Internet access ($15/day), minibar.

Sofitel Chicago Water Tower ★★ This soaring, triangular white tower makes an emphatic design statement, but the place doesn't take itself too seriously, as you'll see when you walk in the airy lobby and check out the luminescent floor tiles that change color in a never-ending light show. The overall feel of the hotel is European modern, and you'll hear French accents from some of the front desk staff. The guest rooms have a neutral-toned, contemporary look, with natural beech wood walls and chrome hardware. Standard doubles are fairly compact, but thanks to large picture windows, they don't feel cramped (the bathrooms' deep marble tubs add a luxurious touch). All the rooms enjoy good views, but the privacy-conscious will want to stay on the upper floors, where they won't be as close to surrounding apartment buildings. Sofitel is popular with younger travelers and international visitors.

20 E. Chestnut St. (at Wabash St.), Chicago, IL 60611. www.sofitel.com. ✆ **800/SOFITEL** (763-4835) or 312/324-4000. Fax 312/324-4026. 415 units. $170–$325 double; suites from $350. AE, DC, DISC, MC, V. Valet parking $47 with in-out privileges; self-parking $35. Subway/El: Red Line to Chicago. Small pets accepted. **Amenities:** Restaurant; bar; concierge; exercise room; room service. *In room:* TV, hair dryer, minibar, free Wi-Fi.

Talbott Hotel ★★ 🎒 With the feel of an upscale European inn—and a loyal clientele of regulars—the Talbott is one of the city's best small, independent hotels. The cozy, wood-lined lobby has the secluded feel of a private club, with roaring fireplaces in the winter and leather couches for curling up with a cup of tea. The larger-than-average rooms are decorated in soothing neutral tones, with furniture chosen for its residential feel (such as carved-wood desks and headboards). The upscale bathrooms vary in size; some have separate shower stalls and bathtubs, and others only tubs. Perhaps surprising for a property that feels so traditional, the Talbott is also at the forefront of guest-service technology; the lights turn on automatically when guests enter their rooms, and a high-tech sensor system shows housekeeping when a room is occupied—so no one will barge in while you're enjoying a late-morning sleep-in.

20 E. Delaware Place (btw. Rush and State sts.), Chicago, IL 60611. www.talbotthotel.com. ℂ **800/TALBOTT** (825-2688) or 312/944-4970. Fax 312/944-7241. 149 units. $219–$329 double; suites from $349. AE, DC, DISC, MC, V. Valet parking $48 with in-out privileges. Subway/El: Red Line to Chicago. **Amenities:** Restaurant; lounge; concierge; complimentary access to nearby health club; room service. *In room:* TV, hair dryer, minibar, MP3 docking station, free Wi-Fi.

W Chicago Lakeshore ★ This property promotes itself as a hip boutique hotel and attracts a relatively young clientele, but sophisticated travelers might feel like it's trying too hard, with dance music in the lobby and black-clad staff members doing their best to be eye candy. The compact rooms are decorated in deep red, black, and gray, a color scheme that will strike you as either refreshingly different from other hotels, or dark and gloomy. Although the Asian-inspired bathrooms are stylish, the wooden shades that separate them from the bedroom don't make for much privacy—so beware if you're sharing a room with a friend. You'll pay more for "Spectacular" rooms (with lake views), but the "Wonderful" city views rooms have great panoramas of the city, especially at night. The on-site outpost of New York's popular Bliss Spa offers a creative range of treatments, but the verging-on-sterile atmosphere won't be to everyone's taste.

644 N. Lake Shore Dr. (at Ontario St.), Chicago, IL 60611. www.whotels.com. ℂ **877/W-HOTELS** (946-8357) or 312/943-9200. Fax 312/255-4411. 520 units. $209–$329 double; from $369 suite. AE, DC, DISC, MC, V. Valet parking $48 with in-out privileges. Subway/El: Red Line to Grand. Pets accepted. **Amenities:** Restaurant; bar; concierge; exercise room w/indoor pool; room service; spa. *In room:* TV/DVD player w/movie library, CD player, hair dryer, minibar, free Wi-Fi.

Whitehall Hotel ★ Staying here is like visiting a wealthy, sophisticated aunt's town house: elegant but understated, welcoming but not effusive. The patrician Whitehall was once Chicago's most exclusive luxury hotel, with rock stars and Hollywood royalty dropping by when in town. Although those glory days have passed, the independently owned Whitehall still attracts devoted regulars who relish its subdued ambience and highly personalized service. Since this is an older property, the hallways are narrow and the bathrooms compact (book a Pinnacle room for a larger, upgraded bath), but the rooms are spacious and bright, with residential-style furniture. Rooms on the north side of the building come with a wonderful straight-on view of the Hancock Building, with Lake Michigan sparkling in the background. Don't miss the hotel's dimly lit, clubby bar, which hasn't changed since the hotel opened in 1928. (Ask the staff to point out Katharine Hepburn's favorite seat.)

105 E. Delaware Place (west of Michigan Ave.), Chicago, IL 60611. www.thewhitehallhotel.com. ℂ **866/753-4081** or 312/944-6300. Fax 312/944-8552. 222 units. $179–$365 double; suites from $600. AE, DC, DISC, MC, V. Valet parking $48 with in-out privileges. Subway/El: Red Line to Chicago. **Amenities:** Restaurant; bar; concierge; executive-level rooms; exercise room (and access to nearby health club for $20/day); room service. *In room:* TV, hair dryer, minibar, Wi-Fi ($9.95/day).

Moderate

The Allerton Hotel ★ A historic hotel that's gotten a stylish modern makeover, the Allerton's charm lifts it a notch above the standard business-traveler hangout. Built in 1924 as a "club hotel," providing permanent residences for single men and women, its Italian Renaissance–inspired exterior has been painstakingly restored to its original dark-red brickwork, stone carvings, and limestone base. Inside, the building has a glam, Art Deco–inspired look. As is the case with many older properties in town, rooms tend to be small, with some not much wider than a queen- or king-sized bed (the "Petite" rooms are the tiniest). Request a room overlooking Michigan Avenue to get the best views, or at least stop by the hotel's Renaissance Ballroom for a peek at the Mag Mile.

701 N. Michigan Ave. (at Huron St.), Chicago, IL 60611. www.theallertonhotel.com. ℰ **866/553-5040** outside Illinois or 312/440-1500. Fax 312/440-1819. 443 units. $109–$259 double; suites from $239. AE, DC, DISC, MC, V. Valet parking $51 with in-out privileges. Subway/El: Red Line to Chicago. **Amenities:** Restaurant; lounge; concierge; exercise room (w/excellent city views); room service. *In room:* TV, hair dryer, minibar, MP3 docking station, Wi-Fi ($9.95/day).

Doubletree Hotel Chicago Magnificent Mile ★ This high-rise hotel is actually a few blocks east of Michigan Avenue, but its location and amenities make it a good pick for vacationers with children, especially during the summer. All rooms have unobstructed city views; book one on the north side for an only-in-Chicago vista of the John Hancock Center. The overall feel is urban chic, with dark wood headboards and burgundy accents; all come with either a couch or a window seat for lounging. In the summer, hang out on the spacious sun deck beside the smallish-but-adequate outdoor pool; the adjoining lounge is a popular spot for pre- or post-dinner drinks. (Unfortunately, you won't be able to take advantage of these amenities if you visit in the winter.) Lake Michigan and kid-friendly Navy Pier are a short walk away.

300 E. Ohio St. (at Fairbanks Court), Chicago, IL 60611. www.chicagomagnificentmile.doubletree. com. ℰ **800/557-2378** or 312/787-6100. Fax 312/787-6259. 500 units. $109–$229 double. AE, DC, DISC, MC, V. Self-parking in attached lot $41. Subway/El: Red Line to Grand. **Amenities:** Restaurant; cafe; bar; concierge; exercise room; outdoor pool; room service. *In room:* TV, hair dryer, minibar, Wi-Fi ($9.95/day).

Homewood Suites ★★ ☺ An excellent choice for families, this hotel offers some nice little freebies that appeal to guests of all ages. Housed just off the Mag Mile in a sleek tower above retail shops, offices, and a health club—and adjacent to ESPN Zone—the hotel includes a mix of one- and two-bedroom suites; there are also a handful of double-double suites, which can connect to king suites. All are decorated in standard long-term stay apartment style and include sleeper sofas (should you need to pack in extra family members), full kitchens, dining room tables that can double as workspaces, and decent-size bathrooms. What sets this place apart are the extras: The hotel provides a complimentary hot breakfast buffet, as well as beverages and hors d'oeuvres on weekday evenings; there are also a free grocery-shopping service and mid-sized indoor pool with views of the city.

40 E. Grand Ave. (at Wabash Ave.), Chicago, IL 60611. www.homewoodsuiteschicago.com. ℰ **800/CALL-HOME** (225-5466) or 312/644-2222. Fax 312/644-7777. 233 units. $179–$299 2-room suite. AE, DC, DISC, MC, V. Valet parking $42 with in-out privileges. Subway/El: Red Line to Grand. **Amenities:** Fitness room w/indoor pool. *In room:* TV, hair dryer, kitchen, free Wi-Fi.

Hotel Cass ★ A hidden gem, the Hotel Cass offers a classic trade-off: You get a great location for the price, but not much space. Some rooms are so small that there's barely room for the flatscreen TV (it's mounted on a mechanical arm that reaches over the bed); others look directly onto the building next door. But the decor is bright and stylish, with masses of pillows (helpfully labeled "soft" and "firm") on the comfortable beds; the compact bathrooms include design-conscious touches such as rectangular sinks. The Cass's relatively low profile means its rates tends to be lower than other hotels in the area, and you can snag very good deals here during the off season. Another bonus for budget travelers: the complimentary buffet breakfast, which includes eggs, bacon, and decadently delicious cinnamon rolls.

640 N. Wabash Ave. (btw. Erie and Ontario sts.), Chicago, IL 60611. www.casshotel.com. © **800/799-4030** or 312/787-4030. Fax 312/787-8544. 175 units. $99–$249 double. AE, DC, DISC, MC, V. Valet parking $40 with in-out privileges; self-parking $34 with no in-out privileges. Subway/El: Red Line to Grand. Small pets accepted for a $25 fee. **Amenities:** Access to nearby health club for $10/day. *In room:* High-definition TV, hair dryer, MP3 docking station, free Wi-Fi.

Millennium Knickerbocker Hotel ★ The real draw of this historic hotel is its superb location, a block from Oak Street Beach and the lakefront (and across the street from the more expensive Drake Hotel). The epitome of Jazz Age indulgence when built in 1927, this hotel was rumored to have shady underworld connections during the Capone era. Its glamour has been long since superseded by newer, splashier properties, and the standard rooms are quite small. (Book a Superior Room if you need more space.) But the overall decor is cheery, and the compact bathrooms have upscale touches such as oversized showerheads and granite countertops. Views are often rather dismal, but you can catch a glimpse of the lake in all rooms ending in 14; corner rooms (ending in 28) look onto Michigan Avenue.

163 E. Walton Place (half-block east of Michigan Ave.), Chicago, IL 60611. www.millennium hotels.com/millenniumchicago/index.html. © **800/621-8140** or 312/751-8100. Fax 312/751-9663. 305 units. $125–$299 double; suites from $289. AE, DC, DISC, MC, V. Valet parking $50 with in-out privileges. Subway/El: Red Line to Chicago. **Amenities:** Restaurant; bar; concierge; exercise room; room service. *In room:* High-definition TV, hair dryer, minibar, Wi-Fi ($9.95/day).

Tremont Hotel The Tremont won't dazzle you with style or amenities, but it fits the bill for anyone looking for a small, European-style hotel. The guest rooms aren't too big—in most, there's space for a bed, a desk, and either a sofa or two chairs—but they are bright, with yellow walls and large windows. Ask for a room facing Delaware Street if you crave natural light (rooms in other parts of the hotel look into neighboring buildings). The hotel also has 12 studio apartments with full kitchens in an annex next door. Penthouse suites include whirlpool tubs, fireplaces, and wet bars. The steak-and-chops restaurant off the lobby, the memorabilia-filled **Mike Ditka's Restaurant** (p. 112), is co-owned by the Chicago Bears' legendary former football coach.

100 E. Chestnut St. (1 block west of Michigan Ave.), Chicago, IL 60611. www.tremontchicago. com. © **800/621-8133** or 312/751-1900. Fax 312/751-8650. 130 units. $119–$279 double; suites from $199. AE, DC, DISC, MC, V. Valet parking $49. Subway/El: Red Line to Chicago. **Amenities:** Restaurant; concierge; small exercise room. *In room:* TV, hair dryer, free Wi-Fi.

Inexpensive

Red Roof Inn ★ ✔ If price is your top concern, this is where you'll find the lowest rates in downtown Chicago. The location couldn't be better: right off the Magnificent Mile (and within blocks of the Ritz-Carlton and the Peninsula, where rooms will cost you about four times as much). The guest rooms are stark and small, but the linens and carpeting are clean and relatively new. Ask for a room facing Ontario Street, where at least you'll get western exposure and some natural light (rooms in other parts of the hotel look right into neighboring office buildings). The bathrooms are tiny but spotless. Upgraded rooms are larger and come with mini-fridges and free Wi-Fi; there are also a few two-room suites that are good for families. The decor won't wow you, and the amenities are minimal (other than free coffee in the lobby), but at these prices, what do you expect?

162 E. Ontario St. (half-block east of Michigan Ave.), Chicago, IL 60611. www.redroof-chicago-downtown.com. © **800/733-7663** or 312/787-3580. Fax 312/787-1299. 195 units. $90–$179 double; suites from $129. AE, DC, DISC, MC, V. Valet parking $36 with in-out privileges. Subway/El: Red Line to Grand. *In room:* TV, hair dryer, free Wi-Fi.

RIVER NORTH

North of the Loop and west of the Magnificent Mile, River North is a former industrial neighborhood that's been transformed into a thriving dining and night-life district.

BEST FOR Night owls. Restaurants in River North stay open late, and there are plenty of clubs and bars within walking distance.

DRAWBACKS Because of its large concentration of hotels, River North can feel overrun with tourists, especially in the summer.

Very Expensive

Trump International Hotel & Tower Chicago ★★★ The 92-story Trump Chicago gives visitors a taste of what it's like to live large Chicago-style. The hotel is housed on the 14th through 27th floors of the glass-walled building (the rest is condos), and though you'll pay more for the "City View" and "River View" rooms, they come with gorgeous panoramas of the city through floor-to-ceiling windows. The overall look is urban contemporary, with none of the flashiness the Trump name might suggest. King and double rooms have kitchenettes and large, limestone-walled bathrooms; suites are more like studio apartments, with separate bedrooms, living rooms, and full kitchens stocked with upscale appliances and cooking supplies. The hotel spa is considered one of the best in the city, and special "Spa Suites" are steps away from the treatment rooms. Chicagoans were suspicious, but Mr. Trump's attractive hotel has become a much-admired addition to the local skyline.

401 N. Wabash Ave. (at the Chicago River), Chicago, IL 60611. www.trumpchicagohotel.com. © **877/458-7867** or 312/588-8000. Fax 312/588-8001. 339 units. $355–$495 double; suites from $645. AE, DC, DISC, MC, V. Valet parking $50 with in-out privileges. Subway/El: Red Line to Grand. **Amenities:** Restaurant; lounge; concierge; fitness center w/spa and indoor pool; room service. *In room:* TV, hair dryer, minibar, free Wi-Fi.

Expensive

Dana Hotel and Spa ★★ This boutique hotel draws younger travelers with its blend of sleek style (a glowing glass elevator tower) and earthy warmth (wood floors in the guest rooms, shower stalls lined with natural stone). You'll feel like you're staying at a friend's downtown loft, complete with floor-to-ceiling windows overlooking the bustle outside. That said, the Dana is definitely an urban experience: If you want to enjoy the views, you'll have to accept that residents of the surrounding high-rises can stare right back at you. (Heavy shades can be pulled down for nighttime privacy.) Befitting a hotel that highlights its spa services, the bathrooms are stylishly modern, with raised basin sinks and oversize shower stalls. The lobby restaurant, **Aja,** focuses on Asian regional cuisine, while the top-floor **Vertigo Sky Lounge** (p. 324) is more nightclub than hotel bar, with a live DJ.

660 N. State St. (at Erie St.), Chicago, IL 60610. www.danahotelandspa.com. ℂ **888/301-3262** or 312/202-6000. Fax 312/202-6033. 216 units. $189–$279 double; suites from $349. AE, DC, DISC, MC, V. Valet parking $38 with in-out privileges. Subway/El: Red Line to Chicago. **Amenities:** Restaurant; lounge; concierge; exercise room and spa; room service. *In room:* TV, hair dryer, minibar, MP3 docking station, free Wi-Fi.

Hotel Felix ★★ 🏠 The city's ultimate eco-chic retreat, the Felix was built with environmental consciousness in mind. Its mix of green credibility and modern style has made it a favorite with travelers in their 20s and 30s, who hang out with their laptops in the small but airy lobby bar. All the materials used in the neutral-toned guest rooms were chosen for their earth-friendly properties, from the carpeting made of recycled plastic bottles to the energy-efficient shower heads (bathrooms come with showers only—no tubs). Rooms are average sized, with built-in drawers under the beds to free up space that would otherwise be filled by a dresser. The compact but tranquil on-site spa offers massages and facials. If you can, snag a room facing east or north; rooms on the south side look onto the wall of an adjacent building and tend to be gloomy.

111 W. Huron St. (at Clark St.), Chicago, IL 60654. www.hotelfelixchicago.com. ℂ **877/848-4040** or 312/447-3440. Fax 312/787-6133. 225 units. $169–$229 double. AE, DC, DISC, MC, V. Valet parking $42 with in-out privileges (free for hybrid cars). Subway/El: Red Line to Chicago. **Amenities:** Restaurant; bar; concierge; exercise room; room service. *In room:* TV, hair dryer, MP3 docking station, free Wi-Fi.

Hotel Palomar ★ The Palomar's contemporary-cool look and eclectic decorative details put it firmly in boutique hotel territory, but its indoor pool and attached deck set it apart from the competition. Standard rooms are moderately sized, with two armchairs; upgrade to a "spa premier" for extra seating space and larger bath (complete with two-person soaking tub). Although you'll get unobstructed city views from most rooms, those on the north side tend to be darker; request one of the upgraded corner rooms for maximum light. Though the Palomar flaunts a grown-up style, the pool has made it a draw for families as well. The hotel's restaurant, **Sable Kitchen & Bar** (p. 127), gives classic American comfort food an upscale-but-approachable twist.

505 N. State St. (at Illinois St.), Chicago, IL 60654. www.hotelpalomar-chicago.com. ℂ **877/731-0505** or 312/755-9703. Fax 312/755-9713. 261 units. $159–$359 double; $309–$509 suite. AE, DC, DISC, MC, V. Valet parking $46 with in-out privileges. Subway/El: Red Line to Grand. Pets allowed. **Amenities:** Restaurant; lounge; concierge; exercise room; room service. *In room:* High-definition TV, hair dryer, minibar, MP3 docking station, Wi-Fi ($10/day, free for hotel loyalty program members).

Hotel Sax Chicago ★★ If you're looking for a hotel that combines unique style with high-tech perks, head for the Hotel Sax. The all-white lobby has a Miami Beach–like feel, but the adjoining lounge, Crimson, goes for a sultry, jewel-toned vibe, with screens and mirrors creating pockets of privacy. The eclectic sensibility carries over to the guest rooms, which feature wingback chairs covered in snakeskin and side tables constructed entirely of mirrored panels. Despite the eye-catching decor, one of the hotel's biggest selling points is its location in the Marina Towers complex; steps away, you've got a bowling alley, the restaurant **Bin 36** (p. 121), and the **House of Blues theater** (p. 315). Designated "technology" rooms come with Xbox video game consoles and MP3 players; you can also try out games like Rock Band in the nightclublike **Studio,** a cozy lounge stocked with refreshments, couches, and laptops.

333 N. Dearborn St. (at the river), Chicago, IL 60610. www.hotelsaxchicago.com. © **877/569-3742** or 312/245-0333. Fax 312/923-2444. 353 units. $169–$319 double; suites from $259. AE, DC, DISC, MC, V. Valet parking $42 with in-out privileges. Subway/El: Brown Line to Clark/Lake, or Red Line to Grand. Pets accepted. **Amenities:** Lounge; concierge; exercise room; room service. *In room:* High-definition TV, hair dryer, minibar, free Wi-Fi.

The James Chicago A boutique hotel of the sleek, minimalist variety, the James is aimed at sophisticated travelers who prefer luxury with a contemporary spin. Guest rooms are neutral-toned and modern, with private dining niches, reproductions of Mies Van der Rohe chairs and Saaranen tables, dark wood floors and walls, and installations by up-and-coming Chicago artists. Studio rooms include a separate sitting area, and lofts include a private media room with projection DVD player. Although interior-view rooms have a fairly dismal view of a neighboring building during the day, it livens up at night, when the wall becomes the backdrop for a black-and-white animated film. The lobby lounge, **J Bar** (p. 326), is a dimly lit, clubby hangout that's popular with locals who live and work in the neighborhood.

55 E. Ontario St. (at Rush St.), Chicago, IL 60611. www.jameshotels.com. © **877/526-3755** or 312/337-1000. 297 units (including 52 studios). $149–$309 double; studios from $189; lofts from $289. AE, DISC, MC, V. Valet parking $42. Subway/El: Red Line to Grand. Pets welcome. **Amenities:** Restaurant; bar; concierge; large exercise room; room service; spa. *In room:* TV, hair dryer, minibar, MP3 docking station, free Wi-Fi.

CHICAGO HOTELS GO green

With their large-scale heating and cooling costs—not to mention all those loads of laundry—Chicago's hotels suck up a considerable amount of energy. Now the city's hospitality industry is taking a leading role in lessening that environmental footprint. About two dozen local hotels have signed up for a city-wide Green Hotels Initiative, signaling their commitment to recycling and energy conservation.

Hotel Allegro (p. 72), **Hotel Burnham** (p. 69), **Hotel Monaco** (p. 69), and **Hotel Palomar** (p. 82)—all part of the Kimpton hotel chain—print all material on recycled paper using soy-based inks. Though all three hotels are located in historic buildings, they've been fitted with energy-efficient lighting and air-conditioning systems.

At the **Talbott Hotel** (p. 77), automatic sensors adjust the lighting, heating, and air-conditioning in low-traffic areas when they're not in use, and unused in-room soaps and shampoos are donated to a charity that recycles them for the needy. The hotel also purchases wind energy credits to offset 100% of the property's carbon footprint.

The **InterContinental Chicago** (p. 77) was the first hotel in the city to receive an Energy Star rating from the Environmental Protection Agency, thanks to its use of water-conserving toilets and sinks and motion-sensitive thermostats in the guest rooms (which lower the heat or air-conditioning when there's no one inside).

Then there's the **Hotel Felix** (p. 82), the first hotel in the city to be built from the ground up with environmentally sensitive practices in mind. Sustainable or recycled materials were used throughout the property, from the flooring to the bedding. Guests who arrive in a hybrid car can even park free.

Westin Chicago River North ★ ☺ The Westin Chicago River North has an understated feel that appeals to those looking for a quiet retreat. The hotel still retains traces of its previous incarnation as the Japanese-owned Hotel Nikko, with a Zen rock garden and bamboo in the lobby; the Hana Lounge also offers a sushi menu. Rooms are understated, with furniture and artwork that give them a residential look. For the best view, get a room facing south, overlooking the Chicago River. If you like to sleep in, the Westin chain is known for its "Heavenly Beds" and piles of pillows. (Believe me, it's more than just a marketing ploy—the beds are *really* comfortable.) Even though it has the personality of a business hotel, the Westin has made an effort to be family-friendly. Many baby and toddler accessories are available, and older kids can while away the hours with an in-room PlayStation.

320 N. Dearborn St. (on the river), Chicago, IL 60610. www.westinchicago.com. ℰ **800/WES-TIN1** (937-8461) or 312/744-1900. Fax 312/527-2650. 424 units. $239–$359 double; suites from $359. AE, DC, DISC, MC, V. Valet parking $52 with in-out privileges. Subway/El: Brown, Orange, or Green line to State/Lake. **Amenities:** Restaurant; lounge; concierge; executive-level rooms; large exercise room ($10/day); room service; sauna. *In room:* TV, hair dryer, high-speed Internet access, minibar.

Moderate

Best Western River North Hotel ☺ ⚓ This former motor lodge isn't going to win any design prizes, but it's got the most affordable rates in the neighborhood. Rooms are generic but spacious (with comfortable bedding and down pillows); the bathrooms, though no-frills, are in good condition. One-room suites have a separate sitting area, while other suites have a separate bedroom; all suites come with a sleeper sofa and fridge. A big selling point for families is the indoor pool, with an adjoining outdoor roof deck (a smallish fitness room looks out onto the pool, for parents who want to work out while the kids splash around). The almost-unheard-of free parking in the hotel's parking lot can add up to significant savings for anyone who drives here for a visit.

125 W. Ohio St. (at LaSalle St.), Chicago, IL 60610. www.rivernorthhotel.com. ℰ **800/528-1234** or 312/467-0800. Fax 312/467-1665. 150 units. $119–$269 double. AE, DC, DISC, MC, V. Free parking for guests (1 car/room) with in-out privileges. Subway/El: Red Line to Grand. **Amenities:** Restaurant; exercise room; indoor pool; room service. *In room:* TV, hair dryer, free Wi-Fi.

Embassy Suites Chicago–Downtown ★ ☺ Although this hotel does a healthy convention business, its vaguely Floridian ambience—a gushing waterfall and palm-lined ponds at the bottom of a huge central atrium—makes it very family-friendly, with plenty of room for the kids to run around. The guest rooms (all suites) have a generic chain-hotel feel but are spacious enough for both parents and kids. Each suite has two rooms consisting of a living room with a sleeper sofa, a round table, and four chairs; and a bedroom with either a king-size bed or two double beds; the rooms also have a minifridge and a microwave. The hotel serves a complimentary cooked-to-order breakfast in the morning and, in the other end of the atrium, complimentary cocktails and snacks in the evening. Off the lobby is an excellent Italian restaurant, **Osteria Via Stato** (p. 123), and next door is a Starbucks with outdoor seating.

600 N. State St. (at W. Ohio St.), Chicago, IL 60610. www.embassysuiteschicago.com. ℰ **800/ EMBASSY** (362-2779) or 312/943-3800. Fax 312/943-7629. 366 units. Suites $199–$249. AE, DC, DISC, MC, V. Valet parking $44 with in-out privileges. Subway/El: Red Line to Grand. **Amenities:** Restaurant (Italian); concierge; exercise room w/whirlpool; indoor pool; limited room service. *In room:* TV, hair dryer, kitchenette, Wi-Fi ($9.95/day).

Hampton Inn & Suites Chicago Downtown ★★ ☺ ✔ This family-friendly hotel manages to appeal to both adults and kids—the Art Deco–style lobby and sleek white breakfast lounge add a touch of sophistication, while the indoor pool and free hot breakfast are a plus for families. While the views aren't spectacular, most rooms get ample natural light and have a bright, cheery look, with white duvets and green decorative accents. You can book a standard room, which includes a desk, armchair, and ottoman; a studio, which has a microwave, sink, and minifridge along one wall; or a suite, which includes a kitchenette with a separate bedroom. The complimentary continental breakfast, which includes two hot items per day, can save families money on food; you won't need much lunch if you fill up here each morning.

33 W. Illinois St. (at Dearborn St.), Chicago, IL 60610. www.hamptonsuiteschicago.com. ⓒ **800/ HAMPTON** (426-7866) or 312/832-0330. Fax 312/832-0333. 230 units. $139–$199 double; suites from $179. AE, DC, DISC, MC, V. Valet parking $42 with in-out privileges. Subway/El: Red Line to Grand. **Amenities:** Restaurant; exercise room w/sauna; indoor pool w/Jacuzzi and sun deck. *In room:* TV, hair dryer, free high-speed Internet access.

THE GOLD COAST

Mansions from the 19th and early 20th centuries line the streets of this exclusive neighborhood. Peaceful and secluded as it feels, the Gold Coast is still within easy walking distance to Michigan Avenue and the lakefront.

BEST FOR Visitors who want to escape the noise and traffic of downtown.

DRAWBACKS There are only a few hotel options in this largely residential district.

Very Expensive

The Elysian ★★★ The Elysian is the current standard-setter for luxury in Chicago, and it attracts the sophisticated, well-traveled guests to match. With its Parisian, Beaux-Arts–style exterior, it looks like an exclusive private club, an impression that continues in the marble-clad lobby. The larger-than-average, elegant rooms come with comfortable armchairs for lounging, imported Italian linens, spacious bathrooms with built-in mini-TVs and several amenities you won't find anywhere else in town, including working fireplaces and furnished terraces. The Elysian has become a popular place for couples celebrating anniversaries, and it's ideal for anyone looking to relax and decompress in style (especially when you factor in the on-site spa). Guests who manage to pry themselves from their rooms can call on the hotel's fleet of luxury cars to whisk them off to a museum or restaurant.

11 E. Walton St. (at State Pkwy.), Chicago, IL 60611. www.elysianhotels.com. ⓒ **800/500-8511** or 312/646-1300. Fax 312/475-1679. 188 units. $395–$570 double; suites from $565. AE, DC, DISC, MC, V. Valet parking $50 with in-out privileges. Subway/El: Red Line to Chicago. **Amenities:** 2 restaurants; lounge; concierge; health club w/spa and indoor lap pool; room service. *In room:* TV, hair dryer, minibar, free Wi-Fi.

Moderate

Ambassador East ★ In its 1930s and '40s heyday, the Ambassador East hosted stars such as Frank Sinatra and Humphrey Bogart, and its recent purchase by boutique hotelier Ian Schrager promises to bring the swagger back to this local landmark. The hotel has been under renovation throughout 2011, which means certain amenities (including the restaurant and fitness room) have been unavailable at times to guests. The upside? Low rates that probably won't last post-rehab. Although the Ambassador East's makeover had yet to be revealed at press time (completion is scheduled for fall 2011), its residential location makes it feel like a great getaway spot. Best of all, you're still within easy walking distance of restaurants, Michigan Avenue, and the lakefront.

1301 N. State Pkwy. (1 block north of Division St.), Chicago, IL 60610. www.theambassadoreast hotel.com. ✆ **888/506-3471** or 312/787-7200. Fax 312/787-4760. 285 units. $129–$259 double; suites from $229. AE, DC, DISC, MC, V. Valet parking $41 with in-out privileges. Subway/El: Red Line to Clark/Division. **Amenities:** Restaurant; concierge; small fitness room; room service. *In room:* TV, hair dryer, minibar, Wi-Fi ($9.95/day).

Flemish House of Chicago ★★ 🏠 Want to pretend you live in a grand historic mansion? Book a room at this B&B, tucked away on one of the Gold Coast's most picturesque (and expensive) streets. The entire building—including the Flemish Revival facade that inspired its name—was renovated in the late 1990s by innkeepers Tom Warnke (an architect) and Mike Maczka (a real estate appraiser). Their architecture experience is evident in the rooms' tasteful decor: a mix of Victorian and Arts and Crafts furniture and decorative details that respect the home's late-19th-century design—along with all the necessary modern amenities. The rooms include spacious studios and one-bedroom suites, all with full kitchens. This isn't the kind of B&B that promotes socializing; there are no common rooms, and breakfast is strictly self-serve (all the fixings are stocked in the fridge). But for independent travelers looking for a quiet getaway, the location and setting are truly unique.

68 E. Cedar St. (at Lake Shore Dr.), Chicago, IL 60611. www.innchicago.com. ✆ **312/664-9981.** Fax 312/664-0387. 7 units. $125–$250 double. AE, MC, V. Valet parking in nearby lot $25/day. Subway/El: Red Line to Clark/Division. *In room:* TV/VCR, hair dryer, kitchen, free Wi-Fi.

Hotel Indigo ★ The Indigo is perfect for anyone looking for a cool (but not too edgy) alternative to the cookie-cutter business hotel. The bright rooms have blonde hardwood floors and white wood furniture; walls have splashes of vibrant color and giant photomurals of seashells, fruit, and other "relaxing" images. King rooms on the north side of the building tend to be larger, but they also look out on neighboring buildings. The queen rooms (on the south side of the building) are small but have lovely views of downtown and plenty of natural light. Hotel Indigo won't overwhelm you with facilities; the hotel's restaurant and bar are both quite small, but there's a decent-size fitness room and a salon/spa with separate facial and massage treatment rooms.

1244 N. Dearborn St. (1 block north of Division St.), Chicago, IL 60610. www.goldcoastchicago hotel.com. ✆ **866/521-6950** or 312/787-4980. Fax 312/787-4069. 165 units. $149–$249 double. AE, DC, DISC, MC, V. Valet parking $37 with in-out privileges. Subway/El: Red Line to Clark/Division. Pets accepted. **Amenities:** Restaurant; lounge; concierge; exercise room; room service; spa services. *In room:* TV, CD player, hair dryer, free Wi-Fi.

LINCOLN PARK & THE NORTH SIDE

The North Side is a general term that encompasses the residential neighborhoods north of the Gold Coast; Lincoln Park is the area that sprawls westward from the lakefront park of the same name.

BEST FOR Experiencing Chicago as a local; few tourists hang out this far from downtown.

DRAWBACKS The distance from cultural institutions such as the Art Institute or Field Museum, both of which are a half-hour bus ride away.

Moderate

Best Western Hawthorne Terrace ★ ☙ Located within walking distance of Wrigley Field, Lake Michigan, and the Lincoln Park walking and bike paths, this neighborhood spot attracts an extremely varied clientele—from business travelers in search of a homey environment, to diehard baseball fans, to gay travelers in town for the annual Gay Pride Parade. Although it's on busy Broadway Avenue, a charmingly landscaped terrace separates the hotel somewhat from the traffic (it's also a good spot to enjoy your complimentary continental breakfast when the weather's nice). Inside, the relatively large rooms come with standard motel decor, but most are bright and cheery, with spotless bathrooms. The ground-level exercise room is especially welcoming, with large windows and a glass-enclosed hot tub.

3434 N. Broadway Ave. (at Hawthorne Place), Chicago, IL 60657. www.hawthorneterrace.com. ☏ **888/401-8781** or 773/244-3434. Fax 773/244-3435. 59 units. $149–$229 double and suite. Rates include continental breakfast. AE, DC, DISC, MC, V. Valet parking $20 with in-out privileges. Subway/El: Red Line to Addison. **Amenities:** Concierge; exercise room w/hot tub and sauna. *In room:* A/C, TV, fridge, hair dryer, free Wi-Fi.

Windy City Urban Inn ★★ 🎁 This grand 1886 home is located blocks away from busy Clark Street and Lincoln Avenue—both full of shops, restaurants, and bars. While the inn is charming enough, the true selling point are its hosts, Andy and Mary Shaw. He's a well-known local television reporter, while she has more than 20 years of experience in the Chicago bed-and-breakfast business. Together they are excellent resources for anyone who wants to get beyond the usual tourist sites. The remodeled Victorian home has five rooms in the main house and three apartment suites in a coach house. Two of the coach-house apartments can sleep four: two in an upstairs bedroom and two on a bed that folds up against the wall. In good weather, guests are invited to eat breakfast on the back porch or in the garden between the main house and the coach house.

607 W. Deming Place, Chicago, IL 60614. www.windycityinn.com. ☏ **877/897-7091** or 773/248-7091. Fax 773/529-4183. 8 units. $115–$225 double; $225–$325 coach-house apt. Rates include buffet breakfast. AE, DISC, MC, V. Parking $6 in nearby lot with in-out privileges. Subway/El: Red Line to Fullerton. *In room:* TV, hair dryer (upon request), kitchenette, free Wi-Fi.

Inexpensive

City Suites Hotel ★ ☙ Steps from the El, this small hotel is a cozy oasis in a busy, semi-gritty stretch of Belmont Avenue. Most rooms are suites, with separate sitting rooms and bedrooms, all decorated in Art Deco shades of black and gold. Whether the hotel's neighborhood setting is a bonus or drawback depends on your point of view. Most rooms can be fairly noisy; those facing north overlook Belmont, where the nightlife continues into the early morning hours, and those facing west look right out over the rumbling El tracks. On your way in and out of the hotel, you'll be able to mingle with plenty of locals, everybody from young professional families to gay couples, to punks in full regalia. Room service is available from **Ann Sather,** a neighborhood institution next door (p. 140).

933 W. Belmont Ave. (at Sheffield Ave.), Chicago, IL 60657. www.chicagocitysuites.com. © **800/248-9108** or 773/404-3400. Fax 773/404-3405. 45 units. $109–$159 double; suites $129–$179. Rates include continental breakfast. AE, DC, DISC, MC, V. Parking $25 in nearby lot with in-out privileges. Subway/El: Red Line to Belmont. **Amenities:** Concierge; free access to nearby health club; limited room service. *In room:* TV, fridge, hair dryer, free Wi-Fi.

Majestic Hotel ★★ 🛏️ Located on a charming tree-lined street—but convenient to the many restaurants and shops of Lincoln Park—the Majestic Hotel is a good choice for anyone looking for a quiet retreat. As at the City Suites (above, which has the same owners), guests receive complimentary continental breakfast, 24-hour coffee and tea service, and afternoon cookies in the lobby. Some of the larger suites offer butler's pantries with a fridge, microwave, and wet bar. If you can, book one with a sun porch; most of the other rooms are fairly dark (since you're surrounded by apartment buildings on almost all sides), and you should avoid the claustrophobic single rooms with alley views. Ideally suited for enjoying the North Side, the Majestic is only a short walk from both Wrigley Field and the lake.

528 W. Brompton St. (at Lake Shore Dr.), Chicago, IL 60657. www.cityinns.com. © **800/727-5108** or 773/404-3499. Fax 773/404-3495. 52 units. $109–$159 double; suites $129–$199. Rates include continental breakfast. AE, DC, DISC, MC, V. Self-parking $25 in nearby garage with no in-out privileges. Subway/El: Red Line to Addison; walk several blocks east to Lake Shore Dr. and then 1 block south. **Amenities:** Free access to nearby health club; limited room service. *In room:* TV, fridge, hair dryer, free Wi-Fi.

NEAR MCCORMICK PLACE

Although the sprawling McCormick Place Convention Center isn't far from downtown, it feels cut off from the rest of the city. The main reason to stay here is the easy access to the center.

BEST FOR Business travelers attending a convention. The Field Museum, Shedd Aquarium, and Adler Planetarium are also close by. It's also ideal for bargain-shoppers looking for a good rate near downtown during the summer, when there are few conventions scheduled.

DRAWBACKS No restaurants or stores within walking distance; you'll have to take a taxi or bus to explore the city.

Expensive

Wheeler Mansion ★ 🛏️ This grand Italianate bed-and-breakfast, located near Chicago's original "Millionaire's Row," allows visitors to go back in time without giving up amenities such as cable TV. The mosaic tile floor in the vestibule and some of the dark walnut woodwork and fixtures are original to the house; welcome additions include good-sized private bathrooms. The rooms—spacious enough to include armoires and armchairs—feel even larger, thanks to the high ceilings. Antique European furniture fills the house, and guests sleep on goose-down feather beds with high-end linens. Adding to the homey ambience is the courtyard garden, where you can relax with a glass of wine after a day of sightseeing. A full gourmet breakfast—served on elegant bone china—is included in the daily room rate. Wheeler Mansion's location—on a residential side street a few blocks from the convention center—mean it's removed from the urban action, but that's the draw for some visitors.

2020 S. Calumet Ave., Chicago, IL 60616. www.wheelermansion.com. © **312/945-2020.** Fax 312/945-2021. 11 units. $230–$285 double; $265–$365 suite. AE, DC, DISC, MC, V. Free parking. Bus: 62 from State St. downtown. **Amenities:** Computer rental available. *In room:* A/C, TV, hair dryer, free high-speed Internet access.

Moderate

Hyatt Regency McCormick Place ★ Rising 33 stories from Chicago's sprawling convention center, the Hyatt Regency is often solidly booked during trade shows and meetings. But it can be a good place to snag bargain rooms during convention lulls in the winter and summer. The trade-off? The hotel is cut off from the rest of the city by highways; although the hotel is relatively close to the Museum Campus, the lakefront, and the Loop, none are easy walks. However, cabs are plentiful, and the hotel offers a complimentary shuttle to downtown shopping areas, the main museums, and Navy Pier. The average-size rooms are decorated in standard business-hotel style; if you can, request one on the north side, which features panoramic views of the city skyline and Lake Michigan.

2233 S. Martin Luther King, Jr. Dr. (at 22nd St.), Chicago, IL 60616. www.mccormickplace.hyatt. com. © **800/233-1234** or 312/567-1234. Fax 312/528-4000. 800 units. $149–$329 double; suites from $650. AE, DC, DISC, MC, V. Valet parking $44 with in-out privileges; self-parking $30. Bus: 3 or 4. **Amenities:** Restaurant; bar; concierge; exercise room; indoor lap pool; room service; sauna. *In room:* TV, hair dryer, MP3 docking station, Wi-Fi ($10/day).

PRACTICAL INFORMATION
The Big Picture

For the most part, Chicago hotels offer a quintessential urban experience: Rooms come with views of surrounding skyscrapers, and the bustle of city life hits you as soon as you step outside the lobby doors. Every major hotel chain is represented here, from the traditionally luxe **Ritz-Carlton** and **Peninsula** to the more casual, family-focused **Embassy Suites** or **Best Western River North.** But many hotels here have their own unique character, from the industrial-chic look of the **Dana Hotel and Spa** to the vibrant in-room art at the **Hotel Indigo.**

Chicago has its share of places that tout themselves as "boutique" hotels, such as the **Hotel Felix** and **The James Chicago,** but these aren't quite the same as their New York, Miami, or Los Angeles counterparts; the so-called beautiful people who frequent these spots on the coasts aren't likely to stop off in Chicago. No matter where you stay in town, you'll likely find that your fellow guests are business travelers or vacationing families, though the boutiques attract a generally younger crowd.

A note about smoking: A number of Chicago hotels, such as **The Drake Hotel** and the **Renaissance Chicago,** are completely nonsmoking. If you want to make sure you can light up in your room, check the hotel's policy when making your reservation.

Getting the Best Deal

Because Chicago's hospitality industry caters first and foremost to the business traveler, rates tend to be higher during the week. The city's slow season is from January to March, when outsiders steer clear of the cold and the threat of being snowed in at O'Hare. If you're not doing a lot of outdoor sightseeing, it's a great time to take advantage of the lowest room rates of the year.

Hotels charge premium prices during major conventions, most notably the International Home & Housewares Show in early March and the Restaurant Show in late May. Other conventions gobble up desirable rooms periodically throughout the year; to find out if an upcoming convention coincides with your trip, check the "Major Convention Dates" calendar in chapter 2 (p. 42).

For all the properties listed in this chapter, the best rates tend to show up on the hotels' websites, which often tout special deals. The only downside to booking online is that you often can't be sure what kind of room you're getting (at older properties in particular, room sizes can vary widely, as can the views). Follow up with a call to the hotel if you want to make sure your windows don't look out on an alley.

A local service, **Hot Rooms** (© **800/468-3500** or 773/468-7666; www. hotrooms.com), offers discounts of 25% to 50% off standard rates at more than 30 downtown hotels. (The rates here aren't always cheaper than the hotels' own websites, but it's worth checking out.) The 24-hour service is free, but if you cancel a reservation, you're assessed a $25 fee.

Most hotels offer discounts of roughly 10% to individuals who are visiting Chicago on business. To qualify for this rate, your company usually must have an account on file at the hotel. In some cases, however, you may be required only to present some perfunctory proof of your commercial status, such as a business card or an official letterhead, to receive the discount. It never hurts to ask.

Reservation Services

The **Chicago Convention & Tourism Bureau**'s website (www.choosechicago. com) allows you to book hotels as well as complete travel packages. Check out the "Immersion Weekends," trips planned around a particular theme (such as fashion or museums) that include behind-the-scenes tours and meals at distinctive local restaurants. For a free copy of the annual *Illinois Hotel-Motel Directory,* which also provides information about weekend packages, call the **Illinois Bureau of Tourism** at © **800/2-CONNECT** [226-6632].

Alternative Accommodations

If you'd prefer to stay in a private home, a centralized reservations service called **At Home Inn Chicago,** P.O. Box 14088, Chicago, IL 60614 (© **800/375-7084** or 312/640-1050; fax 312/640-1012; www.athomeinnchicago.com), lists more than 70 accommodations in the city. Options range from high-rise and loft apartments to guest rooms carved from a former private club on the 40th floor of a Loop office building. Most lie within 3 miles of downtown (many are located in the Gold Coast, Old Town, and Lincoln Park neighborhoods) and will run you about $150 to $300 per night for apartments, and as low as $105 for guest rooms in private homes. Most require a minimum stay of 2 or 3 nights.

A group of local B&B owners has formed the **Chicago Bed and Breakfast Association,** with a website that links to various properties throughout the city: **www.chicago-bed-breakfast.com**.

WHERE TO EAT

5

C hicago has upped its culinary credentials over the past decade, with high-end spots such as Alinea and Moto on the cutting edge of the molecular gastronomy trend (raising the average check price substantially along the way). But the city's thriving deep-dish pizza spots and casual ethnic eateries prove you don't need to be a hard-core foodie to find culinary satisfaction here. Steakhouses continue to be a draw, as they have for decades, and comfort food remains a staple of local restaurant menus.

BEST BETS

- **Best Splurge:** The standard-bearer for Chicago's reinvention as a culinary leader is **Alinea,** where chef Grant Achatz astounds and delights professional critics and amateur foodies with his ability to transform familiar food into unexpected shapes, textures, and presentations. Dishes at Asian-inspired **Moto** are equally inventive—sometimes even the menu itself is edible. With its refined approach and tranquil setting, **L2O** epitomizes the 21st-century approach to fine dining: Though every dish looks like a miniature work of art, the overall experience is welcoming, not snooty. See p. 131, 103, and 134 respectively.

- **Best View:** Forty stories above Chicago, **Everest,** in the heart of Loop, astounds with a spectacular view—and food to match. The panoramas are equally awe-inspiring at the **Signature Room at the 95th,** which is perched on the 95th floor of the John Hancock Center, the city's second-tallest building. Closer to earth, diners on the patio at Greektown's **Athena** get a panoramic view of the city skyline. See p. 94, 113, and 128 respectively.

- **Best Spot for a Romantic Dinner:** Secluded **North Pond** is an Arts and Crafts–style retreat with a postcard-perfect setting in Lincoln Park. Not only does it boast a dramatic vista of the Gold Coast skyline, but the restaurant's out-of-the-way locale also requires diners to begin and end their meals with an idyllic stroll through the park. For charm at a much more affordable price, try **Cyrano's Bistrot & Wine Bar,** a cozy River North spot with warm, personal service and an eclectic Parisian bistro decor that will make you feel like you've jetted off to the romantic City of Love. See p. 134 and 125, respectively.

- **Best Cheap Eats:** It's hard to find a dining bargain downtown, but **food-life,** inside the Water Tower Place shopping center, offers affordable lunch and dinner options in the heart of North Michigan Avenue's shopping district. Yes, it's a food court, but there are no chain fast-food stalls here: Instead you'll find a variety of made-to-order

Price Categories, by Average Entree Price	
Very Expensive	$25–$40
Expensive	$20–$30
Moderate	$15–$20
Inexpensive	$15 or less

PREVIOUS PAGE: **Don't leave Chicago without sampling the deep-dish pizza at the original Pizzeria Uno.**

choices, from stir fry and burgers to fresh salads and pastas. In Lincoln Park and Wicker Park, cash-strapped 20-somethings and families head to **Penny's Noodle Shop** for delicious, low-priced Asian noodle dishes and soups. See p. 118 and 141, respectively.

○ **Best for Kids:** Going out for deep-dish pizza is pretty much a requirement for any family visiting Chicago. **Gino's East** and the original **Pizzeria Uno** have been around for decades, and they're still serving up authentic versions of the city's gooey, gut-busting specialty. For something different from the usual fast food, try **Wishbone** in the West Loop, a family-owned spot specializing in Southern food with a casual vibe and plenty of mix-and-match menu options for fussy eaters. See p. 125, 130, and 108, respectively.

○ **Best American Cuisine:** It's no longer the see-and-be-seen spot it was when it first opened, but **mk** is actually better now that the crowds have moved on, serving up accessible twists on classic American dishes in a space that is both comfortable and sophisticated. **Crofton on Wells** is a true labor of love for Chef Suzy Crofton—and her devoted local fans keep coming back for more. See p. 119 and 118, respectively.

○ **Best French Cuisine:** An updated take on the bistro experience, **Bistronomic** offers classic French dishes in a fresh, modern setting, just a few blocks from the Magnificent Mile. Convivial **Mon Ami Gabi** re-creates the look and feel of a Parisian cafe, steps from Lincoln Park Zoo and the lakefront. See p. 114 and 135, respectively.

○ **Best Italian Cuisine:** Even without the glamorous view of the Magnificent Mile, ultra-elegant **Spiaggia** would draw diners with its gourmet versions of classic Italian cuisine. For a more casual atmosphere, it's hard to beat **Mia Francesca** in Lincoln Park, or its sister restaurant, **Francesca's on Chestnut,** just off the Magnificent Mile. Both are bustling, Americanized twists on classic trattoria dining, where the fresh, seasonal pastas are the main draw. See p. 110 and 140, respectively.

○ **Best Steakhouse:** Legendary Chicago restaurateur Arnie Morton no longer prowls the dining room, but **Morton's** remains the king of the city's old-guard steakhouses, serving up gargantuan wet-aged steaks and baked potatoes. **Gene & Georgetti** is another blast from the past, a long-time hangout for the city's movers and shakers that's barely changed since it opened in 1941—and that's exactly why the regulars like it. See p. 109 and 122, respectively.

ethnic GOES UPSCALE

While the term "ethnic restaurant" is often synonymous with casual, low-priced spots, Chicago chefs have taken world cuisine to new, fine-dining heights. At **Topolobampo** (p. 121), chef Rick Bayless highlights the flavors of Mexico, including little-known regional specialties, with a focus on fresh, sustainably produced ingredients. **Arun's** (p. 139), the namesake restaurant of chef Arun Sampanthavivat, turns Thai dining into a multi-hour, multi-course experience, with a customized menu that varies with the seasons and according to diners' preferences. Ultra-elegant **Spiaggia** (p. 110) gives Italian cuisine a gourmet upgrade, featuring luxe ingredients such as truffles and caviar.

- **Best Pretheater Dinner:** A longtime local favorite in the Loop, the **Italian Village**—three restaurants run by one family under one roof—knows how to get its clientele seated and fed in time for a show. For Chicago Symphony Orchestra audiences, **Rhapsody** is conveniently located in the Symphony Center building. If you're seeing a play in Lincoln Park, stop first for tasty tapas and pitchers of sangria at **Café Ba-Ba-Reeba!** See p. 100, 98, and 136, respectively.

THE LOOP

In keeping with their proximity to the towers of power, many of the restaurants in the Loop feature expense-account-style prices, but it's still possible to dine here for less than the cost of your hotel room. The South Loop—a neighborhood just west of the lake and south of Congress Parkway—has seen a mini-boom in restaurants in the past few years, accompanying a rash of condo conversions and new construction in the area. **Note:** Keep in mind that several of the best downtown spots are closed on Sunday.

Very Expensive

Everest ★★★ ALSATIAN/FRENCH Towering high above the Chicago Stock Exchange, Everest is an oasis of fine-dining civility, a place where you can taste the creations of one of Chicago's top chefs while enjoying one of the city's top views. The decor looks like a high-end corporate dining room, but the focus here is the view, the food, and the tranquil dining experience. Chef Jean Joho draws inspiration from the earthy cuisine of his native Alsace and mixes what he calls "noble" and "simple" ingredients, such as caviar or foie gras, with potatoes or turnips. While the menu changes frequently, the salmon soufflé and cream-of-Alsace-cabbage soup with smoked sturgeon and caviar are popular appetizers; signature entrees include roasted Maine lobster in Alsace Gewürztraminer butter and ginger, and poached tenderloin of beef cooked *pot-au-feu* style and served with horseradish cream. Befitting a restaurant that's been in business for a few decades, service is smooth and polished.

440 S. LaSalle St., 40th floor (at Congress Pkwy.). ✆ **312/663-8920.** www.everestrestaurant. com. Reservations required. Main courses $27–$46; tasting menu $89; 3-course pretheater dinner $49. AE, DC, DISC, MC, V. Tues–Thurs 5:30–9pm; Fri 5:30–9:30pm; Sat 5–10pm. Complimentary valet parking. Subway/El: Brown Line to LaSalle/Van Buren, or Red Line to Adams.

Expensive

Atwood Café ★★ 👤 AMERICAN Located in the historic **Hotel Burnham** (p. 69), this place combines a gracious, 1900-era feel with a fresh take on American comfort food. The dining room is fairly compact but comfortable, with soaring ceilings; lush velvet curtains and settees; and whimsical, colorful china and glassware. Executive chef Derek Simcik dabbles in global influences. Recent entree selections included crab cakes over an asparagus-and-lentil coleslaw; pan-seared striped bass with clams, wilted spinach, and roasted fingerling potatoes; and chicken and pork sausage with lentils and a poached egg. Desserts are a high point, from seasonal fruit cobblers to the rich banana-and-white-chocolate bread pudding. Atwood Café has a timeless quality: It's focused on delivering good food in a grownup setting rather than chasing the latest trends. The restaurant also serves breakfast and lunch daily, as well as brunch on weekends.

Restaurants in the Loop & West Loop

Monroe Harbor

Harbor Dr.

Field Blvd.

E. Randolph Dr.

S. Lake Shore Dr.

E. Jackson Dr.

Columbus Dr.

GRANT PARK

E. Balbo Dr.

E. Monroe Dr.

Art Institute of Chicago

N. Stetson Ave.

MILLENNIUM PARK

N. Michigan Ave.

S. Michigan Ave.

RIVER NORTH

Randolph

N. Wabash Ave.

N. State St.

Madison

Adams

Jackson

Library

E. Congress Pkwy.

E. Harrison St.

Wabash Ave.

E. 8th St.

E. 9th St.

Subway/El stop

1/4 mi

0.25 km

Chicago River

W. Kinzie St.

W. Wacker Dr.

Clark/Lake

State

N. Dearborn St.

N. Clark St.

N. LaSalle St.

N. Wells St.

N. Franklin St.

Monroe

Madison

Washington

W. Lake St.

W. Washington St.

W. Madison St.

W. Monroe St.

W. Adams St.

W. Jackson Blvd.

S. Dearborn St.

S. Clark St.

S. LaSalle St.

S. Sherman St.

S. Wells St.

S. State St.

S. Plymouth Ct.

S. Federal St.

SOUTH LOOP

THE LOOP

Merch Mart

Merchandise Mart

Quincy

Sears Tower

S. Franklin St.

LaSalle

Harrison

Congress Pkwy.

W. Harrison St.

S. Congress

N. Wacker Dr.

S. Wacker Dr.

South Branch Chicago River

Post Office

290

Union Station

CHINATOWN & PILSEN

W. Polk St.

S. Canal St.

S. Clinton St.

S. Jefferson St.

S. Des Plaines St.

N. Canal St.

N. Clinton St.

N. Jefferson St.

N. Milwaukee Ave.

Clinton

W. Fulton St.

W. Lake St.

W. Randolph Dr.

N. Des Plaines St.

N. Halsted St.

N. Green St.

N. Peoria St.

N. Sangamon St.

N. Morgan St.

90 94

90 94

W. Adams St.

W. Jackson Blvd.

W. Van Buren St.

Eisenhower Expwy.

Halsted/U of I

UNIVERSITY OF ILLINOIS AT CHICAGO

LITTLE ITALY

W. Taylor St.

S. Green St.

S. Peoria St.

S. Morgan St.

GREEK-TOWN

Santorini 14
Sepia 12
South Water Kitchen 24
Sushi Wabi 7
Tavern at the Park 25
Trattoria No. 10 28
Wishbone 6

312 Chicago 22
Artopolis 18
Athena 17
Atwood Café 27
Avec 11
The Berghoff 32
Blackbird 10
Carnivale 9
Costas 20
Custom House Tavern36
Edwardo's 37
Everest 35
The Gage 30
Gioco 39
The Girl and the Goat 8
Greek Islands 16
Heaven on Seven 26
The Italian Village 31
La Sardine 5
Lou Mitchell's 21
Mercat a la Planxa 38
Moto 1
Next 2
nine 13
One sixtyblue 4
Park Grill 29
Parthenon 19
Pegasus 15
Petterino's 23
The Publican 3
Rhapsody 34
Russian Tea Time 33

1 W. Washington St. (at State St.). ✆ **312/368-1900.** www.atwoodcafe.com. Main courses $14–$27 lunch; $19–$35 dinner. AE, DC, DISC, MC, V. Mon–Thurs 7–10am, 11:30am–3:45pm, and 5–10pm; Fri 7–10am, 11:30am–3:45pm, and 5–11pm; Sat 8–10am, 11:30am–3:45pm, and 5–11pm; Sun 8am–3pm and 5–10pm. Subway/El: Red Line to Washington.

Custom House Tavern ★★ AMERICAN Custom House's tranquil dining room—with large windows overlooking the surrounding cityscape—is a good pick if you value conversation over crowds. The sophisticated-but-comfortable setting is reflected in the seasonal menu, which ranges from gourmet burgers to seafood to more adventurous offerings (lamb sweetbreads, anyone?). Even seemingly straightforward dishes get a lift from unexpected flavor combinations, such as the arctic char with chickpea spaetzle, Meyer lemon, and almonds; or the venison *osso buco* with wild rice, ancho chilies, celery root, and dark chocolate. If you'd rather go more casual, you can order at the bar, which has its own menu, featuring top-notch hamburgers and other lighter fare.

500 S. Dearborn St. (at Congress Pkwy.), in the Hotel Blake. ✆ **312/523-0200.** www.custom house.cc. Reservations recommended on weekends. Main courses $12–$24 lunch, $14–$35 dinner. AE, DC, DISC, MC, V. Mon–Fri 11:30am–4pm and 5–10pm; Sat noon–4pm and 5–10pm; Sun noon–4pm and 5–9pm. Subway/El: Brown Line to Library.

The Gage ★ IRISH/AMERICAN Downtown's first gastropub feels as if it's been here forever, thanks to an impeccable remodeling of a historic space. The owners, originally from Ireland, have created a place where the food deserves equal billing with the drinks. (This is one of the few places in the Loop that serves decent food late.) The menu leans toward appetizer-size portions, which you can order in any combination. Entrée choices run the gamut from basic roasted Amish chicken to an exotic roast saddle of elk (for which you'll pay an eye-popping $42). The wide range of food on offer means that the Gage is a good choice for groups with different tastes. (No other place in town offers Scotch eggs, caramelized lobster, roasted bone marrow, and Alaskan halibut on the same menu.) The only disappointment—surprisingly—is the bland fish and chips. On weekends, the Gage serves brunch, including a traditional Irish breakfast of eggs, rashers, black and white puddings, sausages, and beans on toast.

24 S. Michigan Ave. (btw. Madison and Monroe sts.). ✆ **312/372-4243.** www.thegagechicago. com. Reservations recommended on weekends. Main courses $10–$38 lunch, $16–$42 dinner. AE, DISC, MC, V. Mon–Fri 11am–11pm (bar till 2am); Sat 10am–midnight (bar till 3am); Sun 10am–11pm (bar till midnight). Subway/El: Red Line to Monroe or Brown, or Orange Line to Madison.

Gioco ★ ITALIAN The South Loop was officially gentrified with the opening of this funky Italian restaurant. The cozy, lively ambience—with exposed brick, mahogany accents, an open kitchen, stacks of wine bottles, and hip music—is par for the course in other restaurant-rich neighborhoods, but it's a welcome addition to this area. Start with one of the wood-fired pizzas, or move on to the fine selection of pastas, including ricotta and spinach tortelloni; mushroom-stuffed ravioli and a hearty pappardelle with braised wild boar. Seafood shows up in various preparations, along with filet of beef in Barolo wine sauce, or the massive *Bistecca alla Fiorentina,* a porterhouse steak served in a portion for two. Even if you're loath to order tiramisu for the umpteenth time, try this heavenly version—light as air and easy on the rum. The lunch menu also has a few panini selections.

1312 S. Wabash Ave. (at 13th St.). ✆ **312/939-3870.** www.gioco-chicago.com. Main courses $13–$22 lunch, $17–$35 dinner. AE, DC, DISC, MC, V. Mon–Thurs 11:30am–2pm and 5–10pm; Fri 11:30am–2pm and 5–11:30pm; Sat 5–11:30pm; Sun 5–10pm. Subway/El: Red Line to Roosevelt.

Mercat a la Planxa ★★ SPANISH & TAPAS South Michigan Avenue, a stretch of offices and venerable old buildings such as the Hilton Chicago and Symphony Center, isn't exactly hip. Mercat's bright, vivacious atmosphere has brought some much-needed culinary diversity to this rather staid neighborhood. The bi-level, loftlike space and loungey dance-music soundtrack give Mercat a younger vibe, and the eclectic drink menu sets the party mood (the Bolero, with tequila, orange liqueur, lime, and fresh avocado sounds odd but gets raves). The extensive menu includes the usual tapas favorites, from traditional *charcuteria* (cured meats) to bacon-wrapped dates, garlic shrimp, and Spanish omelets. The menu also gets creative with heartier entrée options such as slow-cooked pork belly in a cider glaze or curry lamb with garbanzo beans, broccolini, and grilled flatbread.

638 S. Michigan Ave. (at Balbo Dr.), in the Blackstone Hotel. ℰ **312/765-0524.** www.mercat chicago.com. Reservations recommended on weekends. Tapas $6–$12; entrees $16–$26. AE, DC, MC, V. Mon–Thurs 11am–11pm; Fri–Sat 11am–midnight; Sun 11am–10pm. Subway/El: Red Line to Harrison.

Nine ★ AMERICAN/STEAK The sizzle isn't all on the grill at this contemporary steakhouse. You'll feel like you're making a grand entrance as you step down an open staircase into the airy, white and silver dining room, with its dramatic central champagne-and-caviar bar. (The owners have opened another Nine in Las Vegas, a city this glam decor seems meant for.) For a splurge, try the dry-aged steaks, particularly the 24-ounce bone-in rib-eye and 22-ounce porterhouse. You can also sample selections from the extensive raw bar (including wallet-busting caviar). The menu wisely accommodates a variety of tastes; non-red-meat options include a generous chopped salad, roast chicken with chipotle marinade, and seafood selections such as the delicious miso-marinated black cod. If you want to keep hanging with the beautiful people after dinner, head to the sleek Ghost Bar lounge upstairs.

440 W. Randolph St. (at Canal St.). ℰ **312/575-9900.** www.n9ne.com. Reservations recommended. Main courses $9–$22 lunch, $21–$43 dinner. AE, DC, MC, V. Mon–Thurs 11:30am–1:30pm and 5:30–10pm; Fri 11:30am–1:30pm and 5–11pm; Sat 5–11pm. Subway/El: Blue, Orange, Brown, or Green line to Clark/Lake.

Park Grill ★★ AMERICAN Location, location, location—it's what sets Park Grill apart from all the other upscale comfort-food restaurants in town. Set in the middle of Millennium Park, it makes a great stop after a late-afternoon stroll or before a summer concert at the Pritzker Music Pavilion. (You can order from a special three-course pretheater menu.) The dining room itself is simple but welcoming, with floor-to-ceiling windows that look out onto the Michigan Avenue skyline. The menu highlights American favorites, some prepared simply (American lamb chop and rotisserie chicken), others featuring a more international twist, such as house-made ravioli with ricotta, spring peas, mint, Spanish almonds, and brown butter; and black garlic risotto. Lunch selections include a good mix of sandwiches, and there's also a kids' menu.

11 N. Michigan Ave. (at Madison St.). ℰ **312/521-PARK** (7275). www.parkgrillchicago.com. Reservations recommended. Main courses $10–$21 lunch, $18–$26 dinner. AE, DC, MC, V. Sun–Thurs 11am–9:30pm; Fri 11am–10:30pm; Sat 10am–10:30pm Subway/El: Red Line to Washington, or Brown, Orange, Purple, or Green line to Madison.

Petterino's ★★ AMERICAN/STEAK Self-consciously retro, this restaurant re-creates the feeling of downtown dining in the 1940s and '50s. Located in the Goodman Theatre building, Petterino's is a popular pretheater option, so book a table in advance if you have to catch a show. The dimly lit dining room is decorated in dark wood with red leather booths, and the overall feel is relaxed rather than hyped up. The straightforward menu is filled with classic American big-night-out favorites: prime steaks, classic comfort food items such as chicken pot pie and Yankee pot roast, and some fresh fish selections. Among the old-time appetizers, you'll find shrimp *de jonghe,* coated with garlic and bread crumbs, and an excellent tomato bisque soup. In keeping with the restaurant's entertainment connection, some dishes are named after local celebrities—a nicely done salad of chopped mixed greens and blue cheese is named for longtime *Sun-Times* columnist Irv Kupcinet.

150 N. Dearborn St. (at Randolph St.). ✆ **312/422-0150.** www.petterinos.com. Reservations recommended. Main courses $8.95–$25 lunch, $10–$40 dinner. AE, DC, DISC, MC, V. Mon 11am–10pm; Tues–Thurs 11am–10:30pm; Fri–Sat 11am–11pm; Sun 11am–7:30pm. Subway/El: Red Line to Washington, or Brown Line to State/Lake.

Rhapsody ★★ AMERICAN This fine-dining restaurant inside Symphony Center (with floor-to-ceiling windows overlooking an outdoor dining area and a small park) is a hit with the concert-going crowd, as much for the setting as for the food. In the summer, the restaurant's outdoor garden is a mini-oasis of flowers and greenery, definitely the most charming outdoor dining spot in the Loop. (You still have to contend with the squealing wheels of El trains passing overhead.) The menu emphasizes contemporary American dining with a strong Italian influence. Recent entrees included pan-roasted Arctic char with pancetta in a balsamic glaze; grilled pork tenderloin served with parmesan-flavored polenta and topped with a braised pork ragu; and shrimp and scallop ravioli in a caviar cream sauce. The lunch menu features a few lighter choices, such as salads and panini. Preconcert dinners are Rhapsody's specialty, so be sure to make a reservation if you plan to catch a show.

65 E. Adams St. (at Wabash Ave.). ✆ **312/786-9911.** www.rhapsodychicago.com. Reservations recommended before symphony concerts. Main courses $11–$15 lunch, $19–$40 dinner. AE, DC, DISC, MC, V. Mon–Thurs 11:30am–2pm and 5–9pm; Fri 11:30am–2pm and 5–10pm; Sat 5–10pm. During symphony season, mid-Sept to mid-June, the restaurant is also open Sun 4:30–9pm; Thurs–Sat until 10:30pm. Subway/El: Brown, Purple, Green, or Orange line to Adams; or Red Line to Monroe or Jackson.

Russian Tea Time ★★ 🏛 RUSSIAN/TEA Another spot that's popular with Chicago Symphony Orchestra patrons and musicians, Russian Tea Time is far from being the simple cafe that its name implies. Reading through this family-owned restaurant's extensive menu is like taking a tour through the cuisine of czarist Russia and the former Soviet republics. (For Russian neophytes, all the dishes are well described.) The atmosphere is old world and cozy, with lots of woodwork and a friendly staff. Start off a meal with potato pancakes, blini with Russian caviar, or chilled smoked sturgeon; then move on to the beef stroganoff, short rib stew, or whole roasted baby chicken. If you want to extend your meal well into the night, order one of the "vodka flights," three 1-oz. shots of chilled, flavored vodka; the staff will even show you the authentic Russian way to down them.

77 E. Adams St. (btw. Michigan and Wabash aves.). ✆ **312/360-0000.** www.russianteatime. com. Reservations recommended. Main courses $15–$27 lunch, $18–$30 dinner. AE, DC, DISC, MC, V. Sun–Thurs 11am–9pm; Fri–Sat 11am–11pm (the restaurant sometimes closes earlier during the summer months). Tea service daily 2:30–4:30pm. Subway/El: Brown, Purple, Green, or Orange line to Adams; or Red Line to Monroe or Jackson.

South Water Kitchen ★ ☺ AMERICAN Because Loop restaurants mostly cater to office workers and business travelers, there aren't a lot of family-friendly options other than fast food. So while South Water Kitchen's upscale American-favorites menu doesn't break any new culinary ground, it deserves a mention as one of the few places in the area that welcomes kids—while featuring food sophisticated enough for discerning moms and dads. The dining room evokes the spirit of an old-fashioned city saloon, and the menu goes the retro route as well. Entrees include classic meat-and-potatoes dishes such as grilled rack of lamb with a minted pea puree; pan-seared walleye with mussels and wild rice; and grilled salmon served with a sweet corn succotash; there are usually a few vegetarian options as well. The restaurant provides not only kids' menus, but also games to keep the little ones occupied.

In the Hotel Monaco, 225 N. Wabash Ave. (at Wacker Dr.). ✆ **312/236-9300.** www.south waterkitchen.com. Main courses $9–$19 lunch, $19–$28 dinner. AE, DC, MC, V. Mon–Fri 7–10:30am and 11am–3pm; Sat–Sun 7am–2:30pm; daily 5–10pm. Subway/El: Red Line to State/Lake.

Tavern at the Park ★ AMERICAN The "Park" in question is Millennium Park, although—in the interest of full disclosure—the restaurant is actually located across the street. Still, this is a convenient spot for lunch or dinner during a day of sightseeing, even if most tables don't have much of a view (try to snag a seat by the windows, which look out over the rippling steel roof of Frank Gehry's Pritzker Music Pavilion). The staid brown color scheme calls to mind a generic chain-hotel restaurant, but at night white linen tablecloths brighten the space a little. Still, the food itself is more sophisticated than the decor (think comfort food with flair). Menu highlights include the chicken pot pie, barbecue rotisserie chicken, and a tasty prime rib sandwich. The melt-in-your-mouth-tender braised beef short ribs in red-wine demi-glaze are a personal favorite.

130 E. Randolph St. (at Michigan Ave.). ✆ **312/552-0070.** www.tavernatthepark.com. Sand-wiches $12–$18; entrees $22–$37. AE, DC, DISC, MC, V. Mon–Thurs 11am–10pm; Fri 11am–10:30pm; Sat noon–10:30pm. Subway/El: Red Line to Washington, or Brown Line to Randolph.

312 Chicago ★ ITALIAN Although this is technically a hotel restaurant (connected to the Hotel Allegro), it has a homey-yet-sophisticated character all its own—and a clientele that goes beyond hotel guests. Downstairs, the restaurant's dark booths and wood accents give the space a clubby feel; upstairs, the mood is brighter and more contemporary, thanks to large windows that welcome natural light. Italian-born chef Luca Corazzina focuses on fresh, seasonal ingredients and classic Italian preparations with entrees such as homemade spinach-and-ricotta tortellini in a brown butter sage sauce, roast chicken with peppers and polenta, and veal medallions with porcini mushrooms and squash purée (there are also vegetarian and vegan options). Appropriately enough for an Italian restaurant, there's an extensive wine list. The lunch menu includes a selection of panini sandwiches. Because the restaurant caters to hotel guests, it's also open for breakfast and Sunday brunch.

136 N. LaSalle St. (at Randolph St.). ✆ **312/696-2420.** www.312chicago.com. Reservations rec-ommended. Main courses $17–$32. AE, DC, DISC, MC, V. Mon–Fri 7–10am and 11am–10pm; Sat 8–11am and 4:30–10pm; Sun 8am–3pm and 4–9pm. Subway/El: Red Line to Washington.

Trattoria No. 10 ITALIAN Elegant but not pretentious, Trattoria No. 10 is a long-time, dependable favorite with downtown office workers. The burnt-or-ange tones, ceramic floor tiles, and gracefully arched ceilings set a dining-in-Italy mood. The house specialty is the homemade ravioli, which can be ordered as an appetizer or main course (recent fillings included butternut and acorn squash topped with walnut sauce, and homemade Italian sausage and mozzarella served with spicy arrabiata sauce). There are plenty of other worthwhile pasta dishes to choose from, such as farfalle with duck confit, asparagus, caramelized onions, and pine nuts; or the linguine with roasted eggplant, grilled tomatoes, and smoked mozzarella. You'll also find the expected beef, veal, and seafood options, and a weekly changing risotto. For a lighter (and more affordable) meal, stop by between 5 and 7:30pm Tuesday through Friday for an all-you-can-eat buffet at the bar; $15 (with a $6 drink minimum) allows you to fill up on salads, antipasti, shrimp, and various pasta specials.

10 N. Dearborn St. (btw. Madison and Washington sts.). ☎ **312/984-1718.** www.trattoriaten.com. Main courses $16–$22 lunch, $17–$28 dinner. AE, DC, DISC, MC, V. Mon–Thurs 11:30am–2pm and 5:30–9pm; Fri 11:30am–2pm and 5:30–10pm; Sat 5:30–10pm. Subway/El: Red Line to Madison.

Moderate

The Berghoff ★ GERMAN/AMERICAN A Chicago landmark, the Berghoff is housed in one of the first buildings constructed in the Loop after the Great Chicago Fire. Opened in 1898, it also has the honor of holding the first liquor license granted after the repeal of Prohibition in 1933. Unfortunately, much of the city's German heritage has dissipated over the years, and even the menu has moved along with the times, adding multicultural entrees like Cajun chicken salad and mushroom panini. The good news is that you can still order Berghoff classics like Wiener schnitzel and sauerbraten, along with a side of chewy spaetzle (noodles). (For the full Berghoff experience, wash it all down with a glass of the house draft beer or root beer.) Downstairs from the main restaurant, the counter-service **Berghoff Café** serves up sandwiches, panini, and salads to neighborhood office workers (it's open for lunch only on weekdays).

17 W. Adams St. (btw. State and Dearborn sts.). ☎ **312/427-3170.** www.theberghoff.com. Reservations accepted. Main courses $9–$17 lunch, $14–$19 dinner. AE, DC, DISC, MC, V. Mon–Fri 11am–9pm; Sat 11:30am–10pm. Subway/El: Red Line to Jackson.

The Italian Village ★ 🏛 ITALIAN Open since 1927 (and run by the grandchildren of the original owner), this downtown dining landmark houses three separate Italian restaurants that are popular with pre- and post-theater crowds. Each has its own menu and ambience, but the sentimental favorite is the **Village,** on the second floor, a charmingly retro interpretation of alfresco dining in a small Italian town, complete with a midnight-blue ceiling, twinkling "stars," and banquettes tucked into private, cavelike rooms. The food is old-school Italian: eggplant parmigiana, a heavy fettuccine Alfredo that would send your cardiologist into fits, veal scaloppini, and even calves' liver. The food is good rather than great, but the service is outstanding.

Downstairs from the Village, you'll find **Vivere,** a trendier (and more expensive) restaurant experience with a flashy, eye-catching interior (including spiraling bronze sculptures and multicolored, fragmented mosaic floors). Pasta dishes feature upscale and exotic ingredients, from the pappardelle with wild boar and hen of the woods mushrooms to the *agnolottini* filled with pheasant. In the basement of the building, **La Cantina Enoteca** has the feel of a casual wine cellar; the specialty here is steak and seafood, although you can order basic pasta dishes as well.

71 W. Monroe St. (btw. Clark and Dearborn sts.). ☎ **312/332-7005.** www.italianvillage-chicago. com. Reservations recommended (accepted for parties of 3 or more). Main courses (including salad) $9–$23 lunch, $13–$24 dinner. AE, DISC, MC, V. Mon–Thurs 11am–midnight; Fri–Sat 11am–1am; Sun noon–midnight. Subway/El: Red Line to Monroe.

Inexpensive

Heaven on Seven ★★ 🍴 CAJUN & CREOLE/DINER Hidden on the seventh floor of an office building opposite Macy's, this no-frills spot is truly an insider's hangout. Chef/owner Jimmy Bannos's Cajun and Creole specialties come with a cup of soup and include such Louisiana staples as red beans and rice, a catfish po' boy sandwich, and jambalaya. If you don't have a taste for Tabasco,

---

😊 family-friendly **RESTAURANTS**

One of the city's first "theme" restaurants, **Ed Debevic's,** 640 N. Wells St., at Ontario Street (📞 312/664-1707), is a temple to America's hometown lunch-counter culture. The burgers-and-milkshakes menu is kid-friendly, but it's the staff shtick that makes this place memorable. The waitresses play the parts of gum-chewing toughies who make wisecracks, toss out good-natured insults, and even sit right down at your table.

If you're in the mood for something a little more funky, **Wishbone** ★★ (p. 108) is a popular option for local families. The food is diverse enough that both adults and kids can find something to their liking (you can mix and match side dishes, a big plus), and there's also a menu geared just toward children. Another all-American choice in the Loop is **South Water Kitchen** ★ (p. 99), which offers a kids' menu and coloring books.

A fun breakfast-and-lunch spot in Lincoln Park, **Toast** (pictured below), 746 W. Webster St., at Halsted Street (📞 773/935-5600), serves up all-American favorites (pancakes, eggs, sandwiches) and employs an age-old restaurateur's device for keeping idle

hands and minds occupied: Tables at this neighborhood spot are covered with blank canvases of butcher-block paper on which kids of all ages can doodle away with crayons. But be forewarned: This is a very popular spot for weekend brunch.

At **Gino's East** ★★ (p. 125), the famous Chicago pizzeria, long waits can also be an issue during the prime summer tourist season. But once you get your table, the kids can let loose: Patrons are invited to scrawl all over the graffiti-strewn walls and furniture. For fun and games of the coin-operated and basement rec room variety, seek out **Dave & Buster's,** 1024 N. Clark St. (📞 312/943-5151), the Chicago location of the Dallas-based mega entertainment/dining chain.

With heaping plates of pasta served up family style, **Maggiano's,** 516 N. Clark St. (📞 312/644-7700), in River North, and **Buca di Beppo,** 521 N. Rush St., right off Michigan Avenue (📞 312/396-0001), are good choices for budget-conscious families. These Italian-American restaurants (both parts of national chains) serve up huge portions of pasta and meat to be passed and shared.

the extensive coffee-shop-style menu covers all the traditional essentials: grilled-cheese sandwiches, omelets, tuna—the works. Although Heaven on Seven is usually open only for breakfast and lunch, they do serve dinner on the third Friday of the month from 5:30 to 9pm.

Heaven also has another downtown location just off the Mag Mile at **600 N. Michigan Ave.** (𝓒 **312/280-7774**); unlike the original location, they accept reservations and credit cards and are open for dinner. The ambience is more lively than gritty, making it a popular spot for families.

111 N. Wabash Ave. (at Washington St.), 7th floor. 𝓒 **312/263-6443.** www.heavenonseven. com. Reservations not accepted. Sandwiches $10–$14; main courses $10–$14. No credit cards. Mon–Fri 9am–4pm; Sat 10am–3pm; 3rd Fri of each month 5:30–9pm. Subway/El: Red Line to Washington.

THE WEST LOOP

For restaurants listed in this section, see the map "Restaurants in the Loop & West Loop," on p. 95.

The stretch of Randolph Street just west of the Chicago River—once known as the Market District—used to be filled with produce trucks and warehouses that shut down tight after nightfall. In the 1990s, in an echo of New York's Meatpacking District, a few bold restaurant pioneers moved in, bringing their super-hip clientele with them. It wasn't long before industrial buildings began their transformation into condos, and now it seems like there's a construction zone on every corner. Despite the upheaval, the West Loop still feels like a neighborhood in transition. It's home to some of the city's coolest restaurants and clubs, but not much else.

Transportation to the West Loop is easy. You can get there by bus (no. 8 or 9) or El (the Green Line has a stop at Clinton, which is within a few blocks of most restaurants listed here), but takes about 5 minutes and costs less than $10 to take a cab from Michigan Avenue. The walk from the Loop is pleasant and secure in the daytime and early evening, but it's best to catch a cab if you're returning to your hotel late.

Very Expensive

Blackbird ★★★ NEW AMERICAN Stylishly spare, chef Paul Kahan's Blackbird looks like a contemporary art gallery, an appropriate image for a place that creates miniature masterpieces out of traditional American ingredients. The white, narrow room is dense with close-packed tables, and the floor-to-ceiling windows in front frame the urban landscape outside. Blackbird is fun for people who like a scene, but it can feel overcrowded and loud (I'd recommend elsewhere for a romantic dinner). Kahan is a big proponent of local, organic ingredients, so expect top-notch quality and perfectly executed creations. Entrees change seasonally, but recent dishes have included wood-grilled California sturgeon with broccoli, parsley root, and violet mustard spaetzle; and grilled pork belly with royal trumpet mushrooms, melted leeks, pickled turmeric, and chorizo broth. Desserts are similarly original and well worth a splurge; choices might include white honey parfait with coconut sponge, passion fruit, rum, and caramelized white chocolate; or a hazelnut dacquoise with espresso, crispy chicory caramel, and apricot kernel sorbet.

619 W. Randolph St. ✆ **312/715-0708.** www.blackbirdrestaurant.com. Reservations recommended. Main courses $10–$15 lunch, $27–$36 dinner. AE, DISC, MC, V. Mon–Fri 11:30am–2pm and 5:30–10:30pm; Sat 5:30–11:30pm.

Moto ★★★ NEW AMERICAN Chef Homaro Cantu calls his cuisine "avant-garde with Asian influences"—but what he really wants is to take dining beyond just eating. At Moto, you experience food with all the senses, making for some of the most jaw-droppingly original dishes in town. Herbs are entwined in corkscrew-handled spoons, allowing their scent to waft toward diners as they chew, while everyday ingredients show up in unexpected forms (such as a "pizza and salad" soup). Cantu's got a sense of humor, too—during a raw food course, he uses a "virtual aroma device" to emit a smoky scent, and sometimes the menu itself is edible. Diners have a choice of tasting menus, offering from 10 to 20 courses; a la carte is not an option. The restaurant itself has a minimalist Zen look—here, all the drama is on your plate.

945 W. Fulton Market Ave. (at Sangamon St.). ✆ **312/491-0058.** www.motorestaurant.com. Reservations recommended. Prix-fixe dinners $135–$195. AE, DC, DISC, MC, V. Tues–Sat 5–11pm.

Next ★★★ NEW AMERICAN Grant Achatz's restaurant **Alinea** (p. 131) is consistently rated among the best in the world; this appropriately named restaurant is the superstar chef's game-changing next act. The gimmick—and it's a great one—is that menus change four times per year and are based on time and place in history, faithful, for the most part, to the ingredients and dining traditions of the times. Menus could range from "Paris, 1906" (turtle soup; roast duck; truffled egg custard) to "Kyoto, 1946" to "Hong Kong 2056." Wisely, the culinary novelty never overshadows the delicious, perfectly cooked food. Next's reservation process is equally revolutionary. Tickets must be purchased in advance through the website (a few "same night" walk-in tickets are sold on the restaurant's Facebook page), with beverage, tax, and tip included in a set fee that varies depending on the day and time you dine (Wednesday at 6pm costs less than Saturday at 8pm, though the menu is exactly the same).

953 W. Fulton Market Ave. (between Morgan and Sangamon sts.) ✆ **312/226-0858.** www. nextrestaurant.com. Online reservations required. Set menus from $65–$110 (wine pairings $48–$98). AE, DC, DISC, MC, V. Mon–Sun 5:30–9:30pm.

one sixtyblue ★★ AMERICAN If you're looking for a dining experience that is refined without being stuffy—and you prefer reading menus that don't require a thesaurus—then you'll have a memorable meal here. (The restaurant's tag line is "Simple inspiration, every day"). High ceilings, upholstered banquettes, and carpeting keep down the noise level, and there's plenty of space between tables. The contemporary American menu highlights locally sourced ingredients (some from the restaurant's own garden); recent offerings included rhubarb-glazed chicken with raisins, bok choy, and Persian cucumber; seared scallops with pineapple-mango chutney; and wood-grilled duck breast with roasted butternut squash and a citrus glaze. The dessert list mixes sweet and savory flavors in unexpected combinations (for example, basil ice cream and rosemary shortbread). Service is attentive but unobtrusive.

1400 W. Randolph St. (at Loomis St.). ✆ **312/850-0303.** www.onesixtyblue.com. Reservations recommended on weekends. Main courses $21–$29. AE, MC, V. Mon–Thurs 5:30–9pm; Fri–Sat 5:30–10pm.

Expensive

Avec ★ MEDITERRANEAN A casual wine bar owned by chef Paul Kahan of neighboring Blackbird (p. 102), Avec keeps things simple: top-quality ingredients in simple preparations that take inspiration from Italian, French, and Spanish cuisines. The menu focuses on a variety of "small plates" meant for sharing (although there are always five or six entree-size offerings as well). The long, narrow dining room, with its wood walls and floors, will strike you as either cramped or cozy. I know many people who love Avec's convivial spirit; others find it annoyingly crowded and loud. Small plates include salads and appetizer-style dishes such as house-made watercress pasta with lamb confit, zucchini cream, and spring vegetables; and dates stuffed with chorizo sausage. Large plates feature seasonal ingredients and tend to be heartier (prosciutto with honeycomb, orange zest, Marcona almonds, and black peppercorn vinaigrette, for example). There's also a good selection of specialty cheeses and—of course—an extensive European-focused wine list.

615 W. Randolph St. © **312/377-2002.** www.avecrestaurant.com. Reservations not accepted. Small plates $5–$13; large plates $14–$20. AE, DISC, MC, V. Mon–Thurs 3:30pm–midnight; Fri–Sat 3:30pm–1am; Sun 3:30–11pm (bar open later every night).

Carnivale ★ LATIN AMERICAN This sprawling, Pan-Latin spot features a lively soundtrack to accompany its Central and South American–inspired food. If you want to be at the center of the action, head for the two-story central dining room, where brightly colored walls and enormous red-and-yellow lanterns complete the party atmosphere. If you prefer not to shout through your meal, request a table in one of the more intimate side rooms, or try snagging one of the tables just off the central staircase, which give you the best view of the action below. Carnivale's menu features Latin cuisine ranging from rum-glazed pork shoulder with Puerto Rican rice and beans to Argentine-style steaks. Befitting its clubby vibe, there's also an extensive selection of tropical drinks. Overall, the food is good rather than great; Carnivale's main selling point is its bright, buzzy atmosphere.

702 W. Fulton St. (btw. Clinton St. and the Kennedy Expwy./I-94). © **312/850-5005.** www.carnivalechicago.com. Reservations recommended on weekends. Main courses $8–$15 lunch, $16–$38 dinner. AE, DISC, MC, V. Mon–Thurs 11:30am–2:30pm and 5–10pm; Fri 11:30am–2:30pm and 5–11pm; Sat 5–11pm; Sun 5–10pm. Bar Mon–Tues till 11:30pm; Wed–Thurs till midnight; Fri–Sat till 1am; Sun till 10pm. Subway/El: Green Line to Clinton.

Girl and the Goat ★ AMERICAN Chef Stephanie Izard became a foodie celebrity when she won TV's *Top Chef* in 2008, but her bustling, welcoming restaurant proves she'd rather be cooking for regular folks than burnishing her media credentials. Here, the chefs work from an open kitchen that fills one side of the dining room, and the loftlike space—with rustic wood tables and concrete floors—is a fitting backdrop for Izard's bold flavor combinations. The menu is strictly small-plates, which are heavy on meat and fish (and yes, you'll find goat, mixed in sausages or arrayed with cherries on top of a pizza). While adventurous diners may rise to the challenge of the Roasted Pig Face, others will take comfort in more accessible dishes such as grilled octopus with Serrano ham and braised pistachios; escargot ravioli; or the roasted cauliflower with pickled peppers and pine nuts. Desserts focus on savory-sweet combinations, such as a bittersweet chocolate popsicle paired with shiitake mushroom gelato.

809 W. Randolph St. (at Halsted St.). © **312/492-6262.** www.girlandthegoat.com. Reservations strongly recommended on weekends. Small plates $4–$18. AE, DISC, MC, V. Sun–Thurs 4:30–11pm; Fri–Sat 4:30–midnight.

La Sardine ★ 🍽 BISTRO/FRENCH Sister to Jean-Claude Poilevey's popular Le Bouchon (and named after a critic's description of that tiny Bucktown bistro; p. 144), this is a more spacious and gracious destination, with an open, airy feel. Well-prepared versions of bistro standards include the delicate bouillabaisse in a lobster-saffron broth; rabbit stew with mushrooms; steak frites; sensational escargots bourguignon; onion soup; and *salade Lyonnaise* (greens, bacon lardons, croutons, and poached egg). The dessert menu boasts traditional soufflés, with your choice of Grand Marnier or chocolate. At lunch, choose from an abbreviated menu of appetizers and salads, soups, sandwiches, and entrees. There's also a daily $22 three-course lunch that includes soup or salad and your choice of entree and dessert.

111 N. Carpenter St. © **312/421-2800.** www.frenchrestaurantschicago.com. Reservations recommended. Main courses $14–$18 lunch, $17–$25 dinner. AE, DC, DISC, MC, V. Mon–Thurs 11:30am–2:30pm and 5–10pm; Fri 11:30am–2:30pm and 5–11pm; Sat 5–11pm.

The Publican ★ 🍽 BISTRO Along with Avec and Blackbird (see above), this is another of chef Paul Kahan's creations—his take on the Belgian beer hall with a pork- and fish-focused menu. The room is simple and spare, with wooden communal tables and dozens of white globe lights hanging from the ceiling. A large selection of fresh oysters tops the menu, followed by seafood choices ranging from smoked char from southern Iceland with giardiniera (pickled vegetable relish), fingerling potatoes, and *fromage blanc,* to Dungeness crab with yellow Thai curry. "Aged ham" has its own section on the menu (and you can try a sampling of all of them), and "Meats" include a wide array of offerings: pork rinds, duck liver pate, *boudin blanc,* roasted chicken, suckling pig, Wagyu beef cheek, and flank steak. Vegetable side dishes range from radishes and pickles to spicy greens and asparagus. This place also is serious about beer: The extensive list includes selections imported from Germany, the U.K., and numerous Belgian breweries.

837 W. Fulton Market St. © **312/733-9555.** www.thepublicanrestaurant.com. Reservations recommended. Main courses $14–$29. AE, MC, V. Mon–Thurs 3:30am–10:30pm; Fri–Sat 3:30–11:30pm; Sun 10am–2pm (brunch) and 5–9pm.

Sepia ★★★ AMERICAN The elegant dining room, housed in an 1890s print shop, has a palpable sense of history, but the real show here is the honest food prepared with integrity by chef Andrew Zimmerman. He focuses on seasonal, organic, and sustainable ingredients for his cuisine, which is refined with a hint of rusticity. The selection of house-made charcuterie epitomizes Sepia's style: The platter is casual in spirit, but gorgeous and tasteful in execution. After those sausages, you might try an appetizer of ricotta cavatelli with snap peas, pancetta, mint, and pickled lemon zest; or crispy sweetbreads with smoked potato gnocchi and roasted mushrooms. Entrees range from vegetable moussaka with confit garlic puree, braised quince, and fried herbs; to monkfish with chorizo, judion beans, Serrano ham, clams, and piperade broth. Dessert offerings include a rich pecan and chocolate cake with butterscotch, cassis syrup, and coconut ice cream.

123 N. Jefferson St. (at Randolph St.). © **312/441-1920.** www.sepiachicago.com. Reservations recommended. Main courses $23–$31. AE, DC, DISC, MC, V. Mon–Fri 11:30am–2pm; Mon–Thurs 5:15–9:30pm; Fri–Sat 5:15–10:30pm; Sun 5–10pm.

CHINATOWN

Chicago's Chinatown is about 20 blocks south of the Loop. The district is strung along two thoroughfares, Cermak Road and Wentworth Avenue, as far south as 24th Place. Hailing a cab from the Loop is the easiest way to get here, but you can also drive and leave your car in the validated lot near the entrance to Chinatown, or take the Orange Line of the El to the Cermak stop, a well-lit station on the edge of the Chinatown commercial district.

The spacious, fairly elegant **Phoenix,** 2131 S. Archer Ave. (btw. Wentworth Ave. and Cermak Rd.; ✆ **312/328-0848;** www.chinatownphoenix.com), has plenty of room for big tables of family or friends to enjoy the Cantonese (and some Szechuan) cuisine. A good sign: The place attracts lots of Chinatown locals. It's especially popular for dim sum brunch, so come early to avoid the wait. Late night, stop by the more casual **Saint's Alp Teahouse** downstairs (✆ **312/842-1886**), an outpost of the Hong Kong chain, which is open until at least midnight daily.

Open since 1927, **Won Kow,** 2237 S. Wentworth Ave. (btw. 22nd Place and Alexander St.; ✆ **312/842-7500**), is the oldest continually operating restaurant in Chinatown. You can enjoy dim sum in the mezzanine-level dining room from 9am to 3pm daily. Most of the items cost around $3. Other house specialties include Mongolian chicken and duck with seafood.

Two other great spots for daily dim sum are located in Chinatown Square Mall, an open-air walking pavilion of restaurants, shops, and other businesses along Archer Avenue. Try **Shiu Wah,** 2162 S. Archer Ave. (✆ **312/225-8811;** 8am–3pm), or **Happy Chef,** 2164 S. Archer Ave. (✆ **312/808-3689;** 9am–4pm).

They're both great; pick the one with the shortest wait.

LITTLE ITALY

Convenient to most downtown locations, a few blocks' stretch of Taylor Street is home to a host of time-honored, traditional, hearty Italian restaurants. If you're staying in the Loop (an easy cab ride away), the area makes a good destination for dinner.

Regulars return for the straightforward Italian favorites livened up with some adventurous specials at **Francesca's on Taylor,** 1400 W. Taylor St. (at Loomis St.; ✆ **312/829-2828;** www.miafrancesca.com). Standouts include the fresh homemade pastas and the creative fish entrees. This is part of a local chain that includes the popular **Mia Francesca** (p. 140), as well as nearby **Davanti Enoteca,** 1359 W. Taylor St. (✆ **312/226-5550**), a cozy, buzzy smallplates spot that's known for its truffle egg toast, bruschetta, and specialty pizzas.

Expect to wait even with a reservation at **Rosebud on Taylor** ★, 1500 W. Taylor St. (at Laflin St.; ✆ **312/942-1117;** www.rosebudrestaurants.com), but fear not—your hunger will be satisfied. Rosebud is known for enormous helpings of pasta, most of which lean toward heavy Italian-American favorites: deepdish lasagna and a fettuccine Alfredo

5

The West Loop

WHERE TO EAT

that defines the word *rich.* I highly recommend any of the pastas served with vodka sauce. Another location is near the Mag Mile at 720 N. Rush St. (© **312/266-6444**).

Family-owned **Tuscany,** 1014 W. Taylor St. (btw. Morgan and Miller sts.; © **312/829-1990;** www.tuscanychicago. com), has the comfortable feel of a neighborhood restaurant, unlike the city's more fashionable Italian spots. Specialties include anything cooked on the wood-burning grill and Tuscan sausage dishes. A second location is across from Wrigley Field, at 3700 N. Clark St. (at Waveland Ave.; © **773/404-7700**).

GREEKTOWN

A short cab ride across the south branch of the Chicago River will take you to the city's Greektown, a row of moderately priced and inexpensive Greek restaurants clustered on Halsted Street between Van Buren and Washington streets.

To be honest, there's not much here to distinguish one restaurant from the other: They're all standard Greek restaurants with similar looks and similar menus. That said, **Greek Islands,** 200 S. Halsted St. (at Adams St.; © **312/782-9855;** www.greekislands. net); **Santorini,** 800 W. Adams St. (at Halsted St.; © **312/829-8820;** www. santorinichicago.com); **Parthenon,** 314 S. Halsted St. (btw. Jackson and Van Buren sts.; © **312/726-2407;** www. theparthenon.com); and **Costas,** 340 S. Halsted St. (btw. Jackson and Van Buren sts.; © **312/263-0767;** www. costasdining.com), are all good bets for gyros, Greek salads, shish kabobs, and

the classic moussaka. On warm summer nights, opt for either **Athena ★,** 212 S. Halsted St. (btw. Adams and Jackson sts.; © **312/655-0000;** www.athenarestaurantchicago.com), which has a huge outdoor seating area, or **Pegasus,** 130 S. Halsted St. (btw. Monroe and Adams sts.; © **312/226-3377;** www.pegasuschicago.com), with its rooftop patio serving drinks, appetizers, and desserts. Both have wonderful views of the Loop's skyline. **Artopolis,** 306 S. Halsted St. (at Jackson St.; © **312/559-9000;** www.artopolischicago.com), a more recent addition to the neighborhood, is a casual option offering up Greek and Mediterranean specialties, wood-oven pizzas, breads, and French pastries, all of them tasty.

PILSEN

Just south of the Loop and convenient to McCormick Place and Chinatown, Pilsen is a colorful blend of Mexican culture, artists, and bohemians, and pricey new residential developments. The area's nascent restaurant scene is showing signs of life, but for now, the local fare is decidedly casual.

Nuevo Leon, 1515 W. 18th St. (at Laflin St.; © **312/421-1517;** www. nuevoleonrestaurant.com), is a popular Mexican restaurant serving the standard offerings.

On the more bohemian side, linger over a salad, sandwich, cake, or refreshing fruit milkshake *(liquado)* at **Café Jumping Bean,** 1439 W. 18th St. (at Bishop St.; © **312/455-0019;** http:// cafejumpingbean.org), and admire the artwork—from paintings to photographs—hanging on the walls.

Sushi Wabi ★ JAPANESE/SUSHI Artfully presented sushi and chic crowds are the order of the day at this stylish but attitude-free restaurant. The minimal-chic decor is industrial and raw, and the lighting is dark and seductive—giving the restaurant a downtown-lounge feel. Sushi connoisseurs can request the chef's selection sashimi plate or go for specialties such as the sea-scallop roll with smelt roe, mayonnaise, avocado, and sesame seeds; the dragon roll of shrimp tempura, eel, and avocado; or the spiky, crunchy spider roll of soft-shell crab, smelt roe, mayonnaise, and pepper-vinegar sauce. Simple entrees such as seared tuna, grilled salmon, teriyaki beef, and sesame-crusted chicken breast will satisfy landlubbers who are accommodating their sushi-loving companions. Drinks include a selection of teas in cast-iron pots and both chilled and hot sakes, or try a martini with a ginger-stuffed olive.

842 W. Randolph St. © **312/563-1224.** www.sushiwabi.com. Reservations recommended on weekends. Main courses $12–$30. AE, DC, DISC, MC, V. Mon–Fri 11:30am–2pm; Mon–Tues 5–11pm; Wed–Sat 5pm–midnight; Sun 5–11pm.

Inexpensive

Wishbone ★★ ☺ BREAKFAST & BRUNCH/SOUTHERN A down-home, casual spot that inspires intense loyalty, Wishbone blends hearty, country-style choices with healthy and vegetarian items. It's best known around town for its popular Saturday and Sunday brunch, but lunch and dinner are just as good—and less crowded. Seafood lovers will enjoy the blackened catfish or crawfish cakes; other offerings include a hearty jambalaya stew and a daily étouffée special. Entrees come with your choice of two side dishes, which range from healthy (fresh fruit) to heavy (macaroni and cheese, mashed sweet potatoes); there are also several vegetarian options. The tart Key lime pie is a worthy finish to a meal here. Wishbone has a children's menu and actively welcomes families (even toddlers!).

There's a newer location on the North Side, at 3300 N. Lincoln Ave. (at W. School St.; © **773/549-2663**), but the original has more character.

1001 Washington St. (at Morgan St.). © **312/850-2663.** www.wishbonechicago.com. Reservations accepted, except for weekend brunch. Main courses $4–$14 breakfast and lunch, $6–$17 dinner. AE, DC, DISC, MC, V. Mon 7am–3pm; Tues–Thurs 7am–3:30pm and 5–9pm; Fri 7am–3pm and 5–10pm; Sat 8am–3pm and 5–10pm; Sun 8am–3pm.

A Taste of Poland

Chicago has long been a popular destination for Polish immigrants (currently, about one million Chicagoans claim Polish ancestry). It's somewhat mystifying, then, why they haven't made much of an impact on the city's dining scene. There are Polish restaurants here, but they tend to be small, casual, family-run affairs in residential neighborhoods far removed from the usual tourist attractions. If you'd like to try some hearty, stick-to-your-ribs Polish food, the best-known restaurant is **Red**

Apple (Czerwone Jabluszko), 3121 N. Milwaukee Ave. (© 773/588-5781; www.redapplebuffet.com). Dining here is strictly buffet, and the lineup includes Polish specialties such as pirogi (meat- or cheese-stuffed dumplings) and blintzes, as well as a huge selection of roast meats, salads, and bread (there's even fruit, should you feel nutrient starved). Best of all is the price: $13 on weekdays and $15 on weekends for all you can eat (lunch prices are $2 less).

THE MAGNIFICENT MILE & THE GOLD COAST

Many tourists who visit Chicago never stray far from the Magnificent Mile and the adjoining Gold Coast area. From the array of restaurants, shops, and pretty streets, it's not hard to see why. The Gold Coast is home to some of the city's wealthiest, most tradition-bound families, people who have been frequenting the same restaurants for years. But newer places, such as Table Fifty-Two, have carved out their own culinary niches here as well.

Very Expensive

Cape Cod Room ✋ SEAFOOD There's nothing nouvelle about the Cape Cod Room, which is part of the draw for old-timers; the restaurant, located on the lower level of The Drake Hotel, is dimly lit and hasn't changed much since it opened in the 1930s. Although the food is fine, I think the prices are far too steep for what you get. But that doesn't stop Cape Cod loyalists—many of whom have been coming here for decades—from filling up the place and ordering the signature bookbinder soup, a rich seafood-and-vegetable concoction. Classic old-school offerings include the signature Dover sole (boned tableside, naturally), along with oysters Rockefeller, lobster thermidor, and a steak-and-lobster combo plate. If seafood's not your thing, there's also a New York strip and a filet mignon. I wouldn't call the Cape Cod Room a good value, but as with any vintage restaurant, it has a certain timeless charm, and the people-watching can be priceless.
In The Drake Hotel, 140 E. Walton Place (at Michigan Ave.). ✆ **312/932-4615.** Reservations recommended. www.thedrakehotel.com/dine/cape-cod-room. Main courses $28–$60. AE, DC, DISC, MC, V. Daily 5:30–10pm. Subway/El: Red Line to Chicago.

Gibsons Bar & Steakhouse ★★ STEAK Popular with its Gold Coast neighbors, Gibsons is the steakhouse you visit when you want to take in a scene. There are sporty cars idling at the valet stand, photos of celebs and near-celebs who've appeared here, and overdressed denizens mingling and noshing in the bar. The dining rooms evoke a more romantic feel, from the sleek Art Deco decor to the bow-tied bartenders. But Gibsons, which marked its 20th anniversary in 2010, isn't coasting on atmosphere alone; the top-notch steaks deserve some credit, too. This isn't the place for a romantic dinner *à deux*; portions are notoriously enormous, so Gibsons is best for groups who are happy to share dishes. The namesake martinis are served in 10-ounce glasses, and the entrees are outlandishly scaled, from the six-piece shrimp cocktail so huge you swore you downed a dozen, to the turtle pie that comes with a steak knife (and could easily serve eight people).
1028 N. Rush St. (at Bellevue Place). ✆ **312/266-8999.** www.gibsonssteakhouse.com. Reservations strongly recommended. Main courses $25–$80. AE, DC, DISC, MC, V. Daily 11am–midnight (bar open later). Subway/El: Red Line to Clark/Division.

Morton's ★★ STEAK Morton's is a well-known chain with more than 75 locations worldwide, but it's Chicago born and bred, and many still consider it the king of classic, old-time steakhouses. Hidden on the lower level of an undistinguished high-rise, the place hasn't changed its look in decades, and most of the menu has stayed the same for years, too: double filet mignon with béarnaise sauce, and classic porterhouse, New York strip, and rib-eye steaks, with the usual array of a la carte sides. Overall, Morton's steaks are dependable rather than awe inspiring, but the place has a relaxed ambience that welcomes everyone from power-suited businessmen to 20-somethings in jeans.

Morton's also has a Loop location at 65 E. Wacker Place, between Michigan and Wabash avenues (✆ 312/201-0410), with a slightly more upscale, clubby decor; unlike the original location, it's open for lunch.

1050 N. State St. (at Rush St.). ✆ 312/266-4820. www.mortons.com. Reservations recommended. Main courses $26–$44. AE, DC, DISC, MC, V. Mon–Sat 5:30–11pm; Sun 5–10pm. Subway/El: Red Line to Chicago.

Spiaggia ★★★ ITALIAN *Spiaggia* means "beach" in Italian, and the restaurant's name is a tribute to its spectacular view of Lake Michigan and Oak Street Beach. Generally acknowledged as the best fine-dining Italian restaurant in the city, this elegant setting is far removed from your neighborhood trattoria—so dress to impress (jackets are required for men, and jeans are a no-no). Executive chef Tony Mantuano mixes organic, locally grown produce with fresh-from-Italy ingredients to dishes such as spaghetti with squid ink, and wood-roasted pork loin with potato purée and fava beans. The homemade potato gnocchi topped with black truffles is both delicious and indulgent. You're encouraged to order Italian style (appetizer, pasta, meat), which means the bill adds up pretty quickly. But if you're a cheese lover, this is the place to splurge on a cheese course: They'll roll out a cart filled with rare varieties and give you extensive descriptions of each one.

The adjacent, less formal **Café Spiaggia** (✆ 312/280-2755) is also open for lunch.

980 N. Michigan Ave. (at Oak St.). ✆ 312/280-2750. www.spiaggiarestaurant.com. Reservations strongly suggested on weekends. Main courses $34–$41; tasting menu $160. AE, DC, DISC, MC, V. Sun–Thurs 6–9:30pm; Fri–Sat 5:30–10:30pm. Subway/El: Red Line to Chicago.

Tru ★★★ NEW AMERICAN/FRENCH Offering "progressive French cuisine," Tru gives traditional European culinary techniques a creative American twist. The dining room has the elegance of a fine-dining restaurant (and prices to match), but the overall atmosphere is welcoming rather than stiff. Dining is strictly prix fixe, from three to nine courses; choices might include Maine lobster with saffron tagliatelle, Alaskan halibut topped with bacon vinaigrette, or venison served with a cabbage tart and pear chutney. If your wallet and stomach permit, go for the nine-course Chef's Collection ($145), featuring selections inspired by what was available at that day's markets. For an over-the-top splurge, order the visually sensational caviar staircase (caviars and fixin's climbing a glass spiral staircase), which goes for $280. The expansive wine list is a

> ### A Spot of Tea
>
> If you're shopping on the Magnificent Mile and feel like having an elegant afternoon tea complete with finger sandwiches, scones, and pastries, head for the stately **Palm Court** at The Drake Hotel, 140 E. Walton Place (✆ 312/787-2200); the sophisticated beauty of **The Lobby** at The Peninsula hotel, 108 E. Superior St. (✆ 312/573-6695); the cozy **Seasons Lounge** of the Four Seasons Hotel, 120 E. Delaware Place (✆ 312/280-8800); or **The Greenhouse** in the Ritz-Carlton, 160 E. Pearson St. (✆ 312/266-1000), in the sunny 12th-floor lobby above the Water Tower Place mall. In the Loop, the appropriately named **Russian Tea Time** ★★, 77 E. Adams St. (✆ 312/360-0000), serves tea from 2:30 to 4:30pm daily (p. 98).

Restaurants in the Magnificent Mile, Gold Coast, & River North

M Subway/El stop

treat for oenophiles, with 1,200 selections. The restaurant's comfortable lounge, where you can order dessert sampler plates, is a relaxed after-dinner hangout (and you're welcome to stop in even if you've eaten elsewhere).

676 N. St. Clair St. (at Huron St.). ✆ **312/202-0001.** www.trurestaurant.com. Reservations required. Prix-fixe menu $98–$145. AE, DC, DISC, MC, V. Mon–Thurs 6–10pm; Fri 5:30–10pm; Sat 5–11pm. Subway/El: Red Line to Chicago.

Expensive

Bistro 110 FRENCH Although it's too large and pricey to feel like an authentic bistro, this stalwart has a bustling energy that makes dining here an invigorating experience. While other restaurants chase the latest foodie trends, Bistro 110 keeps certain dishes on the menu year after year—such as the hearty cassoulet—and that's just how the regulars like it. The menu also includes French classics such as escargots in puff pastry, mussels in white-wine sauce, onion soup, cassoulet, and steak au poivre. The wood-roasted items, including a savory half chicken and a bountiful roast vegetable plate, are consistently good. A more casual, lighter bar menu is also available. Although the restaurant touts what it calls its "famous crème brûlée," it's worth saving up for the *Gâteau Paradis au Chocolat,* a decadent mix of chocolate cake, caramel, and toffee. On Sunday the restaurant hosts a popular brunch with live jazz music.

110 E. Pearson St. (just west of Michigan Ave.). ✆ **312/266-3110.** www.bistro110restaurant.com. Main courses $20–$32. AE, DC, DISC, MC, V. Mon–Sat 11:30am–10pm; Sun 10:30am–9pm. Subway/El: Red Line to Chicago.

Ditka's ★ AMERICAN/STEAK In this city, Mike Ditka is still known as "Da Coach." Immortalized as such in the classic "Super Fans" sketch on *Saturday Night Live,* "Iron" Mike Ditka remains the quintessential cigar-chomping, hard-nosed Chicagoan—despite the fact that it's been more than 2 decades since he led the Chicago Bears to victory in Super Bowl XX in 1986. Filled with dark wood, leather banquettes, and walls lined with memorabilia, this is man country, with a meat-heavy menu to match—but the food is a good step up from your average sports bar. The "Coach's Meatloaf Stack" is served on a bed of jalapeño cornbread and drenched with barbecue sauce, while "Da Pork Chop" is surrounded by mashed sweet potatoes and Michigan cherry *jus.* You may just see Da Coach himself making the rounds of the dining room; he also broadcasts a radio show from the restaurant on Thursday mornings during football season.

100 E. Chestnut St. (in the Tremont Hotel, btw. Michigan Ave. and Rush St.). ✆ **312/587-8989.** www.

Dessert Tour

Eli's cheesecake is a Chicago icon—the rich, creamy cakes have been served at presidential inaugurations and numerous other high-profile events. For a behind-the-scenes peek at Chicago's most famous dessert, you can take a tour of Eli's Bakery on the northwest side of the city. After watching the cooking and decorating processes, you get to enjoy a full-size slice of your favorite flavor. Tours are given Monday through Friday at 1pm (although reservations aren't necessary, call to make sure the bakery isn't closed for periodic maintenance). The 40-minute tour costs $3 per person; special packages are available for groups. Eli's bakery is at 6701 Forest Preserve Dr., at the corner of Montrose Avenue (✆ **800/ELI-CAKE** [354-2253]; www.elischeesecake.com).

ditkasrestaurants.com. Main courses $10–$17 lunch, $15–$33 dinner. AE, DC, DISC, MC, V. Mon–Thurs 11am–10pm; Fri–Sat 11am–11pm; Sun 10am–10pm. Subway/El: Red Line to Chicago.

The Signature Room at the 95th ★ AMERICAN While its straightforward menu won't win any culinary awards, The Signature Room is worth a visit for its location alone. Perched on the 95th floor of the John Hancock Center, it offers amazing views of the city and lake through floor-to-ceiling windows. Yes, you'll probably be dining with other tourists, but it's a quintessential Chicago experience. While dinner is relatively pricey, lunch is a bargain for a white-tablecloth restaurant in this area (especially the $20 all-you-can-eat buffet), and it also tends to be relatively uncrowded. Lunch menu options include upscale sandwiches, salads, and pastas; dinner includes classics like roast rack of lamb, bacon-wrapped pork tenderloin, and surf and turf. The Sunday buffet brunch is a splurge, at $45 per person, but includes all the usual breakfast favorites, as well as antipasti, a raw bar, and fresh caviar.

875 N. Michigan Ave. (in the John Hancock Center, btw. Chestnut and Delaware sts.). © **312/787-9596.** www.signatureroom.com. Reservations accepted. Main courses $10–$20 lunch, $27–$40 dinner. AE, DISC, MC, V. Mon–Thurs 11am–2:30pm and 5–10pm; Fri–Sat 11am–2:30pm and 5–11pm; Sun 10am–2pm and 5–10pm. Subway/El: Red Line to Chicago.

Table Fifty-Two ★ AMERICAN How does a modest restaurant specializing in non-trendy Southern food become a local favorite? Call it the Oprah effect. The executive chef of this unassuming, cozy spot is Art Smith, Oprah's former

farmers' **MARKETS**

If you're lucky enough to be here during good weather, celebrate by enjoying at least one picnic. Peruse the city's farmers' markets and then carry your lunch off to Grant Park or a spot along the lake front.

The city-sponsored farmers' markets operate from late May through October. Two locations in the Loop are easy for visitors to get to: Daley Plaza (at Washington and Dearborn sts.; open on Thurs) and Federal Plaza (at Adams and Dearborn sts.; open on Tues), both open from 7am to 3pm. Both are good places to pick up fresh fruit or bakery treats. For more information, call the Mayor's Office of Special Events at © **312/744-3315.** At the south end of Lincoln Park (btw. Clark St. and Stockton Dr.), local chefs and civilian foodies head to the **Green City Market** (© **773/880-1266;** greencitymarket.org) for seasonal produce. Pick up some fresh bread, locally produced cheese, and in-season fruit, and enjoy an alfresco meal; Lincoln Park Zoo is just steps away. The market is open Wednesdays and Saturdays from 7am to 1pm, from mid-May through October, and often features cooking demonstrations by chefs from Chicago restaurants.

personal chef, and his association with the talk-show titan was enough to make Table Fifty-Two a hot spot the minute it opened. The fact that it's tiny—only 23 tables on two floors—has kept up the demand. You'll get a taste of Smith's Southern heritage as soon as you're seated, when the server brings out warm goat-cheese biscuits and deviled eggs. Appetizers and entrees include upscale versions of down-home classics, such as shrimp with stone-ground grits; pork chops with chorizo crumble, and fried chicken with garlic mashed potatoes (available only for Sun and Mon dinner). The prices are high for what's essentially comfort food, but devoted regulars find Table Fifty-Two's charm worth the price.

52 W. Elm St. (at Division St.). ✆ **312/573-4000.** www.tablefifty-two.com. Main courses $24–$39 dinner. AE, DISC, MC, V. Mon–Sat 5–10pm; Sun 11am–3pm and 4–9pm. Subway/El: Red Line to Clark/Division.

Moderate

Bistronomic ★★ 🎁 BISTRO/FRENCH The vision of chef and Paris native Martial Noguier, this sophisticated yet unpretentious bistro reinvents traditional French dishes for modern American tastes. Small and medium plates include standouts such as fish soup with mussels, tarragon, and saffron; and oxtail ravioli with celery root puree, Parmesan cheese, and a red wine sauce. Entrees vary from simple but perfectly cooked roast chicken to Lake Superior whitefish to beef au poivre. In true French fashion, there are also cheese flights and single servings of cheese, along with a selection of artisanal charcuterie. Wine is reasonable, but the list also has some pricey depth for oenophiles. At the far end of the stylish red-hued dining room, tucked behind a small bar, is a little room that looks out into the restaurant: Try to snag a seat here for a fun and intimate dining experience. You'll feel like you're getting away with something.

840 N. Wabash Ave. (at Pearson St.). ✆ **312/266-4820.** www.bistronomic.net. Reservations recommended. Main courses $17–$26. AE, DC, DISC, MC, V. Sun–Thurs 5–10pm; Fri–Sat 5–11pm. Subway/El: Red Line to Chicago.

Chicago q ★★ BARBECUE With a kitchen led by 'cue queen Lee Ann Whippen and a dining room that is a little bit roadhouse, a little bit refined dining room, Chicago q is comfortable, pleasant, and serious about barbecue. Meats include baby back ribs, chicken, and Kobe beef brisket, among others. But even before those delicious, heaping, main courses arrive—perhaps with sides such as braised greens or poblano cheddar cornbread—there are the complimentary pig powder potato chips and bread and butter pickles, house specialties so tasty they will have you wondering why the restaurant doesn't charge for them. Portions are large, so try to refrain from eating all those nibbles before your food arrives. The wine and beer lists are varied, but bourbon lovers have special reason to rejoice at the selection available here.

1160 N. Dearborn St. (at Division St.). ✆ **312/642-1160.** www.chicagoqrestaurant.com. Reservations recommended. Main courses $11–$28. AE, DC, DISC, MC, V. Sun–Thurs 11am–10:30pm; Fri–Sat 11am–2am (kitchen open until 1am). Subway/El: Red Line to Clark/Division.

Le Colonial ★★ 🎁 FRENCH/VIETNAMESE Le Colonial has one of the loveliest dining rooms in the city—and the second-floor lounge is a sultry, seductive destination for cocktails. An escapist's paradise, the restaurant is a cleverly crafted re-creation of 1920s Saigon, with bamboo shutters, rattan chairs, potted palms and banana trees, and ceiling fans. While the ambience certainly merits a visit, the flavorful cuisine is a draw on its own. Start with the hearty oxtail soup or the light and refreshing beef-and-watercress salad. Entrees include grilled lime-glazed sea scallops with garlic noodle salad; sautéed jumbo shrimp in curried coconut sauce; and roasted chicken with lemon-grass-and-lime dipping sauce. On Sundays, try tasting-size portions of popular menus items at both lunch and dinner. Le Colonial offers outdoor seating in warm weather; try to reserve one of the coveted romantic mezzanine terrace tables, which look out over the bustling street below.

937 N. Rush St. (just south of Oak St.). ✆ 312/255-0088. www.lecolonialchicago.com. Reservations recommended. Main courses $15–$22 lunch, $18–$29 dinner. AE, DC, MC, V. Mon–Wed 11:30am–2:30pm and 5–11pm; Thurs–Sat 11:30am–2:30pm and 5–midnight; Sun 11:30am–2:30pm and 5–10pm. Subway/El: Red Line to Chicago.

The Purple Pig ★★ MEDITERRANEAN The slogan at this open-kitchen restaurant/wine bar is "Cheese, Swine, and Wine." Chef Jimmy Bannos, Jr., takes all three very seriously. Lively and noisy, The Purple Pig has the attitude of a casual bistro, but the menu is aimed at serious food lovers. You can graze on small to medium-sized portions of milk-braised pork shoulder with mashed potatoes; grilled prawns; and Wagyu sirloin tip with bone marrow vinaigrette, or head into more adventurous territory, such as the pig's tails braised in balsamic vinegar, or pig's ear with crispy kale, marinated cherry peppers, and a fried egg. (Believe it or not, those dishes often sell out.) There is also a large selection of cheeses and cured meats, and dozens of unique beers and wines by the glass. For dessert, try the butterscotch pudding or the Sicilian Iris, a fried brioche bun filled with ricotta cheese and chocolate chips—basically, an insanely delicious doughnut.

500 N. Michigan Ave. (btw. the Chicago River and Ohio St.). ✆ 312/464-1PIG (464-1744). www.thepurplepigchicago.com. Reservations not accepted. Most dishes $8–$17. AE, DC, DISC, MC, V. Sun–Thurs 11:30am–midnight; Fri–Sat 11:30am–1am (bar open till 2am). Subway/El: Red Line to Grand.

Shaw's Crab House ★★ SEAFOOD If you ask average Chicagoans where to go for seafood, chances are, they'll point you here. The dining room—with its red

Kitchens Up Close

Serious food fans can get a firsthand look at how some of the city's culinary stars work by booking a seat at a chef's table. You'll get a personal tour of the kitchen, a special selection of dishes, and—best of all—a front-row seat for dinner-hour drama. At **Tru** ★★★ (✆ 312/202-0001) and **Next** ★★★ (✆ 312/226-0858), four to six people can sit in glass-enclosed rooms just off the kitchen, where they can check out the scene without feeling the heat. The chef's table at **Charlie Trotter's** ★★★ (✆ 773/248-6228) seats four to six

right in the kitchen, so diners can catch Trotter's legendary perfectionism up close. At **Zealous** ★★★ (✆ 312/475-9112), the chef's table seats 8 to 10 and is in the main dining room—but bamboo trees surround it, so other diners won't get jealous when chef Michael Taus stops by for some one-on-one taste tests.

Chef's tables don't come cheap (up to $225 per person), but they're a special splurge for die-hard foodies. Just remember to reserve well in advance because these tables book fast.

leather banquettes, 1930s-era soundtrack, and white-jacketed waitstaff—has a dimly lit, retro feel, but the extensive menu isn't stuck in the past; choices run the gamut from fried calamari to crab cakes, to sushi. Fresh, seasonal seafood (flown in daily) is the main draw, although you can also indulge in surf-and-turf combinations. Overall, you won't go wrong ordering one of the classics: Alaskan king crab, Texas stone-crab claws, or fresh oysters, which you can select according to their provenance (Nova Scotia, British Columbia, and so on). The adjacent Oyster Bar offers a more casual menu and has live music on Sunday, Tuesday, and Thursday nights. The restaurant's Sunday brunch is an excellent weekend option for seafood lovers and includes an indulgent dessert selection.

21 E. Hubbard St. (btw. State St. and Wabash Ave.). ℂ 312/527-2722. www.shawscrabhouse. com. Reservations accepted only for the main dining room. Main courses $14–$35. AE, DC, DISC, MC, V. Mon–Thurs 11:30am–2pm and 5:30–10pm; Fri 11:30am–2pm and 5–11pm; Sat 5–11pm; Sun 10:30am–1:30pm and 5–10pm. Subway/El: Red Line to Grand.

ONLY IN chicago

There is great food to be had in Chicago, but the two dishes that the city truly calls its own are pizza and hot dogs. It may not be haute cuisine, but I promise you've never had anything quite like the city's spin on either of these indulgences.

We have three pizza styles in Chicago: Chicago style, also known as deep-dish, which is thick-crusted and often demands a knife and fork; stuffed, which is similar to a pie, with a crust on both top and bottom; and thin crust.

Three of the best places to try the classic Chicago deep-dish are **Pizzeria Uno ★** (p. 130), **Pizzeria Due** (p. 130), and **Gino's East ★★** (p. 125). In River North, **Lou Malnati's Pizzeria ★**, 439 N. Wells St. (at Hubbard St.; ℂ 312/828-9800), bakes both deep-dish and thin-crust pizza and even has a low-fat-cheese option. **Edwardo's** is a local pizza chain that serves all three varieties, but with a wheat crust and all-natural ingredients (spinach pizza is the specialty here); locations are in the Gold Coast at 1212 N. Dearborn St. (at Division St.; ℂ 312/337-4490), in the South Loop at 521 S. Dearborn St. (btw. Congress Pkwy. and Harrison St.; ℂ 312/939-3366), and in Lincoln Park at 2622

N. Halsted St. (at Wrightwood Ave.; ℂ 773/871-3400). Another popular chain—known for its stuffed pizza—is **Giordano's,** with downtown locations off the Magnificent Mile at 730 N. Rush St. (at Superior St.; ℂ 312/951-0747), and at the Prudential Plaza, 135 E. Lake St. (just east of Michigan Ave.; ℂ 312/616-1200).

For a unique twist on the deep-dish phenomenon, head to **Chicago Pizza & Oven Grinder,** 2121 N. Clark St. (btw. Webster and Dickens aves.; ℂ 773/248-2570), a few blocks from Lincoln Park Zoo. Here the "pizza potpie" is baked in a bowl and then turned over when served. This neighborhood spot stays popular year after year, so plan on showing up early for dinner to avoid a long wait.

The classic Chicago hot dog includes a frankfurter by Vienna Beef (a local food processor and hallowed institution), heaps of chopped onions and green relish, a slather of yellow mustard, pickle spears, fresh tomato wedges,

Inexpensive

Billy Goat Tavern ★ FAST FOOD Viewers of the original *Saturday Night Live* will remember the classic routine "Cheezeborger, Cheezeborger," with John Belushi as a crabby Greek short-order cook. The comic got his material from the Billy Goat Tavern, located under North Michigan Avenue near the bridge that leads to the Loop (walk down the steps across the street from the *Chicago Tribune* building). This is a classic dive: dark, seedy, and no-frills. But unlike the *Saturday Night Live* skit, the guys behind the counter are friendly and this hangout for local newspaper reporters and writers has an insider feel. The menu is pretty basic, but, yes, the cheeseburgers are pretty good. After work, this is a good place to watch a game, chitchat at the bar, and down a few beers.

For the same "cheezeborgers" in less grungy (and more kid-friendly) surroundings, head to the Billy Goat's outpost on Navy Pier (② **312/670-8789**).

a dash of celery salt, and, for good measure, two or three "sport" peppers, those thumb-shaped holy terrors that turn your mouth into its own bonfire.

Chicago is home to many standout hot-dog spots, but one, **Hot Doug's,** 3324 N. California Ave. (at Roscoe St.; ② **773/279-9550**), takes encased meats to a new level, featuring several gourmet sausages on a bun every day except Sunday (plan on standing in line no matter which day you show up—and it's always worth it). Hot Doug's also serves a great classic Chicago dog just like many other stands in town, including **Gold Coast Dogs,** 159 N. Wabash Ave. (at Randolph St.; ② **312/917-1677**), in the Loop just a block from Michigan Avenue. **Portillo's** ★★ (p. 130) is another local chain that specializes in hot dogs but also serves tasty pastas and salads. **Murphy's Red Hots,** 1211 W. Belmont Ave. (at Racine Ave.; ② **773/935-2882**), is a neighborhood spot not too far from Wrigley Field; while **The Wieners Circle,** in Lincoln Park at 2622 N. Clark St. (btw. Wrightwood Ave. and Drummond Place; ② **773/477-7444**),

is a late-night favorite where rude order-takers are part of the shtick.

If you've got a car, head up to **Superdawg Drive-In,** 6363 N. Milwaukee Ave. (at Devon Ave.; ② **773/763-0660**), on the northwest side of the city (look for the giant hot dogs dressed as Tarzan and Jane on the roof). This classic 1950s-style flashback has been run by the same family for three generations, and, yes, they still have carhops who bring out your order.

430 N. Michigan Ave. ✆ **312/222-1525.** www.billygoattavern.com. Reservations not accepted. Menu items $3–$6. No credit cards. Mon–Fri 6am–2am; Sat 10am–2am; Sun 11am–2am. Subway/El: Red Line to Chicago.

foodlife ★★ 👫 FAST FOOD Taking the standard food court up a few notches, foodlife consists of 14 kiosks offering a wide variety of freshly made foods on the mezzanine of Water Tower Place mall. A hostess seats you and gives you an electronic card, and then it's up to you to stroll around and get whatever food strikes your fancy (each purchase is recorded on your card, and you pay on the way out). The beauty of a food court, of course, is that it offers something for everybody, making this a great stop for families with picky eaters. At foodlife, diners can choose from burgers, pizza, south-of-the-border dishes, rotisserie items, sushi, an assortment of stir fry and other Asian fare, and veggie-oriented, low-fat offerings. A lunch or snack is basically inexpensive, but the payment method makes it easy to build up a big tab while holding a personal taste-testing session at each kiosk if you're not careful.

In Water Tower Place, 835 N. Michigan Ave. ✆ **312/335-3663.** www.foodlifechicago.com. Reservations not accepted. Most items $8–$15. AE, DC, DISC, MC, V. Breakfast kiosk daily 8–11:30am. All other kiosks Mon–Thurs 11:30am–8:30pm; Fri–Sat 11:30am–9pm; Sun 11:30am–8pm. Subway/El: Red Line to Chicago.

Oak Tree ★ AMERICAN Though it's located on the sixth floor of the ritzy 900 N. Michigan indoor mall (home of Bloomingdale's, Gucci, and others), Oak Tree isn't exactly high profile. But it's popular with the ladies-who-lunch crowd and local office workers, and makes a convenient stop during a day of downtown shopping. Airy and boutique-hotel sleek, it's a relaxing retreat from the Michigan Avenue madness outside. If you can, snag a table along the windows that overlook the John Hancock Center. The menu focuses on a wide selection of salads and sandwiches. On a cold day, try a duck breast sandwich with mango chutney or a good old-fashioned patty melt with fries. You can also order breakfast all day. The only downside for family travelers: There's no kids' menu.

900 N. Michigan Ave. (at Delaware Place), 6th floor. ✆ **312/751-1988.** www.shop900.com/shop/oak-tree-restaurant. Reservations not accepted. Main courses $8–$16. AE, DISC, MC, V. Daily 7:30am–4pm. Subway/El: Red Line to Chicago.

RIVER NORTH

For restaurants listed in this section, see the map "Restaurants in the Magnificent Mile, Gold Coast & River North " on p. 111.

River North, the area north of the Loop and west of Michigan Avenue, is home to the city's most concentrated cluster of art galleries and a something-for-everyone array of restaurants—from fast food and themed restaurants to chains and some of our trendiest dining destinations. Whether you seek a quick dog or burger, contemporary American fine dining, or world-class Mexican fare, River North has it all—within easy walking distance of many downtown hotels.

Very Expensive

Crofton on Wells ★★ 👫 AMERICAN This unassuming restaurant is the perfect reflection of chef-owner Suzy Crofton, a place that values substance over style. Though the food is considerably more ambitious than your average neighborhood restaurant, it's served in a laid-back setting. The menu is based on seasonally available ingredients: You might start with a chilled cucumber-and-Vidalia-onion soup in the spring, or a roasted squash soup in colder weather. Entree selections run the gamut from seafood to venison and beef; Crofton's signature dish is the pork tenderloin garnished with her smoked apple chutney (you can even buy a jar of the chutney to go). Other

chefs may wow the food critics with their spectacular presentations, but Crofton has built her reputation with accessible dishes that attract a low-key crowd of satisfied regulars.

535 N. Wells St. (btw. Grand Ave. and Ohio St.). ℂ **312/755-1790.** www.croftononwells.com. Reservations recommended. Main courses $29–$39. AE, DC, MC, V. Mon–Sat 5–10pm. Subway/El: Brown Line to Merchandise Mart.

Graham Elliot ★★ AMERICAN The chef/owner of this self-named restaurant has the talent of a gourmet chef, but the soul of a rock-'n-roll party boy. The dining room is warm and welcoming, with large windows and exposed-brick walls. Though pop-rock plays in the background and the servers wear jeans, the prices are in line with far more elegant spots, making it more of a special-occasion destination than a regular-guy hangout. Entrees might be inspired by down-home American classics (sea scallop almondine with caper berry, Meyer lemon, smoked almonds, and brown butter) or showcase a new twist on the standard meat-and-starch combo (Wagyu flat-iron steak with truffled sunchokes, hydroponic watercress, charred cioppolini, and shaved pecorino cheese). Elliot has also been known to toss in far less haute ingredients (such as risotto with crushed Cheez-Its), in a humorous nod to American snack habits.

217 W. Huron St. (btw. Wells and Franklin sts.). ℂ **312/624-9975.** www.grahamelliot.com. Main courses $28–$32; tasting menu $75–$125. AE, DC, MC, V. Mon–Sat 5–10pm. Subway/El: Brown Line to Chicago.

mk ★★★ AMERICAN Even though foodies rank it one of the best American restaurants in the city, mk doesn't flaunt its pedigree. The loftlike dining room is as understated as the lowercase initials that give the restaurant its name. Chef/owner Michael Kornick keeps the menu focused on a straightforward seasonal mix of meat and seafood: Menu selections might range from substantial (grilled veal porterhouse with broccolini and cognac-green peppercorn sauce) to lighter offerings, such as grilled salmon with a Chinese mustard glaze, bok choy, shiitake mushrooms, and ginger-soy vinaigrette. The presentations are tasteful rather than dazzling; Kornick wants you to concentrate on the food, and that's just what the chic, mixed-age crowd does. Service is disciplined yet agreeable, and fine table appointments signal this restaurant's commitment to quality. As for dessert, the Cake & Shake (buttermilk chocolate cake, milk chocolate mousse, bittersweet chocolate pave, chocolate meringue, and buttercream, with a vanilla milkshake) is worth the calories.

868 N. Franklin St. (1 block north of Chicago Ave.). ℂ **312/482-9179.** www.mkchicago.com. Reservations highly recommended. Main courses $27–$46. AE, DC, MC, V. Sun–Thurs 5:30–9:30pm; Fri–Sat 5:30–10pm. Subway/El: Brown Line to Chicago.

5

WHERE TO EAT

River North

Naha ★★ AMERICAN Chef Carrie Nahabedian (who used her nickname for the restaurant's name) did time at four-star hotels in California before returning to her hometown, and a West Coast influence is clear in her use of organic, seasonal ingredients. But she adds Mediterranean flavors to the mix, including dishes that reflect her Armenian heritage. Entrees might include roasted squab and duck liver with mushrooms, young turnips, crisp potatoes, and red cabbage; or Great Lakes whitefish with butter-poached blue crab, hen of the woods mushrooms, caramelized cauliflower, Swiss chard, grits, and lobster–red wine *jus*. The dessert menu features creative combinations, such as coconut, pineapple, and white chocolate with frozen Greek yogurt and coriander.

The front lounge offers a special menu of *meze* (Mediterranean "small dishes"), including feta cheese phyllo triangles made from the chef's mother's recipe.

500 N. Clark St. (at Illinois St.). ✆ **312/321-6242.** www.naha-chicago.com. Reservations recommended. Main courses $16–$25 lunch, $32–$48 dinner. AE, DC, DISC, MC, V. Mon–Thurs 11:30am–2pm and 5:30–9:30pm; Fri 11:30am–2pm and 5:30–10pm; Sat 5:30–10pm. Bar open later every night. Subway/El: Red Line to Grand.

Zealous ★★★ NEW AMERICAN One of the most stylish contemporary restaurants in town, Zealous also has one of the most eclectic menus. Chef Michael Taus's cooking combines American dishes with the subtle complexity of Chinese, Vietnamese, Korean, and Indian flavors. You can order a la carte or from one of three tasting menus; recent entrees have ranged from Asian inspired (sesame-crusted Chilean sea bass with rice noodles and red coconut–curry sauce) to heartland hearty (grilled beef filet with mushroom-potato lasagna and truffle reduction). Zealous is especially welcoming to non–meat eaters; there is always a five-course vegetarian menu available, and the kitchen will prepare vegan entrees on request. The dining room is bright and airy (thanks to a central skylight), and the purple chairs, green banquettes, and silver accents add to the vibrant ambience. The 6,000-bottle wine collection and glass-enclosed wine cellar show that Zealous takes its libations just as seriously as it takes its food.

419 W. Superior St. ✆ **312/475-9112.** www.zealousrestaurant.com. Reservations recommended. Main courses $19–$39; tasting menu $75–$105. AE, DISC, MC, V. Tues–Sat 5–11pm. Subway/El: Brown Line to Chicago.

culinary **MASH-UPS**

Some Chicago chefs find inspiration in the clash of civilizations, combining elements of seemingly unrelated cuisines to create a new, flavorful experience. At **Vermilion** (p. 124) the similarities between Latin American and Indian cooking are highlighted, resulting in dishes such as a tandoori skirt steak with fried plantain chips or shrimp paella served with flattened Indian rice. **SushiSamba Rio** (p. 123) pairs South American flavors with Asian preparations, producing odd-sounding-but-delicious creations such as a salmon-and-jalapeño sushi roll or lobster taquitos garnished with lemongrass. At **Yoshi's Café** in Lincoln Park (p. 140), the menu reflects both chef Yoshi Katsumura's Japanese heritage and his traditional French culinary training, with entrees such as panko-breaded pork loin, smoked salmon salad with Asian pear, and crab cakes paired with wasabi.

Expensive

Bin 36 ★★ AMERICAN In one lofty, airy space, this River North hot spot combines wine, food, and retail in a successful, wine-centric concept—you don't have to be a wine snob to enjoy yourself. You can swirl, sniff, and snack at one of two zinc-topped bars, sample lighter fare or artisanal cheeses; or settle down in the main restaurant for a full meal of American bistro-style dishes. Dishes range from seafood and pastas to heavier dishes such as slow-roasted pork loin or lobster shepherd's pie. For each entree, the menu includes two or three suggested wines, all available by the glass. You can also order creative "wine flights," small glasses organized around a theme (Italian, Australian, and so on). The food–wine pairings continue on the dessert menu; a recommended sherry along with a slice of gingerbread-pear cake here one evening was a delight.

339 N. Dearborn St. ✆ **312/755-9463.** www.bin36.com. Reservations recommended. Main courses $10–$17 lunch, $11–$32 dinner. AE, DC, DISC, MC, V. Mon–Wed 11am–11pm; Thurs 11am–midnight; Fri–Sat 11am–1am; Sun noon–10pm. Subway/El: Red Line to Grand.

Chicago Cut Steakhouse ★★ STEAK Name any type of steakhouse and Chicago has one: classic, trendy, and everything in between. But when Chicago Cut opened in the fall of 2010, it was a restaurant that people spoke of simply as a great restaurant—not just a great new steakhouse. The place delights on every level, from its USDA prime cuts of beef (dry-aged in-house), to pork and lamb chops, to fresh seafood options, including oysters and other shellfish. Appetizers range from light sushi to decadent foie gras. The restaurant also has an extensive wine list presented on iPads: You browse through the options by flicking your finger across the lighted screen. This is a loud, energetic place with two gigantic walls of windows overlooking the buildings along the Chicago River. Every few minutes an El train slowly crosses the River reminding you exactly where you are—in downtown Chicago eating a great steak.

300 N. LaSalle St. (at the Chicago River). ✆ **312/329-1800.** www.chicagocutsteakhouse.com. Reservations recommended. Main courses $12–$55. AE, DC, DISC, MC, V. Mon–Fri 7am–2am; Sat-Sun 10am–2am. Subway/El: Red Line to Grand; Brown Line to Merchandise Mart.

Frontera Grill, Topolobampo & Xoco ★★★ MEXICAN Owners Rick and Deann Bayless are widely credited with bringing authentic Mexican regional cuisine to a wider audience, emphasizing the importance of fresh, organic ingredients supplied by local artisanal farmers. Within one River North building, they oversee three separate establishments, each with its own look and attitude: the casual **Frontera Grill** (plain wood tables, terra-cotta tile floor), the fine-dining **Topolobampo** (white linen tablecloths, a more hushed environment), and the super-casual **Xoco** (pronounced SHO-ko), where you order from a counter and sit at cramped communal tables.

At Frontera, it's worth starting with whatever soup is offered, as Bayless does them extremely well. The ever-changing entree list might include ancho-rubbed pork loin in a black bean sauce flavored with smoky salsa negra, or adobo-marinated Gulf shrimp in guajillo-mango sauce; you can also get delicious, upscale tacos and enchiladas. At adjacent Topolobampo, both the ingredients and presentation are more upscale (think lobster and scallops roasted in an aromatic *mojo* sauce of fermented white and black garlic, chipotle peppers, and lime juice).

Next door at Xoco, Bayless turns out sandwiches (tortas) and made-to-order hot chocolates (soups are also available after 3pm). Expect to stand in line at both Xoco and Frontera during prime dining hours, but you can always do what the locals do: Put your name on the list and order a few margaritas in the large, lively bar area.

For an affordable taste of Frontera downtown, stop by **Frontera Fresco,** a counter-service lunch spot on the seventh floor of Macy's, 111 N. State St. (✆ **312/781-4884**). You can sample authentic Mexican tortas, quesadillas, and tamales, all priced less than $8; it's open Monday through Friday from 11am to 3pm.

445 N. Clark St. (btw. Illinois and Hubbard sts.). ✆ **312/661-1434.** www.fronterakitchens.com. Reservations strongly recommended for Topolobampo; limited reservations accepted at Frontera Grill. Frontera Grill main courses $17–$29. Topolobampo main courses $25–$39; chef's 5-course tasting menu $75 ($120 with wine pairings). Xoco sandwiches and soups $8.50–$13. AE, DC, DISC, MC, V. Frontera Grill Tues–Fri 11:30am–2:30pm; Sat 10:30am–2pm; Tues 5:20–10pm; Wed–Thurs 5–10pm; Fri–Sat 5–11pm. Topolobampo Tues 11:45am–2pm; Wed–Fri 11:30am–2pm; Tues–Thurs 5:30–9:30pm; Fri–Sat 5:30–10:30pm. Xoco Tues–Thurs 8am–9pm; Fri–Sat 8am–10pm. Subway/El: Red Line to Grand.

Gene & Georgetti ★ ITALIAN/STEAK A classic vestige of old Chicago, Gene & Georgetti is a family-run steakhouse that's been serving up steak and Italian fare in a wood-frame house in the shadow of the El since 1941. The restaurant is dark and clubby, and the (exclusively male) waiters seem to have worked here for decades—and they no doubt have been serving some of the same patrons all that time. Gene & Georgetti has a popular following, so expect a wait at the bar if you show up on the weekend without a reservation. Although the place is best known for steaks, classic Italian-American specialties are also an essential part of the menu (mostaccioli, veal parmigiana, and the like). Fans of old-time restaurants will find plenty of local character—some of the regulars have been coming here for half a century.

500 N. Franklin St. (at Illinois St.). ✆ **312/527-3718.** www.geneandgeorgetti.com. Reservations recommended. Main courses $13–$28 lunch, $20–$46 dinner. AE, DC, MC, V. Mon–Thurs 11am–11pm; Fri–Sat 11am–midnight. Subway/El: Brown Line to Merchandise Mart.

Harry Caray's Italian Steakhouse AMERICAN/ITALIAN/STEAK A shrine to the legendary Cubs play-by-play announcer, this landmark building is a repository for Harry's staggering collection of baseball memorabilia. The main dining room, with its high tin ceilings and brick walls, has a certain retro charm, and the food is better than you'd expect from a celebrity restaurant. The menu is a greatest hits list of Italian-American favorites: mounds of pasta with red sauce, bone-in chicken Vesuvio, veal piccata, and a variety of seafood. Harry's is also a good place to order massive plates of meat: dry-aged prime steaks, lamb, veal, and pork chops. If you don't want a full-service meal, the bar is a lively place for watching a game and grabbing some munchies—and, incidentally, the bar is 60 feet, 6 inches long, the same distance from the pitcher's mound to home plate.

Harry Caray's also has a location on Navy Pier, 700 E. Grand Ave. (✆ **312/527-9700**).

33 W. Kinzie St. (at Dearborn St.). ✆ **312/828-0966.** www.harrycarays.com. Main courses $15–$40. AE, DC, DISC, MC, V. Mon–Sat 11:30am–3pm; Mon–Thurs 5–10:30pm; Fri–Sat 5–11pm; Sun 11:30am–4pm (bar only) and 4–10pm. Subway/El: Brown Line to Merchandise Mart or Red Line to Grand.

Nacional 27 ★ 🏮 LATIN AMERICAN Part sleek restaurant, part nightclub, Nacional 27 showcases the cuisine of 27 Latin American nations, including

Venezuela, Argentina, Costa Rica, and Brazil. Rich walnut and bamboo woods and gauzy curtains lend a tropical air to the grand dining room, which has cozy booth seating and tables arranged around a central dance floor. The innovative drink menu will get you in the mood: You'll find classic mojitos, sangrias, and trendy martini variations. For starters, there are a variety of skewers, seviches, and empanadas; entrees are divided into steaks, seafood, and "Latin Comfort Foods," which include stick-to-your-ribs selections such as smoked pork tenderloin with mashed Cuban sweet potatoes or tequila-marinated chicken. (Some of the food can be spicy, so ask before you order if you've got sensitive taste buds.) Nacional 27 heats up on Friday and Saturday nights after 10pm, when a DJ spins Latin tunes and couples hit the dance floor.

325 W. Huron St. (btw. Franklin and Orleans sts.). ✆ **312/664-2727.** www.nacional27.net. Reservations recommended. Main courses $15–$28. AE, DC, DISC, MC, V. Dining room Mon–Thurs 5:30–9:30pm; Fri–Sat 5:30–10:30pm. Bar Mon–Thurs 5pm–9:30pm; Fri 5pm–2am; Sat 5pm–3am. Subway/El: Brown Line to Chicago.

Osteria Via Stato ★★ 🍴 ITALIAN An American take on the classic Italian trattoria, Osteria Via Stato delivers top-quality, authentic dishes in a cozy setting. Where it really shines, I think, is with its "Italian Dinner Party" menu: A set price of $39 buys you a full, European-style meal, including a range of antipasto plates, two pastas, and a meat entree (recent choices included halibut Milanese with lemon-herb breadcrumbs, and braised pork shank with white beans and bacon). They'll bring you unlimited helpings of everything except the entrees, so come with an appetite. If you're not up for a gut-busting meal, you can also order appetizer-only or appetizer-and-pasta versions, or choose from the a la carte menu. To keep drinks simple, request the "Just Bring Me Wine" program, which matches a glass of wine to each course at three different price levels. The adjacent **Pizzeria Via Stato** serves Roman-style thin-crust pizzas with artisanal and classic toppings, and is open for lunch and dinner.

620 N. State St. (at Ontario St.). ✆ **312/642-8450.** www.osteriaviastato.com. Reservations accepted. Fixed-price dinner $39; entrees $16–$29. AE, DC, DISC, MC, V. Mon–Thurs 5–10pm; Fri–Sat 5–11pm; Sun 5–9:30pm. Subway/El: Red Line to Grand.

SushiSamba Rio ★★ LATIN AMERICAN/SUSHI At first glimpse, the menu seems like a gimmick: Latin American ceviche paired with sushi? But it's based on a real culinary tradition: When Japanese immigrants moved to Peru and Brazil in the early 20th century, they combined their native cuisine with South American flavors. I highly recommend the creative "samba rolls," and the El Topo (salmon, jalapeño pepper, mozzarella, and crispy onions wrapped in sticky rice) tastes much better than it sounds. Depending on your appetite and budget, you can order light (seviches, mini seafood tacos) or go all out with a selection of Kobe beef entrees or red snapper (served whole) on a bed of coconut rice with an aromatic red-curry sauce. Part of the fun of dining here is the flashy decor, from the colorful, multilevel dining room with its sunken red conversation pit to the Miami Beach–inspired rooftop patio (a great place to sample the creative cocktail menu).

504 N. Wells St. (at Illinois St.). ✆ **312/595-2300.** www.sushisamba.com. Reservations recommended on weekends. Main courses $8–$17 lunch, $12–$29 dinner. AE, MC, V. Sun–Mon 11:30am–11pm; Tues 11:30am–midnight; Wed–Fri 11:30am–1am; Sat 11:30am–2am; Sun brunch 11:30am–3:30pm. Subway/El: Brown Line to Merchandise Mart or Red Line to Grand.

5

WHERE TO EAT

River North

Vermilion ★ INDIAN/LATIN AMERICAN Owner Rohini Dey and executive chef Maneet Chauhan—both women, both originally from India—have found a common thread between Indian and Latin American cooking: Both feature similar ingredients (rice and chilies), use some of the same seasonings (cumin and coriander), and even share similar preparations (Latin salsas vs. Indian chutneys). The result is a menu that mixes flavors in new ways that still seem somewhat familiar, whether it's empanadas with mango-coconut chutney, ceviche with Indian spices, or tandoori skirt steak served on sautéed garlic spinach with fried plantain. (There are also three different five-course tasting menus, $70–$80.) This isn't your usual Taj Mahal–meets–Bollywood Indian decor, either—the sleek white dining room is brightened with red decorative accents and large black-and-white fashion photographs. The lounge is open late for drinks and dessert, served to a soundtrack of Indian and Latin American tunes.

10 W. Hubbard St. (at State St.). ℂ **312/527-4060.** www.thevermilionrestaurant.com. Reservations recommended on weekends. Main courses $23–$33. AE, DC, DISC, MC, V. Mon–Fri 11:30am–2:30pm; Sun–Thurs 5–10pm; Fri–Sat 5–11pm. Lounge until 11pm. Subway/El: Red Line to Grand.

ZED 451 ★★ AMERICAN If you often find yourself staring indecisively at menus because *everything* sounds good, the ZED 451 concept is made for you. Pay a set price ($48 per person), and you get unlimited trips to the "Harvest Table," a trendy take on the salad bar, with homemade soups, breads, cheeses, and vegetables. Head back to your table, and the main course comes to you: Chefs stroll throughout the restaurant, offering unlimited appetizer-sized portions of the day's specialties, which could be anything from citrus salmon and Mediterranean chicken breast to grilled rib-eye and goat cheese–encrusted rack of lamb (there are usually at least 10 choices, all included in the set price). The space itself is gorgeous, with soaring ceilings and sexy lighting; the extensive use of natural materials gives this distinctly urban environment a warm, sultry vibe. Head to the outdoor rooftop deck for an after-dinner drink: The sparkling lights of the neighborhood high-rises make for a magical setting. The restaurant also offers Sunday brunch ($24 per person).

739 N. Clark St. (1 block south of Chicago Ave.). ℂ **888/493-3451.** www.zed451.com. Prix-fixe meal $48 per person. AE, DC, DISC, MC, V. Mon–Thurs 4:30–10pm; Fri–Sat 4:30–11pm; Sun 10am–2pm and 4:30–10pm. Subway/El: Brown or Red line to Chicago.

Moderate

Carson's ★ AMERICAN/BARBECUE A true Chicago institution, Carson's calls itself "The Place for Ribs," but you won't go wrong if you order anything slathered in the restaurant's sweet-and-tangy barbecue sauce. You can get ribs by the full or half slab, or gorge on one of the signature combo plates, which pair ribs with barbecue chicken, pork chops, or shrimp. (There are also entree-sized salads and sandwiches for smaller appetites.) For dinner, there's often a wait, but don't despair: In the bar area, you'll find a heaping mound of some of the best chopped liver around and plenty of cocktail rye to go with it. When you're seated at your table, tie on your plastic bib and indulge. Carson's popularity has led to something of a factory mentality among management, which sometimes herds diners in and out, but the servers are responsive to requests not to be hurried through the meal.

612 N. Wells St. (at Ontario St.). ℂ **312/280-9200.** www.ribs.com. Reservations accepted. Main courses $13–$34. AE, DISC, MC, V. Mon–Thurs 11:30am–10:30pm; Fri 11:30am–11pm; Sat noon–11pm; Sun noon–10pm. Subway/El: Red Line to Grand.

Cyrano's Bistrot & Wine Bar ★ 🍴 BISTRO/FRENCH Warm and welcoming, Cyrano's exudes authentic bistro charm, due in part to the friendly presence of chef Didier Durand and his wife, Jamie. The cheery blue-and-red wood exterior, eclectic artwork, and personal asides on the menu ("Use of cellular phones may interfere with the stability of our whipped cream") signal the owner's hands-on touch. Start with one of Durand's sensationally flavorful soups (the lobster bisque is a highlight) or the *pommes frites,* served with Dijon mustard, homemade ketchup, and mayonnaise. The house specialties are the rotisserie duck and chicken served with your choice of sauce and classics such as steak frites, roasted rabbit with mustard sauce, and cassoulet. The restaurant's lower-level cabaret has live entertainment most nights of the week, and in warmer months, a sidewalk cafe is open all day.

546 N. Wells St. (btw. Ohio St. and Grand Ave.). ✆ **312/467-0546.** www.cyranosbistrot.com. Main courses $17–$30. AE, DC, DISC, MC, V. Mon–Thurs 4–10pm; Fri 4–10:30pm; Sat 4–11pm. Subway/El: Brown Line to Merchandise Mart.

Gino's East ★★ ☺ PIZZA Many Chicagoans consider Gino's the city's quintessential deep-dish pizza. True to its reputation, the pizza is heavy, so work up an appetite before chowing down (a small cheese pizza is usually enough for two people—unless you're a champion eater). Specialty pizzas include the supreme, stuffed with sausage, onions, green pepper, and mushrooms; and the vegetarian, with onions, peppers, asparagus, summer squash, zucchini, and eggplant. Gino's also offers salads, sandwiches, and pastas. A warning for hungry families: Pizzas are cooked to order, so you'll have to wait about 45 minutes for your food (I highly recommend calling ahead to preorder, which will save you about a half-hour of waiting time, but preorders aren't accepted on Fri or Sat). If you want to take a pizza home, Gino's also has frozen pies for the road.

633 N. Wells St. (at Ontario St.). ✆ **312/943-1124.** www.ginoseast.com. Reservations not accepted. Pizza $12–$29. AE, DISC, MC, V. Mon–Thurs 11am–10pm; Fri–Sat 11am–11pm; Sun noon–9pm. Subway/El: Red Line to Grand.

HUB 51 ★★ AMERICAN This high-energy eatery is definitely a scene—with polished singles and couples lingering over drinks in the dimly lit, clublike dining room. Stylish setting and clientele aside, the place also offers some legitimately good globally inspired food. The large, varied menu ranges from light offerings (sushi rolls with miso-glazed salmon; shrimp ceviche; a Brussels sprout salad with dates, almonds, and Manchego cheese) to hearty options such as a massive "two-handed" turkey meatloaf sandwich, filet mignon steak tacos, or braised short ribs. The hearty green chili cheeseburger, topped with roasted poblano chilies and sharp cheddar, is a satisfying twist on an American classic. There are also several vegetarian and gluten-free options. Lunch and weekend brunch menus are similarly eclectic. A late-night menu is offered beginning at midnight, and a downstairs lounge transforms into a dance club on Wednesday through Saturday nights.

51 W. Hubbard St. (at Dearborn St.) ✆ **312/828-0051.** www.hub51chicago.com. Reservations accepted. Main courses $9–$20 lunch, $13–$30 dinner. AE, MC, V. Mon–Tues 11:30am–midnight; Wed–Fri 11:30am–2am; Sat 10am–3am; Sun 10am–midnight (brunch Sat–Sun 10am–2pm). Subway/El: Red Line to Grand.

Reza's ★★ 🍴 MIDDLE EASTERN Reza's doesn't look like the typical Middle Eastern restaurant. Housed in a former microbrewery, it has high ceilings and expansive, loftlike dining rooms, but the Persian-inspired menu will soon make you forget all about beer. Specialties include a deliciously rich chicken in pomegranate sauce and a variety of kabobs with heaps of dill rice (although, in a nod to carb-conscious diners, they'll substitute a salad if you want). If you can't decide what to order, go for an appetizer combo: a generous sampler of Middle Eastern dishes including hummus, tabbouleh, and other standbys, nicely presented in a red-lacquer bento box. (Despite the menu's meat-heavy emphasis, there's a selection of vegetarian sampler plates, too.) Reza's has another location in Andersonville, at 5255 N. Clark St. (© 773/561-1898), but the River North spot is the most convenient for visitors staying downtown.

432 W. Ontario St. (at Orleans St.). © 312/664-4500. www.rezasrestaurant.com. Main courses $13–$25. AE, DC, DISC, MC, V. Daily 11am–midnight. Subway/El: Red Line to Grand.

Rockit Bar & Grill ★ AMERICAN Take your standard American burger joint, give it an upscale, urban makeover, and you've got Rockit. The dining room is a trendy take on traditional tavern decor, where exposed-brick walls and distressed-wood tables combine with metallic accents and chocolate-brown leather booths. The Rockit Burger combines Kobe beef and melted brie, served with truffle oil french fries, while the wonderfully tender bone-in pork chop is served with country-style red mashed potatoes and grilled asparagus. The "My Sisters" chopped salad—a signature dish—is a filling mix of romaine lettuce, ham, tomatoes, provolone, hot cherry peppers, corn, and egg with balsamic dressing. Rockit is no gourmet destination, but if you're looking to chow down on better-than-decent

BREAKFAST & brunch

NEAR THE LOOP & MAGNIFICENT MILE

You can get a good (and upscale) breakfast at one of the hotels near the Loop or Magnificent Mile. Favorite spots for business travelers looking to impress include **The Café,** at the Four Seasons Hotel, 120 E. Delaware Place (© 312/280-8800); and **Drake Bros. Restaurant** at The Drake Hotel, 140 E. Walton Place, at Michigan Avenue (© 312/787-2200).

A more informal choice in the Loop, overlooking the El tracks, is **Heaven on Seven** ★★ (p. 101), where the Cajun and Creole specialties supplement an enormous diner-style menu.

For brunch with some soul, head to **House of Blues,** 329 N. Dearborn St., at Kinzie Street (© 312/527-2583; p. 315), for its popular Sunday gospel brunch. To guarantee seating, it's a good idea to book a spot 2 weeks in advance.

A local breakfast favorite since 1923 is **Lou Mitchell's,** 565 W. Jackson Blvd. (© 312/939-3111; loumitchellsrestaurant. com), across the south branch of the Chicago River from the Loop, a block farther west than Union Station. You'll be greeted at the door with a basket of

doughnut holes and Milk Duds so that you can nibble while waiting for a table.

For a Southern-style breakfast of spicy red eggs, cheese grits, or biscuits and gravy, head over to **Wishbone** ★★ (p. 108), a family-friendly, laid-back spot in a converted warehouse building in the West Loop.

LINCOLN PARK & THE NORTH SIDE

A perfect breakfast or brunch spot if you're heading up to Wrigleyville for a Cubs game or a walk through Lincoln Park is **Ann Sather** ★★ (p. 140), famous for its homemade cinnamon rolls.

The **Nookies** restaurants are Chicago favorites for all the standard morning fare. Locations include 2114 N. Halsted St., in Lincoln Park (© 773/327-1400;

food in a high-energy setting, Rockit fits the bill. (***Bonus:*** The waitstaff range from good-looking to gorgeous.)

22 W. Hubbard St. (btw. Wabash and State sts.). ☎ **312/645-6000.** www.rockitbarandgrill.com. Reservations accepted. Main courses $10–$21 lunch, $11–$32 dinner. AE, DC, DISC, MC, V. Sun–Wed 11:30am–12:30am; Thurs–Fri 11:30am–1:30am; Sat 10:30am–2:30am. Subway/El: Red Line to Grand.

Sable Kitchen & Bar ★ AMERICAN Walk through Sable's industrial-chic bar, with its black-clad cocktail waitresses, and into the minimalist, neutral-toned dining room, and you might expect a certain amount of culinary posing. Not so. There may be some disconnect between Sable's urban cool decor and its down-to-earth menu of American comfort food, but the contrast works: Sable is a great pick for not-so-adventurous diners who still want to experience a stylish, downtown restaurant scene. With most dishes available in half or whole portions, you can choose to eat tapas-style, or order a more traditional meat-and-side entrée. Twists on standard American favorites include deviled eggs with truffle oil and black trumpet mushrooms; mini bison burgers glazed with root beer; pistachio-cherry duck sausage with Parmesan grits; and spicy fried quail legs served with blue cheese coleslaw (an upscale take on Buffalo wings). There's also an extensive menu of specialty beers and custom cocktails (which cost as much as some of the dishes).

www.nookiesrestaurants.net); 1748 N. Wells St., in Old Town (☎ **312/337-2454**); and 3334 N. Halsted St., in Lakeview (☎ **773/248-9888**). Especially in Old Town, be prepared to stand outside on the weekends until a table opens for you. It's quite a scene on the sidewalk, which is packed with baby strollers, dogs on leashes, large groups chatting, and singles reading the newspaper.

Go to **Orange,** 3231 N. Clark St., at Belmont (☎ **773/549-4400;** orange restaurantchicago.com), for a fun twist on breakfast foods. Try the Green Eggs and Ham—eggs scrambled with pesto, tomatoes, mozzarella, and pancetta. There's a kids' menu, too, making this a popular choice for families. But a warning to all those with hungry kids (and parents): Come early or late; the line for a table winds outside during prime weekend brunch hours.

Lincoln Park's **Toast** (p. 101), 746 W. Webster St., at Halsted Street

(☎ **773/935-5600**), is homey yet slightly funky. Pancakes come in all sorts of tempting varieties, from lemon/poppy seed drizzled with honey to the "pancake orgy," a strawberry, mango, and banana-pecan pancake topped with granola, yogurt, and honey. Come early on weekends, though; by 10:30am or so, there's guaranteed to be a lengthy wait.

WICKER PARK/BUCKTOWN
The brightly colored and artwork-adorned **Earwax Café,** 1561 N. Milwaukee Ave., at North and Damen avenues (☎ **773/772-4019;** www.earwax-cafe. com), is a Wicker Park institution serving everything from salmon Benedict to vegan options such as the popular tofu scramble. Don't let the unappetizing name, the proliferation of hipsters, or the dearth of meat deter you from this place. The food is delicious, the back patio is delightful, and the tattooed and pierced waitstaff could not be nicer.

505 N. State St. (at Illinois St.), in the Hotel Palomar. ☎ **312/755-9704.** www.sablechicago.com. Reservations recommended on weekends. Main courses $14–$25. AE, DC, DISC, MC, V. Mon–Fri 11:30am–2pm, and 5–10pm; Sat 5–10pm; Sun 5–9pm. Subway/El: Red Line to Grand.

DINING alfresco

Cocooned for 6 months of the year, with furnaces and electric blankets blazing, Chicagoans revel in the warm months of late spring, summer, and early autumn. For locals and visitors alike, dining alfresco is an ideal way to experience the sights, sounds, smells, and social fabric of this multifaceted city.

LOOP & VICINITY

Athena ★ This Greektown mainstay offers a stunning three-level outdoor seating area. It's paved with brick and landscaped with 30-foot trees, flower gardens, and even a waterfall. Best of all: An incredible view of the downtown skyline with the Sears Tower right in the middle. It's located at 212 S. Halsted St., between Adams and Jackson streets (☎ **312/655-0000;** www.athena restaurantchicago.com).

Park Grill ★★ Millennium Park's restaurant serves upscale versions of American comfort food with panoramic views of Michigan Avenue. In the summer, you can pick up a sandwich and grab a seat on the large patio (converted into an ice-skating rink come winter). For a review, see p. 97. It's at 11 N. Michigan Ave., at Madison Street (☎ **312/521-PARK** [7275]).

Rhapsody ★★ A tranquil oasis amid the Loop high-rises, Rhapsody's outdoor garden is a great spot for a romantic meal downtown. For more info, see p. 98. 65 E. Adams St., at Wabash Avenue (☎ **312/786-9911**).

MAGNIFICENT MILE & GOLD COAST

Charlie's Ale House at Navy Pier One of several outdoor dining options along Navy Pier, this outpost of the Lincoln Park restaurant has lip-smacking pub fare and a great location on the southern promenade overlooking the lakefront and Loop skyline. It's located at 700 E. Grand Ave., near the entrance to the Pier (☎ **312/595-1440**).

Le Colonial ★★ This lovely French-Vietnamese restaurant, located in a vintage Gold Coast town house and evocative of 1920s Saigon, *does* have a sidewalk cafe, but you'd do better to reserve a table on the tiny second-floor porch, overlooking the street. For a full review, see p. 114. It's located at 937 N. Rush St., just south of Oak Street (☎ **312/255-0088**).

Oak Street Beachstro Suit up and head for this warm-weather-only beachfront cafe—literally on the sands of popular Oak Street Beach—which serves inventive cafe fare (fresh seafood, sandwiches, and pastas). Beer and wine are available. The address is 1000 N. Lake Shore Dr., at Oak Street Beach (☎ **312/915-4100;** www.oakstreet beachstro.com).

Puck's at the MCA This cafe—run by celebrity chef Wolfgang Puck—is tucked in the back of the Museum of Contemporary Art, where, from the terrace, you'll get a view of the museum's sculpture garden. (Restaurant-only patrons can bypass museum admission.) The address is 220 E. Chicago Ave., at Fairbanks Court (☎ **312/397-4034;** www.mcachicago.org).

Inexpensive

Café Iberico ★★ SPANISH & TAPAS This no-frills tapas spot won't win any points for style, but the consistently good food and festive atmosphere make it a longtime local favorite for singles in their 20s and 30s. Café Iberico gets very

---

RIVER NORTH

SushiSamba Rio ★★ For stunning nighttime views of the skyline—accompanied by views of some pretty stunning people—head to the rooftop deck of this Latin-Asian fusion spot. Canopied banquettes and flickering tea lights create a sultry atmosphere, along with a menu of specialty cocktails. See p. 123. You'll find it at 504 N. Wells St., at Illinois St. (☎ **312/595-2300**).

ZED 451 ★★ You'll find another great rooftop deck on top of this funky all-you-can-eat spot. Here the wood decor and laid-back vibe let you imagine you're kicking back at a rich friend's penthouse. See page 124. It's at 739 N. Clark St., 1 block south of Chicago Ave. (☎ **888/493-3451**).

LINCOLN PARK

Charlie's Ale House A true neighborhood hangout, this Lincoln Park pub's wonderful beer garden—surrounded by tall, ivy-covered brick walls—is spacious and buzzing with activity and good vibes. It's located at 1224 W. Webster Ave., at Magnolia Avenue (☎ **773/871-1440**).

North Pond ★★★ Set on the banks of one of Lincoln Park's beautiful lagoons, the excellent North Pond serves upscale, fresh-as-can-be American cuisine in a romantic and sylvan setting. Also see p. 134. The address is 2610 N. Cannon Dr., halfway between Diversey Parkway and Fullerton Avenue (☎ **773/477-5845**).

O'Brien's Restaurant Wells Street in Old Town is lined with several alfresco options, but the best belongs

to O'Brien's, the unofficial nucleus of neighborhood life. The outdoor patio has teakwood furniture, a gazebo bar, and a mural of the owners' country club on a brick wall. Order the dressed-up chips, a house specialty. Located at 1528 N. Wells St., 2 blocks south of North Avenue (☎ **312/787-3131**; www.obriens restaurant.com).

WRIGLEYVILLE & VICINITY

Tapas Gitana ★ The tapas and sangria at this cozy Wrigleyville restaurant can compete with other, better-known Spanish spots, and the intimate, leafy terrace out back glows with lantern light. Located at 3445 N. Halsted St., at Newport Avenue (☎ **773/296-6046**; www.tapasgitana.com).

Moody's For more than 30 years, Moody's has been grilling some of the best burgers in Chicago. It's ideal in winter for its dark, cozy dining room (warmed by a fireplace), but it's better still in summer for its awesome outdoor patio, a real hidden treasure. The address is 5910 N. Broadway Ave., between Rosedale and Thorndale avenues (☎ **773/275-2696**; www.moodyspub.com).

WICKER PARK/BUCKTOWN

Northside Café On a sunny summer day, Northside seems like Wicker Park's town square, packed with an eclectic mix of locals catching up and checking out the scene. The entire front of the restaurant opens onto the street, making it relatively easy to get an "outdoor" table. For more info, see p. 144. Located at 1635 N. Damen Ave., just north of North Avenue (☎ **773/384-3555**).

loud, especially on weekends, so it makes a fun group destination—but plan your romantic *tête-à-tête* elsewhere. Crowds begin pouring in at the end of the work-day, so you'll probably have to wait for a table. ***Not to worry:*** Order a pitcher of fruit-filled sangria at the bar with everyone else. When you get a table, start with the *queso de cabra* (baked goat cheese with fresh tomato-basil sauce). A few standout dishes are the vegetarian Spanish omelet, spicy potatoes with tomato sauce, chicken brochette with caramelized onions and rice, and grilled octopus with potatoes and olive oil.

739 N. LaSalle St. (btw. Chicago Ave. and Superior St.). ✆ **312/573-1510.** www.cafeiberico.com. Reservations accepted for parties of 6 or more; no reservations for Fri-Sat dinner. Tapas $4–$7; main courses $7–$12. AE, DC, DISC, MC, V. Mon-Thurs 11am–11:30pm; Fri 11am–1:30am; Sat 11am–1:30am; Sun 11am–11pm. Subway/El: Red Line to Chicago or Brown Line to Chicago.

Mr. Beef ★ 👫 FAST FOOD Calling Mr. Beef a restaurant may be a stretch: The place is basically a sandwich stand, without much atmosphere or room for seating (the "dining room" has one long communal picnic table). Despite these drawbacks, Mr. Beef is a much-loved Chicago institution. Its claim to fame is the classic Italian beef sandwich, the Chicago version of a Philly cheese steak. The Mr. Beef variety is made of sliced beef dipped in *jus,* piled high on a chewy bun, and topped with sweet or hot peppers. It's heavy, filling, messy, and *very* Chicago. Mr. Beef really hops during lunchtime, when dusty construction workers and suit-clad businessmen crowd in for their greasy fix. While you're chowing, check out the celebrity photos and newspaper clippings covering the walls, and you'll see why this place is considered a local monument.

666 N. Orleans St. (at Erie St.). ✆ **312/337-8500.** Sandwiches $6–$8.50. No credit cards. Mon-Thurs 8:30am–7pm; Fri 8:30am–7pm and 10:30pm–5am; Sat 10:30am–3pm and 10:30pm–5am. Subway/El: Red Line to Grand.

Pizzeria Uno ★ 🍴 PIZZA Pizzeria Uno invented Chicago-style pizza, and many deep-dish aficionados still refuse to accept any imitations. Uno's is now a chain of restaurants throughout the country, but come here if you want to taste the original. You can eat in the restaurant itself on the basement level or, weather permitting, on the outdoor patio right off the sidewalk. Salads, sandwiches, and a house minestrone are also available, but let's be honest—the main reason to come here is for the pizza. As with **Gino's East** (see earlier), pizzas take about 45 minutes to make, so if you're starving, order an appetizer or salad.

Uno was so successful that the owners opened **Pizzeria Due** in a lovely gray-brick Victorian town house nearby at 619 N. Wabash Ave., at Ontario Street (✆ **312/943-2400**). The menu is exactly the same, the atmosphere just a tad nicer (with more outdoor seating).

29 E. Ohio St. (at Wabash Ave.). ✆ **312/321-1000.** www.unos.com. Reservations not accepted. Pizza $7–$27. AE, DC, DISC, MC, V. Mon-Fri 11am–1am; Sat 11am–2am; Sun 11am–11pm. Subway/El: Red Line to Grand.

Portillo's ★★ ☺ AMERICAN/FAST FOOD Although it's known mostly for its Chicago-style hot dogs and Italian beef sandwiches, this local chain has a surpris-ingly well-rounded menu, making it a good, affordable stop for families with varied tastes. At the main counter, you can order from the usual fast-food favorites (hot dogs, hamburgers, fries, and so on); the tasty grilled tuna sandwich is lighter alter-native. Across the room, a separate counter serves up a range of pastas and salads; the generously sized Asian chicken salad and chicken pecan version are both served with a hunk of chewy, addictive homemade bread. If you're in the mood to indulge, the rich chocolate cake is one of the best desserts in town. With its tourist-friendly location, Portillo's can get crowded and loud (especially if you're unlucky enough to arrive at the same time as a high school tour group), but it's an authentic Chicago spot, and a bargain compared to other River North restaurants.

100 W. Ontario St. (at Clark St.). ✆ **312/587-8930.** www.portillos.com. Reservations not accepted. Main courses $3–$9. AE, DC, DISC, MC, V; Mon–Sat 10am–midnight; Sun 10am–11pm. Subway/El: Red Line to Grand.

LINCOLN PARK & OLD TOWN

Singles and upwardly mobile young families inhabit Lincoln Park, the neighborhood roughly defined by North Avenue on the south, Diversey Parkway on the north, the park on the east, and Clybourn Avenue on the west. In the southeast corner of this area is Old Town, a neighborhood of historic town houses that stretches out from the intersection of North Avenue and Wells Street. You'll find a few fine-dining spots, but most restaurants here are more casual, with average prices lower than you'll find in River North or along the Magnificent Mile.

Very Expensive

Alinea ★★★ NEW AMERICAN Alinea—anointed the best restaurant in the country by no less than *Gourmet* magazine—is a place no serious foodie should miss. Like Homaro Cantu at **Moto** (p. 103), chef Grant Achatz revolutionizes the way we eat, presenting familiar foods in new contexts and unexpected forms. (He's been known, for example, to serve dishes on lavender-scented pillows, so the aroma wafts up as you eat.) The 12- or 24-course tasting menus change constantly, but you're guaranteed to taste something new here, whether it's ravioli with a liquid-truffle filling; Wagyu beef with deconstructed A1 steak sauce; or lobster and popcorn served with a cube of butter that's cold on the outside, melted on the inside. Achatz says he wants diners to feel like they're taking a journey, "zigzagging between challenge and comfort." The restaurant itself is certainly comfortable, with shoulder-high chairs you can sink into and soft, flattering lighting. Eat with an open mind (and a full wallet), and you'll be well rewarded.

1723 N. Halsted St. (btw. North Ave. and Willow St.). ✆ **312/867-0110.** www.alinea-restaurant. com. Reservations strongly recommended. Fixed-price menus $150 and $225. AE, DC, DISC, MC, V. Wed–Fri 5:30–9:30pm; Sat–Sun 5–9:30pm. Subway/El: Red Line to North/Clybourn.

Charlie Trotter's ★★★ NEW AMERICAN Charlie Trotter, Chicago's first celebrity chef, still draws foodies to his namesake restaurant after more than 20 years in business. Trotter delights in presenting diners with unfamiliar ingredients and presentations, and prides himself on using only organic or free-range products (so you can feel good about indulging). There is no a la carte menu; your only choice is to decide between the vegetable ($135) or grand ($155) tasting menu. The entree descriptions signal Trotter's attention to detail; sample dishes include steamed Casco Bay cod with cockles, picholine olives, artichokes, and stinging nettles; and roasted squab breast with Alaskan licorice, toasted pistachios and heirloom beets. The dining room may be formal, but the overall attitude is attentive, not intimidating. A sommelier is on hand to help match wines with each course.

For a taste of Trotter's gourmet fare without the high price tag, check out **Trotter's to Go,** his gourmet food store in Lincoln Park at 1337 W. Fullerton Ave. (btw. Lakewood and Wayne aves.; ✆ **773/868-6510**).

Restaurants in Lincoln Park, Old Town, & Wrigleyville

Adobo Grill **34**

Alinea **30**

Ann Sather **8**

Arun's **1**

Bamee Noodle Shop **10**

Bistrot Margot **36**

Boka **29**

Café Ba-Ba-Reeba! **24**

Charlie's Ale House **17**

Charlie Trotter's **25**

The Chicago Diner **2**

Chicago Pizza & Oven Grinder **23**

Edwardo's **14**

Geja's Cafe **26**

Goose Island Brewing Company **28**

Karyn's Raw **27**

L2O **20**

La Creperie **11**

Mia Francesca **4**

Mon Ami Gabi **21**

Murphy's Red Hots **9**

Nookies **5, 22, 32**

North Pond **16**

O'Brien's Restaurant **35**

Orange **7**

Penny's Noodle Shop **12**

Perennial Virant **31**
Potbelly Sandwich Works **19**
RoseAngelis **13**
Thai Classic **3**
Tiparos **37**
Toast **18**
Twin Anchors **33**
The Wieners Circle **15**
Yoshi's Café **6**

M Subway/El stop

1/4 mi
0.25 km

North
Avenue
Beach

Lincoln Statue
N. State St.
N. Dearborn St.
Chicago
Historical
Society
N. Clark St.
37
N. La Salle St.
64
36
35
OLD TOWN
Schiller
St.

Theater
on the
Lake

Lake   Shore   Dr.

Fullerton Beach

LINCOLN   PARK

Café Brauer
South Pond
Farm-in-the-Zoo

N. Cannon Dr.
Lincoln Park
Conservatory
LINCOLN PARK ZOO
Stockton Dr.
Lincoln Park
Cultural Center
26
23

N. Lincoln Park West
21 20

Peggy Notebaert
Nature Museum

Diversey Harbor

North
Pond
16

N. Lakeview Ave.

31   N. Wells   St.
32
34
N. Park   Ave.
33
N.   Sedgwick   St.   Eugenie   St.
M   Sedgwick
N. Cleveland Ave.

Wrightwood

Wayne
13
N.   Southport
N.   Greenview
N.   Ashland

15
Deming
Arlington   Pl.
N.   Orchard   St.
N.   Burling   St.
N.   Halsted   St.
14
Ave.

LINCOLN PARK

Clark   Ave.
N. Cleveland Ave.
N.   Dickens
Belden   Ave.
Fullerton
North
Ave.
Webster

Lincoln
19
OZ PARK
No. 276
Park
18

DEPAUL UNIVERSITY
M
Fullerton
Montana
St.
Ave.
Trebes
Park
17   Magnolia Ave.
Lakewood   Ave.
Ave.
Schubert   Ave.
Altgeld
Ave.

Clifton   St.

Wisconsin   St.
N. Cleveland Ave.
Armitage
N. Orchard   St.
N. Burling   St.
N.   Halsted St.
27
29 30
Willow   St.
N.   Park
22 24 25
N.   Dayton   St.
N.   Fremont   St.
N.   Bissell   St.
N. Sheffield   Ave.
Armitage
Wisconsin St.
Menomonee   St.
Mohawk   St.
Larrabee   St.

North

Clybourn
Marcey St.
North
28
Kingsbury   Ave.
Chicago River
Cortland   St.
Elston
North   Branch
Kennedy Expwy.
90
94
64
Turning
Basin
Stanton
Park
Weed   St.
N.   Clybourn
M
North/clybourn
W.
North

N. Greenview
N. Ashland
N.   Wood   St.

816 W. Armitage Ave. (at Halsted St.). ☎ **773/248-6228.** www.charlietrotters.com. Reservations required. Jackets required, ties requested. Fixed-price menus $135 and $165. AE, DC, DISC, MC, V. Seatings Tues–Thurs at 6 and 9pm; Fri–Sat at 5:30 and 9pm. Subway/El: Brown Line to Armitage.

Geja's Cafe ★ FONDUE A dark, subterranean hideaway, Geja's (pronounced gay-*haz*) regularly shows up on lists of the most romantic restaurants in Chicago. However, the interior might strike some as too gloomy, and the cook-it-yourself technique won't appeal to anyone who wants to be pampered. The best overall option is the Prince Geja's combination dinner, which starts with a Gruyère cheese fondue appetizer. Next, a huge platter arrives, brimming with squares of beef tenderloin, lobster tails, jumbo shrimp, chicken breast, and scallops—all raw—and a caldron of boiling oil to cook them in. These delicacies are accompanied by a variety of raw vegetables and eight different dipping sauces. When the flaming chocolate fondue arrives for dessert, with fresh fruit and pound cake for dipping and marshmallows for roasting, you'll want to beg for mercy. *Caution:* The aroma of cooking oil that fills the restaurant might bother some sensitive noses.

340 W. Armitage Ave. (btw. Lincoln Ave. and Clark St.). ☎ **773/281-9101.** www.gejascafe. com. Reservations accepted. 3-course dinners $28–$49 per person. AE, DC, DISC, MC, V. Mon–Thurs 5–10pm; Fri 5–11pm; Sat 5–11:30pm; Sun 4:30–9:30pm. Bus: 22. Subway/El: Brown Line to Armitage.

L2O ★★★ 🍴 SEAFOOD French chef Laurent Gras leads this kitchen, which gracefully swims the line between traditional fine dining and molecular gastronomy. Although L2O (pronounced "El-Two-Oh") is not afraid of a little liquid nitrogen once in a while, the tricks here are not as dramatic as they are at Alinea or Moto; the cuisine is as refined and carefully prepared as any in town. Recent offerings on the ever-changing menu have included halibut with arugula dumplings and bacon butter; diver scallops with vanilla and passion fruit; and smoked salmon flavored with Earl Gray tea, ginger noodles, and croutons. A tasting menu is your only option here, with most courses featuring seafood, but you also might get a taste of the chef's take on Peking duck or beef short ribs. L2O also has private tatami-floored rooms where groups of up to eight people can enjoy a traditional Japanese meal complete with kimono-clad servers.

2300 N. Lincoln Park West (at Belden Ave.). ☎ **773/868-0002.** www.l2orestaurant.com. Reservations strongly recommended. 4- to 12-course tasting menus $110–$245 (Japanese kaiseki menu $225). AE, DC, DISC, MC, V. Sun–Mon, Wed–Thurs 6–10pm (closed Tues); Fri 6–11pm; Sat 5–11pm. Bus: 151.

North Pond ★★★ 🍴 AMERICAN Tucked away in Lincoln Park, north of the zoo, North Pond truly is a hidden treasure. The building's Arts and Crafts–inspired interior blends perfectly with the park outside, and the addition, with its abundance of windows via French doors, lets you dine "outside" year-round. In keeping with the natural setting, chef Bruce Sherman emphasizes sustainable, locally grown ingredients and favors simple preparations—although the overall result is definitely upscale (at these prices, it'd better be). Examples of seasonal menu items include grilled sturgeon with mascarpone polenta, griddled green asparagus, maple bacon, and arugula; and grilled pork loin and braised pork belly with andouille sausage, cranberry-black bean ragout, charred peppers, and black figs. For dessert, try a plate of artisanal cheeses or dark chocolate mousse with roasted apricots and a hazelnut biscuit. To enjoy the setting with a slightly lower price tag, try the three-course Sunday brunch ($32). The all-American wine list focuses on boutique vintners.

2610 N. Cannon Dr. (south of Diversey Pkwy.). ☎ **773/477-5845.** www.northpondrestaurant.com. Reservations recommended. Main courses $32–$39. AE, DC, MC, V. Tues–Sat 5:30–10pm (closed Tues Jan–April); Sun 10:30am–1:30pm and 5:30–10pm. Lunch served June–Sept Tues–Fri 11:30am–1:30pm. Bus: 151.

Expensive

Boka ★ AMERICAN In a neighborhood full of Irish pubs and casual sandwich joints, Boka is a sophisticated, grown-up alternative. The dimly lit dining room manages to be both romantic and dramatic, thanks to the white fabric "sculptures" stretched across the ceiling. The food—described by the owners as "progressive American"—combines upscale ingredients in creative ways, such as roasted duck breast with golden barley cake; mahimahi with orange gnocchi; pickled tongue; and French fries cooked in duck fat. There are also six- and nine-course tasting menus. The desserts, which look like miniature modern art arrangements, offer a similar mix of flavors, such as a chocolate-caramel terrine with bourbon ice cream and malt meringue. Boka is a good place to grab dinner before a show at the nearby Steppenwolf Theatre, but make a reservation first. Aesthetically, Boka's main claim to fame is its cellphone booth, where diners are encouraged to make calls in private—an idea that many hope will catch on.

1729 N. Halsted St. (btw. North Ave. and Willow St.). ☎ **312/337-6070.** www.bokachicago.com. Reservations recommended on weekends. Main courses $24–$37; tasting menus $85 and $115. AE, MC, V. Daily 5–11pm. Subway/El: Red Line to North/Clybourn.

Mon Ami Gabi ★ BISTRO/FRENCH This "French steakhouse" concept seduces with its aromatic bistro atmosphere, tasty steak preparations, and rolling cart of wines by the glass ("Gabi" refers to executive chef Gabino Sotelino). There are numerous classic starters and hot seafood appetizers, such as plump mussels steamed in white wine and herbs, pâtés, and cheeses, and the simple but impeccably executed entrees include chicken paillard (a crusty, pounded chicken breast in lemon butter) and trout Grenobloise (pan-seared trout in caper butter with a sprinkle of croutons). Steak frites can be customized with *maître d'hôtel* butter, au poivre, Roquefort, or bordelaise (with caramelized onions in mushroom and red wine sauce). For the full Gabi experience, don't skip dessert: The bananas foster crepe or profiteroles topped with warm fudge are the perfect ending to a French meal.

2300 N. Lincoln Park West (at Belden Ave.). ☎ **773/348-8886.** www.monamigabi.com. Reservations recommended. Main courses $15–$30. AE, DC, DISC, MC, V. Mon–Thurs 5:30–10pm; Fri–Sat 5–11pm; Sun 5–9pm. Bus: 151.

Perennial Virant ★★ AMERICAN This elegant charmer stands out for both its airy look and its fresh, seasonal preparations. The bright, light-filled dining room is a loungey-cool space that attracts young singles and couples from the neighborhood, many of whom fill the outdoor patio overlooking Lincoln Park (unfortunately, it also overlooks busy, traffic-filled Clark St.). The menu includes a range of small plates meant to be shared, including roasted chicken sausage with hot pepper vinaigrette; scallops with carrot puree, and other dishes that highlight fresh, seasonal ingredients (the chef, Paul Virant, is a fan of the nearby Green City farmers' market). There's also a nightly three-course prix-fixe meal for $35, as well as a custom-brewed beer on tap.

1800 N. Lincoln Ave. (at Clark St.). ☎ **312/981-7070.** www.perennialchicago.com. Small plates $9–$26; prix-fixe dinner $35. AE, MC, V. Mon–Fri 5–10pm; Sat–Sun 10am–2pm and 5–11pm. Bus: 22 (Clark St.).

Moderate

Adobo Grill MEXICAN A cut above the average taco joint, Adobo Grill showcases the flavors of Mexico in a bright, contemporary setting. If you don't mind noise, join the action on the first floor; head upstairs for a quieter meal. Adobo Grill's signature dish is the fresh guacamole prepared tableside (you choose the spice level, but be warned that even the "medium" will give your tongue a jolt). Entrees include an achiote-marinated pork chop with black beans, pickled purple onions, and molcajete salsa; and the lighter but tangy chipotle-marinated grilled shrimp with plantain, rice, and zucchini noodles. Before ordering a margarita or one of the 60 sipping tequilas, consider a refreshing Michelada (your choice of beer with lime juice in a chili- and salt-dusted glass) or a bittersweet Adobopolitan (tequila, Citrónge, and pomegranate juice). Although the busy bar is a singles' hangout, families are a regular part of the restaurant's clientele; there's even a kids' menu.

1610 N. Wells St. (at North Ave.). © **312/266-7999.** www.adobogrill.com. Reservations recommended. Main courses $14–$25. AE, DC, MC, V. Mon–Thurs 5–10pm; Fri 5–11pm; Sat 11am–11pm; Sun 11am–9pm. Bus: 22, 36, or 156.

Bistrot Margot ★★ 🍴 BISTRO/FRENCH This family-owned-and-operated restaurant is not only one of the best in Old Town, but it's also one of the top bistros in Chicago. The tables are quite close together, but for many, the room's noisy bustle adds to its charm, giving the place the feel of an authentic Parisian cafe. Starters include a traditional preparation of mussels in white wine with fresh herbs; escargot in garlic butter; and country-style pâté. The well-prepared French staples (roasted chicken with garlic and lemon; duck confit; rack of lamb with Dijon mustard; steak frites) are proof that, when done right, it's hard to beat classic bistro cuisine. On warm nights, the restaurant sets about a dozen tables on the sidewalk, which, on this busy stretch of Wells Street, makes for a truly memorable meal.

Bistrot Margot's weekend brunch puts a Gallic twist on this traditionally American meal, with choices such as brioche French toast and croque-monsieur sandwiches.

1437 N. Wells St. (at W. Schiller St.). © **312/587-3660.** www.bistrotmargot.com. Reservations recommended. Main courses $16–$26. AE, DISC, MC, V. Mon 11:30am–9pm; Tues–Thurs 11:30am–10pm; Fri 11:30am–11pm; Sat 10am–11pm; Sun 10am–9pm. Subway/El: Red Line to Clark/Division, or Brown Line to Sedgwick.

Café Ba-Ba-Reeba! ★ SPANISH & TAPAS One of the city's first tapas restaurants, Café Ba-Ba-Reeba! is still going strong decades later. The clientele at this vibrantly colored spot tends to be young and comes to the restaurant in groups, so be prepared: Loud conversations and tipsy toasts over pitchers of sangria may surround you. Tapas lovers will see plenty of old favorites on the menu, including spicy potatoes with tomato aioli, spinach, and Manchego-stuffed mushrooms; chicken and ham *croquetas;* and meatballs with sherry tomato sauce. For even more tasting possibilities, the restaurant offers "pinxtos," which are even smaller than tapas and can be ordered individually or by the platter; bite-sized options include shrimp and egg salad on toast, Serrano ham and caramelized pineapple, and short rib–stuffed piquillo peppers. Got a bigger appetite? Dig into an entree-size portion of paella.

2024 N. Halsted St. (at Armitage Ave.). © **773/935-5000.** www.cafebabareeba.com. Reservations recommended on weekends. Tapas $4.50–$11; main courses $9–$30. AE, DC, DISC, MC, V. Mon–Thurs 4–10pm; Fri 4pm–midnight; Sat 11am–midnight; Sun 11am–10pm. Subway/El: Red or Brown line to Fullerton, or Brown Line to Armitage.

Twin Anchors ★ BARBECUE A landmark in Old Town since 1932, Twin Anchors manages to maintain the flavor of old Chicago. It's a friendly, family-owned pub with Frank Sinatra songs on the jukebox and pictures of Ol' Blue Eyes on the walls (he apparently hung out here on swings through town in the 1960s). But rather than striking a purposefully retro pose, this feels like the real deal, with a long mahogany bar up front and a modest dining room in back with red Formica-topped tables crowded close. Of course, you don't need anything fancy when the ribs—the fall-off-the-bone variety—come this good. The only downside to Twin Anchors' longtime success is that you'll probably have a long wait on weekends. Ribs and other entrees come with coleslaw and dark rye bread, plus your choice of baked potato, tasty fries, and the even-better crisp onion rings. For dessert, there's a daily cheesecake selection.

1655 N. Sedgwick St. (1 block north of North Ave.). © **312/266-1616.** www.twinanchorsribs. com. Reservations not accepted. Sandwiches $7–$11; main courses $13–$26. AE, DC, DISC, MC, V. Mon–Thurs 5–11pm; Fri 5pm–midnight; Sat noon–midnight; Sun noon–10:30pm. Subway/El: Brown Line to Sedgwick.

Inexpensive

Goose Island Brewing Company AMERICAN Some of the best beer in Chicago is produced at this microbrewery on the western edge of Old Town. Goose Island produces about 100 varieties of lagers and ales, which means you're pretty much obligated to taste-test a few while you're here (you can order samplers and flights if you're not up for full pints). Cut-above bar food includes an excellent burger topped with Stilton cheese, a tasty barbecue pulled-pork sandwich, and rabbit sausage. Don't skip the side dishes, either; the homemade potato chips and roasted beets with feta cheese are both deliciously addictive. While the loftlike, exposed-brick main room attracts mostly groups of 20- and 30-somethings, there's also a separate dining area that's a popular Sunday brunch spot for families. While the grownups sample lagers, the kids can order a glass of homemade root beer or orange soda.

Goose Island also has a more sports-oriented location near Wrigley Field, at 3535 N. Clark St. (© **773/832-9040**).

1800 N. Clybourn Ave. (at Willow St.). © **312/915-0071.** www.gooseisland.com. Reservations accepted. Main courses $10–$18. AE, DC, DISC, MC, V. Sun–Thurs 11am–1am; Fri–Sat 11am–2am. Subway/El: Brown Line to Armitage.

La Creperie ★★ 🛉 FRENCH Germain and Sara Roignant opened this intimate cafe in 1972, never straying from the reasonably priced crepes that won them a loyal following. Onion soup, pâté, and escargot are all good starters, but the highlights here are the whole-wheat crepes—prepared on a special grill that Germain imported from his native Brittany. Single-choice fillings include cheese, tomato, egg, or ham; tasty duets feature chicken and mushroom or broccoli and cheese. But I'd suggest going with the richer fillings, such as beef bourguignon, coq au vin, or curried chicken, for the best overall flavor. A popular combination is tomato, goat cheese, and chicken in a Dijon cream sauce. Don't leave without sharing one of the dessert crepes, which tuck combinations of fruit, ice cream, peanut butter, Belgian chocolate, and Nutella within their warm folds.

2845 N. Clark St. (half-block north of Diversey Pkwy.). © **773/528-9050.** www.lacreperieusa. com. Reservations accepted for groups of 6 or more. Main courses $7–$15. AE, DC, DISC, MC, V. Tues–Fri 11:30am–11pm; Sat 11am–11pm; Sun 11am–9:30pm. Subway/El: Brown Line to Diversey.

Potbelly Sandwich Works 🍴 FAST FOOD It doesn't matter what time you stop by Potbelly; there's usually a line of hungry 20- and 30-somethings waiting to get their fix (good thing the behind-the-counter staff is so fast). Yes, there's a potbelly stove inside, along with other Old West saloon-type memorabilia, but fans come here for the made-to-order grilled sub sandwiches (that's all they serve). Prepared on homemade rolls stuffed with your choice of turkey, Italian meats, veggies, pizza ingredients, and more, they're warmed in a countertop toaster oven. Even with all the fixin's, each is under $5 (unlike the massive subs found at other spots, Potbelly's "Originals" are more the size of normal sandwiches; however, "Bigs" and "Skinnys" are also available). Though this is the original location, Potbelly has more than 30 others throughout the city, including 190 N. State St. (✆ 312/683-1234) and in the Westfield North Bridge shopping center, 520 N. Michigan Ave. (✆ 312/664-1008), both of which are convenient to the Loop and Mag Mile.

2264 N. Lincoln Ave. (btw. Belden Ave. and Webster St.). ✆ **773/528-1405.** www.potbelly.com. Reservations not accepted. Sandwiches $4–$5.50. MC, V. Daily 11am–10pm. Subway/El: Brown or Red line to Fullerton.

RoseAngelis ★★ 🍴 ITALIAN What keeps this off-the-beaten path spot busy year after year when there's not exactly a shortage of Italian restaurants in Chicago? The reliably good food, warm ambience, and very reasonable

🎁 A TASTE OF thai

Thai restaurants are to Chicago what Chinese restaurants are to many other American cities: ubiquitous, affordable, and perfect for a quick meal that offers a taste of the exotic. If you've never tried Thai, Chicago is a great place to start. Good introductory dishes are pad thai noodles topped with minced peanuts or the coconut-based mild yellow curry.

Arun's ★★★ (p. 139) is the city's reigning gourmet interpreter of Thai cuisine, but many other low-key places are scattered throughout the residential neighborhoods. Most entrees at these spots don't cost much more $10. A staple of the River North dining scene is the bright and airy **Star of Siam,** 11 E. Illinois St., at North State Street (✆ 312/670-0100; www.starofsiam-chicago.com). On the north end of the Gold Coast where it meets Old Town, **Tiparos,** 1540 N. Clark St. at North Avenue (✆ 312/712-9900; www.tipa-rosthai.com), is a very friendly place that features Thai textiles on its brick interior walls and serves delicious specialties such as massaman curry. **Thai Classic,**

3332 N. Clark St., at Roscoe Street (✆ 773/404-2000; www.thaiclassic restaurant.com), conveniently located between the busy Belmont/Clark intersection and Wrigley Field, offers an excellent all-you-can-eat buffet on weekends if you want to try a taste of everything. While wandering the Lakeview neighborhood, a good stop for a quick, no-frills meal is the **Bamee Noodle Shop,** 3120 N. Broadway, at Wellington Street (✆ 773/281-2641; www.bameethai.com), which offers a wide selection of "Noodles on Plates" and "Noodles in Bowls," as well as a number of soups and fried-rice combinations.

prices—this is neighborhood dining at its best. Hidden on a Lincoln Park side street, the restaurant extends through a series of cozy rooms and garden patios (front and back). The menu emphasizes pasta (rich favorites include a dense lasagna and the ravioli al Luigi, served with a sun-dried-tomato cream sauce). While RoseAngelis is not a vegetarian restaurant, per se, there's little red meat on the menu (a New York strip, and lamb and Italian sausages), and many of the pastas are served with vegetables rather than meat. Finish up with the deliciously decadent bread pudding with warm caramel sauce, which comes in a massive slice big enough to share. Stop by a weeknight to avoid the crowds (who wait up to 2 hr. for a table on weekends).

1314 W. Wrightwood Ave. (at Lakewood Ave.). ✆ **773/296-0081.** www.roseangelis.com. Reservations accepted for parties of 8 or more. Main courses $11–$18. AE, DC, DISC, MC, V. Tues–Thurs 5–10pm; Fri–Sat 5–11pm; Sun 4:30–9pm. Subway/El: Brown or Red line to Fullerton.

WRIGLEYVILLE & THE NORTH SIDE

For restaurants listed in this section, see the map "Restaurants in Lincoln Park, Old Town & Wrigleyville" on p. 132.

The area surrounding Wrigley Field has a long history as a working-class neighborhood, and although housing prices are now beyond the reach of most blue-collar workers, the neighborhood still attracts hordes of recent college grads who prefer chicken wings to truffles. Overall, restaurants here are more affordable and low-key than downtown, though most aren't worth a special trip if you're staying elsewhere. Throughout the North Side—a catch phrase encompassing the neighborhoods north of Lincoln Park—you'll find mostly casual, neighborhood restaurants and a good range of ethnic eats.

Very Expensive

Arun's ★★★ THAI Yes, Arun's is a Thai restaurant, but it's in a whole different league from the noodle shops scattered around the city. Here chef/owner Arun Sampanthavivat prepares a refined version of traditional Thai cuisine: authentic, flavorful, and beautifully presented. Rather than order individual entrees, diners feast on a 12-course chef's menu served family-style, with the dishes varying from night to night (there's also a seven-course menu available Tues–Thurs 5–7pm). You might see courses of delicate dumplings accented with edible, carved dough flowers; traditional spring rolls with morsels of Dungeness crabmeat and filled with seasoned tofu; spicy pork served on an aromatic grilled sweet pepper; or Panang beef curry. The service is as impeccable as the food, and if guests in your group have different tolerances to spicy food, they'll customize each plate and ingredients accordingly. The only downside to Arun's is its out-of-the-way location. You can get here by public transportation, but I recommend a taxi at night.

4156 N. Kedzie Ave. (at Irving Park Rd.). ✆ **773/539-1909.** www.arunsthai.com. Reservations required with credit card. 12-course chef's menu $85; 7-course chef's menu $65. AE, DC, DISC, MC, V. Tues–Thurs 5–10pm; Fri–Sat 5–10:30pm; Sun 5–10pm. Subway/El and bus: Brown Line to Irving Park, and then transfer to westbound bus 80, or take a cab.

Expensive

Yoshi's Café BISTRO Yoshi Katsumura has been a familiar name in the Chicago restaurant scene for years, and this casual bistro has been a neighborhood favorite for more than 2 decades (meaning you may wait for a table during prime weekend hours). The simple, neutral-toned dining room may look straightforward, but the menu is an intriguingly creative mix of Yoshi's native Japan and his French training. For an appetizer, tuna tartare is served on top of homemade guacamole and accompanied by tortilla chips and an oyster shooter with sake, jalapeño, and a salty-sweet sauce made from Japanese yuzu fruit; Japanese pumpkin ravioli is served with creamy garlic goat cheese sauce and herb-infused oil. Entrees include steak frites au poivre and grilled Australian lamb chops. There are always a number of vegetarian options, ranging from pasta to grilled tofu with brie and basil, topped with sweet-sesame paste and miso sauce. While the food is certainly a draw, it's the friendly, personal service that has turned many Wrigleyville residents into regulars.

3257 N. Halsted St. (at Aldine St.). ✆ **773/248-6160.** www.yoshiscafe.com. Reservations recommended. Main courses $15–$27. AE, DC, MC, V. Tues–Thurs 5–10:30pm; Fri–Sat 5–11pm; Sun 11am–2:30pm and 5–9:30pm. Subway/El: Brown or Red line to Belmont.

Moderate

Mia Francesca ★★ ITALIAN Though it's been open since 1992, Mia Francesca remains a hot dining spot—one that has spawned close to 20 sister restaurants throughout the city and suburbs. The restaurant's clean, modern take on the Italian trattoria concept attracts lots of local singles and couples, and the affordable prices keep them coming back. The food—unpretentious but never dull—includes a range of homemade pastas, thin-crust pizzas, chicken, veal, and standout seafood (even if you don't usually order fish in an Italian restaurant, it's worth trying here). Tables are packed close together, so you can't help eavesdropping on your neighbors—and checking out their food. Yes, it does get loud, but the place has an undeniable energy.

You'll find mostly the same menu at the other Francesca's locations in the city: **Francesca's on Chestnut,** 200 E. Chestnut St., just off the Magnificent Mile (✆ **312/482-8800**); **Francesca's on Taylor,** 1400 W. Taylor St., in Little Italy (✆ **312/829-2828**); and **Francesca's Bryn Mawr,** 1039 W. Bryn Mawr Ave., north of Wrigleyville (✆ **773/506-9261**).

3311 N. Clark St. (1½ blocks north of Belmont Ave.). ✆ **773/281-3310.** www.miafrancesca.com. Reservations recommended. Main courses $13–$22. AE, DISC, MC, V. Sun–Thurs 5–10pm; Fri–Sat 5–11pm; Sat–Sun 11:30am–2pm. Subway/El: Brown or Red line to Belmont.

Inexpensive

Ann Sather ★★ AMERICAN/BREAKFAST/BRUNCH/SWEDISH This is a real Chicago institution, with an old-fashioned diner-look to match. You can't go wrong ordering one of the Swedish specialties—such as meatballs with buttered noodles and brown gravy, or the Swedish sampler of duck breast with lingonberry glaze, meatball, potato-sausage dumpling, sauerkraut, and brown beans—but there are plenty of American choices, too, from catfish and crab cakes to pork chops and shepherd's pie. Sather's popular (and very affordable) weekend brunch can get frenzied, but you should be okay if you arrive before 11am. The restaurant's sticky cinnamon rolls are definitely a highlight (if you crave more—and you probably will—you can buy them at a counter up front on your way out). Sather's attracts a truly diverse crowd, and the people-watching at brunch is especially priceless: a cross-section of gay and straight, young and old, from club kids to elderly couples and families.

There are smaller cafes with similar menus at 3411 N. Broadway (☎ 773/305-0024) and 3416 N. Southport Ave. (☎ 773/404-4475).

929 W. Belmont Ave. (btw. Clark St. and Sheffield Ave.). ☎ **773/348-2378.** www.annsather.com. Reservations accepted for parties of 6 or more. Main courses $7–$11 breakfast and lunch; $11–$15 dinner. AE, DC, MC, V. Mon–Fri 7am–3pm; Sat–Sun 7am–4pm. Free parking with validation. Subway/El: Brown or Red line to Belmont.

Penny's Noodle Shop ★ 🖋 ASIAN/THAI Penny Chiamopoulous, a Thai native, has assembled a concise menu of delectable dishes, all of them fresh and made to order—and all at prices that will make you do a double take. The two dining rooms are clean and spare; single diners can usually find a seat along the bar that wraps around the grill. The Thai spring roll, filled with seasoned tofu, cucumber, bean sprouts, and strips of cooked egg, makes a refreshing starter. Of course, noodles unite everything on the menu, so your main decision is choosing among the options (crispy wide rice, rice vermicelli, Japanese udon, and so on) served in a soup or spread out on a plate.

The original Penny's, tucked under the El tracks at 3400 N. Sheffield Ave., near Wrigley Field (☎ 773/281-8222), is smaller and often has long waits. You stand a better chance of scoring a table at the Diversey Avenue location or the one in Wicker Park at 1542 N. Damen Ave. (at W. Pierce Ave.; ☎ 773/394-0100).

950 W. Diversey Ave. (at Sheffield St.). ☎ **773/281-8448.** www.pennysnoodleshop.com. Reservations not accepted. Main courses $5.50–$8.50. MC, V. Sun–Thurs 11am–10pm; Fri–Sat 11am–10:30pm. Subway/El: Brown Line to Diversey.

WICKER PARK/BUCKTOWN

The booming Wicker Park/Bucktown area followed closely on the heels of Lincoln Park and Wrigleyville in the race to gentrification. First came the artists and musicians, followed by armies of yuppies and young families—all attracted by cheap rents and real estate. The result is a well-established, happening scene, which includes some of the city's hippest restaurants and clubs. Get yourself to the nexus of activity at the intersection of North, Damen, and Milwaukee avenues, and you won't have to walk more than a couple of blocks in any direction to find a hot spot. Cab fares from downtown are reasonable, or you can take the El's Blue Line to Damen.

Expensive

Mirai Sushi ★★ JAPANESE/SUSHI Blending a serious devotion to sushi and sake with a decidedly youthful, funky-chic ambience, Mirai is a hot destination for cold raw fish (though it serves other Japanese fare as well). The futuristic second-floor lounge is the hippest place in town to slurp down sushi, chilled sakes, and "red ones," the house cocktail of vodka with passion fruit, lime, and cranberry juices. The bright main-floor dining room offers a comparatively traditional environment. Fish is flown in daily for the sushi bar, where several chefs are hard at work master-crafting a lovely list of offerings—from the beginner sushi standards such as California rolls and *ebi* (boiled shrimp) to escalating classifications of tuna (including *toro,* or fatty tuna), three types of salmon, red snapper, caviar, and four different roes.

2020 W. Division St. (at Damen Ave.). ✆ **773/862-8500.** www.miraisushi.com. Reservations recommended on weekends. Sushi $2–$6 per piece. AE, DC, DISC, MC, V. Mon–Wed 5–10pm; Thurs–Sat 5–11pm; Sun 5–10pm. Upstairs lounge until 2am. Subway/El: Blue Line to Division.

Moderate

Club Lucky ★ 🍸 ITALIAN Club Lucky is the 21st-century re-creation of a '50s-era corner tavern, with an Italian mamma cooking up family recipes in the back. The Naugahyde banquettes and Formica-topped bar and tables give the place a fun retro flair. The scene here changes throughout the evening: Young families gradually give way to stylish couples posing with glasses of the restaurant's signature martinis (be prepared to wait on weekends). The menu offers real Italian home-style cooking, such as the giant meant-to-be-shared calamari appetizer; *pasta e fagioli* (a thick macaroni-and-bean soup that's actually closer to a stew); homemade tortellini filled with chicken and herbs, served with English peas and pine nuts in vodka sauce; and spicy grilled boneless pork chops served with peppers and roasted potatoes. The lunch menu includes about a dozen Italian sandwiches, such as scrambled eggs and pesto, meatball, and Italian sausage.

1824 W. Wabansia Ave. (1 block north of North Ave., btw. Damen and Ashland aves.). ✆ **773/227-2300.** www.clubluckychicago.com. Reservations accepted. Sandwiches $8–$11; main courses $10–$36. AE, DC, DISC, MC, V. Mon–Tues 11:30am–10pm; Wed–Thurs 11:30am–10pm; Fri 11:30am–11pm; Sat 5–11pm; Sun 10:30–2:30 and 3:30–10pm; cocktail lounge later. Subway/El: Blue Line to Damen.

Hot Chocolate ★ AMERICAN Owner Mindy Segal built her reputation as a pastry chef, so no matter what you order here, make sure you save room for dessert. Though it has the sleek, contemporary look of a late-night lounge, the menu focuses on comfort food prepared with upscale, seasonal ingredients. The Tuna Melt, for example, comes with wild capers and havarti cheese on a fresh-baked baguette, while a brined and grilled pork chop is served with house-made pork sausage with sauerkraut, apples, and fennel. There's also a wide selection of specialty ales, lagers, and wines aimed at late-night diners. However, desserts are the main event here. They range from warm brioche doughnuts served with caramel corn and hot fudge to a gourmet take on peanut butter cups, accompanied by rich peanut butter cookie-dough truffles. You can even order a flight of homemade ice creams. In the winter, finish up with a cup of the signature hot chocolate.

1747 N. Damen Ave. (at Willow St.). ✆ **773/489-1747.** Reservations accepted for dinner only. www.hotchocolatechicago.com. Main courses $10–$13 lunch, $12–$27 dinner. AE, MC, V. Tues 5:30–10pm; Wed 11:30am–2pm and 5:30–10pm; Thurs 11:30am–2pm and 5:30–11pm; Fri 11:30am–2pm and 5:30pm–midnight; Sat 10am–2pm and 5:30–midnight; Sun 10am–2pm and 5:30–10pm. Subway/El: Blue Line to Damen.

Jane's ★ 🎁 AMERICAN Jane's may be overlooked by dining critics, but that does not mean snagging a table at this cozy charmer is easy. On the contrary; this is a hugely popular destination among Wicker Park/Bucktown locals, who'd prefer to keep it a secret. (Wait for your table at the friendly Bucktown Pub across the street.) Ensconced in an old house, Jane's encompasses two distinct dining rooms—the first with simple wood tables running parallel to the front bar; and a brighter back room, where the white furniture and floors create the feel of an elegant ice-cream parlor. (In the summer, a few tables are set up on

Restaurants in Wicker Park/Bucktown

BUCKTOWN

WICKER PARK

Flat Iron Building

CLEMENTE PARK

WICKER PARK

M Subway/El stop

Club Lucky **5**	Mirai Suishi **9**
Earwax Café **8**	Northside Café **6**
Hot Chocolate **3**	Piece **7**
Jane's **2**	Silver Cloud **4**
Le Bouchon **1**	

CHICAGO

THE LOOP

Wrigley Field

Map area

U.S. Cellular Field

✈ Midway

Lake Michigan

an outside patio.) The dinner menu offers upscale comfort food, including both meat (ancho barbecue spare rib with grilled pineapple and coleslaw) and vegetarian options (goat cheese, tofu, and veggie burrito). Creative sandwich options are offered at lunch, such as seared marlin topped with tarragon aioli.

1655 W. Cortland St. (1 block west of Ashland Ave.). ✆ **773/862-5263.** www.janesrestaurant. com. Reservations recommended. Main courses $14–$24. AE, MC, V. Tues–Thurs 5–10pm; Fri 11am–3pm and 5–10pm; Sat–Sun 8am–10pm. Subway/El: Blue Line to Damen.

Le Bouchon ★★ 🎁 BISTRO/FRENCH Jean-Claude Poilevey's tiny storefront restaurant is popular for both its intimate yet boisterous atmosphere and affordable, authentic bistro fare. Whatever the season, the food here is fairly heavy, although specials are lighter in warmer months. Poilevey could pack this place every night just with regulars addicted to the house specialty of roast duck for two, bathed in Grand Marnier–orange marmalade sauce. The fare covers bistro basics, with tasty versions of steak frites, sautéed rabbit in white wine sauce, veal kidneys in mustard sauce, and beef Bourguignon, most affordably priced at around $20; there's also a $25-per-person prix-fixe menu. The piped-in music and voices from the closely packed tables create an atmosphere that some perceive as convivial, and others as claustrophobic and noisy. There's a small bar where you can wait—something you might have to do even if you have a reservation.

1958 N. Damen Ave. (at Armitage Ave.). ✆ **773/862-6600.** www.lebouchonofchicago.com. Reservations recommended. Main courses $12–$15 lunch; $14–$24 dinner. AE, DC, DISC, MC, V. Mon–Sat 11:30–2:30pm; Mon–Thurs 5:30–10pm; Fri–Sat 5–11pm. Subway/El: Blue Line to Damen, and then a short cab ride.

Inexpensive

Northside Café AMERICAN Among the best cheap eats in the neighborhood, Northside cooks up great oversized burgers, sandwiches, and salads—most for $10 or less. This is strictly neighborhood dining, without attitude and little in the way of decor; the back dining room looks like a rec room circa 1973, complete with a fireplace, video games, and a pool table. In nice weather, Northside opens up its large front patio for dining, and a sky-lit cover keeps it in use during the winter. You're always sure to be entertained by people-watching here, as Northside attracts all sorts. During the week, the cafe is a neighborhood hangout, while on weekends groups of friends from Lincoln Park and the suburbs pile in. A limited late-night menu is available from 10pm to 1:30am.

1635 N. Damen Ave. (at North and Milwaukee aves.). ✆ **773/384-3555.** www.northsidechicago. com. Reservations not accepted. Menu items $8–$15. AE, DC, DISC, MC, V. Mon–Fri 11am–2am; Sat 10:30am–3am; Sun 10:30am–2am. Subway/El: Blue Line to Damen.

Piece ★ AMERICAN/PIZZA Piece finally proved to deep-dish-loving Chicagoans that thin-crust pizza deserves respect. The large, airy dining room—a former garage that's been outfitted with dark wood tables and ceiling beams—is flooded with light from the expansive skylights overhead; even when it's packed, the soaring space above keeps the place from feeling too crowded. Piece offers a selection of salads and sandwiches on satisfyingly crusty bread, but crunchy, super-thin-crust pizza in the style of New Haven, Connecticut (hometown of one of the owners), is the house specialty. Pick from four styles—plain (tomato sauce and garlic), red (tomato sauce and mozzarella), white (olive oil, garlic, and mozzarella), or barbecue (smoked barbecue sauce and mozzarella), then add on your favorite toppings. Sausage and/or spinach work well with the plain or red, but the adventurous should sample a more offbeat choice: clam and bacon on white pizza.

1927 W. North Ave. (at Milwaukee Ave.). © **773/772-4422.** www.piecechicago.com. Reservations accepted for groups of 10 or more. Pizza $11–$17. AE, DISC, MC, V. Mon–Wed 11am–10:30pm; Thurs 10:30am–11pm; Fri–Sat 11am–12:30am; Sun 11am–10pm. Subway/El: Blue Line to Damen.

Silver Cloud ★★ AMERICAN The motto of this casual cafe is "Food like Mom would make if she was gettin' paid." Indeed, Silver Cloud is comfort food central, with a laid-back pub-meets-diner decor and suitably laid back clientele. If intimate conversation is your priority, try to snag one of the roomy red-leather

---

hold the meat, PLEASE

Yes, Chicago may have a reputation as a carnivore's paradise, but that doesn't mean vegetarians should stuff their bags with dried tofu before coming here. In recent years, more and more local restaurants have made an effort to accommodate non–meat eaters. While you can order a green salad or vegetable pasta almost anywhere, here are some places where veggie offerings are the main event.

At **Green Zebra** (1460 W. Chicago Ave. [at Greenview St.]; © **312/243-7100;** www.greenzebrachicago.com), the menu is almost exclusively meat-free, and the creative small-plates menu gives diners a wide range of flavors to sample. **Reza's** ★★ (p. 125), a sprawling Middle Eastern spot in River North, may specialize in giant mixed-meat kebabs, but their vegetarian plates are generous, flavorful mixes of hummus, tabbouleh, and other traditional dishes, nicely presented in red bento boxes. At the Southern spot **Wishbone** ★★ (p. 108), in the West Loop, veggie lovers can create their own sampler plates by selecting from a wide range of side dishes.

Going vegetarian also doesn't mean giving up on gourmet dining. Two of the city's best, most creative chefs in town— **Charlie Trotter** ★★★ at his namesake restaurant (p. 131) and Michael Taus at **Zealous** ★★★ (p. 120)—offer multicourse vegetarian tasting menus. At **Crofton on Wells** ★★, in River North (p. 118), chef Suzy Crofton always includes a few meat-free options on her nightly menu. (She'll customize them for vegans, too.) In Wrigleyville, chef Yoshi

Katsumura of **Yoshi's Café** (p. 140) also offers a regular selection of vegetarian dishes featuring his signature blend of French and Asian flavors.

Vegans may find their options extremely limited on most menus, but local holistic health devotee Karyn Calabrese operates two vegan-friendly restaurants. **Karyn's Raw,** 1901 N. Halsted St. (© **312/255-1590**), in Old Town, encompasses both a casual cafe and juice bar and a white-tablecloth restaurant specializing in raw food; **Karyn's Cooked,** 738 N. Wells St. (© **312/587-1050**), in River North, offers globally inspired vegan dishes. You can check out both menus at www.karynraw. com. Farther north in Wrigleyville, **The Chicago Diner,** 3411 N. Halsted St. (© **773/935-6696;** www.veggiediner. com), might sound like the kind of place you load up on greasy burgers, but it's actually one of the city's best and longest-lasting vegetarian restaurants. (Most dishes are vegan, too.) The wide-ranging menu includes salads, sandwiches (including a "California Reuben" with seitan instead of corned beef), tacos, and pastas; for dessert, try a peanut butter or vanilla chai vegan milkshake.

booths. While the food isn't extraordinary, the restaurant does deliver consistently reliable home-style favorites: chicken potpie, grilled-cheese sandwiches with tomato soup, pot roast, sloppy Joes with a side of tater tots, s'mores, and root beer floats. While Silver Cloud attracts a mix of families, couples, and groups of friends during the day and early evening hours, it becomes more of a cocktail lounge at night. *A **warning for those with sensitive ears:*** The jukebox volume gets turned up at night, too. The Sunday brunch is especially popular; the "Hangover Helpers" attract a fair amount of hip young things recovering from nightly adventures.

1700 N. Damen Ave. (at Wabansia St.). © **773/489-6212.** www.silvercloudchicago.com. Main courses $6–$10 lunch, $10–$16 dinner. AE, DC, MC, V. Mon–Thurs 11:30am–11pm; Fri 11:30am–midnight; Sat–Sun 10am–11pm. Bar stays open later every night except Sun. Subway/El: Blue Line to Damen.

RESTAURANTS BY CUISINE

ALSATIAN
Everest ★★★ ($$$$, p. 94)

AMERICAN
Ann Sather ★★ ($, p. 140)
Atwood Café ★★ ($$$, p. 94)
The Berghoff ★ ($$, p. 100)
Bin 36 ★★ ($$$, p. 121)
Boka ★ ($$$, p. 135)
Carson's ★ ($$, p. 124)
Charlie's Ale House ($, p. 129)
Charlie's Ale House at Navy Pier
    ($, p. 128)
Crofton on Wells ★★ ($$$$, p. 118)
Custom House Tavern ★★
    ($$$, p. 96)
Dave & Buster's ($, p. 101)
Ditka's ★ ($$$, p. 112)
The Gage ★ ($$$, p. 96)
Girl and the Goat ★ ($$$, p. 104)
Goose Island Brewing Company
    ($, p. 137)
Graham Elliot ★★ ($$$$, p. 119)
Harry Caray's Italian Steakhouse
    ($$$, p. 122)
Hot Chocolate ★ ($$, p. 142)
Hot Doug's ($, p. 117)
HUB 51 ★★ ($$, p. 125)
Jane's ★ ($$, p. 142)
Lou Mitchell's ($, p. 126)
mk ★★★ ($$$$, p. 119)
Moody's ($, p. 129)
Naha ★★ ($$$$, p. 120)
Nine ★ ($$$, p. 97)
North Pond ★★★ ($$$$, p. 134)

Northside Café ($, p. 144)
Oak Street Beachstro ($$, p. 128)
Oak Tree ★ ($, p. 118)
O'Brien's Restaurant ($, p. 129)
one sixtyblue ★★ ($$$$, p. 103)
Orange ($, p. 127)
Park Grill ★★ ($$$, p. 97)
Perennial Virant ★★ ($$$, p. 135)
Petterino's ★★ ($$$, p. 97)
Piece ★ ($, p. 144)
Portillo's ★★ ($, p. 130)
Rhapsody ★★ ($$$, p. 98)
Rockit Bar & Grill ★ ($$, p. 126)
Sable Kitchen & Bar ★ ($$, p. 127)
Sepia ★★★ ($$$, p. 105)
The Signature Room at the 95th ★
    ($$$, p. 113)
Silver Cloud ★★ ($, p. 145)
South Water Kitchen ★ ($$$, p. 99)
Superdawg Drive-In ($, p. 117)
Table Fifty-Two ★ ($$$, p. 113)
Tavern at the Park ★ ($$$, p. 99)
Toast ($, p. 101)
ZED 451 ★★ ($$$, p. 124)

ASIAN
Penny's Noodle Shop ★ ($, p. 141)

BARBECUE
Carson's ★ ($$, p. 124)
Chicago q ★★ ($$, p. 114)
Twin Anchors ★ ($$, p. 137)

BISTRO
Bistronomic ★★ ($$, p. 114)
Bistrot Margot ★★ ($$, p. 136)

WHERE TO EAT   Restaurants by Cuisine

Cyrano's Bistrot & Wine Bar ★
($$, p. 125)
La Sardine ★ ($$$, p. 105)
Le Bouchon ★★ ($$, p. 144)
Mon Ami Gabi ★ ($$$, p. 135)
The Publican ★ ($$$, p. 105)
Yoshi's Café ($$$, p. 140)

BREAKFAST/BRUNCH/ BAKERY

Ann Sather ★★ ($, p. 140)
The Café, Four Seasons Hotel ($$$, p. 126)
Drake Bros. Restaurant, The Drake Hotel ($$, p. 126)
Earwax Café ($, p. 127)
Eli's Bakery ($, p. 112)
House of Blues ($$, p. 315)
Lou Mitchell's ($, p. 126)
Nookies ($, p. 126)
Orange ($, p. 127)
Toast ($, p. 101)
Wishbone ★★ ($, p. 108)

CAJUN & CREOLE

Heaven on Seven ★★ ($, p. 101)
House of Blues ($$, p. 315)

CALIFORNIAN

Puck's at the MCA ($, p. 128)

CHINESE

Happy Chef ($, p. 106)
Phoenix ($$, p. 106)
Saint's Alp Teahouse ($, p. 106)
Shiu Wah ($, p. 106)
Won Kow ($, p. 106)

DINER

Ed Debevic's ($, p. 101)
Heaven on Seven ★★ ($, p. 101)
Lou Mitchell's ($, p. 126)
Nookies ($, p. 126)

FAST FOOD

Billy Goat Tavern ★ ($, p. 117)
foodlife ★★ ($, p. 118)
Gold Coast Dogs ($, p. 117)
Mr. Beef ★ ($, p. 130)
Murphy's Red Hots ($, p. 117)
Portillo's ★★ ($, p. 130)
Potbelly Sandwich Works ($, p. 138)

Superdawg Drive-In ($, p. 117)
The Wieners Circle ($, p. 117)

FONDUE

Geja's Cafe ★ ($$$$, p. 134)

FRENCH

Bistro 110 ($$$, p. 112)
Bistronomic ★★ ($$, p. 114)
Bistrot Margot ★★ ($$, p. 136)
Cyrano's Bistrot & Wine Bar ★ ($$, p. 125)
Everest ★★★ ($$$$, p. 94)
La Creperie ★★ ($, p. 137)
La Sardine ★ ($$$, p. 105)
Le Bouchon ★★ ($$, p. 144)
Le Colonial ★★ ($$, p. 114)
Mon Ami Gabi ★ ($$$, p. 135)
Tru ★★★ ($$$$, p. 110)

GERMAN

The Berghoff ★ ($$, p. 100)

GREEK

Artopolis ($, p. 107)
Athena ★ ($$, p. 128)
Costas ($$, p. 107)
Greek Islands ($$, p. 107)
Parthenon ($$, p. 107)
Pegasus ($$, p. 107)
Santorini ($$, p. 107)

INDIAN

Vermilion ★ ($$$, p. 124)

IRISH

The Gage ★ ($$$, p. 96)

ITALIAN

Buca di Beppo ($$, p. 101)
Club Lucky ★ ($$, p. 142)
Davanti Enoteca ($$, p. 106)
Francesca's on Taylor ($$, p. 140)
Gene & Georgetti ★ ($$$, p. 122)
Gioco ★ ($$$, p. 96)
Harry Caray's Italian Steakhouse ($$$, p. 122)
The Italian Village ★ ($$, p. 100)
Maggiano's ($, p. 101)
Mia Francesca ★★ ($$, p. 140)
Osteria Via Stato ★★ ($$$, p. 123)
RoseAngelis ★★ ($, p. 138)

Rosebud on Taylor ★ ($$, p. 106)
Spiaggia ★★★ ($$$$, p. 110)
312 Chicago ★ ($$$, p. 99)
Trattoria No. 10 ($$$, p. 99)
Tuscany ($$, p. 107)

JAPANESE

Mirai Sushi ★★ ($$$, p. 141)
Sushi Wabi ★ ($$$, p. 108)

LATIN AMERICAN

Carnivale ★ ($$$, p. 104)
Nacional 27 ★ ($$$, p. 122)
SushiSamba Rio ★★ ($$$, p. 123)
Vermilion ★ ($$$, p. 124)

MEDITERRANEAN

Avec ★ ($$, p. 104)
The Purple Pig ★★ ($$, p. 115)

MEXICAN

Adobo Grill ($$, p. 136)
Café Jumping Bean ($, p. 107)
Frontera Grill, Topolobampo & Xoco
 ★★★ ($$$, p. 121)
Nuevo Leon ($, p. 107)

MIDDLE EASTERN

Reza's ★★ ($$, p. 125)

NEW AMERICAN

Alinea ★★★ ($$$$, p. 131)
Blackbird ★★★ ($$$$, p. 102)
Charlie Trotter's ★★★ ($$$$, p. 131)
Moto ★★★ ($$$$, p. 103)
Next ★★★ ($$$, p. 103)
Tru ★★★ ($$$$, p. 110)
Zealous ★★★ ($$$$, p. 120)

PIZZA

Chicago Pizza & Oven Grinder ($, p. 116)
Edwardo's ($, p. 116)
Gino's East ★★ ($$, p. 125)
Giordano's ($, p. 116)
Lou Malnati's Pizzeria ★ ($, p. 116)
Piece ★ ($, p. 144)
Pizzeria Due ($, p. 130)
Pizzeria Uno ★ ($, p. 130)

POLISH

Red Apple ($, p. 108)

RUSSIAN

Russian Tea Time ★★ ($$$, p. 98)

SEAFOOD

Cape Cod Room ($$$$, p. 109)
La Cantina Enoteca ($$, p. 100)
L20 ★★★ ($$$$, p. 134)
Shaw's Crab House ★★ ($$, p. 115)

SOUTHERN

House of Blues ($$, p. 315)
Wishbone ★★ ($, p. 108)

SPANISH & TAPAS

Café Ba-Ba-Reeba! ★ ($$, p. 136)
Café Iberico ★★ ($, p. 129)
Mercat a la Planxa ★★ ($$$, p. 97)
Tapas Gitana ★ ($, p. 129)

STEAK

Chicago Cut Steakhouse ★★
 ($$$, p. 121)
Ditka's ★ ($$$, p. 112)
Gene & Georgetti ★ ($$$, p. 122)
Gibsons Bar & Steakhouse ★★ ($$$$,
 p. 109)
Harry Caray's Italian Steakhouse
 ($$$, p. 122)
Morton's ★★ ($$$$, p. 109)
Nine ★ ($$$, p. 97)
Petterino's ★★ ($$$, p. 97)

SUSHI

Mirai Sushi ★★ ($$$, p. 141)
SushiSamba Rio ★★ ($$$, p. 123)
Sushi Wabi ★ ($$$, p. 108)

SWEDISH

Ann Sather ★★ ($, p. 140)

TEA

The Greenhouse, Ritz-Carlton Hotel ($$$,
 p. 110)
The Lobby, The Peninsula Hotel ($$$,
 p. 110)
Palm Court, The Drake Hotel ($$$, p. 110)
Russian Tea Time ★★ ($$$, p. 98)
Seasons Lounge, Four Seasons Hotel
 ($$$, p. 110)

THAI
Arun's ★★★ ($$$$, p. 139)
Bamee Noodle Shop ($, p. 138)
Penny's Noodle Shop ★
  ($, p. 141)
Star of Siam ($, p. 138)
Thai Classic ($, p. 138)
Tiparos ($, p. 138)

VEGETARIAN
Green Zebra ($, p. 145)
Karyn's Cooked ($, p. 145)
Karyn's Raw ($, p. 145)
The Chicago Diner ($, p. 145)

New on the Scene

To find out more about restaurants that have opened since this book went to press, check out the *Chicago Tribune*'s entertainment website (**www.metromix.com**), the websites for the monthly magazine *Chicago* (**www.chicagomag.com**) and the weekly *Time Out Chicago* (**www.timeoutchicago. com**), and the local foodie website LTH Forum (**www.lthforum.com/bb/index.php**).

VIETNAMESE
Le Colonial ★★ ($$, p. 114)

PRACTICAL INFORMATION
The Big Picture

Most restaurants in Chicago are open 7 days a week. A few in the Loop are closed on Sunday evenings, while some others are closed on Mondays (traditionally a slow night). In general, Chicago is not a late-night dining town. Most locals head out to dinner between 6 and 7pm, and the majority of restaurants are closed by 10pm on weeknights and 11pm on weekends. If you plan on heading out for a late dinner, you should definitely check the restaurant's closing time first.

A few restaurants with popular bar areas—such as **Rockit Bar and Grill** and **HUB 51**—keep their kitchens open until midnight or later on weekends. For suggestions on where to eat when most other restaurants have closed, see "Late-Night Bites," in chapter 9 (p. 322).

Overall, the restaurant scene in Chicago is casual; the locals go out to enjoy their food, not to score style points or check each other out. Only a handful of restaurants require jackets for men; even ties are optional at all but the most formal places. A business-casual look is appropriate for just about every restaurant in town, and at the moderately priced places, most customers show up in jeans and sneakers. That said, the higher the average entrée price, the more you're expected to make a modest effort: Showing up at Alinea or Blackbird in scuffed Nikes or shorts won't impress the waitstaff or your fellow diners.

Getting the Best Deal

Prices at Chicago restaurants are among the highest in the country. But there are a few ways you can bring down the price of your bill. The website Restaurant. com allows members to purchase $25 worth of gift certificates to select restaurants for only $10; it's free to join, and there are usually a few dozen places in Chicago to choose from.

It's also worth checking a restaurant's website to see if they're offering any discounts or specials; occasionally, restaurants will also post coupons online.

Restaurants that cater to the theater-going crowd in the Loop sometimes offer prix-fixe meals that cost less than ordering the same courses separately. Such deals tend to be available in the early evening, before the main dinner rush.

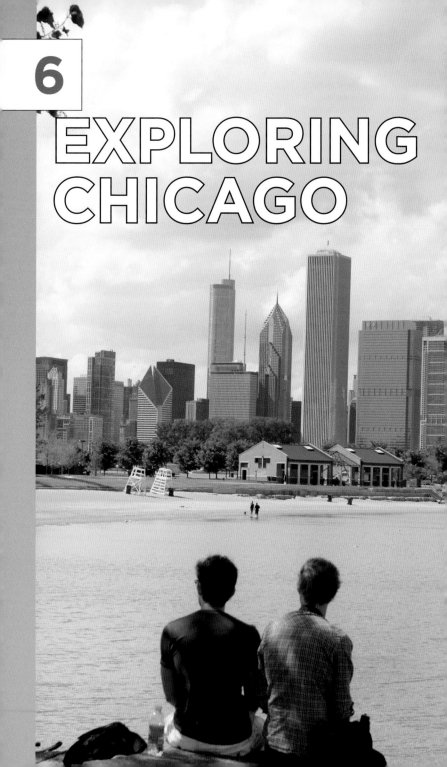

6

EXPLORING CHICAGO

F rom the bustle of the Loop on a weekday morning to the tranquility of Lake Michigan on a cool fall afternoon, Chicago is an experience in contrasts. Its cultural offerings and historic attractions draw seasoned international travelers, but the city's mix of family-friendly museums, beautiful parks, and iconic skyscrapers also attract vacationers of all ages. The fun—and the challenge—is to fit everything in one trip. You can put together a full itinerary each day and still have plenty left over for your next visit.

What you see will depend on your interests and stamina. The city's museums alone could keep you busy for at least a week. (If you don't have that much time, the top three exhibits that shouldn't be missed are the Impressionist masterpieces at the Art Institute of Chicago; Sue, the biggest *Tyrannosaurus rex* fossil ever discovered, at the Field Museum of Natural History; and the U-505 submarine at the Museum of Science and Industry). Come summertime, a stroll through picturesque Lincoln Park Zoo on the Near North Side is the perfect way to spend an afternoon; the setting makes it worth visiting even if you don't have kids along. (**Added bonus:** It's free!)

From a traveler's perspective, visiting Chicago is especially hassle-free because the majority of the places you'll want to see are in or near downtown, making it easy to plan your day and get from place to place. And because this is a town with a thriving tourist economy, you have plenty of guided sightseeing options: walking tours of famous architecture, boat cruises on Lake Michigan, and even bus tours of notorious gangster sites. If you're lucky enough to visit when the weather's nice, you can join the locals at the parks and the beaches along Lake Michigan.

Extensive public transportation makes it simple to reach almost every tourist destination, but some of your best memories of Chicago may come from simply strolling along the sidewalks. Chicago's neighborhoods have their own distinct styles and looks, and you'll have a more memorable experience if you don't limit yourself solely to the prime tourist spots. And if you *really* want to talk about da Bears or da Cubs, chances are, you'll find someone who's more than happy to join in.

IN & AROUND THE LOOP: THE ART INSTITUTE, THE SEARS TOWER & GRANT PARK

The heart of the Loop is Chicago's business center, where you'll find some of the city's most famous early skyscrapers, the Chicago Board of Trade (the world's largest commodities, futures, and options exchange), and the Sears Tower (officially renamed the Willis Tower, though Chicagoans still refer to the landmark high-rise by its original name). If you're looking for an authentic big-city

FACING PAGE: **In the summer, Chicagoans flock to the Lake Michigan.**

Chicago Attractions

STREETER-
VILLE

RIVER
NORTH

THE LOOP

SOUTH
LOOP

GREEK-
TOWN

UNIVERSITY
OF ILLINOIS
AT CHICAGO

*Monroe
Harbor*

**Shedd
Aquarium** 33

**Field Museum
of Natural History** 32

Chicago River

Harbor Dr.

Field Blvd.

E. Randolph Dr.

S. Lake Shore Dr.

Columbus Dr.

E. Monroe Dr.

Art Institute
of Chicago

E. Jackson Dr.

E. Congress Pkwy.

E. Harrison St.

E. Balbo Dr.

GRANT PARK

Roosevelt Rd.
Station

E. North Water St.
E. Wacker Dr.
E. Illinois St.
E. Grand Ave.
E. Ohio St.

Columbus Dr.

N. Stetson Ave.

MILLENNIUM
PARK

Randolph

Madison

Monroe

Adams

Jackson

Library

S. Michigan Ave.

S. Wabash Ave.

S. E. 8th St.

S. State St.

S. Plymouth Ct.

Dearborn St.

S. Federal St.

S. Clark St.

S. LaSalle St.

S. Sherman St.

S. Wells St.

W. Congress Pkwy.

S. Branch Chicago River

W. Polk St.

Roosevelt/
Wabash

S. Roosevelt Rd.

N. Wabash Ave.

N. State St.

N. Dearborn St.

N. Clark St.

N. LaSalle St.

N. Wells St.

N. Franklin St.

State
Clark/Lake

W. Madison St.

W. Monroe St.

W. Quincy

Washington

W. Monroe St.

Franklin St.

**Sears
Tower**

N. Wacker Dr.
S. Wacker Dr.

N. Canal St.

N. Clinton St.

N. Jefferson St.

N. Des Plaines St.

**Union
Station**

W. Adams St.

W. Jackson Blvd.

W. Van Buren St.

Eisenhower Expwy.

Halsted/U of I

S. Canal St.

S. Clinton St.

S. Jefferson St.

S. Des Plaines St.

S. Green St.

S. Peoria St.

S. Morgan St.

S. Halsted St.

W. Taylor St.

N. Kingsbury

N. Milwaukee Ave.

W. Grand Ave.

W. Hubbard St.

W. Kinzie St.

N. Sangamon St.

N. Peoria St.

N. Green St.

W. Fulton St.

W. Lake St.

W. Randolph St.

W. Washington Blvd.

W. Madison St.

W. Monroe St.

N. Morgan St.

W. Ohio St.
W. Grand Ave.
W. Illinois St.
W. Hubbard St.

N. Kinzie St.

Merch Mart

Clinton

W. Harrison St.

Subway/El stop

1/4 mi

0.25 km

153

and Outsider Art **7**

Jane Addams Hull-House
Museum **30**

John G. Shedd Aquarium **33**

Lincoln Park Conservatory **1**

Lincoln Park Zoo **2**

McCormick Tribute Bridgehouse
& Chicago River Museum **15**

Museum of Contemporary Art **11**

Museum of Contemporary
Photography **28**

National Veterans Art Museum **31**

Navy Pier **13**

Newberry Library **8**

North Avenue Beach **3**

Oak Street Beach **6**

Peggy Notebaert
Nature Museum **1**

Polish Museum of America **7**

Pritzker Music Pavilion **17**

The Rookery **20**

Sears Tower Skydeck **18**

The Seated Lincoln **23**

Spertus Institute of
Jewish Studies **29**

experience, wander the area on a weekday, when commuters are rushing to catch trains and businesspeople are hustling to get to work. The Loop is also home to one of the city's top museums, the Art Institute of Chicago, as well as a number of cultural institutions including the Symphony Center (home of the Chicago Symphony Orchestra), the Auditorium Theatre, the Civic Opera House, the Goodman Theatre, and two fabulously restored historic theaters along Randolph Street. On

the eastern edge of the Loop in Grant Park, three popular museums are conveniently located within a quick stroll of each other on the landscaped Museum Campus. Busy Lake Shore Drive, which brings cars zipping past the Museum Campus, was actually rerouted a few years ago to make the area easier to navigate for pedestrians.

The Top Attractions in the Loop

For a map of these attractions (or this neighborhood), see p. 152.

Art Institute of Chicago ★★★ ☺ You can't—and shouldn't—miss the Art Institute. No matter what medium or century interests you, the Art Institute has something in its collection to fit the bill. Japanese *ukiyo-e* prints, ancient Egyptian bronzes, Greek vases, 19th-century British photography, masterpieces by most of the greatest names in 20th-century sculpture, and modern American

The Art Institute of Chicago.

textiles are just some of the works on display, but for a general overview of the museum's collection, take the free "Highlights of the Art Institute" tour, offered at 2pm on Tuesday, Saturday, and Sunday.

If time is limited, head straight to the museum's renowned galleries of **Impressionist art ★★★**, which include one of the world's largest collections of Monet paintings; this is one of the most popular areas of the museum, so arriving early pays off. Among the treasures, you'll find Seurat's pointillist masterpiece *Sunday Afternoon on the Island of La Grande Jatte.* The **Modern Wing ★★** houses works by modern masters such as Picasso, Matisse, de Kooning, and Pollock, as well as rotating exhibits of contemporary art. Confusingly, American modern art from before 1950 is tucked into a separate gallery in the main building, but it's well worth making a detour to see the icons

The Art Institute of Chicago's Impressionist Art Gallery includes masterpieces by artists like Monet and Seurat.

that hang there (Grant Wood's *American Gothic,* Edward Hopper's *Nighthawks*).

Often overlooked but worth seeing are the Arthur Rubloff collection of delicate mid-19th-century **glass paperweights,** and the great hall of **European arms and armor ★**, dating from the 15th to the 19th centuries. Composed of more than 1,500 objects, including armor, horse equipment, swords and daggers, polearms, and maces, the collection is one of the most important assemblages of its kind in the country. (If you do head down here, you'll see Marc Chagall's stunning stained-glass windows at the end of the gallery.)

The **Ryan Education Center** on the first floor of the Modern Wing has workstations where children can create their own works of art or pick up a list of "gallery games" to make visiting the museum more fun. Another good stop for children is the **Thorne Miniature Rooms ★**, filled with tiny reproductions of furnished interiors from European and American history (heaven for dollhouse fanatics).

The museum has a cafeteria, an elegant full-service restaurant with Millennium Park views, and a large gift shop. It offers a busy schedule of lectures, films, and other special presentations, as well as guided tours. The museum also has a research library. Allow 3 hours.

Touring the Art Institute

If you want to enjoy your favorite masterpieces in something resembling peace and quiet, put some thought into the timing of your visit to the Art Institute, a museum so popular that it draws as much traffic as our jammed expressways.

Some tips for avoiding the rush hour: Many people don't realize the museum is open on Monday; keep this secret to yourself, and visit when the galleries are relatively subdued. Also, many visitors aren't aware that the museum stays open late on Thursdays, so consider stopping by after an early dinner.

111 S. Michigan Ave. (at Adams St.). (*C*) **312/443-3600.** www.artic.edu. Admission $18 adults, $12 seniors and students with ID, free for children 13 and under. Free admission 1st and 2nd Wed of the month. Mon–Fri 10:30am–5pm (Thurs until 8pm year-round, Fri until 8pm Memorial Day to Labor Day); Sat–Sun 10am–5pm. Closed Jan 1, Thanksgiving, and Christmas. Bus: 3, 4, 60, 145, 147, or 151. Subway/El: Green, Brown, Purple, or Orange line to Adams, or Red Line to Monroe/State or Jackson/State.

Sears Tower Skydeck First Sears sold the building and moved to cheaper suburban offices in 1992. Next, the Petronas Towers in Kuala Lumpur, Malaysia, claimed the title of world's tallest building, followed by the Burj Khalifa in Dubai. Then came the final blow: In 2009, this iconic landmark was officially renamed Willis Tower, after the international insurance company that became its main tenant. Real-estate deals aside, Chicagoans stubbornly insist on calling it the Sears Tower, so feel free to do so as well.

Despite the fact that this observation area on the 103rd floor is called a "skydeck," you can't actually walk outside, but the panoramas are impressive nonetheless: On a clear day, visibility extends up to 50 miles and you can catch glimpses of four surrounding states. The most nerve-wracking viewing spot is the Ledge, a series of clear observation boxes that jut out from the side of the building: Step out, and there's nothing between you and the ground but a layer of see-through glass. Inside the Skydeck, multimedia exhibits on Chicago history and *Knee High Chicago,* an exhibit for kids, add some perspective to what you're seeing outside. Be forewarned that in the summer you may be stuck in a very long, very noisy line in the lobby, so by the time you make it to the top, your patience could be as thin as the atmosphere up there. (Come in the late afternoon or early evening to avoid most of the crowds.) The 70-second high-speed elevator trip will feel like a thrill ride for some, but it's a nightmare for anyone with even mild claustrophobia. Allow 1 hour, more if there's a long line.

Step out onto the Sears Tower Skydeck's "Ledge", a nerve-wracking (and exciting!) vantage point.

The panoramic view from the Skydeck.

233 S. Wacker Dr. (enter on Jackson Blvd.). © **312/875-9696.** www.the-skydeck.com. Admission $17 adults, $11 seniors and children 3–11, free for children 2 and under. Apr–Sept daily 9am–10pm; Oct–Mar daily 10am–8pm. Bus: 1, 7, 126, 146, 151, or 156. Subway/El: Brown, Purple, or Orange line to Quincy, or Red or Blue line to Jackson; and then walk a few blocks west.

The Loop Sculpture Tour

Grand monuments, statues, and contemporary sculptures are scattered in parks throughout Chicago, but the concentration of public art within the Loop and nearby Grant Park is worth noting. The best known of these works are by 20th-century artists including Picasso, Chagall, Miró, Calder, Moore, and Oldenburg. The newest addition is the massive elliptical sculpture *Cloud Gate* (known as "The Bean" because it looks like a giant silver kidney bean) by British artist Anish Kapoor. The sculpture, in Millennium Park, was Kapoor's first public commission in the U.S.

A free brochure, *The Chicago Public Art Guide* (available at the Chicago Cultural Center, 78 E. Washington St.), can help steer you toward the best examples of monumental public art. You can also conduct a self-guided tour of the city's best public sculptures by following "The Loop Sculpture Tour" map (p. 159).

The single most famous sculpture in Chicago is **Pablo Picasso's *Untitled,*** located in Daley Plaza and constructed out of Cor-Ten steel, the same gracefully rusting material used on the exterior of the Daley Center behind it. Viewed from various perspectives, its enigmatic shape suggests a woman, bird, or dog; the artist himself never discussed its inspiration or meaning. Perhaps because it was the first monumental modern sculpture in Chicago's conservative business center, its installation in 1967 was met with hoots and heckles, but today "The Picasso" enjoys semiofficial status as the logo of modern Chicago. It is by far the city's most popular photo opportunity among visiting tourists. At noon on weekdays during warm weather, you'll likely find a dance troupe, musical group, or visual-arts exhibition here as part of the city's long-running "Under the Picasso" multicultural program. Call ℰ 312/346-3278 for event information.

Grant Park & Millennium Park

For a map of these attractions (or this neighborhood), see p. 152.

Thanks to architect Daniel Burnham and his coterie of visionary civic planners—who drafted the revolutionary 1909 Plan of Chicago—the city boasts a wide-open lakefront park system unrivaled by most major metropolises. Modeled after the gardens at Versailles, **Grant Park** (ℰ 312/742-**PLAY** [7529]; www.chicago parkdistrict.com) is Chicago's front yard, composed of giant

FROM TOP: Anish Kapoor's *Cloud Gate*. ABOVE: The single most famous sculpture in Chicago is Pablo Picasso's *Untitled*.

The Loop Sculpture Tour

1 *Untitled ("The Picasso")*, Pablo Picasso (1967)
2 *Chicago*, Joan Miro (1981)
3 *Monument with Standing Beast*,
   Jean Dubuffet (1984)
4 *Freeform*, Richard Hunt (1993)
5 *Flight of Daedalus and Icarus*, Roger Brown (1990)
6 *Dawn Shadows*, Louise Nevelson (1983)
7 *Loomings* and *Knights and Squires*, Frank Stella
8 *Batcolumn*, Claes Oldenburg (1977)
9 *The Universe*, Alexander Calder (1974)
10 *Gem of the Lakes*, Raymond Kaskey (1990)
11 *San Marco II*, Ludovico de Luigi (1986)

12 *The Town-Ho's Story*, Frank Stella (1993)
13 *Ruins III*, Nita K. Sutherland (1978)
14 *Flamingo*, Alexander Calder (1974)
15 *Lines in Four Directions*, Sol Lewitt (1985)
16 *The Four Seasons*, Marc Chagall (1974)
17 *Untitled Sounding Sculpture*, Harry Bertoia (1975)
18 *Cloud Gate*, Anish Kapoor (2004)
19 *Large Interior Form*, Henry Moore (1983)
20 *Celebration of the 200th Anniversary
   of the Founding of the Republic*,
   Isamu Noguchi (1976)
21 *The Fountain of the Great Lakes*, Lorado Taft (1913)

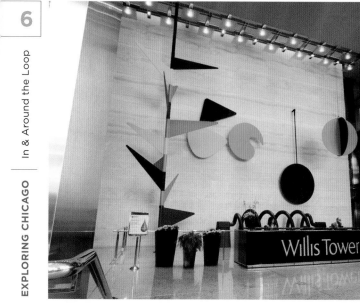

Alexander Calder's *The Universe,* in the Willis Tower.

Joan Miro's *Chicago.*

Henry Moore's *Large Interior Form.*

Grant Park.

lawns segmented by *allées* of trees, plantings, and paths, and pieced together by major roadways and a network of railroad tracks. Incredibly, the entire expanse was created from sandbars, landfill, and debris from the Great Chicago Fire; the original shoreline extended all the way to Michigan Avenue. A few museums are spread out inside the park, but most of the space is wide open (a legacy of mail-order magnate Aaron Montgomery Ward's late-19th-c. campaign to limit municipal buildings).

The northwest corner of Grant Park (bordered by Michigan Ave. and Randolph St.) is the site of **Millennium Park ★★★**, one of the city's grandest public works projects. Who cares that the park cost hundreds of millions more than it was supposed to, or the fact that it finally opened a full 4 years *after* the actual millennium? It's a winning combination of beautiful landscaping, elegant architecture (the classically inspired peristyle), and public entertainment spaces (including an ice rink and theater). The park's centerpiece is the dramatic Frank Gehry–designed **Pritzker Music Pavilion,** featuring massive curved ribbons of steel. The Grant Park Symphony Orchestra and Chorus stages a popular series of free outdoor classical music concerts here most Wednesday through Sunday evenings in the summer. For a schedule of concert times and dates, contact the **Grant Park Music Festival** (© **312/742-7638;** www.grantparkmusicfestival. com). Two public artworks well worth checking out are the kidney bean–shaped sculpture *Cloud Gate* and the *Crown Fountain,* where children splash in the shallow water between giant faces projected on video screens. Free walking tours of the park are offered daily from May through October at 11:30am and 1pm, starting at the park's Welcome Center, 201 E. Randolph St. (© **312/742-1168;** www.millenniumpark.org).

During the summer, a variety of music and food festivals take over central Grant Park. Annual events that draw big crowds include a blues music festival (in June) and a jazz festival (Labor Day). The **Taste of Chicago** (© 312/744-3315; www.cityofchicago. org/specialevents) is purportedly the largest food festival in the world, with attendance estimated at 3.5 million people during the 10 days leading up to the 4th of July. Local restaurants serve up more ribs, pizza, hot dogs, and beer than you'd ever want to see, let alone eat. (See chapter 3 for a comprehensive listing of summer events in Grant Park.)

Head south to the lake via Congress Parkway, and you'll find **Buckingham Fountain** ★, the baroque centerpiece of Grant Park, composed of pink Georgia marble and patterned after—but twice the size

TOP: Millennium Park's centerpiece, the Frank Gehry-designed Pritzker Music Pavilion.
ABOVE: An outdoor concert at the Pritzker Pavilion.

of—the *Latona Fountain* at Versailles, with adjoining esplanades beautified by rose gardens in season. From April through October, the fountain spurts columns of water up to 150 feet in the air every hour on the hour, and beginning at 4pm, a whirl of colored lights and dramatic music amps up the drama. The fountain shuts down at 11pm; concession areas and bathrooms are available on the plaza.

Sculptures and monuments stand throughout the park, including a sculpture of two Native Americans on horseback, *The Bowman and the Spearman* (at Congress Pkwy. and Michigan Ave.), which was installed in 1928 and has become the park's trademark. Also here are likenesses of Copernicus, Columbus, and Lincoln, the latter by the great American sculptor Augustus Saint-Gaudens, located on Congress Parkway between Michigan Avenue and Columbus Drive. On the western edge of the park, at Adams Street, is the **Art Institute** (see above), and at the southern tip, in the area known as the Museum Campus, are the **Field Museum of Natural History,** the **Adler Planetarium,** and the **Shedd Aquarium** (see below for all three).

To get to Grant Park, take bus no. 3, 4, 6, 146, or 151. If you want to take the subway/El, get off at any stop in the Loop along State or Wabash streets, and walk east.

TOP: **The Loop's Buckingham Fountain spurts columns of water 150 feet in the air on the hour.** ABOVE: *The Bowman and the Spearman.*

💬 Did You Know?

Croatian sculptor Ivan Mestrovic titled his bronze sculpture of Indian warriors on horseback *The Bowman and the Spearman;* however, Mestrovic intentionally omitted the warriors' bows, arrows, and spears to make an antiwar statement.

Along South Michigan Avenue

For a map of these attractions (or this neighborhood), see p. 152.

The high-fashion boutiques may be clustered along the Magnificent Mile, but aesthetically, Chicago's grandest stretch of boulevard is still the stretch of Michigan Avenue that runs south of the river. Running from the Michigan Avenue Bridge all the way down to the Field Museum, it serves as the boundary between Grant Park on one side and the Loop on the other. A stroll along this boulevard in any season offers both visual and cultural treats. Particularly impressive is the great wall of buildings from Randolph Street south to Congress Parkway (beginning with the Chicago Cultural Center and terminating at the Auditorium Building) that architecture buffs refer to as the "Michigan Avenue Cliff."

The following attractions are listed from north to south.

McCormick Tribune Bridgehouse & Chicago River Museum 🎁 Chicago has more moveable bridges than any other city in the world, and this modest museum provides a glimpse into the machinery that operates them. Although it's located on one of the busiest corners in town—at the southwest corner of the Michigan Avenue Bridge—the entrance is easy to miss. (You have to walk down a flight of stone steps to river level.) Inside, as you walk up the bridgehouse's five floors, historic engravings and photos trace the history of the city as it relates to the river (including the engineering feat that reversed the river's flow). The coolest part is the observation deck directly under the bridge, where you can gawk at the massive gears while listening to the pounding of traffic overhead. To see the gears in action, reserve a spot during one of the scheduled bridge lifts, which take place about six times a month; admission is $10 per person. (Check the museum's website for dates.)

376 N. Michigan Ave. (at the Chicago River). ✆ **312/977-0227.** www.bridgehousemuseum. org/home. Admission $4, seniors and children 6–12 $3, free for children 5 and under. May–Oct

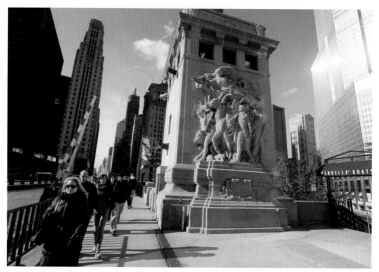

Michigan Avenue Bridge.

The Chicago Cultural Center's Tiffany dome.

Thurs–Mon 10am–5pm. Bus: 3, 4, 20, 56, 145, 146, 147, 151, or 157. Subway/El: Brown, Green, Orange, or Purple line to Randolph, or Red Line to Washington.

Chicago Cultural Center ★ 📱 The Chicago Cultural Center was built in 1897 as the city's public library, and in 1991, it was transformed into a show-place for visual and performing arts. Today it's an often-overlooked civic treasure with a formal Beaux Arts exterior and a sumptuous interior of rare marble; fine hardwood; stained glass; and mosaics of Favrile glass, colored stone, and mother-of-pearl inlaid in white marble. The crowning centerpiece is the **Tiffany dome** ★ inside Preston Bradley Hall on the 2nd floor, said to be the largest of its kind in the world.

The building also houses a **Chicago Office of Tourism** visitor center, which makes it an ideal place to kick-start your visit. If you stop in to pick up tourist information and take a quick look around, your visit won't take longer than 15 minutes, but the Cultural Center also schedules an array of art exhibitions, concerts, films, lectures, and other special events (many free), which might convince you to extend your time here. A long-standing tradition is the 12:15pm Dame Myra Hess Memorial classical concert every Wednesday in the Preston Bradley Hall.

Free guided architectural tours of the Cultural Center run at 1:15pm on Wednesday, Friday, and Saturday.

78 E. Washington St. ✆ **312/FINE-ART** [744-6630] for weekly events. www.chicagocultural center.org. Free admission. Mon–Thurs 9am–7pm; Fri 8am–6pm; Sat 9am–6pm; Sun 10am–6pm. Closed major holidays. Bus: 3, 4, 20, 56, 145, 146, 147, 151, or 157. Subway/El: Brown, Green, Orange, or Purple line to Randolph, or Red Line to Washington.

The Beaux Arts Grand Staircase in the Chicago Cultural Center.

Chicago Architecture Foundation Chicago's architecture is one of the city's main claims to fame, and a quick swing through this non-profit foundation's visitor center (conveniently located across the street from the Art Institute) will help you understand why. Permanent exhibits include a scale model of downtown Chicago, profiles of the people and buildings that shaped the city's look, and a searchable database with information on many of Chicago's best-known skyscrapers. Two galleries also feature changing exhibits about ongoing Chicago design projects, so you can see firsthand how local architecture continues to evolve. "Architecture ambassadors" are on hand to provide information on the excellent tours run by the foundation, which are well worth experiencing, especially for visitors new to the city (see "Sightseeing Tours," p. 224). An appealing gift shop is filled with architecture-focused books, well-designed decorative accessories, and an eclectic array of gifts. Allow a half-hour, more if you want to browse in the store.

224 S. Michigan Ave. © **312/922-3432,** ext. 241. www.architecture.org. Free admission. Exhibits daily 9:30am–5pm. Shop and tour desk daily 9am–6:30pm. Bus: 3, 4, 145, 147, or 151. Subway/El: Brown, Green, Purple, or Orange line to Adams, or Red Line to Jackson.

Fine Arts Building A worthwhile brief stop for architecture and history buffs, this 1885 building was originally a showroom for Studebaker carriages. In 1917 it became an arts center, with offices, shops, two theaters, and studios for musicians, artists, and writers. Its upper stories sheltered a number of well-known publications (the *Saturday Evening Post, Dial*) and provided offices for such luminaries as Frank Lloyd Wright, sculptor Lorado Taft, and L. Frank Baum, author of *The Wonderful Wizard of Oz*. Harriet Monroe published her magazine, *Poetry,* here, and introduced American readers to Carl Sandburg, T. S. Eliot, and Ezra Pound. Before the literary lions prowled its halls, the building served as a rallying base for suffragettes. Located throughout the building are a number of interesting studios and musical instrument shops. Take at least a quick walk through the marble-and-wood lobby, and ride the vintage elevator to the top floor to see the **Art Nouveau–era murals.** Allow a half-hour.

> **Photo Op**
>
> For a great photo op, walk on Randolph Street toward the lake in the morning. The sun, rising in the east over the lake, hits the cliff of buildings along South Michigan Avenue, giving you the perfect backdrop for an only-in-Chicago picture.

410 S. Michigan Ave. ✆ **312/566-9800.** www.fineartsbuilding.tv. Free admission. Mon–Fri 7am–10pm; Sat 7am–9pm; Sun 9am–5pm. Bus: 3, 4, 145, 147, or 151. Subway/El: Brown, Green, Purple, or Orange line to Adams, or Red Line to Jackson.

Auditorium Building and Theatre ★★ A truly grand theater with historic landmark status, the Auditorium gives visitors a taste of late-19th-century Chicago opulence. Because it's still a working theater—not a museum—it's not usually open to the public during the day; to make sure you'll get in, schedule a guided tour, which are offered on Monday at 10:30am and noon, and Thursday at 10:30am. (Call ✆ **312/431-2389** to confirm the date and time.) Tours cost $10 per person.

Designed and built in 1889 by Louis Sullivan and Dankmar Adler, the 4,000-seat Auditorium was a wonder of the world: The heaviest (110,000 tons) and most massive modern edifice on earth, the most fireproof building ever constructed, and the tallest building in Chicago. It was also the first large-scale building to be lit by electricity, and its theater was the first in the country to install air-conditioning. Originally the home of the Chicago Opera Company, Sullivan and Adler's masterpiece is defined by powerful arches lit by thousands of bulbs

The Auditorium Theatre gives visitors a taste of late-19th-century opulence.

and features Sullivan's trademark ornamentation—in this case, elaborate golden stenciling and gold plaster medallions. It's equally renowned for otherworldly acoustics and unobstructed sightlines.

During World War II, the building sheltered GIs, and its theater stage was turned into a bowling alley. The theater reopened in 1967 following a $3-million renovation made possible through the fundraising efforts of the nonprofit Auditorium Theatre Council. Remnants of the building's halcyon days remain in the Michigan Avenue lobby, with its faux-marble ornamental columns, molded ceilings, mosaic floors, and Mexican onyx walls.

An insider tip: If you can't get in for a tour, you can still get a glimpse of the building's historic past. Around the corner on Michigan Avenue, walk in the entrance that now houses Roosevelt University, and you'll get a sense of the building's grand public spaces. Take the elevator to the school's 10th-floor library reading room to see the theater's original dining room, with a barrel-vaulted ceiling and marvelous views of Grant Park.

Allow 1 hour for the guided tour.

50 E. Congress Pkwy. ✆ **312/922-2110.** www.auditoriumtheatre.org. For tickets to a performance at the Auditorium, call Ticketmaster at ✆ **312/902-1500.** Bus: 145, 147, or 151. Subway/El: Brown, Green, Orange, or Purple line to Library/Van Buren, or Red Line to Jackson.

Museum of Contemporary Photography Ensconced in a ground-floor space at Columbia College—a progressive arts- and media-oriented institution that boasts the country's largest undergraduate film department and a highly respected photojournalism-slanted photography department—the Museum of Contemporary Photography is the only museum in the Midwest of its kind. As the name indicates, it exhibits, collects, and promotes modern photography, with a special focus on American works from 1959 to the present. Rotating exhibitions showcase images by both nationally recognized and "undiscovered" regional artists. Related lectures and special programs take place during the year. Allow 1 hour.

600 S. Michigan Ave. ✆ **312/663-5554.** www.mocp.org. Free admission. Mon–Sat 10am–5pm (Thurs until 8pm); Sun noon–5pm. Bus: 6, 146, or 151. Subway/El: Red Line to Harrison.

The Spertus Institute of Jewish Studies This educational center and museum collects and preserves historic Jewish ceremonial objects, textiles, and sculpture, but its stunning modern building is firmly ensconced in the present. A glass facade fills the airy, white interior with light (even on cloudy days), and an outdoor terrace off the 10th-floor exhibition space lets you gaze out over Grant Park and the lake beyond. Art from the institute's collection is showcased throughout the building and temporary exhibits examine aspects of Jewish culture. The building also includes a 400-seat theater for lectures, films, and performances. Researchers can register to visit the Asher Library or study the Chicago Jewish Archives collection. The well-stocked gift shop carries a large selection of art, books, music, videos, and contemporary and traditional Jewish ceremonial gifts. Allow 1 hour.

610 S. Michigan Ave. ✆ **312/322-1700.** www.spertus.edu. Free admission Sun–Thurs 10am–5pm. Closed for major national holidays and Jewish religious holidays. Bus: 3, 4, 6, 145, 147, or 151. Subway/El: Red Line to Harrison, or Brown, Purple, Orange, or Green line to Adams. Validated parking in nearby lots.

Elsewhere in the Loop

For a map of these attractions (or this neighborhood), see p. 152.

MUSEUM free DAYS

If you time your visit right, you can save yourself some admission fees—but not during prime tourist season. While some major museums offer free admission at specific times year-round, others schedule free days only during the slowest times of the year (usually late fall and the dead of winter); keep in mind that you will still have to pay for special exhibitions and films on free days. The good news? Some smaller museums never charge admission.

Monday: Field Museum of Natural History (2nd Monday of every month), and Shedd Aquarium (mid-Sept to Nov and Jan–Feb; Oceanarium admission extra).

Tuesday: International Museum of Surgical Science, Museum of Contemporary Art, and Shedd Aquarium (mid-Sept to Nov and Jan–Feb; Oceanarium admission extra).

Wednesday: Art Institute of Chicago (first and second Wed of each month); The Spertus Institute of Jewish Studies (10am–noon).

Thursday: Chicago Children's Museum (5–8pm), and Spertus Institute of Jewish Studies (2–6pm).

Always Free: Chicago Cultural Center, Garfield Park Conservatory, David and Alfred Smart Museum of Art, Jane Addams Hull-House Museum, Lincoln Park Conservatory, Lincoln Park Zoo, National Museum of Mexican Art, Museum of Contemporary Photography, and Newberry Library.

Chicago Fed Money Museum It's not worth a special trip unless you're a monetary-policy megageek, but the visitor center at the Federal Reserve Bank of Chicago is worth a quick stop during a walk around the Loop. More than just the standard history-of-banking displays, the center has kid-friendly features such as a giant cube that holds a million dollars, an exhibit that lets you try to detect counterfeit bills, and a section where visitors can play Fed chairman, showing how changes in interest rates affect the economy. A suitcase packed with $1 million makes for a fun family photo op. Free guided tours begin at 1pm on weekdays. Allow a half-hour.

230 S. LaSalle St. (at Quincy St.). ✆ **312/322-2400.** www.chicagofed.org. Free admission. Mon–Fri 9am–5pm. Closed federal holidays. Bus: 134, 135, 136, or 156. Subway/El: Brown Line to Quincy/Wells or Red Line to Jackson.

Chicago Public Library/Harold Washington Library Center A massive, hulking building that looks like an Italian Renaissance fortress, Chicago's main public library is the largest in the world. Named for the city's first and only African-American mayor, who died of a heart attack in 1987 at the beginning of his second term in office, the building fills an entire city block at State Street and Congress Parkway. The interior design has been criticized for feeling cold and impersonal (you have to go up a few floors before you even see any books), but the stunning 52-foot glass-domed **Winter Garden ★** on the top floor is worth a visit. On the second floor is another treasure: The vast Thomas Hughes Children's Library, which makes an excellent resting spot for families traveling with kids. The library also offers an interesting array of events and art exhibitions

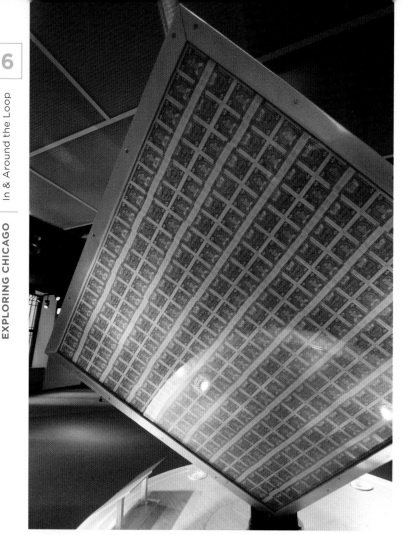

This giant cube at the Chicago Fed Money Museum holds a million dollars.

that are worth checking out. A 385-seat auditorium is the setting for a unique mix of dance and music performances, author talks, and children's programs. Want to check your e-mail? Stop by the third-floor Computer Commons, which has about 75 terminals available for public use. Allow a half-hour.

400 S. State St. (C) **312/747-4300.** www.chipublib.org. Free admission. Mon–Thurs 9am–9pm; Fri–Sat 9am–5pm; Sun 1–5pm. Closed major holidays. Bus: 2, 6, 11, 29, 36, 62, 145, 146, 147, or 151. Subway/El: Red Line to Jackson, or Brown Line to Van Buren/Library.

The Rookery ★ From the outside, this gloomy building gives no hint of the beauty within. Designed by master architect Daniel Burnham in the 1880s, it was one of Chicago's largest and most expensive office buildings when it was

The Chicago Public Library's facade.

The stunning glass-domed Winter Garden on the Public Library's top floor.

completed. (The name was a carryover from the old City Hall that previously occupied the site, a favorite of roosting birds.) In 1898, a young architect starting up an independent practice, Frank Lloyd Wright, rented an office here; a few years later, he was commissioned to update the building's interior. The resulting work is one of the loveliest commercial interiors in the city, a two-story glass pavilion filled with natural light and gleaming white marble. Free half-hour tours are offered on Mondays and Fridays at noon; longer tours, including the on-site library, start at noon on Wednesdays and cost $10 (no advance reservations required). The ShopWright store stocks a well-edited collection of books and decorative accessories. Allow 5 minutes for a quick look, up to 45 minutes if you stay for a tour.

209 S. LaSalle St. (at Adams St.). ☎ **312/994-4000.** www.gowright.org/visit/rookery.html. Free admission. Mon–Fri 9am–5pm. Closed federal holidays. Bus: 134, 135, 136, or 156. Subway/El: Brown Line to Quincy/Wells or Red Line to Jackson.

THE GRANT PARK MUSEUM CAMPUS'S BIG THREE

For a map of these attractions (or this neighborhood), see p. 152.

With terraced gardens and broad walkways, the Museum Campus at the southern end of Grant Park makes it easy for pedestrians to visit three of the city's most beloved institutions: the Field Museum of Natural History, Shedd Aquarium, and Adler Planetarium. To get to the Museum Campus from the Loop, walk south on Michigan Avenue to East Balbo Drive. Head east on Balbo, across Grant Park, then trek south along the lakeshore path to the museums (about a 15-min. walk).

Or follow 11th Street east from South Michigan Avenue, which takes you across a walkway spanning the Metra train tracks. Cross Columbus Drive, and then pick up the path that will take you under Lake Shore Drive and into the Museum Campus. The CTA no. 146 bus will take you from downtown to all three of these attractions; it also stops at the Roosevelt El stop on the Red Line. Call ✆ 312/836-7000 (from any city or suburban area code) for the stop locations and schedule.

A large indoor parking lot is accessible from Lake Shore Drive southbound; you can park there for $16 for up to 4 hours, $19 all day. Be aware that there is no public parking during Chicago Bears games in the fall; Soldier Field is next to the Museum Campus, and football fans get first dibs on all the surrounding parking spaces.

The Adler Planetarium and Astronomy Museum.

Adler Planetarium and Astronomy Museum ★★

The building may be historic (it was the first planetarium in the Western Hemisphere), but some of the attractions here will hold the attention of even the most jaded video game addict.

Your first stop should be the modern Sky Pavilion, where the don't-miss experience is the **Space Theater ★★**. Settle down under the massive dome, and you'll take a half-hour interactive virtual-reality trip through the Milky Way and into deep space, featuring a computer-generated 3-D-graphics projection system and controls in the armrest of each seat. Six high-resolution video projectors form a seamless image above your head—you'll feel as if you're literally floating in space. If you're looking for more entertainment, the **Sky Theater** shows movies with an astronomical bent, and the **Universe Theater** presents 3-D features, most shot in outer space.

The planetarium's exhibition galleries feature a variety of displays and interactive activities. If you're going to see only one exhibit, check out *Shoot For the Moon* ★★, an exhibit on lunar exploration that's full of interactive stations. (It also showcases the personal collection of astronaut Jim Lovell, captain of the infamous Apollo 13 mission, who now lives in the Chicago suburbs.) If you've got little ones in

Museums for Less

If you're planning on visiting lots of Chicago museums, you should invest in a **CityPass,** a prepaid ticket that gets you into the biggest attractions (the Art Institute, Field Museum of Natural History, Shedd Aquarium, Adler Planetarium, Museum of Science and Industry, and Hancock Observatory). The cost at press time was $76 for adults and $59 for children, which is about 50% cheaper than paying all the museums' individual admission fees. You can buy a CityPass at any of the museums listed above or purchase one online before you get to town (www.citypass.com).

Website Extras

Scanning the websites of museums and other attractions before you visit can enhance your trip when you get here. At the **Field Museum of Natural History** website (www.fieldmuseum.org), you can download an MP3 audio tour of the museum's permanent collection; you can also print out a Family Adventure Tour, which sends kids on a scavenger hunt throughout the museum. The **Millennium** **Park** MP3 audio tour (available at www. millenniumpark.org) includes interviews with the artists who created the park's eye-catching artwork. And if you're intimidated by the massive size of the **Museum of Science and Industry,** check out the website's Personal Planner, which will put together a customized itinerary based your family's interests (www.msi chicago.org).

tow, your first stop should be **_Planet Explorers_** ★★, a series of immersive play stations where kids can experience a simulated rocket launch and crawl through the caves and tunnels of a mysterious "Planet X." Other exhibits worth checking out include **_Bringing the Heavens to Earth_** ★, which traces the ways different cultures have tried to make sense of astronomical phenomena, and **_Universe in Your Hands,_** which includes artifacts from the planetarium's extensive collection of astronomical instruments. (Although suitable for older children, these can get a bit boring for little ones unless they're real astronomy nuts.)

The museum's cafe provides views of the lakefront and skyline. On the third Thursday evening of the month, the museum stays open until 10pm, and visitors can view dramatic close-ups of the moon, the planets, and distant galaxies through a closed-circuit monitor connected to the planetarium's Doane Observatory telescope.

Allow 2 hours, more if you want to see more than one show.

1300 S. Lake Shore Dr. © **312/922-STAR** (7827). www.adlerplanetarium.org. Admission $10 adults, $8 seniors, $6 children 3–14, free for children 2 and under; admission including 2 shows $27 adults, $21 children. Memorial Day to Labor Day daily 9:30am–6pm; early Sept to late May Mon–Fri 10am–4pm; Sat–Sun 10am–4:30pm; 3rd Thurs of every month until 10pm. StarRider Theater and Sky Shows run throughout the day; call main number for current times. Bus: 146.

Field Museum of Natural History ★★★ ☺ Is it any wonder that Steven Spielberg thought the Field Museum of Natural History was a suitable home turf for the intrepid archaeologist and adventurer hero of his _Indiana Jones_ movies? Spread over the museum's 9 acres of floor space are scores of permanent and temporary exhibitions—some interactive, but most requiring the old-fashioned skills of observation and imagination.

Navigating all the exhibits can be daunting, so pace yourself and prioritize what you want to see. Start in the grand Stanley Field Hall, where you'll stand face-to-face with **Sue** ★★★, the largest, most complete _Tyrannosaurus rex_ fossil ever unearthed. The museum acquired the specimen—named for the paleontologist who discovered it in South Dakota in 1990—for a cool $8.4 million after a high-stakes bidding war. The real skull is so heavy that a lighter copy had to be mounted on the skeleton; the actual one is on display nearby.

Families should head downstairs for the most popular kid-friendly exhibits. Walking through **_Inside Ancient Egypt_** ★★, visitors explore scenes and rituals of everyday life, viewing actual mummies and realistic burial scenes, a living marsh environment and canal works, the ancient royal barge, a religious shrine, and a reproduction of a typical marketplace of the period. Next door, you'll find **Underground Adventure ★**, a "total immersion environment" populated by giant robotic earwigs, centipedes, wolf spiders, and other subterranean critters. It's a hit with kids but—annoyingly—carries an extra admission charge ($7 on top of regular admission).

You might be tempted to skip the "peoples of the world" exhibits, but the ones here are not only mind opening and well designed, but also great fun. **Africa ★★**, an assemblage of African artifacts and provocative interactive multimedia presentations, takes viewers to Senegal, a Cameroon palace, and the wildlife-rich savanna, and on a "virtual" journey aboard a slave ship to the Americas. **Traveling the Pacific ★**, hidden up on the second floor, is definitely worth a stop. Hundreds of artifacts from the museum's oceanic collection re-create scenes of island life in the South Pacific. (There's even a full-scale model of a Maori Meeting House.) Native Chicagoans will quickly name two more signature highlights

TOP: Stand face-to-face with Sue, the most complete *Tyrannosaurus rex* fossil ever unearthed; ABOVE: The Crown Family PlayLab is full of hands-on activities for kids.

Getting the Most from Your Field Museum Visit

You could easily spend a day at the Field Museum—so don't waste half of it trying to decide where to go. The Field is one of Chicago's must-see destinations for families, but it can get crowded, especially during school vacations in the winter and summer. Remember that the museum opens earlier than most people realize—at 9 in the morning—and you'll get a jump on the crowds as long as you arrive by 10am. Head for two of the most popular exhibits first: **Inside**

Ancient Egypt (on the ground floor) and the **Dinosaur Hall** (on the upper level). It also pays to take an early lunch break: The Field has two on-site restaurants (McDonald's and Corner Bakery) but no cafeteria, and both places are often full by noon. If you plan ahead and bring your own food, you can eat in relative peace and quiet at the **Siragusa Center** on the lower level, a large, bright room with benches, tables, and vending machines.

that have been here for years: the taxidermies of **Bushman** (a legendary lowland gorilla that made international headlines while at the city's Lincoln Park Zoo) and the **Man-Eating Lions of Tsavo** (the pair of male lions that munched nearly 140 British railway workers constructing a bridge in East Africa in 1898; their story is featured in the film *The Ghost and the Darkness*).

If you've got little kids along (ages 7 and under), don't miss the **Crown Family PlayLab,** which is full of hands-on activities, including an art room, dress-up station and a soundproofed space filled with drums and other percussion instruments. (**Note:** The PlayLab is closed Tues and Wed.)

The museum books special traveling exhibits (recent blockbusters included shows on King Tut and ancient Pompeii), but be forewarned: The high-profile exhibits are usually crowded and—again—have an additional admission charge. A much better deal is a free tour of the museum highlights; tours begin daily at 11am and 2pm.

When you're ready to take a break, the **Corner Bakery** cafe, just off the main hall, serves food a cut above the usual museum food court—although there's also a McDonald's on the lower level. Allow 3 hours (although you could easily spend all day).

Roosevelt Rd. and Lake Shore Dr. *(C)* **312/922-9410.** http://fieldmuseum.org. Admission $15 adults, $12 seniors and students with ID, $10 children 3–11, free for children 2 and under. Extra fees apply for special exhibits. Free admission the second Mon of every month. Daily 9am–5pm. Closed Christmas. Bus: 146.

John G. Shedd Aquarium ★★★ The Shedd is one of the world's largest indoor aquariums and houses thousands of river, lake, and sea denizens in standard aquarium tanks and elaborate new habitats within its octagon-shaped marble building. The only problem with the Shedd is its relatively steep admission price. You can keep your costs down by buying "Aquarium Only" tickets; the tradeoff is that you'll miss some of the most stunning exhibits. A CityPass (see "Museums for Less," above) can save you money if you visit enough of the other included attractions.

The first thing you'll see as you enter is the **Caribbean Coral Reef** ★. This 90,000-gallon circular tank occupies the Beaux Arts–style central rotunda, entertaining spectators who press up against the glass to ogle divers feeding nurse sharks, barracudas, stingrays, and a hawksbill sea turtle. A roving camera

Inside the Caribbean Coral Reef exhibit at the John G. Shedd Aquarium.

connected to video monitors on the tank's periphery gives visitors close-ups of the animals inside, but I'd recommend sticking around to catch one of the daily feedings, when a diver swims around the tank and (thanks to a microphone) talks about the species and their eating habits.

The exhibits surrounding the Caribbean coral reef re-create marine habitats around the world. The best is *Amazon Rising: Seasons of the River* ★, a rendering of the Amazon basin that showcases frogs and other South American species, as well as fish (the sharp-toothed piranhas are pretty cool).

You'll pay extra to see the other Shedd highlights, but they're quite impressive, so I'd suggest shelling out for them if you plan to spend more than an hour here. The *Oceanarium* ★★★, with a wall of windows revealing the lake outside, replicates a Pacific Northwest coastal environment and creates the illusion of one uninterrupted expanse of sea. On a fixed performance schedule in a large pool flanked by an amphitheater, a crew of friendly trainers puts dolphins through their paces of leaping dives, breaches, and tail walking (there's an extra charge of $2 per person to see the show). If you're visiting during a summer weekend, consider buying tickets in advance to make sure you can catch a show that day.

Wild Reef—Sharks at Shedd ★★ is a series of 26 connected habitats that house a Philippine coral reef patrolled by sharks and other predators. The floor-to-ceiling windows bring the toothy swimmers up close and personal (they even swim over your head at certain spots). And if you're here with kids, you'll want to stop by the **Polar Play Zone,** where little ones can pet a starfish, try on a penguin suit, or get a good look at the real thing—the Play Zone is home to a dozen rockhopper penguins.

HISTORIC HOMES OF Prairie Avenue

Prairie Avenue, south of the Loop, was the city's first "Millionaire's Row," and its most famous address is **Glessner House,** 1800 S. Prairie Ave. (② **312/326-1480;** www.glessnerhouse.org). A must-see for anyone interested in architectural history, and the only surviving Chicago building designed by Boston architect Henry Hobson Richardson, the 1886 structure represented a dramatic shift from traditional Victorian architecture (and inspired a young Frank Lloyd Wright).

The imposing granite exterior gives the home a forbidding air. (Railway magnate George Pullman, who lived nearby, complained, "I do not know what I have ever done to have that thing staring me in the face every time I go out my door.") But step inside, and the home turns out to be a welcoming, cozy retreat, filled with Arts and Crafts furnishings. Visits are by guided tour only; tours begin at 1 and 3pm Wednesday through Sunday (except major holidays) on a first-come, first-served basis (advance reservations are taken only for groups of 10 or more). Tours cost $10 for adults,

$9 for students and seniors, and $6 for children 5 to 12.

A visit to Glessner House can also be combined with a tour of the nearby **Clarke House Museum,** a Greek Revival home that's the oldest surviving house in the city; tours are given at noon and 2pm. Combination tickets for both Glessner House and Clarke House cost $15 for adults, $12 student and seniors, and $8 for children 5 to 12. Admission for all tours is free on Wednesday.

To get to Prairie Avenue, catch the no. 1, 3, or 4 bus from Michigan Avenue at Jackson Boulevard; get off at 18th Street and walk 2 blocks east.

If you want a quality sit-down meal in a restaurant with a spectacular view of Lake Michigan, check out Soundings. There's also a family-friendly cafeteria. Allow 2 to 3 hours.

1200 S. Lake Shore Dr. ☏ **312/939-2438.** www.sheddaquarium.org. Shedd Pass (for all exhibits) $29 adults, $20 seniors and children 3–11, free for children 2 and under; aquarium only $8 adults, $6 seniors and children. Free admission to aquarium only Mon–Tues mid-Sept to Oct and Jan–Feb. Memorial Day to Labor Day daily 9am–6pm; early Sept to late May Mon–Fri 9am–5pm, Sat–Sun 9am–6pm. Bus: 146.

NORTH OF THE LOOP: THE MAGNIFICENT MILE & BEYOND

For a map of these attractions (or this neighborhood), see p. 152.

Most of these sights are either on the Magnificent Mile (North Michigan Ave.) and its surrounding blocks or close by on the Near North Side.

💬 A river RUNS THROUGH IT

The **Chicago River** remains one of the most visible of the city's major physical features. It's spanned by more movable bridges within the city limits (52 at last count) than any other city in the world. An almost-mystical moment occurs downtown when all the bridges spanning the main and south branches—connecting the Loop to both the Near West Side and the Near North Side—are raised, allowing for the passage of some ship, barge, or contingent of high-masted sailboats. The Chicago River has long outlived the critical commercial function that it once performed.

Most of the remaining millworks that occupy its banks no longer depend on the river alone for the transport of their materials, raw and finished.

The river's main function today is to serve as a fluvial conduit for sewage, which, owing to an engineering feat that reversed its flow inland in 1900, no longer pollutes the waters of Lake Michigan. Recently, Chicagoans have begun to discover other roles for the river, including water cruises, park areas, cafes, public art installations, and a riverside bike path that connects to the lakefront route near Wacker Drive. Actually, today's developers aren't the first to wonder why the river couldn't be Chicago's Seine. A look at the early-20th-century Beaux Arts balustrades lining the river along Wacker Drive, complete with comfortably spaced benches and Parisian-style bridge houses, shows

that Chicago architect and urban planner Daniel Burnham knew full well what a treasure the city had.

The Hancock Observatory ★ The Hancock may not be quite as famous as the Sears Tower, but the view from the city's third-tallest building is as good as any in town. A high-speed elevator carries passengers to the observatory in 40 seconds, and on a clear day, you can see portions of the three states surrounding this corner of Illinois (Michigan, Indiana, and Wisconsin), for a radius of 40 to 50 miles. The view up the North Side is particularly dramatic, stretching from nearby Oak Street and North Avenue beaches, along the green strip of Lincoln Park, to the suburbs that trace the shoreline beyond. During your visit, you're given a handheld PDA that delivers a **"Sky Tour,"** using audio and video to highlight features of interest across the skyline (kids get their own version). The Skywalk open-air viewing deck, surrounded on all sides by a safety screen, allows visitors to feel the rush of the wind at 1,000 feet. There's also a cafe with an adjoining kids' play area if you want to linger over a cappuccino and snack, and a complimentary concierge service. Allow 1 hour.

"Big John," as some locals call the building, also has a restaurant, the **Signature Room at the 95th** (p. 113), and a bar, the **Signature Lounge** (p. 325). For about the same cost as the observatory, you can take in the views with a libation in hand.

94th floor, John Hancock Center, 875 N. Michigan Ave. (enter on Delaware St.). ℭ **888/875-VIEW** (8439), or 312/751-3681. www.hancock-observatory.com. Admission $15 adults, $10 children 3–11, free for children 2 and under. Daily 9am–11pm. Bus: 145, 146, 147, or 151. Subway/El: Red Line to Chicago.

Museum of Contemporary Art (MCA) ★★ The MCA's gloomy, imposing building, designed by the German architect Josef Paul Kleihues, doesn't offer a warm welcome, but the interior spaces are more appealing, with a bright, sun-drenched two-story central corridor, elliptical staircases, and three floors of exhibition space. Although the MCA is one of the largest contemporary art museums in the country, theaters and hallways seem to take up much of the space, making it relatively easy to see the whole collection, which emphasizes experimentation in a variety of media, including painting, sculpture, photography, video and film, and performance. Although you can see the main highlights in about an hour, art

Rock Around the World

The impressive Gothic **Tribune Tower,** just north of the Chicago River on the east side of Michigan Avenue, is home to the *Chicago Tribune* newspaper. It's also notable for an array of architectural fragments jutting out from the exterior. The newspaper's notoriously despotic publisher, Robert R. McCormick, started the collection shortly after the building's completion in 1925, gathering pieces during his world travels. *Tribune* correspondents then began supplying building fragments that they acquired on assignment. Each one now bears the name of the structure and the country from whence it came. There are 138 pieces in all, including chunks and shards from the Great Wall of China; the Taj Mahal; the White House; the Arc de Triomphe; the Berlin Wall; the Roman Colosseum; London's Houses of Parliament; the Great Pyramid of Cheops in Giza, Egypt; and the original tomb of Abraham Lincoln in Springfield, Illinois.

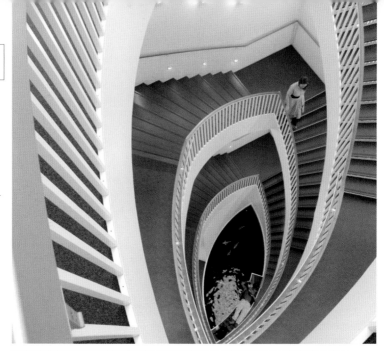

Elliptical staircases connect the Museum of Contemporary Art's three floors of exhibition space.

lovers will want more time to wander, especially if a high-profile exhibit is in town (the MCA has tried to raise its national profile to the level of New York's Museum of Modern Art by booking major touring retrospectives of working artists such as Jeff Koons and Cindy Sherman).

Your first stop should be the handsome barrel-vaulted galleries on the **top floor,** dedicated to pieces from the permanent collection. Visitors who'd like a little guidance with making sense of the rather challenging works can rent an audio tour or take a free tour (1 and 6pm Tues; 1pm Wed–Fri; noon, 1, 2, and 3pm Sat–Sun). In addition to a range of special activities and educational programming, including films, performances, and a lecture series in a 300-seat theater, the museum features **Puck's at the MCA,** a cafe operated by Wolfgang Puck of Spago restaurant fame, with seating that overlooks a 1-acre terraced sculpture garden. The store, with one-of-a-kind gift items, is worth a stop even if you don't make it into the museum. The museum's **First Friday** program, featuring after-hours performances, live music, and food and drink, takes place on the first Friday of every month. Allow 1 to 2 hours.

220 E. Chicago Ave. (1 block east of Michigan Ave.). ✆ **312/280-2660.** www.mcachicago.org. Admission $12 adults, $7 seniors and students with ID, free for children 12 and under. Free admission Tues. Tues 10am–8pm; Wed–Sun 10am–5pm. Closed Jan 1, Thanksgiving, and Christmas. Bus: 3, 10, 66, 145, 146, or 151. Subway/El: Red Line to Chicago.

Navy Pier ★ ☺ Built during World War I, this 3,000-foot-long pier served as a Navy training center for pilots during World War II. The military aura is long gone, and Navy Pier now thrives as a major tourist attraction, complete with carnival rides, a large food court, T-shirt shops, and boat rides. Whether or not you enjoy Navy Pier depends on your tolerance for crowds (especially in the

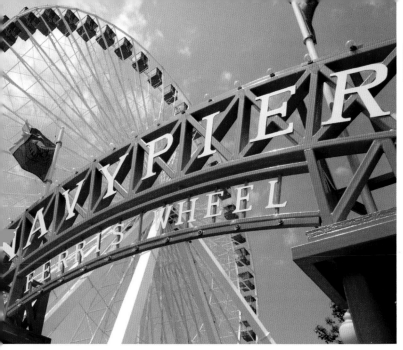

Navy Pier's Ferris wheel is a replica of the one built for the 1893 World's Fair.

summer), but even if you decide to bypass the souvenir stands, it's worth walking to the very end, where you'll be rewarded with great views of the city.

Midway down the pier are the **Crystal Gardens ★**, a lovely glass-enclosed atrium with 70 full-size palm trees, dancing fountains, and other flora; a carousel and kiddie carnival rides; and a 15-story Ferris wheel, a replica of the original that made its debut at Chicago's 1893 World's Fair. The pier is also home to the **Chicago Children's Museum** (p. 221), a **3-D IMAX theater** (*C* **312/595-5629**), a small ice-skating rink, and the **Chicago Shakespeare Theatre** (p.

Free Fireworks!

Yes, Navy Pier can be chaotic, crowded, and loud, but come summer, it's also a prime gathering spot for visitors from around the world. From Memorial Day through Labor Day, the pier sponsors twice-weekly **fireworks** shows, where you can watch spectacular light displays reflected in the water of Lake Michigan below. It's a great way to appreciate the city at night (along with a few thousand of your fellow travelers). The shows start at 9:30pm on Wednesday and 10:15pm on Saturday.

301). The shops tend to be bland and touristy, but there are a number of good dining options. They include the white-tablecloth seafood restaurant Riva; a beer garden with live music; and outposts of two popular local restaurants, **Charlie's Ale House** (p. 129), a casual pub with top-notch burgers, and the sports-themed **Harry Caray's Tavern** (p. 122). Summer is one long party at the pier, with fireworks on Wednesday and Saturday evenings.

The **Smith Museum of Stained Glass Windows** ★★ may sound dull, but decorative-art aficionados shouldn't miss this remarkable installation of more than 150 stained-glass windows set in illuminated display cases. Occupying an 800-foot-long expanse on the ground floor of Navy Pier, the free museum features works by Frank Lloyd Wright, Louis Sullivan, John LaFarge, and Louis Comfort Tiffany.

If the noise and commercialism get overwhelming, take the half-mile stroll to the end of the pier, where you

A Tiffany copy of a medieval window at the Smith Museum of Stained Glass Windows.

can enjoy the wind, the waves, and the city view, which is the real delight of a place like this. Or unwind in **Olive Park,** a small sylvan haven with a sliver of beach just north of Navy Pier.

You'll find more than half a dozen sailing vessels moored at the south dock, including a couple of dinner-cruise ships, the pristine white-masted tall ship *Windy,* and the 70-foot speedboats *Seadog I, II,* and *III.* In the summer months, water taxis speed between Navy Pier and other Chicago sights. For more specifics on sightseeing and dinner cruises, see "Lake & River Cruises," p. 226. Allow 1 hour.

600 E. Grand Ave. (at Lake Michigan). ⓒ **800/595-PIER** (7437; outside 312 area code), or 312/595-PIER [7437]. www.navypier.com. Free admission. Summer Sun–Thurs 10am–10pm, Fri–Sat 10am–midnight; fall–spring Mon–Thurs 10am–8pm, Fri–Sat 10am–10pm, Sun 10am–7pm. Parking: $20/day Mon–Thurs; $24/day Fri–Sun (lots fill quickly). Bus: 29, 65, 66, 120, or 121. Subway/El: Red Line to Grand; transfer to city bus no. 65 or board a free pier trolley bus.

Newberry Library The Newberry Library, housed in a stately five-story granite building, is a bibliophile's dream. Established in 1887, thanks to a bequest by Chicago merchant and financier Walter Loomis Newberry, the noncirculating research library contains many rare books and manuscripts (such as Shakespeare's first folio and Jefferson's copy of *The Federalist Papers*). The library is also a major destination for genealogists digging at their roots, with holdings that are free to the public (over the age of 16 with a photo ID). The collections include more than 1.5 million volumes and 75,000 maps, many of which are on display during an ongoing series of public exhibitions. For an overview, take a free 1-hour tour

Thursday at 3pm or Saturday at 10:30am. The Newberry operates a fine book-store and also sponsors a series of concerts (including those by its resident early music ensemble, the Newberry Consort), lectures, and children's story hours throughout the year. One popular annual event is the **Bughouse Square debates ★**. Held across the street in Washington Square Park in late July, the debates re-create the fiery soapbox orations of the left-wing agitators in the 1930s and 1940s. Allow a half-hour.

60 W. Walton St. (at Dearborn Pkwy.). ✆ **312/943-9090,** or 312/255-3700 for programs. www.newberry.org. Reading room Tues–Fri 9am–5pm; Sat 9am–1pm. Exhibit gallery Mon, Fri, and Sat 8:15am–5pm; Tues–Thurs 8:15am–7:30pm. Bus: 22, 36, 125, 145, 146, 147, or 151. Subway/El: Red Line to Chicago.

WHAT TO SEE & DO IN LINCOLN PARK

For a map of these attractions (or this neighborhood), see p. 152.

Lincoln Park is the city's largest park, and certainly one of the longest. Straight and narrow, the park begins at North Avenue and follows the shoreline of Lake Michigan north for several miles. Within its 1,200 acres are a world-class zoo; half a dozen beaches; a botanical conservatory; two excellent museums; a golf course; and the meadows, formal gardens, sporting fields, and tennis courts typical of urban parks. To get to the park, take bus no. 22, 145, 146, 147, 151, or 156.

Augustus Saint-Gaudens's statue of the standing Abraham Lincoln.

Sit and relax at the Park Place Cafe, next to Cafe Brauer.

The park, named after Abraham Lincoln, is home to the **statue of the standing Abraham Lincoln** (just north of the North Ave. and State St. intersection), one of the city's two Lincoln statues by Augustus Saint-Gaudens (the seated Lincoln is in Grant Park). Saint-Gaudens also designed the *Bates Fountain* near the conservatory.

Cafe Brauer This landmark 1900 building is not technically open to the public, aside from a restaurant on the ground floor. (The lovely second-floor Great Hall, flanked by two curving loggias, is one of the city's most popular wedding reception spots; if you stop by on a weekend, chances are, you can sneak a peek while the caterers are setting up.) Even if you don't make it inside, Cafe Brauer is a nice stopping-off point during a walk around the park. Best of all, though, is the picture-postcard view from the adjacent bridge spanning the pond of the John Hancock Center and neighboring skyscrapers beyond Lincoln Park's treetops. Allow a quarter-hour.

2021 Stockton Dr. ✆ **312/742-2400.** Daily 10am–5pm. Bus: 151 or 156.

Chicago History Museum ★ This museum at the southwestern tip of Lincoln Park is one of the city's oldest cultural institutions (founded in 1856), but it's reinvented itself for the 21st century. The main, must-see exhibit is *Chicago: Crossroads of America* ★★, which fills the museum's second floor. A survey of the city's history—from it s founding as a frontier trading post to the riots at the 1968 Democratic Convention—it's filled with photos, artifacts, and newsreels

Inside the Chicago History Museum.

that make the past come alive; surrounding galleries track the development of local sports teams, architecture, music, and art. Although the exhibit is geared toward families with older children (you can even download an MP3 audio tour for teenagers from the museum's website), little ones love the re-creation of an 1890s El station, where they can run inside the city's first elevated train. The Children's Gallery on the ground floor has interactive exhibits for kids, including a giant table where you can experience the "Smells of Chicago" (both good and bad!).

Another museum highlight is the hall of dioramas that re-create scenes from Chicago's past. Although they've been around for decades (and are decidedly low-tech), they're a fun way to trace the city's progression from a few small cabins to the grand World's Columbian Exposition of 1893. The museum's Costume and Textile Gallery showcases pieces from the museum's renowned collection of historic clothing; recent exhibitions included couture gowns by French designer Christian Dior and a survey of American quilts.

There's a small cafe with sandwiches and salads that makes a convenient lunch stop. The History Museum also presents a wide range of lectures, seminars, and tours, including walking tours of the surrounding neighborhood; check the museum's website for details, as the schedules change frequently. Allow 1 to 2 hours.

1601 N. Clark St. (at North Ave.). 𝄢 **312/642-4600.** www.chicagohistory.org. Admission $14 adults, $12 seniors and students, free for children 12 and under. Mon–Sat 9:30am–4:30pm; Sun noon–5pm. Bus: 11, 22, 36, 72, 151, or 156.

The Lincoln Park Conservatory's expansive lawn is the perfect place for a picnic.

Lincoln Park Conservatory ★ Just beyond the zoo's northeast border is a lovely botanical garden housed in a soaring glass-domed structure. Inside are four great halls filled with thousands of plants. If you're visiting Chicago in the wintertime, this lush haven of greenery provides a welcome respite from the snow and ice outside. The Palm House features giant palms and rubber trees (including a 50-ft. fiddle-leaf rubber tree dating back to 1891); the Fernery nurtures plants that grow close to the forest floor; and the Tropical House is a shiny symphony of flowering trees, vines, and bamboo. The fourth environment is the Show House, where seasonal flower shows take place.

Even better than the plants inside, however, might be what lies outside the front doors. The expansive lawn, with its French garden and lovely fountain on the conservatory's south side, is one of the best places in town for an informal picnic (especially nice if you're visiting the zoo and want to avoid the congestion at its food concession venues).

The Lincoln Park Conservatory has a sister facility on the city's West Side, in Garfield Park, that is even more impressive. In fact, the 2-acre **Garfield Park Conservatory,** 300 N. Central Park Ave. (✆ **312/746-5100**), designed by the great landscape architect Jens Jensen in 1907, is one of the largest gardens under glass in the world. Unfortunately, it's surrounded by a pretty rough neighborhood with a high crime rate, so it's best to visit if you have a car, rather than using public transportation to get there. It's open 365 days a year from 9am to 5pm.

Allow a half-hour for the Lincoln Park Conservatory.

Fullerton Ave. (at Stockton Dr.). ✆ **312/742-7736.** Free admission. Daily 9am–5pm. Bus: 73, 151, or 156.

Lincoln Park Zoo ★★★ ✍ One of the city's treasures, this family-friendly attraction is not only open every day of the year, but it's also free. Even if you don't have time for a complete tour of the various habitats, it's worth at least

The Regenstein Center for African Apes at the Lincoln Park Zoo.

a quick stop during a stroll through Lincoln Park. The term *zoological gardens* truly fits here: Landmark Georgian Revival brick buildings and modern structures sit among gently rolling pathways, verdant lawns, and a kaleidoscopic profusion of flower gardens. The late Marlon Perkins, legendary host of the *Mutual of Omaha's Wild Kingdom* TV series, got his start here as the zoo's director and filmed a pioneering TV show called *Zoo Parade* (*Wild Kingdom*'s predecessor) in the basement of the old Reptile House.

The **Regenstein African Journey ★★★**, a series of linked indoor and outdoor habitats that's home to giraffes, rhinos, and other large mammals, shouldn't be missed. Large glass-enclosed tanks allow visitors to go face-to-face with swimming pygmy hippos, meerkats, colobus monkeys, and other exotic species, including (not for the faint of heart) a rocky ledge filled with Madagascar hissing cockroaches.

Your second stop should be the **Regenstein Center for African Apes ★★**. Lincoln Park Zoo has had remarkable success breeding gorillas and chimpanzees, and watching these ape families interact can be mesmerizing (and touching). **One caveat:** The building can get incredibly noisy when it's crowded, so be prepared.

Other exhibits worth a visit are the **Small Mammal–Reptile House,** which features a glass-enclosed walk-through ecosystem simulating river, savanna, and forest habitats; and the popular **Sea Lion Pool** in the center of the zoo, which is home to harbor seals, gray seals, and California sea lions (walk down the ramp and take a look at the underwater viewing area). The zoo's large carousel features beautifully rendered figures of endangered species. If you're here for a while and need nourishment, there's an indoor food court, as well as the Big Cats Café, located on a terrace above the gift shop. Allow 3 hours. For the adjoining children's zoo, see "Kid Stuff," p. 221.

2200 N. Cannon Dr. (at Fullerton Pkwy.). ☎ **312/742-2000.** www.lpzoo.com. Free admission. Buildings daily 10am–5pm (Memorial Day to Labor Day until 6:30pm Sat–Sun). Grounds Memorial Day to Labor Day daily 9am–7pm; Apr to late May and early Sept to Oct daily 9am–6pm; Nov–Mar daily 9am–5pm. Parking $17 for up to 3 hr. in on-site lot. Bus: 22, 36, 151, or 156.

Peggy Notebaert Nature Museum ★ ☺ Built into a slope that was once the site of an ancient sand dune—and part of the shoreline of Lake Michigan—this museum bills itself as "an environmental museum for the 21st century." Many of the exhibits are hands-on and designed for kids, making this a good stop for families.

The uniquely designed Peggy Notebaert Nature Museum resembles a sand dune.

Shaded by huge cottonwoods and maples, the sand-colored exterior, with its horizontal lines composed of interlocking trapezoids, resembles a sand dune. Rooftop-level walkways give strollers a view of birds and other urban wildlife below, and paths wind through gardens planted with native Midwestern wildflowers and grasses. Inside, large windows create a dialogue between the outdoor environment and the indoor exhibits designed to illuminate it. The museums' best known exhibit is the *Butterfly Haven* ★★, a greenhouse habitat where about 25 Midwestern species of butterflies and moths carry on their complex life cycles (wander through as a riot of color flutters all around you). If you're traveling with little ones, I'd also recommend the **Extreme Green House** ★, a bungalow where kids can play while learning how they can be environmentally friendly, and **RiverWorks,** a water play exhibit that gives children an excuse to splash around while building dams and maneuvering boats along a mini river. Allow 1 to 2 hours.

Fullerton Ave. and Cannon Dr. ☎ **773/755-5100.** www.chias.org. Admission $9 adults, $7 seniors and students, $6 children 3–12, free for children 2 and under. Free admission Thurs. Mon–Fri 9am–5pm; Sat–Sun 10am–5pm. Closed Jan 1, Thanksgiving, and Christmas. Bus: 22, 36, 151, or 156.

○ A Great View

After a visit to Lincoln Park Zoo or the Peggy Notebaert Nature Museum, take a quick stroll along the south side of Fullerton Avenue toward the lakefront. Standing on the bridge that runs over the lagoon (just before you get to Lake Shore Dr.), you'll have a great view of the Chicago skyline and Lincoln Park behind you—an excellent backdrop for family souvenir photos. This path can get very crowded with bikers and runners on summer weekends, so this photo op works best during the week. You'll also get good pictures if you continue on to Lake Michigan.

EXPLORING HYDE PARK

Hyde Park, south of the Loop, is the birthplace of atomic fission, home to the University of Chicago and the popular Museum of Science and Industry, and definitely worth a trip. It's gotten an added boost of publicity ever since a certain former resident, Barack Obama, came to national prominence. The Obamas are such fans of the area that they've kept their house here. (For more about the Obama connection, see "Obama's Chicago" in chapter 2, p. 44.) Allow at least half a day to explore the University of Chicago campus and surrounding neighborhood (one of Chicago's most successfully integrated). If you want to explore a museum or two as well, plan on a full day.

SOME HYDE PARK HISTORY When Hyde Park was settled in 1850, it became Chicago's first suburb. A hundred years later, in the 1950s, it added another first to its impressive résumé, one that the current neighborhood is not particularly proud of: an urban-renewal plan. At the time, a certain amount of old commercial and housing stock—just the kind of buildings that would be prized today—was demolished rather than rehabilitated and replaced by projects and small shopping malls that actually make some corners of Hyde Park look more like a post–World War II suburb than an urban neighborhood.

What Hyde Park can be proud of is that, in racially divided Chicago, this neighborhood has found an alternative vision. As Southern blacks began to migrate to Chicago's South Side during World War I, many whites fled. But most whites here, especially those who wanted to stay near the university, chose integration as the only realistic strategy to preserve their neighborhood. The 2000 census proved that integration still works: About 40% of the residents are white and 37% are black; there is also a significant Asian population. Hyde Park is decidedly middle class, with pockets of affluence that reflect the early-20th-century period when the well-to-do moved here to escape the decline of Prairie Avenue. A well-known black resident from the area is the late Elijah Muhammad, and numerous Nation of Islam families continue to worship in a mosque, formerly a Greek Orthodox cathedral, that is one of the neighborhood's architectural landmarks. Surrounding this unusual enclave, however, are many marginal blocks where poverty and slum housing abound. For all its nobility, Hyde Park's achievement in integration merely emphasizes that socioeconomic differences are even more unwieldy than racial ones.

The University of Chicago is widely hailed as one of the more intellectually exciting institutions of higher learning in the country and has been home to some 73 Nobel laureates, including physicist Enrico Fermi, novelist Saul Bellow, and economist Milton Friedman. (Almost one-third of all the Nobel Prizes in Economics have gone to University of Chicago professors, twice as many as any other institution.) Another long-time faculty member was English professor Norman Maclean, author of *A River Runs Through It*. Though they may joke about the school's staid social life, U of C undergrads take pride in their school's nerdy reputation.

The year the university opened its doors in 1892 was a big one for Hyde Park, but 1893 was even bigger. In that year, Chicago, chosen over other cities in a competitive international field, played host to the World's Columbian Exposition, commemorating the 400th anniversary of Columbus's arrival in America. To create a fairground, the landscape architect Frederick Law Olmsted was enlisted to fill in the marshlands along

Hyde Park's lakefront and link what was to become Jackson Park to existing Washington Park on the neighborhood's western boundary with a narrow concourse called the Midway Plaisance. On the resulting 650 acres—at a cost of $30 million—12 exhibit palaces, 57 buildings devoted to U.S. states and foreign governments, and dozens of smaller structures were constructed under the supervision of architect Daniel Burnham. Most of the buildings followed Burnham's preference for the Classical Revival style and white stucco exteriors. With the innovation of outdoor electric lighting, the sparkling result was the "White City," which attracted 27 million visitors in a single season, from May 1 to October 31, 1893. The exposition sponsors, in that brief time, had remarkably recovered their investment, but within a few short years of the fair's closing, vandalism and fire destroyed most of its buildings. Only the Palace of Fine Arts, occupying the eastern tip of the midway, survives to this day, and it now houses the Museum of Science and Industry. (For more on the behind-the-scenes drama at the Exposition, read *The Devil in the White City*, by Erik Larson, a nonfiction history book that reads like a thriller.)

GETTING THERE From the Loop, the ride to Hyde Park on the **no. 6 Jeffrey Express bus** takes about 30 minutes. The bus originates on Wacker Drive, travels south along State Street, and ultimately follows Lake Shore Drive to Hyde Park. The bus runs daily from early morning to late evening, with departures about every 5 minutes on weekdays and every 10 minutes on weekends and holidays. The southbound express bus fare adds a surcharge of 25¢ to the normal fare of $2.25 (there's no surcharge if you use a CTA

The University of Chicago.

transit card). The **no. 1 local bus** originates at Union Station on Jackson Boulevard and Canal Street and takes about an hour.

For a faster trip, take the **Metra Electric train** on the South Chicago line, which goes from downtown to Hyde Park in about 15 minutes. Trains run every hour (more frequently during rush hour) Monday through Saturday from 5:15am to 12:50am, and every 30 to 90 minutes on Sunday and holidays from 5am to 12:55am. Downtown stations are at Randolph Street and Michigan Avenue, Van Buren Street and Michigan Avenue, and Roosevelt Road and Michigan Avenue (near the Museum Campus in Grant Park). Printed schedules are available at the stations. The fare is approximately $2.50 each way.

For CTA bus and Metra train information, call © **312/836-7000,** or visit **www.transitchicago.com** or **www.metrarail.com**.

For taxis, dial © **312/TAXI-CAB** (829-4222) for **Yellow Cab** or © **312/CHECKER** (243-2537) for **Checker.** The one-way fare from downtown is around $15 to $20.

A SUGGESTED ITINERARY A long 1-day itinerary for Hyde Park should include the following: a walk through the University of Chicago campus (including a stroll along the Midway Plaisance); a visit to the Museum of Science and Industry (for families), Frank Lloyd Wright's Robie House, or one of the other local museums; and lunch or dinner in the neighborhood's commercial center.

The Top Attractions

DuSable Museum of African-American History The DuSable Museum is a repository of the history, art, and artifacts pertaining to the African-American experience and culture. Named for Chicago's first permanent settler, Jean Baptiste Point du Sable, a French-Canadian of Haitian descent, it was founded in 1961 in the home of Dr. Margaret Burroughs, an art teacher at the city's DuSable High School. In 1973, as a result of a community-based campaign, the museum took up residence in its present building (a former parks administration facility and police lockup), on the eastern edge of Washington Park. Despite beginning with no major endowment, the DuSable Museum has managed to accumulate a wide range of artifacts, including an excellent collection of paintings, drawings, and sculpture by African-American and African artists.

In 1993, the DuSable Museum added a 25,000-square-foot wing named in honor of the city's first and only African-American mayor, Harold Washington. The permanent exhibit on Washington contains memorabilia and personal

---

Hyde Park Bites

When you're ready to take a break, Hyde Park has an eclectic selection of restaurants. As in any university town, you'll find plenty of affordable, student-friendly hangouts. The most famous University of Chicago gathering spot is **Jimmy's Woodlawn Tap,** 1172 E. 55th St. (© **773/643-5516**). This 50-year-old bar and grill doesn't offer much in the way of atmosphere, but the hamburgers and sandwiches are cheap, and the person sitting next to you might just be a Nobel Prize–winning professor. Another casual spot near campus is **Medici,** 1327 E. 57th St. (© **773/667-7394;** www.medici57.com), where a few generations' worth of students have carved their names into the tables while chowing down on pizza, the house specialty. About a block from the main Hyde Park Metra station you'll find **La Petite Folie,** 1504 E. 55th St. (© **773/493-1394;** www.lapetitefolie. com), a French bistro that offers a refined escape from student life.

The U-505, a German submarine displayed in the Museum of Science and Industry.

effects, and surveys important episodes in his political career. Other recent exhibits have included "Red, White, Blue and Black," an examination and celebration of the African-American experience in the armed forces, as well as showings of African art. The museum also has a gift shop, a research library, and an extensive program of community-related events, such as a jazz and blues music series, poetry readings, film screenings, and other cultural events, all presented in a 466-seat auditorium. Allow 1 to 2 hours.

740 E. 56th Place. © **773/947-0600.** www.dusablemuseum.org. Admission $10 adults, $6 students and seniors, $3 children 6–11, free for children 5 and under. Free admission Sun. Tues–Sat 10am–5pm; Sun noon–5pm. Closed major holidays. Bus: 6 or Metra Electric train to 57th St. and Lake Park Ave., and then a short cab ride.

Museum of Science and Industry ★★ ☺ Even if you don't plan on spending the day in Hyde Park, you'll likely pass through the neighborhood on your way to one of Chicago's most popular tourist attractions. The massive Museum of Science and Industry is the granddaddy of interactive museums, with some 2,000 exhibits. Schedule at least 3 hours here; a comprehensive visit can take all day, especially if you catch an OMNIMAX movie.

While the museum is constantly adding new displays to cover the latest scientific breakthroughs, you shouldn't miss certain tried-and-true exhibits that have been here for years and epitomize the museum for Chicagoans. The **U-505 ★★★**, a German submarine that was captured in 1944 and arrived at the museum 10 years later, brings home the claustrophobic reality of underwater naval life. The sub is displayed in a dramatic indoor arena with exhibits and newsreel footage that put the U-boat in historical context. (A guided tour of the sub's interior costs $8 extra, but the surrounding exhibit is worth visiting even

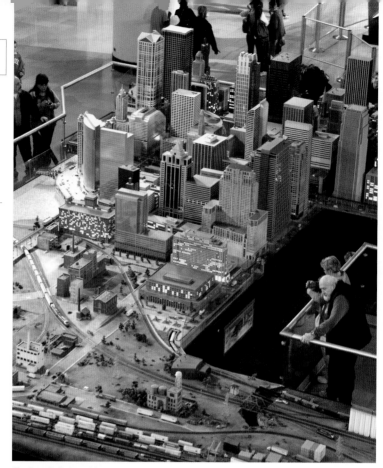

The Great Train Story, a massive model train exhibit.

if you pay for the add-on tour.) The full-scale **Coal Mine ★★**, which dates back to 1934, incorporates modern mining techniques into the exhibit—but the best part is the simulated trip down into a dark, mysterious mine and the clattering mini-trains that transport you through the shadowy tunnels. Get to these exhibits quickly after the museum opens because they attract amusement-park-length lines during the day, with waits for the Coal Mine sometimes running up to an hour.

Kids who love planes, trains, and automobiles shouldn't miss *All Aboard the Silver Streak,* a refurbished Burlington Pioneer Zephyr train with onboard interactive exhibits; the massive model-train exhibit that makes up *The Great Train Story ★★*; or *Take Flight,* an aviation exhibit featuring a full-size 727 airplane that revs up its engines and replays the voice recordings from a San Francisco–Chicago flight periodically throughout the day. In *Networld ★*, you create an avatar who guides you through the technology that makes the Internet possible. More low-tech—but fun for kids—are *The Farm* (where children can sit at the wheel of a giant combine) and the **chick hatchery** inside the exhibit *Genetics: Decoding Life,* where you can watch as tiny newborn chicks poke their way out of eggs. ***Enterprise*** ★ immerses mini-capitalists in the goings-on of a virtual company and includes an entire automated toy-making assembly line. If you have really little ones (under age 5), head for the ***Idea Factory,*** which is filled with hands-on play equipment (admission is limited to a set number of kids, so pick up a free timed ticket in advance).

Girly girls will love **Colleen Moore's Fairy Castle** ★★, a lavishly decorated miniature palace filled with priceless treasures (yes, those are real diamonds and pearls in the chandeliers). It's hidden on the lower level, but worth the effort. Also tucked away in an inconspicuous spot—along the Blue stairwell between the Main Floor and the Balcony—are the ***Human Body Slices,*** actual slivers of human cadavers that are guaranteed to impress teenagers in search of something truly gross.

The **Henry Crown Space Center** ★★ is a museum-within-the-museum that documents the story of space exploration in copious detail, highlighted by a simulated space-shuttle experience through sight and sound at the center's five-story OMNIMAX Theater. The theater offers double features on the weekends; call for show times.

When you've worked up an appetite, you can visit the museum's large food court or the old-fashioned ice-cream parlor; there's also an excellent gift shop.

Although it's quite a distance from the rest of Chicago's tourist attractions, the museum is easy enough to reach without a car. During the summer, the no. 10 bus runs from downtown to the museum's front entrance; you can find a route map and schedule on the museum's website. At other times of the year, your best options are the no. 6 Jeffrey Express bus and the Metra Electric train.

57th St. and Lake Shore Dr. © **800/468-6674** outside the Chicago area, 773/684-1414, or TTY 773/684-3323. www.msichicago.org. Admission to museum only: $15 adults, $14 seniors, $10 children 3–11, free for children 2 and under. Free admission weekdays in Jan. Memorial Day to Labor Day daily 9:30am–5:30pm; early Sept to late May daily 9:30am–4pm. Closed Christmas. Bus: 6 or Metra Electric train to 57th St. and Lake Park Ave.

Oriental Institute Museum ★ Near the midpoint of University of Chicago's campus, the Oriental Institute houses one of the world's major collections of Near Eastern art. Although most of the

This 16-foot sculpture, displayed at the Oriental Institute Museum, once stood in the palace of Assyrian King Sargon II.

galleries have been renovated within the last few years, this is still a very traditional museum: lots of glass cases and very few interactive exhibits (in other words, there's not much to interest young children). A few impressive pieces make it worth at least a brief stop, although history and art buffs should allow more time to linger.

Your first stop should be the **Egyptian Gallery ★★**, which showcases the finest objects among the museum's 35,000 Egyptian artifacts. At the center stands a monumental 17-foot solid-quartzite statue of the boy king Tutankhamen; the largest Egyptian sculpture in the Western Hemisphere, it tips the scales at 6 tons. The surrounding exhibits have a wonderfully accessible approach that emphasizes themes, not chronology. Among them are mummification (there are 14 mummies on display, 5 people and 9 animals), kingship, society, and writing (including a deed for the sale of a house, a copy of the *Book of the Dead*, and a schoolboy's homework).

The Oriental Institute also houses important collections of artifacts from civilizations that once flourished in what are now Iran and Iraq. The highlight of the **Mesopotamian Gallery ★** is a massive 16-foot-tall sculpture of a winged bull with a human head, which once stood in the palace of Assyrian king Sargon II. The gallery also contains some of the earliest man-made tools ever excavated, along with many other pieces that have become one-of-a-kind since the destruction and looting of the National Museum in Baghdad in 2003. Allow 1 hour.

1155 E. 58th St. (at University Ave.). © **773/702-9514.** www.oi.uchicago.edu. Free admission; suggested donation $7 adults, $4 children. Tues–Sat 10am–6pm (Wed until 8:30pm); Sun noon–6pm. Closed major holidays. Bus: 6 or Metra Electric train to 57th St. and Lake Park Ave.

Robie House ★★ For architectural history buffs, Robie House is a must-see. Frank Lloyd Wright designed this 20th-century American architectural masterpiece for Frederick Robie, a bicycle and motorcycle manufacturer. The home, which was completed in 1909, is a classic example of Wright's Prairie School of design, with its open layout and linear geometry of form. Wright prided himself on creating all-encompassing, stylistically harmonious environments, and he oversaw everything from the furniture to the exquisite leaded- and stained-glass doors and windows. It was among the last of Wright's Prairie School–style homes: During its construction, he abandoned both his family and his Oak Park practice to follow other pursuits, most prominently the realization of his Taliesin home and studio in Spring Green, Wisconsin. Docents from Oak Park's Frank Lloyd Wright Home and Studio Foundation lead 1-hour tours of the interior, and after a massive, 10-year restoration in honor of the house's 100th anniversary, it looks better than ever. *Note:* Advance reservations are a good idea in the summer.

A **Wright specialty bookshop** is in the building's former three-car garage—which was highly unusual for the time in which it was built. Advance reservations are recommended in the summer;

🎁 More Frank Lloyd Wright Homes

In addition to Robie House, several of Wright's earlier works, still privately owned, dot the streets of Hyde Park. They include the **Heller House,** 5132 S. Woodlawn Ave. (1897); the **Blossom House,** 1332 E. 49th St. (1882); and the **McArthur House,** 4852 S. Kenwood Ave. (1892). *Note:* These houses are not open to the public, so they can only be admired from the outside.

The Robie House is a classic example of Frank Lloyd Wright's Prairie School of design.

you can order tickets through Robie House's website. Allow 1 hour per tour, plus time to browse the gift shop.

5757 S. Woodlawn Ave. (at 58th St.). © **773/834-1847.** www.gowright.org/visit/robie-house. html. Admission $15 adults, $12 seniors and children 4–17, free for children 3 and under. Thurs–Mon tours at 11am, noon, 1, and 2pm. Bookshop daily 10am–5pm. Bus: 6 or Metra Electric train to 57th St. and Lake Park Ave.

Rockefeller Memorial Chapel To call the Rockefeller Memorial Chapel a chapel is false modesty, even for a Rockefeller. When the university first opened its doors, the students sang the following ditty:

John D. Rockefeller, wonderful man is he

Gives all his spare change to the U of C.

John D. was a generous patron, indeed. He founded the university (in cooperation with the American Baptist Society), built the magnificent mini-cathedral that now bears his name, and shelled out an additional $35 million in donations over the course of his lifetime. Memorial Chapel, designed by Bertram Goodhue, an architect known for his ecclesiastical buildings—including the Cadet Chapel at West Point and New York City's St. Thomas Church—was dedicated in 1928.

In keeping with the rest of the campus, which is patterned after Oxford, the chapel is reminiscent of English Gothic structures; however, it was built from limestone using modern construction techniques. Its most outstanding features are the circular stained-glass window high above the main altar (the windows, in general, are among the largest of any church or cathedral anywhere) and the world's second-largest carillon, which John D. Rockefeller, Jr., donated in 1932 in memory of his mother, Laura. The chapel's organ is nearly as impressive, with four manuals, 126 stops, and more than 10,000 pipes. Choir concerts, carillon performances, and other musical programs run throughout the year, usually for a small donation. Allow a half-hour.

The Rockefeller Memorial Chapel.

5850 S. Woodlawn Ave. ✆ **773/702-2100.** http://rockefeller.uchicago.edu. Free admission. Daily 8am–4pm (except during religious services). Bus: 6 or Metra Electric train to 57th St. and Lake Park Ave.

The Smart Museum of Art ★ The University of Chicago's fine-arts museum looks rather modest, but it packs a lot of talent into a compact space. Its permanent collection of more than 7,000 paintings and sculptures spans Western and Eastern civilizations, ranging from classical antiquity to the present day. Bona fide treasures include ancient Greek vases, Chinese bronzes, and Old Master paintings; Frank Lloyd Wright furniture; Tiffany glass; sculptures by Degas, Matisse, and Rodin; and 20th-century paintings and sculptures by Mark Rothko, Arthur Dove, Diego Rivera, Henry Moore, and Chicago sculptor Richard Hunt. Built in 1974, the contemporary building doesn't really fit in with the campus's Gothic architecture, but its sculpture garden and outdoor seating area make a nice place for quiet contemplation. The museum also has a gift shop and cafe. Allow 1 hour.

5550 S. Greenwood Ave. (at E. 55th St.). ✆ **773/702-0200.** www.smartmuseum.uchicago.edu. Free admission. Tues–Fri 10am–4pm (Thurs until 8pm); Sat–Sun 11am–5pm. Closed major holidays. Bus: 6 or Metra Electric train to 57th St. and Lake Park Ave.

The Smart Museum's sculpture garden.

Exploring the University of Chicago

Walking around the Gothic spires of the University of Chicago campus is bound to conjure up images of the cloistered academic life. Allow about an hour to stroll through the grassy quads and dramatic stone buildings. (If the weather's nice, do as the students do, and chill out for a while on the grass.) If you're visiting on a weekday, your first stop should be the university's **Visitors Information Desk** (*©* **773/702-9739**), on the first floor of Ida Noyes Hall, 1212

Henry Moore's *Nuclear Energy.*

The charming, intimate Bond Chapel.

E. 59th St., where you can pick up campus maps and get information on university events. The center is open Monday through Friday from 10am to 7pm. If you stop by on a weekend when the Visitors Information Desk is closed, you can get the scoop on campus events at the **Reynolds Clubhouse** student center (© **773/702-8787**).

Start your tour at the **Henry Moore statue, *Nuclear Energy,*** on South Ellis Avenue between 56th and 57th streets. It's next to the Regenstein Library, which marks the site of the old Stagg Field, where, on December 2, 1942, the world's first sustained nuclear reaction was achieved in a basement laboratory below the field. Then turn left and follow 57th Street until you reach the grand stone Hull Gate; walk straight to reach the main quad, or turn left through the column-lined arcade to reach **Hutchinson Court** (designed by John Olmsted, son of revered landscape designer Frederick Law Olmsted). The Reynolds Clubhouse, the university's main student center, is here; you can take a break at the C-Shop cafe or settle down at a table at Hutchinson Commons. The dining room and hangout right next to the cafe will bring to mind the grand dining halls of Oxford and Cambridge.

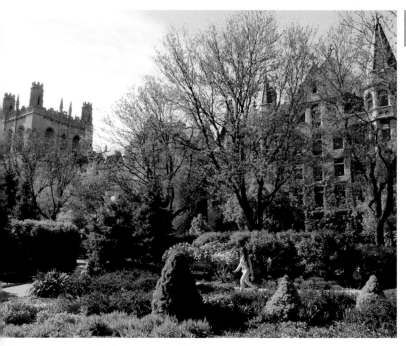

The University of Chicago's Midway Plaisance.

Other worthy spots on campus include the charming, intimate **Bond Chapel,** behind Swift Hall on the main quad, and the blocks-long **Midway Plaisance,** a wide stretch of green that was the site of carnival sideshow attractions during the World's Columbian Exposition in 1893. (Ever since, the term *midway* has referred to carnivals in general.)

The **Seminary Co-op Bookstore,** 5757 S. University Ave. (© **773/752-4381;** www.semcoop.com), is a treasure trove of academic and scholarly books. Its selection of more than 100,000 titles has won it an international reputation as "the best bookstore west of Blackwell's in Oxford." It's open Monday through Friday from 8:30am to 8pm, Saturday from 10am to 6pm, and Sunday from noon to 6pm.

Enjoying the Outdoors in Hyde Park

Hyde Park is not only a haven for book lovers and culture aficionados; the community also has open-air attractions. Worthy outdoor environments near Lake Michigan include **Lake Shore Drive,** where many stately apartment houses follow the contour of the shoreline. A suitable locale for a quiet stroll during the day is **Promontory Point,** at 55th Street and Lake Michigan, a bulb of land that juts into the lake and offers a good view of Chicago to the north and the seasonally active 57th Street beach to the south.

Farther south, just below the Museum of Science and Industry, is **Wooded Island** in Jackson Park, the site of the Japanese Pavilion during the Columbian

Exposition and today a lovely garden of meandering paths. In the **Perennial Garden** at 59th Street and Stony Island Avenue in Jackson Park, more than 180 varieties of flowering plants display a palette of colors that changes with the seasons.

Kenwood Historic District

A fun side trip for architecture and history buffs is the Kenwood Historic District, a short walk north of Hyde Park. The area originally developed as a suburb of Chicago, when local captains of industry (including Sears founder Julius Rosenwald) began building lavish mansions in the mid-1850s. The neighborhood's large lots and eclectic mix of architecture (everything from elaborate Italianate to Prairie-style homes) make it unique in Chicago, especially compared to the closely packed buildings in Hyde Park. Although many of the fine homes here became dilapidated after the South Side's "white flight" of the 1950s and '60s, a new generation of black and white middle-class homeowners has lovingly renovated these one-of-a-kind mansions. Today the blocks between 47th and 51st streets (north-south) and Blackstone and Drexel boulevards (east-west) make for a wonderful walking tour, with broad, shady streets full of newly restored buildings.

TOP: **Promontory Point.** ABOVE: **The lovely, meandering paths at Wooded Island.**

The Kenwood Historic District's eclectic architecture.

MORE MUSEUMS

City Gallery Along with the pumping station across the street, the **Chicago Water Tower** is one of only a handful of buildings to survive the Great Chicago Fire of 1871. It has long been a revered symbol of the city's resilience and fortitude, although today the building is dwarfed by the high-rise shopping centers and hotels of North Michigan Avenue. The Gothic-style limestone building is now an art gallery. The spiffed-up interior is intimate and sunny, and it's a convenient, quick pit stop of culture on your way to the Water Tower shopping center or the tourist information center across the street in the pumping station. Exhibits focus mostly on photography, usually featuring Chicago-based artists such as the fashion photographer Victor Skrebneski. Allow 15 minutes.

806 N. Michigan Ave. (btw. Chicago Ave. and Pearson St.). ✆ **312/742-0808.** Free admission. Mon–Sat 10am–6:30pm; Sun 10am–5pm. Bus: 3, 145, 146, 147, or 151.

Driehaus Museum Investment advisor Richard H. Driehaus is one of Chicago's leading philanthropists and a passionate supporter of historic

City Gallery, housed in the 19th-century Chicago Water Tower.

architecture (given that only the most avant-garde buildings tend to win design awards, he even awards his own prize for the best new uses of traditional architecture). This museum, a few blocks from the Magnificent Mile, is his personal love letter to the Gilded Age—an immaculate restoration of a grand 19th-century mansion that re-creates the sumptuousness of the era. Throughout, the decorative details astound, from the two-story marble-clad front hall to the huge stained-glass dome in the Gallery ceiling; the museum also houses one of the largest collections of objects by designer Louis Comfort Tiffany. Visits are by guided tour only, with no advance reservations taken. Allow 1 hour.

50 E. Erie St. (at Wabash Ave.). *C* **312/932-8665.** www.driehausmuseum.org. Admission $25 adults, $18 seniors, $12.50 students and children 12–16. Tours offered Tues, Wed, and Sat at 10am, 1pm, and 3pm. Subway/El: Red Line to Grand.

Historic Pullman ★★ Railway magnate George Pullman may have been a fabulously wealthy industrialist, but he fancied himself more enlightened than his 19th-century peers. So when it came time to build a new headquarters for his Pullman Palace Car Company, he dreamed of something more than the standard factory surrounded by tenements. Instead, he built a model community for his workers, a place where they could live in houses with indoor plumbing and abundant natural light—amenities almost unheard of for industrial workers in the 1880s. Pullman didn't do all this solely from the goodness of his heart: He hoped that the town, named after him, would attract the most skilled workers (who would be so happy that they wouldn't go on strike). As one of the first "factory towns," Pullman caused an international sensation and was seen as a model for other companies to follow. The happy workers that Pullman envisioned did

The Hotel Florence in Historic Pullman.

go on strike in 1894, however, frustrated by the company's control of every aspect of their lives.

Today the Pullman district makes a fascinating stop for anyone with a historical or architectural bent. While most of the homes remain private residences, a number of public buildings (including the Hotel Florence, the imposing Clock Tower, and the two-story colonnaded Market Hall) still stand. You can walk through the area on your own (stop by the visitor center for a map), or take a guided a tour at 1:30pm on the first Sunday of the month from May through October ($7 adults, $5 seniors, $4 students). Allow 1½ hours for the guided tour.

11141 S. Cottage Grove Ave. ℂ **773/785-8901.** www.pullmanil.org. Visitor center Tues–Sun 11am–3pm. Free admission. Train: Metra Electric line to Pullman (111th St.), turn right on Cottage Grove Ave., and walk 1 block to the visitor center.

International Museum of Surgical Science ★ 🏛 This unintentionally macabre shrine to medicine may be the oddest tourist attraction in town. Not for the faint of stomach, it occupies a historic 1917 Gold Coast mansion designed by the noted architect Howard Van Doren Shaw, who modeled it after Le Petit Trianon at Versailles. Displayed throughout its four floors are surgical instruments, paintings, and sculptures depicting the history of surgery and healing practices in Eastern and Western civilizations. (It's run by the International College of Surgeons.) The exhibits are old-fashioned (no interactive computer displays here), but that's part of the museum's offbeat charm.

You'll look at your doctor in a whole new way after viewing the trepanned skulls excavated from an ancient tomb in Peru. The accompanying tools bored holes in patients' skulls, a horrific practice thought to release the evil spirits causing their illness. (Some skulls show signs of new bone growth, meaning that some lucky headache-sufferers actually survived the low-tech surgery.) There are also battlefield amputation kits, a working iron-lung machine in the polio exhibit, and oddities such as a stethoscope designed to be transported inside a top hat. Other attractions include an apothecary shop and dentist's office (ca. 1900) re-created in a historic street exhibit, and the hyperbolically titled *Hall of Immortals,* a sculpture gallery depicting 12 historic figures in medicine, from Hippocrates to Madame Curie. Allow 1 hour.

1524 N. Lake Shore Dr. (btw. Burton Place and North Ave.). ℂ **312/642-6502.** www.imss.org. Admission $10 adults, $6 seniors, students, and children ages 4–13. Free admission Tues. Tues–Sat 10am–5pm; May–Sept Sun 10am–5pm. Closed major holidays. Bus: 151.

Intuit: The Center for Intuitive and Outsider Art Chicago is home to an active community of collectors of "outsider art," a term attached to a group of unknown, unconventional artists who do their work without any formal training or connection to the mainstream art world. Often called folk or self-taught artists, they produce highly personal and idiosyncratic work using a range of media, from bottle caps to immense canvases. Intuit was founded in 1991 to bring attention to these artists through exhibitions and educational lectures. It's in the warehouse district northwest of the Loop, and has two galleries and a performance area. The museum offers a regular lecture series, and if you time your visit right, you might be here for one of the center's tours of a private local art collection. Allow 1 hour.

756 N. Milwaukee Ave. (at Chicago and Ogden aves.). ℂ **312/243-9088.** www.art.org. Admission $5 adults, free for children 11 and under. Tues–Sat 11am–5pm (Thurs until 7:30pm). Bus: 56 or 66. Subway/El: Blue Line to Chicago.

Jane Addams Hull-House Museum In 1889, a young woman named Jane Addams bought a mansion on Halsted Street surrounded by the shanties of poor immigrants. Here, Addams and her co-worker, Ellen Gates Starr, launched the American settlement-house movement with the establishment of Hull-House, a place where residents of the surrounding slums could learn English, find affordable childcare, and receive social services; eventually, Addams was awarded the Nobel Peace Prize for her work in social justice. In 1963, most of the settlement, along with the entire residential neighborhood in its immediate vicinity, was demolished to make room for the University of Illinois at Chicago campus, which now owns the museum buildings. Of the original settlement, what remain today are the Hull-House Museum, located in the original man-

The Jane Addams Hull-House Museum, located in the original mansion.

sion, and the residents' dining hall, snuggled among the ultramodern, poured-concrete buildings of the university campus. Inside are the original furnishings, Addams's office, and numerous settlement maps and photographs. Rotating exhibits re-create the history of the settlement and the work of its residents, showing how Addams was able to help transform the dismal streets around her into stable inner-city environments worth fighting over. Public tours are given on Wednesdays and Sundays at 1pm. Allow a half-hour.

University of Illinois at Chicago, 800 S. Halsted St. (at Polk St.). © **312/413-5353.** www.uic.edu/jaddams/hull. Free admission. Tues–Fri 10am–4pm; Sun noon–4pm. Closed university holidays. Bus: 8. Subway/El: Blue Line to Halsted/University of Illinois.

National Museum of Mexican Art ★ Chicago's vibrant Pilsen neighborhood, just southwest of the Loop, is home to one of the nation's largest Mexican-American communities. Ethnic pride emanates from every doorstep, *taqueria,* and bakery, and colorful murals splash across building exteriors and alleyways. This institution—the only Latino museum accredited by the American Association of Museums—may be the neighborhood's most prized possession. That's quite an accomplishment, given that it was founded in 1987 by a passel of public school teachers who pooled $900 to get it started.

Exhibits showcase Mexican and Mexican-American visual and performing artists, often drawing on the permanent collection of more than 5,000 works, but the visiting artists, festival programming, and community participation make the museum really shine. Its **Day of the Dead** celebration, which runs for about 8 weeks beginning in September, is one of the most ambitious in the country. The **Del Corazon Mexican Performing Arts Festival,** held in the spring, features programs by local and international artists here and around town; the **Sor Juana Festival,** presented in the fall, honors Mexican writer and pioneering feminist

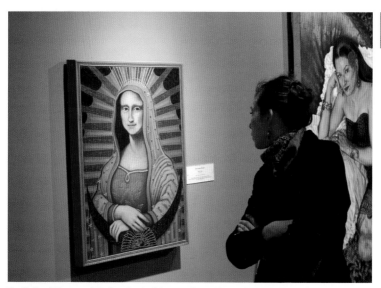

The National Museum of Mexican Art, in Chicago's vibrant Pilsen neighborhood.

Sor Juana Ines de la Cruz with photography and painting exhibits, music and theater performances, and poetry readings by Latina women.

The museum is very family oriented, with educational workshops for kids and parents. It also has an excellent gift shop and stages a holiday market, featuring items from Mexico, on the first weekend in December. Allow 1 hour.

1852 W. 19th St. (a few blocks west of Ashland Ave.). © **312/738-1503.** www.nationalmuseum ofmexicanart.org. Free admission. Tues–Sun 10am–5pm. Closed major holidays. Bus: 9. Subway/ El: Blue Line to 18th St.

National Veterans Art Museum ★ 🎁 This museum houses a stirring collection of art by American war veterans and is the only one of its kind in the world. It opened in 1981 as the National Vietnam Veterans Art Museum, when a small group of former soldiers who had made art as personal therapy began showing their work together in Chicago and in touring exhibitions. The collection has since grown to more than 1,500 paintings, drawings, photographs, and sculptures from all over the world; titles such as *We Regret to Inform You, Blood Spots on a Rice Paddy,* and *The Wound* give you an idea of the power of the images. Eventually, as the museum started exhibiting work by veterans who returned from Iraq, it changed its name and expanded its mission. Housed in a former warehouse in the Prairie Avenue district south of the Loop, the building is modern and well organized. An installation suspended from the ceiling, ***Above & Beyond ★***, comprises more than 58,000 dog tags with the names of the men and women who died in the Vietnam War—it creates an emotional effect similar to that of the Wall in Washington, D.C. The complex also houses a small theater, a gift shop, and an outdoor plaza with a flagpole that has deliberately been left leaning because that's how veterans saw them in combat. Allow 1 hour.

1801 S. Indiana Ave. (at 18th St.). © **312/326-0270.** www.nvam.org. Admission $10 adults, $7 seniors and students with ID. Tues–Sat 10am–5pm. Closed major holidays. Bus: 3 or 4.

Polish Museum of America One million people of Polish ancestry live in Chicago, giving the city the largest Polish population outside of Warsaw, so it's no surprise that the Polish Museum of America is here, in the neighborhood where many of the first immigrants settled. The museum has one of the most important collections of Polish art and historical materials outside Poland. (It is also the largest museum in the U.S. devoted exclusively to an ethnic group.) The museum's programs include rotating exhibitions, films, lectures, and concerts, and a permanent exhibit about Pope John Paul II. There's also a library with a large Polish-language collection, and archives where visitors can research genealogical history. (Call in advance if you want to look through those records.) Allow a half-hour.

984 N. Milwaukee Ave. (at Augusta Blvd.). ✆ **773/384-3352.** www.polishmuseumofamerica. org. Admission $7 adults, $6 students and seniors, $5 children 11 and under. Fri–Wed 11am–4pm. Subway/El: Blue Line to Division.

EXPLORING THE 'BURBS
Oak Park

Architecture and literary buffs alike make pilgrimages to Oak Park, a nearby suburb on the western border of the city that is easily accessible by car or train. Bookworms flock here to see the town where Ernest Hemingway was born and grew up, while others come to catch a glimpse of the Frank Lloyd Wright–designed homes that line the well-maintained streets.

GETTING THERE

BY CAR Oak Park is 10 miles due west of downtown Chicago. By car, take the Eisenhower Expressway (I-290) west to Harlem Avenue (Ill. 43) and exit north. Continue on Harlem north to Lake Street. Take a right on Lake Street and continue to Forest Avenue. Turn left here, and immediately on your right you'll see the **Oak Park Visitor Center** (see below).

BY PUBLIC TRANSPORTATION Take the Green Line west to the Harlem stop, roughly a 25-minute ride from downtown. Exit the station onto Harlem Avenue, and proceed north to Lake Street. Take a right on Lake Street, follow it to Forest Avenue, and then turn left to the **Oak Park Visitor Center** (see below).

BY TOUR The **Chicago Architecture Foundation** regularly runs guided tours from downtown Chicago to Oak Park. For details, see "Sightseeing Tours," p. 224.

VISITOR INFORMATION

The **Oak Park Visitor Center,** 158 Forest Ave. (✆ **888/OAK-PARK** [625-7275]; www.visitoakpark.com), is open daily from 10am to 5pm April through October, and from 10am to 4pm November through March. Stop here for an orientation, maps, and guidebooks. There's a city-operated parking lot next door. The heart of the historic district and the Frank Lloyd Wright Home and Studio are only a few blocks away.

An extensive tour of Oak Park's historic district leaves from the **Ginkgo Tree Bookshop,** 951 Chicago Ave., on weekends from 11am to 3:30pm (exact departure times vary, depending on how many people show up). The tour lasts

Oak Park Attractions

Commuter Railroad and CTA Green Line

ⓜ EL/Subway Stop

ⓘ Information

ⓟ Parking

✉ Post Office

Chicago Ave.

Superior St.

Superior St.

Marion St.

Erie St.

Forest Ave.

Elizabeth Ct.

Kenilworth Ave.

Grove Ave.

Oak Park Ave.

Euclid Ave.

Erie St.

Ontario St.

AUSTIN GARDENS

Ontario St.

SCOVILLE PARK

Lake St.

North Blvd.

Harlem

South Blvd.

Forest Ave.

Home Ave.

Clinton Ave.

Kenilworth Ave.

Grove Ave.

Oak Park Ave.

Euclid Ave.

Pleasant St.

Oak Park

Frank Lloyd Wright Home and Studio **1**
Ginkgo Tree Bookshop **2**
Hemingway Birthplace **6**
Hemingway Museum **5**
Oak Park Visitors Center **3**
Unity Temple **4**

3 mi

3 km

Wrigley Field

CHICAGO

OAK PARK

Map area

THE LOOP

U.S. Cellular Field

✈ Midway

1 hour and costs $15 for adults, $12 for seniors and children ages 4 to 17 (free for children 3 and under). If you can't make it to Oak Park on the weekend, you can follow a self-guided map and audiocassette tour of the historic district for the same price; the audio tour is available at the Ginkgo Tree Bookshop from 10am to 3:30pm. In addition to homes designed by Wright, you will see work by several of his disciples, as well as some charming examples of the Victorian styling that he so disdained. A more detailed map, *Architectural Guide Map of Oak Park and River Forest*, includes text and photos of all 80 sites of interest in Oak Park and neighboring River Forest.

THE WRIGHT STUFF

Frank Lloyd Wright Home and Studio ★★★ For the first 20 years of Wright's career, this remarkable complex served first and foremost as the sanctuary where he designed and executed more than 130 of 430 completed buildings. The home began as a simple shingled cottage that the 22-year-old Wright built for his bride in 1889, but it became a living laboratory for his revolutionary reinvention of interior spaces. Wright remodeled the house constantly until 1911, when he moved out permanently. During Wright's fertile early period, the house was Wright's showcase, but it also embraces many idiosyncratic features molded to his own needs rather than those of a client. With many add-ons—including a

wright's **OAK PARK**

Oak Park has the highest concentration of Frank Lloyd Wright–designed and –built houses or buildings anywhere. People come here to marvel at the work of a man who saw his life as a twofold mission: to wage a single-handed battle against excessively ornamental architecture (Victorian, in particular), and to create in its place a new form that would be, at the same time, functional, appropriate to its natural setting, and stimulating to the imagination.

Not everyone who comes to Oak Park shares Wright's architectural philosophy, but scholars and enthusiasts admire him for being consistently true to his vision, out of which emerged a unique and genuinely American architectural statement. The reason for Wright's success could stem from the fact that he was a living exemplar of a quintessential American type. In a deep sense, he embodied the ideal of the self-made and self-sufficient individual who had survived, even thrived, in the frontier society—qualities that he expressed in his almost-puritanical insistence that each spatial or structural form in his buildings serve some useful purpose.

He was also an aesthete in Emersonian fashion, deriving his idea of beauty from natural environments, where apparent simplicity often belies a subtle complexity.

The three principal ingredients of a tour of Wright-designed structures in Oak Park are the **Frank Lloyd Wright Home and Studio Tour,** the **Unity Temple Tour,** and a **walking tour**—guided or self-guided—to view the exteriors of homes throughout the neighborhood that were built by the architect. Oak Park has 25 homes and buildings by Wright, constructed between 1892 and 1913, which constitute the core output of his Prairie School period.

Frank Lloyd Wright's modest home became a living laboratory for his revolutionary work.

barrel-vaulted children's playroom and a studio with an octagonal balcony suspended by chains—the place has a certain whimsy that others might have found less livable. This was not an architect's masterpiece, but rather the master's home, and visitors can savor every room for the view it offers into of the workings of a remarkable mind.

Advance reservations are recommended, especially during the busy summer months; you can book online or by phone (© **800/514-3849**). Allow 1 hour for the tour, more time if you want to browse in the bookshop.

951 Chicago Ave. © **708/848-1976.** www.gowright.org. Admission $15 adults, $12 seniors and children 4–17, free for children 3 and under; combined admission for the home and studio tour and guided or self-guided historic district tour $25 adults, $20 seniors and students 4–17. Admission to the home and studio is by guided tour only; tours depart from bookshop daily 11am–4pm. Closed Jan 1, last week in Jan, Thanksgiving, and Christmas. Facilities for people with disabilities are limited; please call in advance.

Unity Temple ★ After a fire destroyed its church around 1900, a Unitarian Universalist congregation asked one of its members, Frank Lloyd Wright, to design an affordable replacement. Using poured concrete with metal reinforcements—a necessity due to a small $40,000 budget—Wright created a building that on the outside seems as forbidding as a mausoleum but inside contains all the elements of the Prairie School that has made Wright's name immortal. Wright believed conventional church architecture was overpowering—he complained that he didn't feel a part of the Gothic-style cathedral across the street, for example—and Unity Temple was intended to offer a new model for houses of worship.

Yet his vision in this regard was somewhat confused and contradictory. He wanted Unity Temple to be "democratic," but perhaps Wright was unable to subdue his own personal hubris and hauteur in the creative process, for the ultimate effect of his chapel, and much of the building's interior, is grand and imperial.

Wright's Unity Temple still feels groundbreaking, 100 years later.

This is no simple meetinghouse; instead, its principal chapel looks like the chamber of the Roman Senate.

Wright was a true hands-on, can-do person; he knew his materials as intimately as the artisans who carried out his plans. He added pigment to the plaster (rather than the paint) to achieve a pale, natural effect. His use of wood trim and other decorative touches is still exciting to behold; his sensitivity to grain, tone, and placement was akin to that of an exceptionally gifted woodworker. His stunning, almost minimalist use of form is what still sets him apart as a relevant and brilliant artist. Unity Temple still feels groundbreaking 100 years later—which Wright would consider the ultimate compliment. Allow a half-hour.

875 Lake St. © **708/383-8873.** www.unitytemple-utrf.org. Self-guided tours $9 adults; $7 seniors, children 6-12, and students with ID; free for children 5 and under. Mon–Fri 10:30am–4:30pm; Sat 10am–2pm; Sun 1–4pm. Closed New Year's Day, Thanksgiving, and Christmas. Church events can alter schedule; call in advance.

ON THE TRAIL OF HEMINGWAY

Hemingway Museum Frank Lloyd Wright isn't Oak Park's only famous native son; the town was also the birthplace of writer Ernest Hemingway. Hemingway had no great love for Oak Park;

The Wright Plus Tour

Die-hard fans of the architect will want to be in town on the third Saturday in May for the annual Wright Plus Tour. The public can tour several Frank Lloyd Wright–designed homes and other notable Oak Park buildings, in both the Prairie School and Victorian styles, in addition to Wright's home, his studio, and the Unity Temple. The tour includes 10 buildings in all. Tickets, which go for $100, go on sale March 1 and can sell out by mid-April. Call the Frank Lloyd Wright Home and Studio (© 708/848-1976; www.gowright.org) for details and ticket information.

he moved away right after high school and later referred to his hometown as a place of "wide lawns and narrow minds." But that hasn't stopped Oak Park from laying claim to the great American writer. A portion of the ground floor of this former church, now the Oak Park Arts Center, holds a small but interesting display of Hemingway memorabilia. A 6-minute video sheds considerable light on Hemingway's time in Oak Park, where he spent the first 18 years of his life, and covers his high school experiences particularly well.

The **Ernest Hemingway Birthplace Home** is 2 blocks north, at 339 N. Oak Park Ave. The lovely Queen Anne house—complete with wraparound porch and turret—was the home of Hemingway's maternal grandparents, and it's where the writer was born on July 21, 1899. Its connection to Hemingway is actually pretty tenuous—he spent most of his boyhood and high school years at 600 N. Kenilworth Ave., a few blocks away (that house is still privately owned)—but the birthplace has been carefully restored to replicate its appearance at the end of the 19th century, making this an appealing stop for fans of historic house tours (whether they're Hemingway fans or not). The hours are the same as the Hemingway Museum's. Allow 1 hour.

200 N. Oak Park Ave. © **708/848-2222.** www.ehfop.org. Combined admission to Hemingway Museum and Ernest Hemingway Birthplace Home $10 adults, $8 seniors and children 6–12, free for children 5 and under. Sun–Fri 1–5pm; Sat 10am–5pm. Closed major holidays.

The North Shore

Between Chicago and the state border of Wisconsin is one of the nation's most affluent residential areas, a swath of suburbia known as the North Shore. Although towns farther west like to co-opt the name for its prestige, the North Shore proper extends from Evanston, Chicago's nearest neighbor to the north, along the lakefront to tony Lake Forest, originally built as a resort for Chicago's aristocracy. Dotted with idyllic, picture-perfect towns such as Kenilworth, Glencoe, and Winnetka, this area has long attracted filmmakers such as Robert Redford, who filmed *Ordinary People* in Lake Forest, and the North Shore's own John Hughes, who shot most of his popular coming-of-age comedies (*Sixteen Candles, Ferris Bueller's Day Off, Home Alone,* and so on) here.

Although a Metra train line extends to Lake Forest and neighboring Lake Bluff, I highly recommend that you rent a car and drive north along **Sheridan Road,** which winds its leisurely way through many of these communities, past palatial homes and mansions designed in a startling array of architectural styles. Aside from Lake Shore Drive in Chicago, you won't find a more impressive stretch of roadway in the entire metropolitan area.

EXPLORING EVANSTON

Despite being frequented by Chicagoans, Evanston, the city's oldest suburb, retains an identity all its own. A unique hybrid of sensibilities, it manages to combine the tranquillity of suburban life with a highly cultured, urban charm. It's great fun to wander amid the shops and cafes in its downtown area or along funky Dempster Street at its southern end. The beautiful lakefront campus of **Northwestern University** (© 847/491-3741; www.northwestern.edu) is here, and many of its buildings—such as Alice Millar Chapel, with its sublime stained-glass facade, and the Mary and Leigh Block Gallery, a fine-arts haven that offers a top-notch collection and intriguing temporary exhibitions—are well worth several hours of exploration.

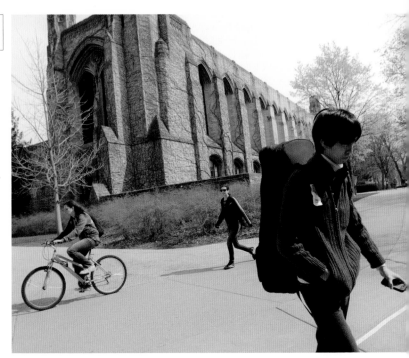

Northwestern University.

Evanston was also the home of Frances Willard, founder of the Women's Christian Temperance Union (WCTU). The **Francis Willard House Museum,** 1730 Chicago Ave. (© **847/328-7500;** www.franceswillardhouse.org), is open to visitors on the first and third Sundays of every month from 1 to 4pm ($10 adults, $5 children 12 and under). Nine of the 17 rooms in this old Victorian "Rest Cottage" (as Willard called it) have been converted into a museum of period furnishings and temperance memorabilia. Among her personal effects is the bicycle she affectionately called "Gladys" and learned to ride late in life, in the process spurring women across the country to do the same. The headquarters of the WCTU are still on-site.

Tucked away in north Evanston, a few miles from the Northwestern campus, is the unusual and informative **Mitchell Museum of the American Indian,** 2600 Central Park Ave. (© **847/475-1030;** www.mitchellmuseum.org). The collection ranges from stoneware tools and weapons to the work of contemporary Native-American artists. The museum is open Tuesday through Saturday from 10am to 5pm (Thurs until 8pm), and Sunday from noon to 4pm. It's closed on holidays and during the last 2 weeks of August. Admission is $5 for adults, $2.50 for seniors and children. Call in advance to arrange a volunteer-led tour.

For a bit of serenity, head to **Grosse Point Lighthouse and Maritime Museum,** 2601 Sheridan Rd. (© **847/328-6961;** www.grossepointlighthouse. net), a historic lighthouse built in 1873, when Lake Michigan still teemed with cargo-laden ships. Tours of the lighthouse, situated in a nature center, take place on weekends from June to September at 2, 3, and 4pm ($6 adults, $3 children 8–12; children 7 and under not admitted, for safety reasons). The adjacent Lighthouse Beach is a favorite spot for local families during the summer. If you're here between Memorial Day and Labor Day, you'll have to pay to frolic on the sand ($7 adults, $5 children 1–11), but it's a great place for a (free) stroll on a sunny spring or fall day.

OTHER AREA ATTRACTIONS

Bahá'í House of Worship Up the road from Evanston in Wilmette is the most visited of all the sights in the northern suburbs, the Bahá'í House of Worship, an ethereal edifice that seems not of this earth. The gleaming white stone temple, designed by the French-Canadian Louis Bourgeois and completed in 1953, is essentially a soaring, nine-sided, 135-foot dome, draped in a delicate lace-like facade, that reveals the Eastern influence of the Bahá'í faith's native Iran. Surrounded by formal gardens, it is one of seven Bahá'í temples in the world and the only one in the Western Hemisphere. The dome's latticework is even more beautiful as you gaze upward from the floor of the sanctuary, which, during the day, is flooded with light. Downstairs, displays in the visitor center explain the Bahá'í faith. Temple members offer informal tours of the building and exhibits to anyone who inquires. Allow a half-hour.

100 Linden Ave. (at Sheridan Rd.), Wilmette. ℭ **847/853-2300.** www.bahai.us/bahai-temple. Free admission. Daily 7am–10pm; visitor center 10am–5pm (until 8pm May–Sept). From Chicago, take the El Red Line north to Howard St. Change for the Evanston train and go to the end of the line, Linden Ave. (Or take the Purple/Evanston Express and stay on the same train all the way.) Turn right on Linden and walk 2 blocks east. If you're driving, go north on the Outer Dr. (Lake Shore Dr.), which feeds into Sheridan Rd.

Tours of the historic Grosse Point Lighthouse are offered on summer weekends.

Wilmette's Bahá'í temple is a soaring, nine-sided dome, one of only seven such temples in the world.

Chicago Botanic Garden ★★ 🗲 Despite its name, the world-class Chicago Botanic Garden is 25 miles north of the city in the suburb of Glencoe. This 385-acre living preserve includes eight large lagoons and a variety of distinct botanical environments, including the Illinois prairie, an English walled garden, and a three-island Japanese garden. Also on the grounds are a large fruit-and-vegetable garden, an "enabling garden" (which shows how gardening can be adapted for people with disabilities), and a 100-acre old-growth oak woodland. If you're here in the summer,

📎 **A Suburban Respite**

If you've made it to the Bahá'í temple, take a stroll across Sheridan Road to the 60-acre **Gillson Park** for a taste of north suburban life. Check out the sailors prepping their boats for a day cruise, families picnicking and playing Frisbee, and kids frolicking on the sandy beach. (Boats are also available for rent at the harbor from $38–$79/hour [📞 847/256-9656] if you'd like to explore Lake Michigan from the water.) Access to the beach is restricted to local residents in the summer, but in the fall and spring, you're welcome to wander (just don't expect to take a dip in the frigid water).

don't miss the extensive rose gardens, with more than 7,750 plants. The Botanic Garden also has an exhibit hall, auditorium, museum, library, education greenhouses, outdoor pavilion, carillon, cafe, designated bike path, and garden shop. Carillon concerts take place at 7pm Monday evenings from late June through August; tours of the carillon are offered beforehand.

Every summer the Botanic Garden stages a special outdoor exhibition. (One year giant animal-shaped topiaries stood in unexpected locations throughout the grounds; another year, model railroads wound through miniature versions of

The Chicago Botanic Garden's serene Japanese garden.

American national parks.) Check the website or call for event schedules. Allow 3 hours.

1000 Lake-Cook Rd. (just east of Edens Expwy./I-94), Glencoe. ✆ **847/835-5440.** www.chicago-botanic.org. Free admission. Daily 8am–sunset. Tram tours Apr–Oct. Closed Christmas. From Chicago, take Sheridan Rd. north along Lake Michigan or the Edens Expwy. (I-94) to Lake-Cook Rd. Parking $20/day.

Ravinia Festival ★★ 👔 Want to know where the natives get away from it all? Come summertime, you'll find them chilling on the lawn at Ravinia, the summer home of the highly regarded Chicago Symphony Orchestra in suburban Highland Park. In operation since 1904, Ravinia started off as an amusement park. The **Martin Theatre**—built in the Prairie style—still remains and is the only building still standing from the early days. Over the years, the festival has hosted an amazing array of performers, from Louis Armstrong, Duke Ellington, George Gershwin, and Ella Fitzgerald to Janis Joplin and Steven Sondheim. The season runs from mid-June to Labor Day and includes far more than classical concerts: You can also catch pop acts, dance performances, operatic arias, and blues concerts. Tickets are available for the lawn or the covered pavilion, where you get a reserved seat and a view of the stage. The lawn is the real joy of Ravinia: sitting under the stars and a canopy of leafy branches while listening to music and indulging in an elaborate picnic. (It's a local tradition to try to outdo everyone else by bringing candelabras and fine china.)

Don't let the distance from downtown discourage you from visiting, because Ravinia is served by an extremely convenient public-transportation system. On concert nights, a special Ravinia Metra commuter train leaves at 5:50pm from the North Western train station at Madison and Canal streets (just west of the Loop). The train stops at the festival at 6:30pm, allowing plenty of time to enjoy a picnic before an 8 o'clock show. After the concert, trains wait right outside the gates to take commuters back to the city. The round-trip train fare is $6, a real bargain, considering that traffic around the park can be brutal.

Dining options at the park range from the fine-dining restaurant **Mirabelle** (✆ **847/432-7550** for reservations) to prepacked picnic spreads from the **Gatehouse,** featuring gourmet items to go. For $10, you can rent a pair of lawn chairs and a table from booths set up near the park entrance. In case you're wondering about the weather conditions at concert time, dial Ravinia's Weather Line (✆ **847/433-5010**).

Green Bay and Lake-Cook rds., Highland Park. ✆ **847/266-5100.** www.ravinia.org. Pavilion tickets $20–$90; lawn $10–$25. Most concerts are in the evening.

Visit historic Long Grove's many specialty stores, galleries and restaurants.

The North & Northwest Suburbs

The North Shore is only one slice of life north of Chicago. To its west lies a sprawling thicket of old and new suburbs, from the bucolic environs of equestrian-minded **Barrington** and its ring of smaller satellite communities in the far northwest, to near-northwest shopping mecca **Schaumburg,** home to the gigantic Woodfield Mall. While Woodfield attracts a steady stream of dedicated shoppers—allowing it to tout its status as one of the top tourist destinations in Illinois—it's not that distinctive; you'll find most of the same stores at your local megamall back home.

A more pastoral option for visitors with time on their hands might be a day trip to the **historic village of Long Grove,** about 30 miles northwest of Chicago. Settled in the 1840s by German immigrants and pioneers traveling west from New England, Long Grove has assiduously preserved its old-fashioned character. Set amid 500 acres of oak- and hickory-tree groves, the village maintains nearly 100 specialty stores, galleries, and restaurants, many of which are in former smithies, wheelwright barns, and century-old residences. (Don't skip the **Long Grove Confectionery Company,** a local institution.) By village ordinance, all new buildings constructed in the shopping district must conform to the architecture of the early 1900s. The village schedules several cultural and entertainment events, festivals, and art fairs throughout the year. The biggest and best is the annual **Strawberry Festival,** held during the last weekend in June. Call the village's information center or check the town's website (© **847/634-0888;** www.longgroveonline.com) for updates on coming events. To get there from the Chicago Loop, take the I-94 tollway (also known as the Kennedy Expwy.) north until it separates at I-90, another tollway that runs northwest. Follow I-90 until

Arlington International Racecourse.

you reach Rte. 53, and drive north on 53 until it dead-ends at Lake-Cook Road. Take the west exit off 53, and follow Lake-Cook Road to Hicks Road. Turn right on Hicks Road and then left on Old McHenry Road, which will take you right into the center of town.

Arlington International Racecourse With its gleaming-white, palatial, six-story grandstand and lush gardens, this racecourse is one of the most beautiful showcases for thoroughbred horse racing in the world. Its storied history stretches back to 1927, and such equine stars as Citation, Secretariat, and Cigar have graced the track. The annual Arlington Million (the sport's first million-dollar race, held in mid-Aug) attracts top jockeys, trainers, and horses, and is part of the World Series Racing Championship, which includes the Breeders Cup races. Arlington's race days are thrilling to behold, with all of racing's time-honored pageantry on display—from the bugler in traditional dress to the parade of jockeys.

Arlington likes to say that it caters to families, and the ambience is more Disney than den of iniquity. "Family days" throughout the summer include live music and entertainment ranging from petting zoos to puppet shows.

2200 W. Euclid Ave., Arlington Heights. © **847/385-7500.** www.arlingtonpark.com. May–Sept Wed–Sun gates open 11am, 1st post 1pm. No racing Oct–Apr. General admission $6 adults, $3–$6 additional per person for reserved seating. Take the Kennedy (I-94) Expwy. to the I-90 tollway, and exit north on Rte. 53. Follow 53 north to the Euclid exit. Or take Metra train to Arlington Heights. Free parking.

The Western Suburbs

So many corporations have taken to locating their offices beyond the city limits that today more people work in the suburbs than commute into Chicago. Much of the suburban sprawl in counties such as DuPage and Kane consists of seas of aluminum-sided houses that seem to sprout from cornfields overnight. But there are also some lovely older towns, such as upscale **Hinsdale** and, much farther west, the quaint tandem of **St. Charles** and **Geneva,** which lie across the Fox River from each other. Perhaps there is no more fitting symbol of this booming area than the city of **Naperville.** A historic, formerly rural community with a Main Street U.S.A. downtown district worthy of Norman Rockwell, Naperville has exploded from a population of about 30,000 residents in the early 1970s to approximately 145,000 today—which makes it the third-largest municipality in the state. Naperville maintains a collection of 19th-century buildings in an outdoor setting known as Naper Settlement, and its river walk is the envy of neighboring village councils. But much of its yesteryear charm seems to be disappearing bit by bit as new subdivisions and strip malls ooze forth across the prairie.

Brookfield Zoo ★★ ☺ In contrast to the more modest Lincoln Park Zoo, Brookfield is enormous, spreading out over 216 acres and housing thousands of animals—camels, dolphins, giraffes, baboons, wolves, tigers, green sea turtles, Siberian tigers, snow leopards, and more—in naturalistic environments that put them side by side with other inhabitants of their regions. These creative indoor and outdoor settings, filled with activities to keep kids interested, are what set Brookfield apart.

Start out at *Habitat Africa!* ★★, a multiple-ecosystem exhibit that encompasses 30 acres—about the size of the entire Lincoln Park Zoo. Then wander through some of the buildings that allow you to see animals close up; my personal favorites are **Tropic World ★★**, where you hang out at treetop level with monkeys, and **Australia House,** where fruit bats flit around your head. **The Living Coast ★** explores the west coast of Chile and Peru, and includes everything from a tank of plate-size moon jellies to a rocky shore where Humboldt penguins swim and nest as Inca terns and gray gulls fly freely overhead. **The Swamp** re-creates the bioregions of a southern cypress swamp and an Illinois river scene, and discusses what people can do to protect wetlands. The dolphins at the **Seven Seas Panorama ★★** put on an amazing show that has been a Brookfield Zoo fixture for years. If you go on a weekend, buy tickets to the dolphin show at least a couple of hours before the one you plan to attend, because they tend to sell out quickly.

The **Hamill Family Play Zoo** is a wonderful stop for kids. They not only get to pet animals, but can also build habitats, learn how to plant a garden, and even play animal dress-up. The only catch: the separate admission fee ($3.50 adults, $2.50 children). Allow 3 hours.

First Ave. and 31st St., Brookfield. © **708/485-0263.** www.brookfieldzoo.org. Admission $14 adults, $9.50 seniors and children 3–11, free for children 2 and under. Parking $9. Free admission Tues and Thurs Oct–Feb. Memorial Day to Labor Day daily 9:30am–6pm (Sun until 7:30pm); fall–spring daily 10am–5pm. Bus: 304 or 311. Take the Stevenson (I-55) and Eisenhower (I-290) expressways 14 miles west of the Loop.

Morton Arboretum Feel like getting away from it all? This suburban oasis, covering almost 2,000 acres, is dedicated to preserving an amazing variety of trees and shrubs in a peaceful, welcoming setting. You can follow walking trails through solemn forests, explore a re-creation of an original Illinois prairie, or wander the twisting pathways of the **Maze Garden.** (If you'd rather watch others wander,

Wander the twisting pathways of the Morton Arboretum's Maze Garden.

climb up to the viewing platform built around the trunk of a 60-ft.-tall sycamore tree.) Covering the arboretum's vast acreage requires some driving—and you'll need a car to get here, since it's not accessible by public transportation.

The arboretum's modestly named **Children's Garden** is more like a family wonderland, with dozens of nature-friendly attractions. Highlights include streams built for splashing, hidden grottoes, and a wooden walkway suspended between evergreen trees. Morton Arboretum also offers regular nature talks, as well as special exhibits at the Sterling Morton Library. The Visitor Center has an attractive gift shop and restaurant.

4100 Illinois Rte. 53, Lisle. ✆ **630/968-0074.** www.mortonarb.org. Grounds open daily year-round 7am–7pm (or sunset, whichever comes soonest). Visitor Center 9am–5pm (until 6pm May–Oct). Admission $11 adults, $10 seniors, $8 children 2–17. Take the Stevenson (I-290) Expwy. west from downtown Chicago to I-88. Exit north onto Rte. 53 and follow the signs for ½ mile to the entrance.

KID STUFF

Chicago Children's Museum ★ ★ ☺ Located on tourist-filled Navy Pier, this museum is one of the most popular family attractions in the city. The building has areas especially for preschoolers as well as for children up to age 10, and several permanent exhibits allow kids a maximum of hands-on fun. *Dinosaur Expedition* re-creates an expedition to the Sahara, allowing kids to experience camp life, conduct scientific research, and dig for the bones of Suchomimus, a Saharan dinosaur discovered by Chicago paleontologist Paul Sereno (a full-scale model stands nearby).

Kids dig for the bones of Suchomimus, a Saharan dinosaur, at the Chicago Children's Museum *Dinosaur Expedition.*

The ***Inventing Lab*** will appeal to budding scientists—here kids can take the *Alarm Clock Challenge* and wake up the sleeping bear or slide down the musical *Grand Piano Slide.* The **BIG Backyard** is an urban garden filled with enormous insects, giggling flowers, and giant toadstools.

There's also a three-level **schooner** that children can board for a little climbing, from the crow's nest to the gangplank; ***PlayMaze,*** a toddler-scale cityscape with everything from a gas station to a city bus that children 4 and under can touch and explore; and an **arts-and-crafts area** where visitors can create original artwork to take home. Allow 2 to 3 hours.

Navy Pier, 700 E. Grand Ave. ℭ **312/527-1000.** www.chichildrensmuseum.org. Admission $10 adults and children, $9 seniors. Free admission Thurs 5–8pm; free for ages 15 and under the first Sun of every month. Daily 10am–5pm (Thurs until 8pm). Closed Thanksgiving and Christmas. Bus: 29, 65, or 66. Subway/El: Red Line to Grand; transfer to city bus or Navy Pier's free trolley bus.

Lincoln Park Pritzker Children's Zoo & Farm-in-the-Zoo ★ 🐾 ☺ After hours of looking at animals from afar in the rest of Lincoln Park Zoo, kids can come here to get up close and personal. Unlike many other children's zoos, there are no baby animals at the **Pritzker Children's Zoo;** instead, the outdoor habitats feature wildlife of the North American woods, including wolves, beavers, and otters. Although there are a few interactive displays outside, most kids head inside to the Treetop Canopy Climbing Adventure, a 20-foot-high wood-and-fabric tree (encased in soft safety netting) that kids can scramble up and down. There are also a few small padded play areas for little ones.

The **Farm-in-the-Zoo ★** is a working reproduction of a Midwestern farm, complete with a white-picket-fenced barnyard, chicken coops, and

The playground at Lake Shore Park.

Downtown Playgrounds

As anyone who's traveled with little kids well knows, children can take only so much museum-going. Sometimes they have to let loose and run around—luckily, there are playgrounds tucked away in unassuming spots, as long as you know where to look. The **Seneca Playlot,** 228 E. Chicago Ave., is directly east of the Chicago Water Works Visitor Center and across the street from Water Tower Place mall. The play structures are mostly low-to-the-ground, making it a good choice for toddlers. Walk a few blocks east and you'll come to **Lake Shore Park,** 808 N. Lake Shore Dr., which has a good assortment of slides and climbing equipment. As an added bonus, you'll enjoy views of the lake. An adjoining athletic field has a running track and plenty of space for impromptu soccer or football games. Occupying a large corner lot on the ritzy Gold Coast, **Goudy Square Park,** at the corner of Astor and Goethe streets, is a tranquil oasis surrounded by high-rises. There are three separate play areas, along with plenty of benches for parents to lounge.

demonstrations of butter churning and weaving. You'll also spot plenty of livestock, including cows, sheep, and pigs. Inside the Main Barn (filled with interactive exhibits), the main attraction is the huge John Deere tractor that kids can climb up into and pretend to drive. (Can you say "photo opportunity"?) Allow 1 hour.

2200 N. Cannon Dr. ✆ **312/742-2000.** www.lpzoo.com. Free admission. Daily 9am–5pm. Bus: 151 or 156.

Six Flags Great America ★ ☺ One of the Midwest's biggest theme and amusement parks, Six Flags is midway between Chicago and Milwaukee on I-94 in Gurnee, Illinois. The park has more than 100 rides and attractions and is a favorite of roller coaster devotees. There are a whopping 10 of them here, including the nausea-inducing Déjà Vu, where riders fly forward and backward over a twisting, looping inverted steel track; and Superman, where you speed along hanging headfirst (with your legs dangling). Other don't-miss rides for the strong of stomach include the Iron Wolf, where you do corkscrew turns and 360-degree loops while standing up, and the American Eagle, a classic wooden coaster. Because this place caters to families, you'll also find plenty to appeal to smaller visitors. The Looney Tunes National Park is full of kiddie rides with a cartoon theme; other worthwhile stops include the double-decker carousel and bumper cars. Hurricane Harbor, a massive water park with a giant wave pool, is fun on a hot day, but you risk heatstroke waiting in the long lines. Six Flags also has live shows, IMAX movies, and restaurants. If you take the trouble to get out here, allow a full day.

I-94 at Rte. 132 E., Gurnee. ✆ **847/249-4636.** www.sixflags.com. Admission (including unlimited rides, shows, and attractions) $55 adults, $35 children under 54 in. tall, free for children 3 and under. May daily 10am–7pm; June–Aug daily 10am–10pm; Sept Sat–Sun 10am–7pm. Parking $10. Take I-94 or I-294 W. to Rte. 132 (Grand Ave.). Approximate driving time from Chicago city limits: 45 min.

SIGHTSEEING TOURS

If you're in town for a limited time, an organized tour may be the best way to get a quick overview of the city's highlights. Some tours—such as the boat cruises on Lake Michigan and the Chicago River—can give you a whole new perspective on the city's landscape. Many tours go beyond sightseeing to explore important historical and architectural landmarks in depth. These specialized tours can help you appreciate buildings or neighborhoods that you might otherwise have passed by without a second glance.

For information about touring Eli's bakery, which manufactures Chicago's most famous cheesecake, see the "Dessert Tour" box on p. 112.

Carriage Rides

Noble Horse (© 312/266-7878; www.noblehorsechicago.com/carriages.html) maintains the largest fleet of antique horse carriages in Chicago, stationed around the old Water Tower Square at the northwest corner of Chicago and Michigan avenues. Each of the drivers, outfitted in a black tie and top hat, has his or her own variation on the basic Magnificent Mile itinerary (you can also do tours of the lakefront, river, Lincoln Park, and Buckingham Fountain). The charge is $40 for each half-hour, for up to four people. The coaches run year-round, with convertible coaches in the warm months and enclosed carriages furnished with wool blankets on bone-chilling nights. There are several other carriage operators, all of whom pick up riders in the vicinity.

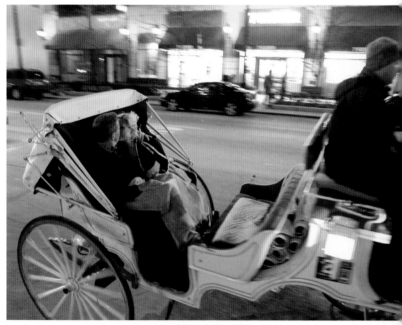

Hop in an antique carriage for a romantic tour of the Magnificent Mile.

An all-day pass allows you to hop on and off these London-style red buses as you please.

Orientation Tours

Chicago Trolley Company Chicago Trolley Company offers guided tours on a fleet of rubber-wheeled "San Francisco–style" trolleys that stop at a number of popular spots around the city, including Navy Pier, the Grant Park museums, the historic Water Tower, and the Sears Tower. You can stay on for the full 2-hour ride or get on and off at each stop. During the summer, the trolleys also offer trips to residential neighborhoods, including Hyde Park, the West Loop, and Wrigleyville. The trolleys operate year-round, but winter visitors won't need to wear a snowsuit: The vehicles are enclosed and heated during the chilliest months. The same company also operates the **Chicago Double Decker Company,** which has a fleet of London-style red buses. The two-level buses follow the same route as the trolleys; if you buy an all-day pass, you can hop from bus to trolley at any point. *An added bonus:* With each ticket, you'll get a free T-shirt and a coupon book with discounts at local restaurants and shops.

615 W. 41st St. ℂ **773/648-5000.** www.chicagotrolley.com. All-day hop-on, hop-off pass $29 adults, $24 seniors, $15 children 3–11; family package (2 adults, 2 children) $64 (tickets are 10% cheaper if purchased in advance online). Apr–Oct daily 9am–6:30pm; Nov–Mar daily 9am–5pm. No tours New Year's Day, Thanksgiving, or Christmas.

Gray Line Part of a worldwide bus tour company, Gray Line Chicago offers professional tours in well-appointed buses. Excursions run 2 to 5 hours and feature highlights of downtown or various neighborhoods. For an additional fee, some tours include a cruise on Lake Michigan or a visit to the Sears Tower Skydeck.

27 E. Monroe St., Ste. 515. ℂ **800/621-4153** or 312/251-3107. www.grayline.com. Tours $20– $50.

Lake & River Cruises

Chicago Line Cruises This company runs two types of 90-minute cruises: a tour of architecture along the Chicago River, and excursions that travel on the lake and river to explore the development of the city. The atmosphere is more upscale-educational than party-hearty, with knowledgeable guides who make no attempt to double as stand-up comedians. The price includes coffee (Starbucks, no less), soft drinks, cookies, and muffins. During the summer, "cocktail" cruises run daily at 6 and 8pm. For tickets, call or stop by the company's ticket office on the lower level on the east end of River East Plaza. Advance reservations are recommended.

465 N. McClurg Court, at the end of E. Illinois St. ✆ **312/527-1977.** www.chicagoline.com. Tickets $38 adults, $32 seniors, $22 children 7–18, free for children 6 and under. May–Oct daily. Tours depart hourly 9am–4pm Memorial Day to Labor Day and every 2 hr. 10am–4pm May, Sept, and Oct.

Mystic Blue Cruises A more casual alternative to fancy dinner cruises, this is promoted as more of a "fun" ship (that means DJs at night, although you'll have to put up with some kind of "live entertainment" no matter when you sail). Daily lunch and dinner excursions are available, as are midnight voyages on weekends. The same company offers more formal (and expensive) cruises aboard the ***Odyssey*** (www.odysseycruises.com) and motorboat rides on the 70-passenger ***Seadog*** (www. seadogcruises.com), if you really want to feel the water in your face.

Departing from Navy Pier. ✆ **877/299-7783.** www.mysticbluecruises.com. Lunch cruise $36; dinner cruise $78–$89; midnight cruise $37. Cruises run year-round.

Shoreline Sightseeing ★ Shoreline launches 30-minute lake cruises every half-hour from its two dock locations at the Shedd Aquarium and Navy Pier. Shoreline has also gotten in on the popularity of architecture tours. Narrated by architectural guides, they cost more than regular tours. A **water taxi** also runs every half-hour between Navy Pier and the Sears Tower, Michigan Avenue, and the Shedd Aquarium. Tickets for the water taxi cost $5 to $7, depending how far you travel.

Departing from Navy Pier, Shedd Aquarium, and Buckingham Fountain in Grant Park. ✆ **312/222-9328.** www.shorelinesightseeing. com. Tickets weekdays $14 adults, $13 seniors, $6 children 11 and under ($1 more per ticket on weekends); architectural tours $24 adults, $21 seniors, $12 children 11 and under ($2 more per ticket on weekends). May–Sept daily. Tours depart hourly 10am–7pm Memorial Day to Labor Day and every 30 min. 10am–4pm May and Sept.

A cruise boat on the Chicago River.

The Spirit of Chicago This luxury yacht offers a variety of wining-and-dining harbor cruises, from a lunch buffet to the "Moonlight Dance Party." This can be a fairly pricey night out if you go for the dinner package; the late-night moonlight cruises are a more affordable option for insomniacs.

Departing from Navy Pier. ☏ **866/211-3804.** www.spiritcruises.com. Lunch cruise $40–$50; dinner cruise (seated) $80–$110; sunset and midnight cruises $32. Ask about children's rates. Year-round daily.

Wendella Sightseeing Boats ★ Started in 1935, Wendella is the granddaddy of Chicago sightseeing operators (it's now run by the original owner's grandsons). The company operates a 1-hour tour along the Chicago River and a 1½-hour tour along the river and out onto Lake Michigan. (One of the most dramatic events during the boat tour is passing through the locks that separate the river from the lake.) Boats run from late April to early October. The 2-hour sunset tour runs Memorial Day to Labor Day starting at 7:45pm. Scheduling depends on the season and the weather, but cruises usually leave every hour during the summer.

Departing from Michigan Ave. and Wacker Dr. (north side of the river, at the Wrigley Building). ☏ **312/337-1446.** www.wendellaboats.com. Tickets $26 adults, $25 seniors, $13 children 3–11, free for children 2 and under. Apr–Oct daily.

Windy ★★ One of the more breathtaking scenes on the lake is this tall ship approaching the docks at Navy Pier. The 148-foot four-masted schooner sets sail for 90-minute cruises two to five times a day, both day and evening. (Because the boats are sometimes booked by groups, the schedule changes each week; check their website or call first to confirm sailing times.) The boats are at the whims of the wind, so every cruise charts a different course. Passengers are welcome to help raise and trim the sails and occasionally take turns at the ship's helm (with the captain standing close by). The boats are not accessible for people with disabilities.

Departing from Navy Pier. ☏ **312/595-5555.** www.tallshipadventuresofchicago.com. Tickets $24 adults, $20 seniors and students, $10 children 3–12. Tickets may be purchased online in advance or bought in person 1 hr. before the 1st sail of the day at the ticket office, on the dock at Navy Pier.

Special-Interest Tours

Chicago Architecture Foundation (CAF) ★★★ Chicago's architecture is world famous. Luckily, the Chicago Architecture Foundation offers first-rate guided tours to help visitors understand what makes this city's skyline so special. The foundation offers walking, bike, boat, and bus tours to more than 60 architectural sites and environments in and around Chicago, led by nearly 400 trained and enthusiastic docents (all volunteers). I highly recommend taking at least one CAF tour while you're in town—they help you look at (and appreciate) the city in a new way. Tours are available year-round but are scheduled less frequently in winter.

One of the CAF's most popular tours is the 1½-hour **Architecture River Cruise,** which glides along both the north and the south branches of the Chicago River. Although you can see the same 50 or so buildings by foot, traveling by water lets you enjoy the buildings from a unique perspective. The excellent docents also provide interesting historical details, as well as some fun facts. (David Letterman once called the busts of the nation's retailing legends that

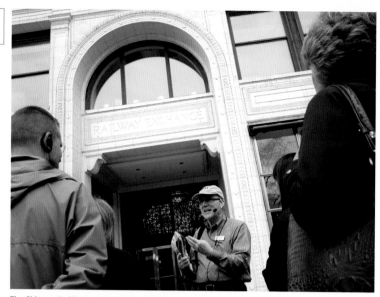

The Chicago Architecture Foundation offers engaging and informative tours of the city.

face the Merchandise Mart the "Pez Hall of Fame.") The docents generally do a good job of making the cruise enjoyable for visitors with all levels of architectural knowledge. In addition to pointing out buildings—Marina City, the Civic Opera House, the Sears Tower—they approach the sites thematically, explaining, for example, how Chicagoans' use of and attitudes toward the river have changed over time.

In the summer (June–Sept), cruises run hourly from 10am to 3pm weekdays and from 9am to 5pm weekends (with more limited schedules in May, Oct, and Nov); the cost is $35 per person. The trips are popular in the summer, so I'd definitely purchase tickets in advance if you're hoping for a particular date or time. You can buy them online through the Architecture Foundation's website, but it means shelling out an annoying service charge to Ticketmaster; instead, I'd suggest buying tickets at one of the foundation's tour centers or from the boat launch on the southeast corner of Michigan Avenue and Wacker Drive.

If you have a limited amount of time in Chicago and want to squeeze in a lot of sightseeing, try the **Highlights by Bus** tour, a 3½-hour overview that covers the Loop, Hyde Park—including a visit to the interior of Frank Lloyd Wright's Robie House—and the Gold Coast, plus several other historic districts. Tours start at 9:30am on Friday and Saturday year-round, with additional tours on Wednesdays and Sundays from April through October; tickets are $42 per person.

A 4-hour bus tour of Frank Lloyd Wright sights in **Oak Park** ($42) is available on the first Saturday of the month from May to October. The tour includes walks through three neighborhoods and commentary on more than 25 houses—but does not take visitors inside Wright's home and studio. A separate 4-hour bus tour ($52), on Tuesday and Thursday at 9:30am (May–Oct), takes Wright fans inside the master's home and Oak Park's Unity Temple.

The CAF offers a variety of guided walking tours. For first-time visitors, I highly recommend two tours for an excellent introduction to the dramatic architecture of the Loop. **Historic Downtown: Rise of the Skyscraper** (daily 10am) covers buildings built between 1880 and 1940, including the Rookery and the Chicago Board of Trade; **Modern Skyscrapers** (daily 1pm) includes modern masterpieces by Mies van der Rohe and postmodern works by contemporary architects. The 2-hour tours cost $16 each for adults and $13 each for seniors and students.

The CAF also offers more than 50 **neighborhood tours** (see website for full list), visiting the Gold Coast, River North, Grant Park, Old Town, the Jackson Boulevard Historic District, and even Lincoln Park Zoo. Most cost $10 and last a couple of hours.

Departing from the Chicago ArchiCenter, 224 S. Michigan Ave.; a few tours leave from the John Hancock Center, 875 N. Michigan Ave. ✆ **312/922-3432,** or 312/922-TOUR [8687] for recorded information. www.architecture.org. Tickets for most walking tours $12–$16. Subway/El: Brown, Green, Purple, or Orange line to Adams, or Red Line to Jackson.

Chicago Supernatural Tours An offbeat way to experience the real "spirit" of Chicago is to take a narrated bus tour of cemeteries, murder sites, Indian burial grounds, haunted pubs, and other spooky places. Richard Crowe, who bills himself as a "professional ghost hunter," spins ghost stories, legends, and lore on the 4-hour trip. Yes, there's plenty of shtick, but Crowe really knows his stuff, so you'll get an informative history lesson along the way. Reservations are required; Crowe's tours get especially popular around Halloween, so you'll definitely want to call ahead.

Crowe also leads 2-hour **supernatural boat excursions** from July through Labor Day weekend; the tour costs $27 per person and boards at 9:30pm at the Mercury boat dock at Michigan Avenue and Wacker Drive.

Departs from Goose Island Restaurant, 1800 N. Clybourn Ave. ✆ **708/499-0300.** www.ghost tours.com. $44 per person. Tours offered once or twice a month Fri–Sat nights; call for exact schedule. Subway/El: Red Line to North/Clybourn and short walk.

Untouchable Tours The days of Al Capone are long gone, but Chicago's notorious past is still good for business, it seems, given the popularity of these "Gangster Tours." The 2-hour bus trip takes you to all of the city's old hoodlum

---

The Wright Stuff in the Gold Coast

Architecture junkies may want to visit the **Charnley-Persky House,** 1365 N. Astor St., in the Gold Coast (✆ **312/915-0105** or 312/573-1365; www.charnleyhouse.org), designed by Frank Lloyd Wright and Louis Sullivan in 1891. Sullivan was Frank Lloyd Wright's architectural mentor, and although Wright was a junior draftsman on this project, Sullivan allowed him to become involved in the design process. The result is an important landmark in modern architecture that rejected Victorian details and embraced symmetry and simplicity. Free 45-minute tours of the interior are given on Wednesday at noon. A 90-minute tour of the home and the surrounding neighborhood is offered Saturdays at 10am year-round ($10); an additional tour is given at noon April through November. Reservations are not accepted.

hangouts from the Prohibition era, including O'Bannion's flower shop and the site of the St. Valentine's Day massacre. The focus is definitely more on entertainment than history (guides with names such as "Al Dente" and "Ice Pick" appear in costume and role-play their way through the tour), but the trip does give you a pretty thorough overview of the city.

Departs from the southeast corner of Clark and Ohio sts. ✆ **773/881-1195.** www.gangstertour.com. Tickets $30. Tours depart Mon–Wed 10am; Thurs 10am and noon; Fri 10am, noon, 2pm, and 7:30pm; Sat 10am, noon, 2, and 4pm; Sun 10am and noon.

NEIGHBORHOOD TOURS

It's a bit of a cliché to say that Chicago is a city of neighborhoods, but if you want to see what really makes the place special, that's where you have to go.

Sponsored by the city's Department of Cultural Affairs, **Chicago Neighborhood Tours ★** (✆ **312/742-1190;** www.chicagoneighborhoodtours.com) are 4- to 5-hour narrated bus excursions to about a dozen diverse communities throughout the city. Departing at 10am from the **Chicago Cultural Center** (p. 165), 77 E. Randolph St., every Saturday, the tours visit different neighborhoods, from Chinatown and historic Bronzeville on the South Side to the ethnic enclaves of Devon Avenue and Uptown on the North Side. Neighborhood representatives serve as guides and greeters along the way as tour participants visit area landmarks, murals, museums, and shopping districts. Tickets (including a light snack) are $30 for adults and $25 for seniors, students, and children 8 to 18. Tours do not run on major holidays (call first) or, usually, in January. Regularly available specialty tours include Literary Chicago; the Great Chicago Fire; Roots of Blues, Gospel & Jazz; Irish Chicago; and Magnificent Churches. These tours, which generally run about 4 to 6 hours and include lunch, are more expensive ($50 adults, $45 seniors and children 8–18).

On Saturday mornings in the summer, the **Chicago History Museum** offers 2-hour walking tours of the neighborhoods surrounding the museum: the **Gold Coast, Old Town,** and **Lincoln Park.** Led by museum docents, they average about four per month June through August. Day and evening tours are available, and a few specialty walking tours are usually offered as well. Tours are $15 per person, and registration is recommended but not required. Tours depart from the museum at Clark Street and North Avenue, and light refreshments are served afterward. In the summer and fall, the museum also offers a few half-day trolley tours that cover unique themes or aspects of the metropolitan area's history. Led by historians and scholars, they take place in the city and surrounding areas ($45). Tours depart from the Chicago History Museum at Clark Street and North Avenue. Call ✆ **312/642-4600,** or visit the museum's website (www.chicagohistory.org) for schedules and to order tickets online.

Groups interested in African-American history should visit **Bronzeville** (also known as the "Black Metropolis"), the South Side neighborhood where immigrants from the South created a flourishing business-and-artistic community in the 1930s and '40s. Walking and bus tours of the area can be arranged through the **Bronzeville Visitor Information Center,** 3501 S. Martin Luther King Dr. (✆ **773/373-2842;** www.bviconline.info). A locally based company that specializes in black heritage tours, **Black CouTours** (✆ **773/233-8907;** www.blackcoutours.com) offers a "Soul Side of the Windy City" tour, which includes Obama-related sites. **Tour Black Chicago** (✆ **773/684-9034;** www.tourblackchicago.com) sells self-guided tours on CD, which are best if you're visiting with a car.

CEMETERY TOURS

Don't be scared away by the creepy connotations. Some of Chicago's cemeteries are as pretty as parks, and they offer a variety of intriguing monuments that are a virtual road into the city's history.

One of the best area cemeteries is **Graceland,** stretching along Clark Street in the Swedish neighborhood of Andersonville, where you can view the tombs and monuments of many Chicago notables. When Graceland was laid out in 1860, public parks were rare. The elaborate burial grounds that were constructed in many large American cities around that time had the dual purpose of relieving the congestion of the municipal cemeteries closer to town and providing pastoral recreational settings for the Sunday outings of the living. Indeed, cemeteries like Graceland were the precursors of such great municipal green spaces as Lincoln Park.

The **Chicago Architecture Foundation** (☎ 312/922-TOUR [8687]; www.architecture.org) offers walking tours of Graceland on select Sundays during August, September, and October. The tour costs $15 and lasts about 2 hours. Among the points of interest in these 121 beautifully landscaped acres are the Ryerson and Getty tombs, famous architectural monuments designed by Louis Sullivan. Sullivan himself rests here in the company of several of his distinguished colleagues: Daniel Burnham, Ludwig Mies van der Rohe, and Howard Van Doren Shaw. Chicago giants of industry and commerce buried at Graceland include Potter Palmer, Marshall Field, and George Pullman. The Chicago Architecture Foundation offers tours of other cemeteries, including Rosehill Cemetery, suburban Lake Forest Cemetery, and Oak Woods Cemetery, the final resting place for many famous African-American figures, including Jesse Owens, Ida B. Wells, and Mayor Harold Washington.

STAYING ACTIVE

Perhaps because winters can be brutal, Chicagoans take their summers seriously. In the warmer months, with the wide blue lake and the ample green parks, it's easy to think that the city is one big grown-up playground. Whether you prefer your activity in the water or on dry ground, you'll probably find it here. For information, contact the city's **park district** (☎ 312/742-PLAY [7529]; www.chicago parkdistrict.com); for questions about the 29 miles of beaches and parks along Lake Michigan, call the park district's lakefront region office at ☎ 312/747-2474.

Beaches

Public beaches line Lake Michigan all the way up north into the suburbs and Wisconsin, and southeast through Indiana and into Michigan. The best known is **Oak Street Beach.** Its location, at the northern tip of the Magnificent Mile, creates some interesting sights as sun worshippers sporting swimsuits and carting coolers make their way down Michigan Avenue. The most popular is massive **North Avenue Beach,** about 6 blocks farther north, where Lincoln Park singles come to play, check each other out, and fly by on bikes and in-line skates. Rows of beach volleyball courts stretch out beside a vintage steamship-shaped beach house; there's also a Venice Beach–style outdoor gym; **Hollywood-Ardmore Beach** (officially Kathy Osterman Beach), at the northern end of Lake Shore Drive, is a lovely crescent that's less congested and has steadily become more popular with gays who've moved up the lakefront from the Belmont Rocks, a longtime hangout. For more seclusion, try **Ohio Street Beach,** an intimate sliver of sand in tiny Olive Park, just north of Navy Pier, which, incredibly enough, remains largely ignored despite its central location. If you have a car, head up to **Montrose Beach,** a beautiful unsung treasure about midway between North Avenue Beach and Hollywood-Ardmore Beach (with plenty of free parking). It has an expanse of beach mostly uninterrupted by piers or jetties, and a huge adjacent park with soccer fields, one big hill that's great for kite flying, and even a small bait shop where anglers can go before heading to a nearby long pier designated for fishing.

If you've brought the pooch along, you might want to take him for a dip at the **doggie beach** south of Addison Street, at about Hawthorne and Lake

TOP: **Volleyball on North Avenue Beach.** ABOVE: **Relaxing in the sun at the doggie beach on Hawthorne and Lake Shore Drive.**

Shore Drive (although this minute spot aggravates some dog owners because it's in a harbor where the water is somewhat fouled by gas and oil from nearby boats). *A tip:* Try the south end of North Avenue Beach in early morning, before it opens to the public for the day. (Also consider that, in the off season, all beaches are fair game for dogs. The police won't hassle you, I promise.)

Beaches officially open with a full retinue of lifeguards on duty around June 20, though swimmers can wade into the chilly water from Memorial Day to Labor Day. Only the bravest souls venture into the water before July, when the temperature creeps up enough to make swimming an attractive proposition. Please take note that the entire lakefront is not beach, and don't go do anything stupid such as dive off the rocks.

Biking

Biking is a great way to see the city, particularly along the lakefront bike path that extends for more than 18 miles. The stretch between Navy Pier and North Avenue Beach gets extremely crowded in the summer (you're jostling for space with in-line skaters, joggers, and dawdling pedestrians). If you're looking to pick up some speed, I recommend biking south (once you're past the Museum Campus, the trail is relatively wide open, and you can zip all the way to Hyde Park). If you want a more leisurely tour with people-watching potential, head north (through the crowds). After you pass Belmont Harbor, the traffic lets up a bit. Ride all the way to Hollywood Beach (where the lakefront trail ends) for a good but not exhausting workout.

To rent bikes, try **Bike and Roll Chicago** (www.bikechicago.com), which has locations at Navy Pier (✆ **312/595-9600**), North Avenue Beach (✆ **773/327-2706**), and Millennium Park (✆ **888/BIKE-WAY** [245-3929]). Open from 8am to 8pm May through October (weather permitting), Bike Chicago stocks mountain and touring bikes, kids' bikes, strollers, and—most fun of all—quadcycles, which are four-wheel contraptions equipped with a steering wheel and canopy that can accommodate four or five people. Rates for bikes start

Chicago's lakefront bike batch extends for more than 18 miles.

at $10 an hour, $30 a day, with helmets, pads, and locks included. If you'd like to cycle your way past some Chicago landmarks, guided tours are also available.

Both the park district (☎ 312/742-PLAY [7529]) and the **Active Transportation Alliance** (☎ 312/427-3325; www.activetrans.org) offer free maps that detail popular biking routes. The latter, which is the preeminent organization for cyclists in Chicago, sells a much larger, more extensive map ($10) that shows routes within a seven-county area. The federation sponsors a number of bike rides throughout the year, including the highly enjoyable **Boulevard Lakefront Tour,** held in September, which follows the historic circle of boulevards that had their genesis in the Chicago Plan of 1909. It starts in Hyde Park at the University of Chicago campus.

A word of caution: Never head anywhere on the city's streets without first strapping on a helmet. Designated bike lanes have been added to many main thoroughfares, but most cabbies and drivers tend to ignore them. Bike with extreme caution on city streets (you can get a ticket for biking on the sidewalk), and stick to the lakefront path if you're not an expert rider. Locking your bike anywhere you go is a no-brainer.

Golfing

For a major metropolis, Chicago has an impressive number of golf options within the city limits (not to mention many plush and pricey suburban courses). The closest you'll get to golfing downtown is the **Green at Grant Park** (☎ 312/987-1818; www.thegreenonline.com), an 18-hole putting course on Monroe Street between Columbus Avenue and Lake Shore Drive, just east of Millennium Park. It's not exactly tournament-level play, but it's more challenging than miniature golf—and the setting can't be beat. The course is open daily from May through October from 10am to 10pm, and putters and golf balls are provided. Rates are $12 per round for adults, $6 for children 12 and under.

To warm up your swing, head to the **Diversey Driving Range,** 141 W. Diversey Pkwy. (☎ 312/742-7929), in Lincoln Park just north of Diversey Harbor. This two-level range attracts all levels—from show-off heavy hitters to beginners—and is very popular on weekends with young singles who live in the surrounding apartment buildings. The price is right ($14 for a bucket of 100 balls), and the setting is pretty much perfect.

The Chicago Park District runs six golf courses in the city. One of the most popular is the 9-hole **Sydney Marovitz Course,** 3600 N. Lake Shore Dr. (at Waveland Ave.), which many Chicagoans simply call Waveland. Thanks to its picturesque lakefront location, it's always full on weekends, so make a reservation well in advance (and don't expect a quick game—this is where beginners come to practice). Another good bet—and usually less crowded—is the 18-hole course in **Jackson Park** on the South Side (63rd St. and Stoney Island Ave.). These city-run courses are open from mid-April through November; for information on greens fees, location, and hours, call the **Chicago Park District** golf office (☎ 312/245-0909; www.cpdgolf.com).

For information about suburban golf courses, visit the website of the **Chicago District Golf Association** (www.cdga.org).

Ice Skating

The city's premier skating destination is the **McCormick-Tribune Ice Rink** at Millennium Park, 55 N. Michigan Ave. (☎ 312/742-5222). The location is pretty much perfect: You're skating in the shadows of grand skyscrapers and within view of the lake. The rink is open daily from 10am to 10pm November through March. Admission is free, and skate rentals are $10.

The park district runs dozens of other skating surfaces throughout the city, along the lakefront and in neighborhood parks. Call 𝄢 **312/742-PLAY** [7529] for locations. There's also a relatively small rink at **Navy Pier,** 600 E. Grand Ave. (𝄢 **312/595-PIER** [7437]).

In-Line Skating

The wheeled ones have been battling bikers over control of Chicago's lakefront paths since the early 1990s. If you want to join in the competition, **Londo Mondo,** 1100 N. Dearborn St. (𝄢 **312/751-2794;** www.londomondo.com), on the Gold Coast, rents blades for $7 an hour or $20 a day. The best route to skate is the lakefront trail that leads from Lincoln Park down to Oak Street Beach. Beware, though, that those same miles of trail are claimed by avid cyclists, and collisions between distracted 'bladers and bikers have been known to happen. On busy summer days, approach Chicago lakefront traffic as carefully as you would a major expressway.

Sailing

It seems a shame just to sit on the beach and watch all those beautiful sailboats gliding across the lake, so go on, get out there. **Chicago Sailing,** in Belmont Harbor (𝄢 **773/871-SAIL** [7245]; www.chicagosailing.com), rents J-22 and J-30 boats from 9am to sunset, weather permitting, May through October. A J-22, which holds four or five adults, rents for $55 to $75 an hour; a J-30, which accommodates up to 10 people, costs $95 to $110 per hour. If you want to take the boat out without a skipper, you need to demonstrate your skills first (for an additional $15 fee). If you'd rather sit back and relax, you can charter a boat. Reservations are recommended.

Swimming

The Chicago Park District maintains about 30 indoor pools for lap swimming and general splashing around, but none is particularly convenient to downtown. The lakefront is open for swimming until 9:30pm Memorial Day to Labor Day in areas watched over by lifeguards (no swimming off the rocks, please). **But *be forewarned:*** The water is usually freezing. If you're willing to take a dip anyway, a good place for lake swimming is the water along the wall beginning at Ohio Street Beach, slightly northwest of Navy Pier. The

Be forewarned: The water in Lake Michigan is usually freezing!

Chicago Triathlon Club marks a course here each summer with a buoy at both the quarter- and half-mile distances. This popular swimming route follows the shoreline in a straight line. The water is fairly shallow. For more information, call the park district's beach and pool office (📞 **312/742-PLAY** [7529]).

IN THE GRANDSTAND: WATCHING CHICAGO'S ATHLETIC EVENTS
Baseball

Baseball is imprinted on the national consciousness as part of Chicago, not because of victorious dynasties, but because of the opposite—the Black Sox scandal of 1919 and the perennially losing Cubs.

The **Chicago Cubs** haven't made a World Series appearance since 1945 and haven't been world champs since 1908, but that doesn't stop people from catching games at historic **Wrigley Field ★★**, 1060 W. Addison St. (📞 **773/404-CUBS** [2827]; www.cubs.mlb.com), with its ivy-covered outfield walls, its hand-operated scoreboard, its view of the shimmering lake from the upper deck, and its "W" or "L" flag announcing the outcome of the game to the unfortunates who couldn't attend. After all the strikes, temper tantrums, and other nonsense, Wrigley has managed to hold on to something like purity. Yes, Wrigley finally installed lights (it was the last major-league park to do so), but by agreement with the residential neighborhood, the Cubs still play most

Despite the Cubs' losing record, locals and visitors alike flock to scenic Wrigley field.

games in the daylight, as they should. Because Wrigley is small, just about every seat is decent.

No matter how the Cubs are doing, tickets ($15–$90) go fast; most weekend and night games sell out by Memorial Day. Your best bet is to hit a weekday game, or try your luck buying a ticket on game day outside the park, when you'll often find some season ticket holders looking to unload a few seats.

Wrigley's easy to reach by El; take the Red Line to the Addison stop, and you're there. Or take the no. 22 bus, which runs up Clark Street. To buy tickets in person, stop by the ticket windows at Wrigley Field Monday through Friday from 9am to 6pm, Saturday from 9am to 4pm, and on game days. Call ✆ **800/ THE-CUBS** [843-2827] for tickets through **Tickets.com** (✆ **866/652-2827** outside Illinois); you can also order online through the team website.

Despite their stunning World Series win in 2005, the **Chicago White Sox** still struggle to attract the same kind of loyalty (despite the fact that they regularly win more games than the Cubs). Longtime fans rue the day owner Jerry Reinsdorf replaced admittedly dilapidated Comiskey Park with a concrete behemoth that lacks the yesteryear charm of its predecessor. That said, the current stadium, **U.S. Cellular Field,** 333 W. 35th St. (✆ **312/674-1000;** www. whitesox.mlb.com), in the South Side neighborhood of Bridgeport, has spectacular sightlines from every seat (if you avoid the vertigo-inducing upper deck), and the park has every conceivable amenity, including above-average food concessions, shops, and plentiful restrooms. The White Sox's endearing quality is the blue-collar aura with which so many Cubs-loathing Southsiders identify. Games rarely sell out—an effect, presumably, of Reinsdorf's sterile stadium and the blighted neighborhood that surrounds it. All of this makes it a bargain for bona fide baseball fans. Tickets cost $20 to $68 and are half-price on Monday.

To get Sox tickets, call **Ticketmaster** (✆ **866/SOX-GAME** [769-4263]), or visit the ticket office, open Monday through Friday from 10am to 6pm, Saturday and Sunday from 10am to 4pm, with extended hours on game days. To get to the ballpark by El, take the Red Line to Sox/35th Street.

○ Field of Dreams

Built in 1914, Wrigley Field is the second-oldest major-league ballpark, after Boston's Fenway Park, and remains one of the only surviving old-time baseball stadiums in the country (no luxury boxes here!). Known as the "friendly confines," Wrigley Field was the site of Babe Ruth's "called shot," when Ruth allegedly pointed to a bleacher location in the 1932 World Series and then hit a home run to that exact spot. For an intimate look at the historic ballpark, take one of the behind-the-scenes tours offered almost daily throughout the summer; stops include the visitors'

and home team locker rooms, press box, security headquarters, and, yes, a walk around the field itself (be sure to check out the original scoreboard, built in 1937). Some dates do sell out, so buy tickets ($25) in advance online, if possible. Keep in mind that if you take a tour on a game day, some areas (such as the locker rooms) will be off-limits. Call ✆ **773/404-CUBS** [2827], or stop by the box office at 1060 W. Addison St.; you can also buy tickets online through the Cubs website (www.mlb.com/chc/ball park/wrigley_field_tours.jsp).

Basketball

When it comes to basketball, Chicagoans still live in the past, associating the **Chicago Bulls** (✆ 312/455-4000; www.nba.com/bulls) with the glory days of Michael Jordan and the never-ending championships of the 1990s. The fact that Jordan chose to remain in town after his playing days were over—a decision almost unheard of in professional sports—has only burnished his image here, and locals are still wowed by occasional Jordan sightings. The downside is that he's a constant reminder of our ever-more-distant winning past.

Although the current players don't inspire the same city-wide fervor, the Bulls have rebounded somewhat from the dismal seasons following Jordan's departure and even made some respectable showings in post-season play. The Bulls don't consistently sell out, which means you might be able to catch a game at the cavernous **United Center,** 1901 W. Madison St. (✆ 312/455-4500; www. unitedcenter.com). Yes, the space is massive and impersonal, but the pre-game buildup, with flashing lights and thumping music, is undeniably dramatic. Most tickets run $20 to $100 through **Ticketmaster** (✆ 312/559-1212), although be aware that the cheap seats are practically in the rafters. If money is no object, you can usually score good seats through local ticket brokers without much advance notice.

Football

The **Chicago Bears** play at **Soldier Field,** Lake Shore Drive and 16th Street (✆ 847/295-6600; www.chicagobears.com), site of a controversial renovation that added what looks like a giant space ship on top of the original stadium's elegant colonnade. Architecturally, it's a disaster, but from a comfort perspective, the place is much improved—although that doesn't impress longtime fans who prided themselves on surviving blistering-cold game days and horrifying bathrooms. The Bears themselves have been inspiring high hopes—most recently, winning a trip to the Super Bowl in 2007. But even during losing seasons, tickets are hard to come by. (Most are snapped up by season ticket holders long before the season starts.) If you plan ahead, individual tickets run $45 to $300; expensive seats are usually available through ticket brokers or online sites.

The **Northwestern Wildcats** play Big Ten college ball at **Ryan Field,** 1501 Central St., in nearby Evanston (✆ 847/491-CATS [2287]). Unfortunately, Northwestern grads are not particularly loyal to their long-suffering team. In fact, fans of the visiting team often outnumber NU supporters in the stands.

Hockey

The **Chicago Blackhawks** have devoted, impassioned fans who work themselves into a frenzy with the first note of "The Star-Spangled Banner," but for years, they had to put up with mediocre play and less-than-stellar management. Over the past few seasons, though, the team that once boasted legends such as Bobby Hull and Tony Esposito has made a comeback, winning the Stanley Cup in 2010. Going to a Hawks games has once again become a rousing—and sometimes rowdy—experience. The Blackhawks play at the **United Center,** 1901 W. Madison St. (✆ 312/455-7000; www.chicagoblackhawks.com). Tickets cost $15 to $100.

For a more affordable and family-friendly outing, catch the semipro **Chicago Wolves** at Allstate Arena, 6920 N. Mannheim Rd., Rosemont

(© 847/724-GOAL [4625]; www.chicagowolves.com). The team has been consistently excellent over the past few years, and the games are geared toward all ages, with fireworks beforehand and plenty of on- and off-ice entertainment (tickets $13–$30).

Horse Racing

Thoroughbreds race at **Arlington International Racecourse,** 2200 W. Euclid Ave., Arlington Heights (© 847/385-7500; www.arlingtonpark.com), in the northwest suburbs. Live local bands and DJs add to the party atmosphere on Fridays and Saturdays from Memorial Day weekend until Labor Day, starting at 2:30pm. For more details, see p. 219. The Chicago area's other major race-track, **Hawthorne Race Course,** 3501 S. Laramie Ave., Stickney (© 708/780-3700; www.sportsmanspark.com), is located in the southwest suburbs, about a half-hour drive from downtown.

Soccer

Chicago's Major League Soccer team, the **Chicago Fire,** plays at its own 20,000-seat stadium in suburban Bridgeview (about 12 miles southwest of downtown). The season runs from late May through October (© 888/MLS-FIRE [657-3473]; www.chicago-fire.com). Games have a family feel, with plenty of activities for kids and affordable ticket prices ($15–$60).

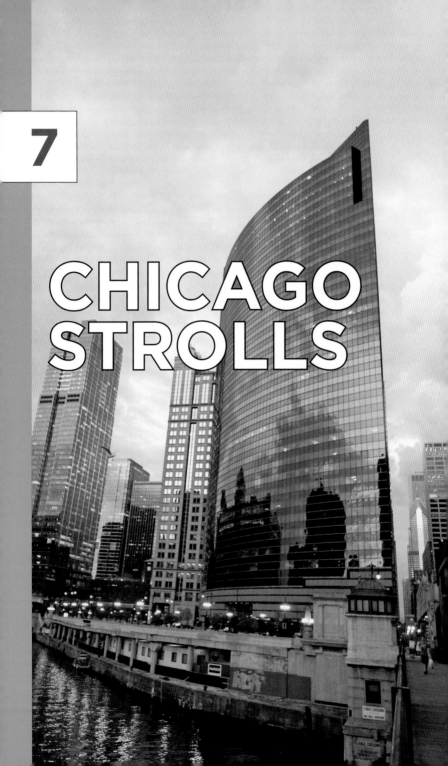

7

CHICAGO
STROLLS

A ccording to novelist Nelson Algren, "Chicago is an October kind of city even in spring." Actually, October happens to be a great month to wander around town: The weather is cool but not freezing, most of the tourist hoards have moved on, and the crisp air is invigorating. But you can meander through Chicago in any season. With the right coat, scarf, and mittens, you can even brave the streets in January or February—then brag about it to friends back home. The following tours give a taste of Chicago's diversity, from the bustling downtown business center to a couple of distinctive residential neighborhoods.

WALKING TOUR 1: **THE LOOP**

START:	**The Sears Tower.**
FINISH:	**Harold Washington Library Center.**
TIME:	**1½ hours.**
BEST TIME:	**Daytime, particularly weekdays when downtown businesses are open.**
WORST TIME:	**Late evening, after shops and offices have closed.**

Walk through the Loop's densely packed canyon of buildings, and you'll feel the buzzing pulse of downtown. While you'll pass plenty of modern high-rises, you'll also get a minilesson in architectural history as you survey the progression of the city's skyscrapers.

Start the tour at:

1 The Sears Tower

Okay, so this 110-story megatower is no longer the world's tallest building. It's not even the Sears Tower anymore, since the naming rights were bought by the London-based insurance broker Willis Group in early 2009. But "Willis Tower" (gulp) is still referred to as the Sears Tower by defiant Chicagoans and remains a bold symbol of the city. If it's a clear day (and you've got the time), take a trip up to the **Skydeck** (p. 156) before heading off on your tour: To the east you'll look out over the lake, to the northwest you can watch planes take off from O'Hare Airport, and to the north you'll be able to see all the way to Wisconsin.

Walk north along Wacker Drive until you arrive at:

2 333 W. Wacker Dr.

Proof that Chicago inspires architectural creativity, this 1983 office building was designed to fit a rather awkward triangular plot (previously thought suitable only for a parking lot). But architectural firm Kohn Pedersen Fox

FACING PAGE: **Chicago's stunning architecture is a mix of old and new.**

came up with a brilliant solution, designing a curved facade that echoes the bend of the Chicago River. Walk out to the Franklin Street Bridge to get the full effect of the building's mirrored surface, which reflects the surrounding cityscape in ever-changing shades of blue, green, and gray.

Across the river you'll see:

3 The Merchandise Mart

Touted as the world's largest commercial building, the Mart is a Chicago landmark as much for its place in the history of American merchandising as for its hulking institutional look. Completed in 1931, it's occupied mostly by furniture and interior-design businesses. Perched on top of the pillars that run the length of the building are oversized busts of American retail icons, including Julius Rosenwalk (Sears), Frank W. Woolworth, and Aaron Montgomery Ward.

Walk 2 blocks east along Wacker Drive. At LaSalle Street, turn right and continue 2 blocks to Randolph Street. Turn left (east), go half a block, and you'll be standing in front of:

4 The James R. Thompson Center

This postmodern cascade of glass and steel is—depending on your point of view—the pinnacle or the low point of architect Helmut Jahn's career. Home to offices of the Illinois state bureaucracy, it was designed to promote the idea of open government: The transparent glass walls inside allow

The postmodern glass and steel of the James R. Thompson Center.

**Walking Tour 1:
The Loop**

1 The Sears Tower
2 333 W. Wacker Dr.
3 The Merchandise Mart
4 The James R. Thompson
   Center
5 Daley Plaza
6 The Reliance Building
7 The Berghoff 🍺
8 The Rookery
9 Chicago Board of Trade
10 Monadnock Building
11 Manhattan Building
12 Harold Washington
   Library Center

Ⓜ Subway/El stop

0   1/4 mi
0   0.25 km

citizens to see their tax dollars at work. Step into the atrium to check out the beehivelike atmosphere; you can even ride a glass elevator up to the 17th floor if you're not afraid of heights.

Cross Randolph Street and head south along Clark Street. On the left you'll come to an open space known as:

5 Daley Plaza

Shadowed by the looming tower of the Richard J. Daley Center—a blocky dark monolith of government offices—this square was named for the legendary mayor and longtime czar of Cook County politics. While you're here, go ahead and do what tourists do: Take a picture in front of the Picasso sculpture (p. 157).

Walk back up to Randolph Street and head east. At the corner of Randolph and State sts., you'll see two local landmarks: the marquee of the Chicago Theatre to your north and the block-long Macy's (previously Marshall Field's) to the south. Continue south along State Street until you reach:

6 The Reliance Building

Now known as the Burnham Hotel, this building may not look impressive, but it's famous in the world of architecture. Completed in 1895, it had a remarkably lighter look than its bulky predecessors, thanks to steel framing that allowed for the extensive use of glass on the facade. It also marked the first use of the "Chicago window": a large central pane of glass flanked by two smaller, double-hung windows used for ventilation. To get a glimpse of what it looked like when it was an office building, take one of the hotel elevators up to one of the guest room floors, which still have the original tile flooring and glass-windowed office doors.

Continue south along State Street until you reach Adams Street. Ready to pause for a bite or a drink? Then turn right (west), go half a block, and stop at:

7 Take a Break ☕
In a world of chain coffee shops and fast-food joints, the **Berghoff,** 17 W. Adams St. (☎ **312/427-3170;** p. 100), feels like a flashback to Old Chicago. The bar of this 100-year-old restaurant serves several different house brews on tap, along with sandwiches and appetizers. (For a nonalcoholic treat, try the homemade root beer.) If it's lunchtime, grab a table in the main dining room; although the menu has been modified for modern, lighter tastes, the Wiener schnitzel and spaetzle are house classics.

Go 2 blocks west along Adams Street until you reach LaSalle Street. Turn left (south) and you'll be at:

8 The Rookery

Built between 1885 and 1888, the Rookery represents a dramatic transition in Chicago architecture. (It's also one of the only surviving buildings designed by noted architect Daniel Burnham, along with the Reliance Building, above.) The name refers to the previous building that sat on this site, Chicago's original City Hall, which was a favorite spot for nesting birds; today it's an office building. The imposing Romanesque exterior has thick masonry walls, but the inside is surprisingly open and airy, thanks to an innovative use of iron framing. The building is essentially a square built around an open interior court that rises the full height of the building's 11 stories. Walk upstairs and follow the staircase to get a glimpse of the Rookery's interior courtyard and the sublime stairway spiraling upward.

Continue south along LaSalle Street. At Jackson Boulevard, the street appears to dead-end at the:

9 Chicago Board of Trade

The city's temple to high finance, this building houses the city's commodities exchange, an echo of the days when corn and wheat from the prairie passed through Chicago on its way east. Opened in 1930, the setbacks on the upper stories are typical of the Art Deco styling of the era, as are the geometric decorative elements over the entrance. Along the building's rear (southern) wall, a 24-story postmodern addition by Helmut Jahn repeats the original's pyramid-shaped roof, maintaining the symmetry between old and new. When it was built, the 45-story Board of Trade was considered so tall that the aluminum sculpture of Ceres, the Roman goddess of architecture who adorns the building's peak, was left faceless, because the builders figured no one in neighboring buildings would ever be high enough to see it.

Head 2 blocks east along Jackson Boulevard to the southwest corner of Dearborn Street and Jackson Boulevard. At 53 W. Jackson Blvd. is the:

10 Monadnock Building

This mass of stonework forms two office buildings that occupy an entire narrow block all the way to Van Buren Street. Only 2 years separate the construction of these architectural twins, but they are light-years apart in design and engineering. (You'll need to step across Dearborn Street to fully appreciate the differences.)

Monadnock I, on the northern end, was built by the architectural firm of

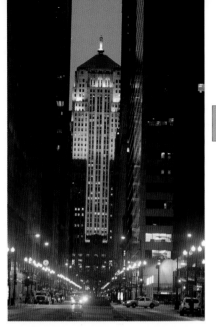

The Chicago Board of Trade.

Burnham and Root between 1889 and 1891. To support a building of this size at the time, the masonry walls had to be built 6 to 8 feet thick (note the deeply recessed windows at street level). Monadnock II, on the southern wing, was built by Holabird & Roche in 1893. Here steel framing was used, allowing the lower walls to be significantly narrower. The second building may have been an engineering marvel at the time, but the original Monadnock has a certain gravitas that the later addition lacks.

Walk south along Dearborn Street until you reach Congress Parkway. At 431 S. Dearborn St. you'll find the:

11 Manhattan Building

Constructed in 1891 by William Le Baron Jenny, this broad structure was viewed as an architectural wonder by many who visited Chicago during the Columbian Exposition 2 years later. To some, the eclectic use of materials and varied design of the façade give the Manhattan Building an appearance of complete chaos; others see a dynamic rhythm in the architect's choices. Today this former office building has been converted into condos.

From the corner of Dearborn and Van Buren streets, look a few blocks west along Van Buren until you spot a triangular tower, carved with slivers of window. That building is the Metropolitan Correctional Center, a 27-story jail for defendants preparing for trial in federal court downtown. The building's three-sided design derives from an attempt by the U.S. Bureau of Prisons to reform prison conditions: Cells were built along the edges surrounding a central lounge area. But it's still not a great place to hang out: To foil jailbreaks, the windows are only 5 inches wide (and have bars, to boot); although there's a recreation yard on the roof, it's enclosed on the sides and topped with wire mesh.

Walk 2 blocks east along Congress Parkway until you reach State Street. Turn left (north) to reach the entrance of the:

12 Harold Washington Library Center

This block-long behemoth, named for the city's first African-American mayor, is the world's largest municipal library (p. 169). Designed by a firm led by Thomas Beeby, then dean of Yale University's School of Architecture, and completed in 1991, it self-consciously echoes the city's original grand buildings, such as the Auditorium Theater a few blocks east. Many Chicagoans think the place looks more like a fortress than a welcoming library—but judge for yourself. The Winter Garden on the ninth floor—a lovely retreat drenched with natural light—is a good place to relax at the end of your walking tour.

WALKING TOUR 2: THE GOLD COAST

START:	**Oak Street Beach.**
FINISH:	**Bellevue Place and Michigan Avenue.**
TIME:	**1 hour, more if you stop to eat along the way.**
BEST TIME:	**Weekends are ideal for this walk at any time of the year. On weekdays, wait until after the morning rush before setting out.**
WORST TIME:	**After dusk, when it's too dark to appreciate the buildings' decorative elements.**

The Gold Coast, as its name implies, is Chicago's ritziest neighborhood, site of its most expensive and exclusive houses. Its reputation dates back to 1882, when Potter Palmer, one of the city's richest businessmen, built a lakeshore castle here, in what was then a relative wilderness north of the city. The mere presence of the Palmers served as an instant magnet, drawing other social climbers in their wake (and Palmer, who owned vast parcels of northside land, saw his holdings shoot up in value). This itinerary begins with a walk overlooking Lake Michigan before heading down charming tree-lined residential streets.

Begin the tour at:

1 Oak Street Beach

This confluence of city and lakeshore epitomizes what Chicagoans love about the city: Facing downtown, you've got the ultimate urban vista; stare at the shoreline, and the seemingly endless expanse of water makes you feel like you've escaped the city completely. You can stroll along the sand or keep to the concrete path (but beware of speeding bikes and rollerbladers). As you head north, look across Lake Shore Drive to see a few remaining historic mansions scattered among the more modern high-rises.

The first mansion you'll pass, just north of Scott Street, is:

2 The Carl C. Heissen House

Both the Heissen House (1250 N. Lake Shore Dr.), built in 1890, and its neighbor, the Starring House (1254 N. Lake Shore Dr.), built in 1889, show the popularity of the sturdy Romanesque style among wealthy Chicagoans.

The juxtaposition of city and lakeshore defines Chicago.

A second cluster of former private mansions, all vaguely neoclassical in outline, faces Lake Michigan north of Burton Place. The first of these is:

3 1516 N. Lake Shore Dr.

This building is home to the International College of Surgeons; its neighbor at 1524 N. Lake Shore Dr. is a museum belonging to the same institution. **The International Museum of Surgical Science** (p. 205) houses a fascinating collection of exhibits and artifacts that portray the evolution of medical surgery, but it's worth visiting for its elegant interior as well, designed by Chicago architect Howard Van Doren Shaw in 1917 as a private mansion (highlights include a massive stone staircase and the second-floor library, with fine wood paneling). A third structure, 1530 N. Lake Shore Dr., is today the Polish Consulate.

The International Museum of Surgical Science houses exhibits that show the evolution of surgery.

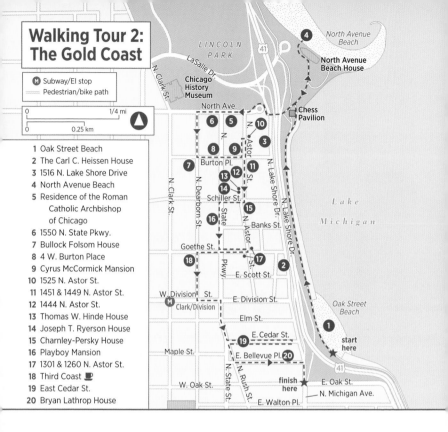

Follow the lakefront path to the Chess Pavilion on your left, and continue past the patch of green where the jetty leads out to a harbor light and into the parking lot. Straight ahead is:

4   North Avenue Beach

One of the city's prime summer spots, North Avenue Beach swarms with beach volleyball players and sun worshippers from June through August. But I think it's just as worth a visit—maybe more so—in spring and fall, when you can take in the view without the crowds. Check out the retro-style beach house, which was designed to look like an old ocean liner.

Double back and cross Lake Shore Drive by way of the North Avenue underpass, directly west of the Chess Pavilion. From the cul-de-sac here, continue west on North Avenue 2 blocks to North State Parkway. The imposing residence on your left, surrounded by spacious grounds, is the:

5   Residence of the Roman Catholic Archbishop of Chicago

Catholicism has strong roots in Chicago, thanks to generations of German, Irish, and Polish immigrants who brought their faith along with them; the city's current archbishop, Francis Cardinal George, is a well-known local figure who receives regular press coverage. This Queen Anne–style mansion was built in 1885 for the first archbishop of Chicago, Patrick Fee-han; it sits on the site of what used to be a cemetery that stretched between present-day North Avenue and Schiller Street. Of the 19 chimneys that march across the roofline, only 3 are still in use.

Across the street on the opposite corner of North Avenue is:

6 1550 N. State Pkwy.

Each apartment in this 1912 vintage luxury high-rise, known as the Ben-jamin Marshall Building, originally occupied a single floor and contained 15 rooms spread over 9,000 square feet. The architects were Marshall & Fox, highly regarded in their day as builders of fine hotels. There was once a garden entryway at the ground-floor level. Among the noteworthy architectural features adorning the exterior of this Beaux Arts classic are the many small balconies and the bowed windows at the corners of the building.

Continue west for 1 block on North Avenue and turn left, following Dearborn Street to Burton Place and the:

7 Bullock Folsom House

As its mansard roof reveals, this 1877 landmark, at 1454 N. Dearborn St., on the southwest corner, takes its inspiration from the French Second Em-pire. (That roof, incidentally, is shingled in slate, not asphalt.) Neighboring houses at nos. 1450 and 1434 have some of the same French-influenced ornamentation and styling. Across Burton Place just to the north, at 1500 N. Dearborn St., is another example of a rival architectural fashion of the day, the Richardsonian or Romanesque Revival.

The 1877 Bullock Folsom House.

Return to the east along Burton, but before crossing North State Parkway, stop at:

8 4 W. Burton Place

Built as a private residence in 1902 by Richard E. Schmidt for a family named Madlener, this striking building today houses the Graham Foundation for Advanced Studies in the Fine Arts. There is something very modern about its appearance: The structure's clean lines and the ornamentation around the entrance were inspired by the work of architects Louis Sullivan and Frank Lloyd Wright. The Society of Architectural Historians offers tours of the home on Saturdays, along with the Charnley-Persky house (see stop no. 15, below).

Continue 1 block farther east to Astor Street. On the northwest corner, at 1500 N. Astor St., is the former:

9 Cyrus McCormick Mansion

New York architect Stanford White designed this building, which was constructed for the Patterson family in 1893. Cyrus McCormick, Jr., bought it in 1914, and David Adler's north addition doubled the size of the building in 1927. The senior McCormick made his fortune by inventing the mechanical reaper, which made it possible to farm vast tracts of wheat on the prairie without depending on seasonal labor at harvest time. Cyrus Sr.'s heirs shared in the wealth, and eventually so many members of the family owned homes near Rush and Erie streets, just south of the Gold Coast, that the neighborhood was known as "McCormicksville."

Like the Fifth Avenue mansions White and his contemporaries built in New York, the McCormick palazzo is an essay in neoclassical detailing. Square and grand, like a temple of antiquity, the construction combines Roman bricks of burnt yellow with touches of terra-cotta trim. The building now is divided into condominiums.

Head north briefly on Astor Street to check out a home with a connection to presidential history:

10 1525 N. Astor St.

This attractive town house was once the residence of Robert Todd Lincoln, the only surviving child of Abraham and Mary Todd Lincoln. The younger Lincoln started a private law practice after the Civil War. He remained in Chicago for much of his life, leaving twice during the 1880s and 1890s

This town house was once the residence of Robert Todd Lincoln, the son of Abraham and Mary Todd Lincoln.

to serve under presidents James Garfield and Chester Arthur as Secretary of War, and later under Benjamin Harrison as ambassador to Britain. On the death of George Pullman, one of his major corporate clients, Lincoln became president of the Pullman Palace Car Company in 1897 (for more about the Pullman Company, see "Exploring Chicago," p. 150).

Reversing direction, walk south along Astor Street. Notice the houses at:

11 1451 & 1449 N. Astor St.

The former, occupying the corner lot, is the work of Howard Van Doren Shaw, built in 1910 according to the so-called "Jacobethan" fashion; a combination of Jacobean and Elizabethan, it revives certain 16th- and 17th-century English architectural features, including narrow, elongated windows, split-level roofs, and multiple chimney stacks. The house at no. 1449 was built around the turn of the century, but the architect of this glorious chateau remains a mystery. Guarding the home's entrance is a somewhat intimidating stone porch, seemingly out of scale. Among the home's other unique characteristics are the big front bay and frieze below the cornice, a scroll decorated with a pattern of shells.

Another neighboring home of interest across the street is:

12 1444 N. Astor St.

While most of the homes in this area were built in the late 1800s and early decades of the 1900s—and most took their cues from architectural fashions from centuries before—this house was on the cutting edge of style when it was built in 1929. An Art Deco masterpiece, it was designed by Holabird & Roche, the same firm that designed Soldier Field football stadium a few years earlier.

Next, walk to 1412 N. Astor St., site of the:

13 Thomas W. Hinde House

This 1892 home, designed by Douglas S. Pentecost, is an homage to the Flemish architecture of the late Middle Ages. The facade has been altered, but some of the original stone ornamentation remains, as do such dominant features as the multipaned diamond-shaped windows.

On the same side of the street, at 1406 N. Astor St., is the:

14 Joseph T. Ryerson House

David Adler designed this 1922 landmark home in the manner of a Parisian hotel. Adler himself supervised the 1931 addition of the top floor and the mansard roof. Woven into the wrought-iron grillwork above the entrance are the initials of the original owners.

Walk to 1365 N. Astor St. to see the landmark:

15 Charnley-Persky House

Shortly before he left the firm of Adler & Sullivan, a then-obscure draftsman, Frank Lloyd Wright, played a major role in designing this 1892 home. The house's streamlined structure gives it a far more contemporary look than its neighbors, making the case that there is something timeless in

Wright's ideas. The building—appropriately enough—is now the headquarters of the **Society of Architectural Historians,** which gives tours of the house on Wednesday and more extensive tours including the surrounding area on Saturday. (Visit www.sah.org or call ✆ **312/915-0105** for details.)

Walk back to Schiller Street. Cross the street and turn left on North State Parkway, continuing south until the middle of the block to 1340 N. State Pkwy., the original:

Rest your weary feet at cozy Third Coast coffeehouse.

16 Playboy Mansion

Little did the original owner of this building, an upright Calvinist named George S. Isham, know how his house would be transformed a mere half-century after it was built in 1899. Playboy founder Hugh Hefner lived here from 1959 to 1974, romping with his Bunnies and celebrities in the indoor pool and lounging in silk pajamas while perusing page layouts in his bedroom. Today that hedonistic past has been erased, and the building has been converted into high-priced condos.

Continue south on State Parkway, then swing east on Goethe Street, back to Astor Street. On opposite corners diagonally across Goethe Street are apartment towers that represent the trend toward high-rise living that began in the 1930s:

17 1301 & 1260 N. Astor St.

Constructed by architect Philip B. Maher in 1932 and 1931, respectively, these apartment buildings are classics of the sleek modernism that characterized American commercial architecture after World War I. Contrast their timeless style with the 1960s apartment tower at 1300 N. Astor St., by architect Bertrand Goldberg; avant-garde at the time, it has not aged as well.

If you're ready for a snack, turn back north to Goethe Street and head west 2 blocks to Dearborn Street. Turn left (south) and go halfway down the block until you reach:

18 Take a Break 🍴

The welcoming **Third Coast coffeehouse,** 1260 N. Dearborn St. (✆ **312/649-0730**), is more laid-back than the elegant neighborhood surrounding it. Tucked below street level, it has a shabby-cozy vibe and makes a good stop for midmorning coffee or lunch (there's a full menu of sandwiches and salads).

Head south on Dearborn Street to Division Street. Walk 1 block east to State Street, then turn right (south), staying on the east side of the street where State and Rush streets merge, and proceed 2 blocks south to:

19 East Cedar Street

This long block between Rush Street and Lake Shore Drive deserves a look because much of its turn-of-the century scale has been so well preserved, in particular the two clusters of "cottages," nos. 42 to 48 (built in 1896 by businessman Potter Palmer) and 50 to 54 (built in 1892).

Return to Rush Street, walk to the next block south, and turn left on Bellevue Place. At 120 E. Bellevue Place stands the:

20 Bryan Lathrop House

New York architect Charles F. McKim, partner of Stanford White, built this mansion for a local real estate agent and civic leader while staying in Chicago as a lead designer of the World's Columbian Exposition. It helped introduce the Georgian fashion in architecture that replaced the Romanesque Revival throughout the Gold Coast.

WALKING TOUR 3: WICKER PARK

START & FINISH:	**The Damen El stop (Blue Line).**
TIME:	**1 hour, not including shopping or eating stops.**
BEST TIME:	**Any time during the day.**
WORST TIME:	**After dark, when you'll have trouble seeing homes' decorative details.**

Wicker Park, along with adjacent Bucktown, is mostly known today as a place to shop at edgy clothing boutiques or try out the latest hip restaurant. This tour takes you along the residential side streets that many tourists overlook but that testify to the rich history of this neighborhood. Middle-class artisans, mostly Germans and Scandinavians, began settling here around 1870. In the following decades, wealthy families whose foreign roots made them unwelcome along the Gold Coast built luxurious homes here as well. In the 20th century, the neighborhood's respectability gradually declined, and many of the grandest homes were converted into rooming houses. It was not until the 1980s that the distinctive homes here began to be rediscovered and renovated, just as the gritty main streets of Milwaukee and Damen avenues began sprouting new shops and cafes.

Walk south along Damen Avenue to:

1 Wicker Park

Two brothers who were beginning to develop their extensive real estate holdings in the area donated this land to the city in 1870, hoping the green space would make the surrounding area more attractive to prospective builders. Unfortunately, little remains of the 19th-century landscaping, which once included a pond spanned by a rustic bridge.

Cross the park to the corner of Damen Avenue and Schiller Street. Follow Schiller east, along the park, stopping first at:

2   1959–1961 W. Schiller St.

Built in 1886 for a ship's captain and a medical doctor, this double home reflects the fashionable Second Empire style. The building became a rooming house in the 1920s but has been restored to its original style. Note the lively Victorian colors of the cornices, tower, and trim. Other distinctive features are the large mansard roof and the decorative saw-toothed pattern in the brickwork.

Next move to:

3   1941 W. Schiller St.

Built for clothing manufacturer Harris Cohn in 1888, this home is also known as the Wicker Park Castle. Essentially Queen Anne in design, its limestone facade made it pricier and more luxurious than its neighbors. Granite columns were polished to look like marble, and a turret rests on a shell-shaped base.

At the end of the block, turn right on Evergreen Avenue until you come to:

4   1958 W. Evergreen Ave.

Novelist Nelson Algren lived in a third-floor apartment here from 1959 to 1975. After he was caught stealing a typewriter in 1933, Algren (1909–81) spent 3 months in jail. This experience, which brought him in contact with criminals, outsiders, drug addicts, and prostitutes, was a strong influence on his work. Algren is best remembered for his two dark novels of the urban semiunderworld, *A Walk on the Wild Side* and *The Man with the Golden Arm* (which was set near here, around Division St. and Milwaukee Ave.), and for his tough but lyrical prose poem Chicago: City on the Make.

Continue to Damen Avenue, then turn right (north) back to Schiller Street. Take Schiller west 1 block to Hoyne Avenue, then turn right (north), where you'll see:

5   1407 N. Hoyne Ave.

Built by German wine and beer merchant John H. Rapp in 1880, this was the largest single-family estate in Wicker Park at the time. The original coach house, behind the mansion, is now a separate residence. This was not a happy home. Mrs. Rapp went insane, a son was convicted of embezzlement, and Rapp was murdered by his female bookkeeper. The home itself is of Second Empire style, with a large, curved mansard roof. The original wrought-iron fence defines the boundaries of the original grounds.

Heading north, you'll pass other late 19th-century mansions and, at 1426 N. Hoyne Ave., an example of a worker's cottage, a reminder that in these immigrant neighborhoods, artisans and their patrons often lived side by side. On the next corner, at Hoyne Avenue and Le Moyne Street, is the:

6   Wicker Park Lutheran Church

The city's oldest Lutheran church, it was modeled from plans of Holy Trinity Church in Caen, France, dating from the 12th century. The stone for this Romanesque structure was recycled from a demolished brothel. When one of the scandalized parishioners protested, the pastor remarked that the

building material "has served the devil long enough; now let it serve the
Lord."

Walk on to:

7   1558 N. Hoyne St.

The building permit for this Queen Anne–style home was issued in 1877,
making it one of the oldest homes in the area. It was built for C. Hermann
Plautz, founder of the Chicago Drug and Chemical Company. Ever con-
scious of the Great Chicago Fire, the builders created all the decorative trim
on both towers, the cornices, and the conservatory of the south side from
ornamental pressed metal. The seemingly misplaced cannon in the front
yard is a relic of the years (1927–72) when the building housed the local
American Legion.

Return to Pierce Avenue and walk west to:

8   2137 W. Pierce Ave.

This well-preserved gem is one of the highlights of historic Wicker Park.
Built for the German businessman Hermann Weinhardt in 1888, it's a fan-
ciful combination of elements that defies categorization. Notable details

include the elaborate carved-wood balcony and the unusual juxtaposition of green stone and redbrick limestone around the large front window. The large lot used to be flooded in the winter for ice-skating.

Across the street is another notable home:

9 2138 W. Pierce Ave.

The original owner of this home, Hans D. Runge, was treasurer of a wood milling company, so it's no surprise that elaborate wood carvings characterize the home inside and out; among the unique designs are the Masonic symbols flanking the pair of dragon heads under the rounded arch. A well-heeled local banker and politician, John F. Smulski, acquired the house in 1902, about the time many Poles were moving into the neighborhood. Smulski committed suicide here after the stock market crash in 1929, and the house served for a time as the Polish consulate.

The well-preserved house at 2137 Pierce Ave. features an unusual combination of green stone and redbrick limestone around its large front window.

Continue west until you reach Leavitt Street. Turn right (north) and walk 3 blocks until you reach:

10 Caton Street

Many of the houses on this street were built in the early 1890s by the same architectural firm, each with its own style, including German Burgher (no. 2156) and Renaissance (no. 2152). The Classical Revival home at 2147 W. Caton St. was built by the owner of a metal company, hence the extensive metal ornamentation on the exterior. (If you peek at the porch, you'll see it has a tin ceiling.)

Retrace your steps along Caton Street and Leavitt Street to North Avenue, and turn left (east). As you pass Hoyne Street, take a quick look at 1617–1619 N. Hoyne Ave.; the building used to house the neighborhood livery stables, where local families kept their horses and carriages. (It's now condos.) The final stop on the tour is at 2039 W. North Ave., an address that used to house the:

11 Luxor Baths

These public baths were built in the 1920s and were reportedly once a hangout for local politicians and wheeler-dealers. Today the building has been transformed into—what else?—condos. Still, it's a fitting end to the tour, a reminder of the days when this was a neighborhood of European immigrants trading news from home in the Luxor Baths steam room.

Head east to the three-way intersection of Milwaukee, Damen, and North avenues. From here, you can hop on the Blue Line El train, or walk a block and a half north on Damen toward a favorite local hangout:

12 Take a Break ☕

Long-time residents gripe about the encroaching suburbanization of Wicker Park, where sterile bank branches have replaced funky-divey coffee shops and million-dollar houses no longer raise eyebrows. Still, many independently owned businesses remain, among them **Caffe de Luca,** 1721 N. Damen Ave. (✆ **773/342-6000**), an Italian-inspired hangout where you can grab a coffee and pastry in the morning, a salad or panini at lunchtime, or a midafternoon dessert pick-me-up. Best of all, it's a place the locals come, where you can check out a cross-section of Wicker Park residents, from grungy wannabe artists to hip moms.

SHOPPING

8

F orget Rodeo Drive or Fifth Avenue—Chicago is the country's original shopping center, the place that helped the United States expand westward by transporting goods to the frontier. Today, the city is the commercial capital of the Midwest, attracting out-of-towners with its mix of designer boutiques, quirky independent clothing shops and cutting-edge home design stores.

The big names in fashion—from Prada to Louis Vuitton—are all represented here, but you don't have to be a big spender to enjoy a Chicago shopping spree. Indeed, the city's commercial success comes from offering something for everyone. Oak Street is known for its luxury boutiques, while bustling Michigan Avenue has everything from designer labels at Giorgio Armani to low-priced fashion trends at H&M. In the Loop, you can wander the massive Macy's (built in the 19th century as Marshall Field's and a Chicago architectural landmark), or bargain shop at a range of discount department stores. River North is home to a cluster of interior-decor shops, while the fashion-forward can find inspiration at the independent boutiques of Wicker Park.

Shopping Hours As a general rule, store hours are 10am to 6 or 7pm Monday through Saturday, and noon to 6pm Sunday. Stores along Michigan Avenue tend to keep later hours, since they cater to after-work shoppers as well as tourists. Almost all stores have extended hours during the holiday season. Nearly all of the stores in the Loop are open for daytime shopping only, generally from 9 or 10am to no later than 6pm Monday through Saturday. (The few remaining big downtown department stores have some selected evening hours.) Many Loop stores not on State Street are closed Saturday; on Sunday the Loop—except for a few restaurants, theaters, and cultural attractions—shuts down.

Sales Tax You might do a double-take after checking the total on your purchase: At 9.75%, the local sales tax on nonfood items is one of the steepest in the country.

SHOPPING THE MAGNIFICENT MILE

The nickname "Magnificent Mile"—hyperbole to some, an understatement to others—refers to the roughly mile-long stretch of North Michigan Avenue between Oak Street and the Chicago River.

In terms of density, the area's first-rate shopping is, quite simply, unmatched. Even jaded shoppers from other worldly capitals are delighted at the ease and convenience of the stores concentrated here. Taking into account that tony Oak Street (see below) is just around the corner, the overall area is a little like New York's Fifth Avenue and Beverly Hills's Rodeo Drive rolled into one. Whether your passion is Bulgari jewelry, Prada bags, or Salvatore Ferragamo footwear, you'll find

FACING PAGE: Sleek, stylish home goods at Orange Skin in River North, Chicago.

it on this stretch of concrete. And don't think you're seeing everything by walking down the street: Michigan Avenue is home to several indoor, high-rise malls, where plenty more boutiques and restaurants are tucked away. Even if you're not the shop-till-you-drop type, it's worth a stroll because this stretch is, in many ways, the heart of the city, a place that bustles with life year-round (although it's especially crowded around Christmas and during the summer).

For the ultimate Mag Mile shopping adventure, start at one end of North Michigan Avenue and try to work your way to the other. Below I've listed some of the best-known shops on the avenue and nearby side streets.

A North Michigan Avenue Shopper's Stroll

This shopper's stroll begins at Oak Street at the northern end of the avenue and heads south toward the river. It just hits the highlights; you'll find much more to tempt your wallet as you meander from designer landmarks to well-known chain stores. (In general, this is not the place to pick up distinctive, one-of-a-kind items—other neighborhoods described later in this chapter cater more to shoppers searching for something unique.) North Michigan Avenue's three vertical malls—each a major shopping destination in its own right—are discussed below under "The Magnificent Malls."

The parade of designer names begins at the intersection of Michigan Avenue and Oak Street, including a couple housed in The Drake Hotel, such as the legendary Danish silversmith **Georg Jensen,** 959 N. Michigan Ave. (📞 312/642-9160; www.georgjensenstore.com), known for outstanding craftsmanship in sterling silver and gold, including earrings, brooches, watches, tie clips, and flatware; and **Chanel,** 935 N. Michigan Ave. (📞 312/787-5500; www.chanel.com). One block south is another luxury emporium, the spacious **Louis Vuitton** store at 919 N. Michigan Ave. (📞 312/944-2010; www.louisvuitton.com), where you'll find trendy handbags and the company's distinctive monogrammed luggage.

On the other side of the street, opposite the dark, soaring Hancock Building, you'll find a quiet oasis that's worth a quick peek. The **Fourth Presbyterian Church,** 126 E. Chestnut St. (📞 312/787-4570; www.fourthchurch.org), looks like something out of an English country village, with a Gothic stone exterior and a peaceful, flower-filled courtyard.

One block south, you'll notice a steady stream of mothers and daughters toting distinctive red shopping bags from **American Girl Place,** on the ground floor of the Water Tower Place mall, 835 N. Michigan Ave. (📞 877/AG-PLACE [247-5223]; www.americangirl.com/stores). The multistory doll emporium is one of the most-visited attractions in town, thanks to the popularity of the company's historic character dolls. The store's cafe is a nice spot for a special mother-daughter lunch or afternoon tea (but be sure to book ahead during Christmas and summer).

Across the street, overlooking a small park next to the historic Water Tower, is **Giorgio Armani's** sleek boutique, 800 N. Michigan Ave., in the Park Hyatt Hotel (📞 312/573-4220; www.armanistores.com). Offering an alternative to high-style minimalism is the **Hershey's Chicago** candy store, 822 N. Michigan Ave. (📞 312/337-7711; www.thehersheycompany.com), a multisensory overload of colors and chocolate.

The next block of Michigan Avenue has a New York vibe, thanks to the world's largest **Polo Ralph Lauren,** 750 N. Michigan Ave. (📞 312/280-1655;

Magnificent Mile & Gold Coast Shopping

American Girl Place 8
Barneys New York 2
Burberry 17
Chanel 4
Crate & Barrel 16
Fourth Presbyterian Church 7
Garrett Popcorn Shop 18
Georg Jensen 5
Giorgio Armani 9
Hershey's Chicago 10

Ikram 14
La Perla 19
Louis Vuitton 6
Madison & Friends 3
Neiman Marcus 13
Niketown 15
Polo Ralph Lauren 11
Prada 1
Tiffany & Co. 12

http://stores.ralphlauren.com), a four-floor, wood-paneled mini-mansion, and **Tiffany & Co.,** 730 N. Michigan Ave. (© **312/944-7500;** www.tiffany.com), with its signature clock, jewels, and tabletop accessories.

A few doors south are high-end department store **Neiman Marcus** and **Niketown,** a multilevel complex that helped pioneer the concept of retail as entertainment. Across the street, at the intersection of Michigan Avenue and Erie Street, is the appropriately barrel-shaped **Crate & Barrel,** 646 N. Michigan Ave. (© **312/787-5900**). Crate & Barrel was started in Chicago, so this is the company's flagship location. Countless varieties of glassware, dishes, cookware, and kitchen gadgets for everyday use line the shelves. The top two floors are devoted to furniture.

Continuing south, you'll find the iconic British design house **Burberry,** 633 N. Michigan Ave. (© **312/787-2500**), where the classic beige plaid shows up on chic purses, shoes, and bathing suits. (If you're looking for luxury souvenirs, check out the collection of baby clothes and dog accessories.) Across Ontario Street, you'll probably see a line of people trailing out from the **Garrett Popcorn Shop,** 645 N. Michigan Ave. (© **312/944-2630**), a 50-year-old landmark. Join the locals in line and pick up some caramel corn for a quick sugar rush. Beautifully made (but pricey) Italian lingerie is the draw at **La Perla,** 535 N. Michigan Ave. (© **312/494-0400**), a popular stop around Valentine's Day.

The Magnificent Malls

Many of the Magnificent Mile's shops are tucked away inside high-rise malls, most of which take up a whole city block. Here's a quick guide to the stores you'll find inside.

900 North Michigan Shops The most upscale of the Magnificent Mile's four vertical malls, 900 North Michigan is often called the Bloomingdale's building, for its most prominent tenant. Compared to boisterous Water Tower Place (below), it tends to be relatively tranquil and appeals to more well-heeled shoppers. In addition to about 70 stores, there are a few decent restaurants and a ground-level cafe that's convenient for a quick caffeine stop.

The Chicago outpost of **Gucci** (ground floor; © **312/664-5504**) has the same sophisticated-but-sexy attitude as the label's body-conscious clothing and much-in-demand purses. Also on the ground floor is **MaxMara** (© **312/475-9500**), the Italian women's fashion house known for elegantly constructed coats and separates (some of which will cost you about as much as a flight to Italy). Other goodies worth checking out include funky European footwear at **Charles David** (second floor; © **312/944-9013**), classic American fashion at **Michael Kors** (ground floor; © **312/640-1122**), and an eclectic selection of hats, mittens, scarves, and other accessories at **Glove Me Tender** (fifth floor; © **312/664-4022**), which should be your first stop if you're caught here during an unexpected cold spell. 900 N. Michigan Ave. (btw. Walton St. and Delaware Place). © **312/915-3916.** www.shop900.com. Subway/El: Red Line to Chicago.

Water Tower Place In 1975, Water Tower was the first big indoor mall to open downtown, and 35 years ago its glass elevators and shiny gold trim gave the place a glamorous air. These days the mall remains popular but doesn't have much to distinguish it from any other upscale big-city shopping center. Water Tower is a magnet for suburban teenagers—just like your mall back home—and can get quite crowded during prime summer tourist season. Most of its stores are part of national chains (Ann Taylor, Victoria's Secret, and so on). There are also a few souvenir shops that are popular with visitors picking up last-minute gifts, including a small **Oprah Store** on the second floor, where you can buy "O"-branded clothing, mugs, and books. The complex is anchored on one end by the Mag Mile outpost of **Macy's** (see "Department Stores" in "Shopping A to Z," later in this chapter) and on the other by busy **American Girl Place** (p. 260). One of Water Tower's best features is its funky mezzanine-level food court, **foodlife,** a place I often recommend for families in search of an affordable meal downtown (p. 118). 835 N. Michigan Ave. (btw. Pearson and Chestnut sts.). © 312/440-3166. www.shopwatertower.com. Subway/El: Red Line to Chicago.

The Shops at North Bridge The anchor of this development—and its most popular draw for shoppers—is a four-story **Nordstrom** department store (p. 279). The rest of the mall is bright and open, thanks to high ceilings and a wide central walkway, but it can also feel somewhat deserted compared to the bustling street outside. The stores are a mix of clothing, jewelry, and bath-and-body shops (in a midrange to upscale price bracket). Distinctive stores that are worth checking out include the high-style chocolate cafe **Vosges Haut-Chocolat,** on the second floor (p. 275), and the **LEGO** store, on the third floor (© 312/494-0760), which features a mini re-creation of the Chicago skyline. The third-floor food court is a good stop for lunch, with a food station run by Tuscany, a local Italian restaurant, and other stands that offer Japanese tempura, grilled wraps, and Chicago-style hot dogs. 520 N. Michigan Ave. (btw. Grand Ave. and Illinois St.). © 312/327-2300. www.theshopsatnorthbridge.com. Subway/El: Red Line to Grand.

Chic Shopping on Nearby Oak Street

Oak Street has long been a symbol of designer-label shopping; if a store has an Oak Street address, you can count on it being expensive. The shopping district itself is actually quite limited, taking up only 1 block at the northern tip of the Magnificent Mile (where Michigan Ave. ends and Lake Shore Dr. begins). While big-name designer showcases such as Giorgio Armani and Louis Vuitton pride themselves on having a Michigan Avenue address, Oak Street features smaller, more personal shops (most of them high-priced). Since the stores are tucked into converted town houses, it's also more tranquil than Michigan Avenue. It's well worth a stroll for people-watching: This is Main Street for Chicago socialites. Most of Oak Street is closed on Sunday, except during the holiday season.

Just around the corner from Michigan Avenue, footwear fans can browse Italian shoemaker **Tod's,** best known for its luxuriously soft (and pricey) driving

Shop the chic boutiques on Oak Street for unique, high-quality goods.

shoes (p. 286). Shoes, stationery, and handbags are available at **kate spade,** 101 E. Oak St. (☎ 312/654-8853), along with the Jack Spade line of men's accessories. The priciest accessories on this very pricey block can likely be found at French luxury house **Hermès of Paris,** 110 E. Oak St. (☎ 312/787-8175). Thread-count fanatics swear by the sheets from **Pratesi,** 67 E. Oak St. (☎ 312/943-8422), and **Frette,** 41 E. Oak St. (☎ 312/649-3744), both of which supply linens to top hotels (and where sheet sets cost more than what some people pay in rent).

> **An Oak Street Bargain**
>
> Oak Street is not the place to come shopping for bargains, with one exception— **Bravco,** 43 E. Oak St. (☎ 312/943-4305). This crowded, narrow drugstore seems out of place among the luxury boutiques, but it's a popular spot among Chicago hairstylists and makeup artists. You'll find an excellent selection of professional hair and beauty products (including Aveda, Sebastian, and Bumble and bumble) here for much less than they cost at salons. Even if you haven't heard of some of the brands, trust me, if Bravco carries them, they're hot.

Anchoring the western end of the block are two haute heavyweights, hip Italian designer **Prada,** 30 E. Oak St. (☎ 312/951-1113), which offers three floors of sleek, postmodern fashions for men and women and plenty of the designer's signature handbags; and the equally style-conscious department store **Barneys New York** (p. 278). When you're ready to take a break, stop for a coffee and treat at **Sarah's Pastries & Candies,** a cheery cafe where chocolate lovers will find plenty to tempt them (p. 275).

MORE SHOPPING NEIGHBORHOODS
State Street & the Loop

Shopping in the Loop is mostly concentrated along State Street, from Randolph Street south to Congress Parkway. State Street was Chicago's first great shopping district—by World War I, seven of the largest and most lavish department stores in the world were competing for shoppers' loyalties along this half-mile stretch. The area has long since been eclipsed by Michigan Avenue, but one grand old department store makes it worth a visit: **Macy's at State Street** (formerly Marshall Field's; see p. 279). A city landmark and one of the largest department stores in the world, it occupies an entire city block and features the largest Tiffany glass mosaic dome in the U.S. If you're in Chicago between Thanksgiving and New Year's, Macy's has maintained a long-time Marshall Field's tradition: lavishly decorated holiday windows and lunch under the Great Tree in the store's restaurant, the Walnut Room.

Aside from Macy's, State Street has become a hot destination for bargain hunters in recent years, thanks to the opening of discount stores such as **Loehmann's,** 151 N. State St. (☎ 312/705-3810);

> **Point Zero**
>
> If the quick change from north to south in the Loop confuses you, keep in mind that in Chicago, point zero for the purpose of address numbering is the intersection of State and Madison streets.

Nordstrom Rack, 24 N. State St. (✆ 312/377-5500); **T.J. Maxx,** 11 N. State St. (✆ 312/553-0515); and **Filene's Basement,** 1 N. State St. (✆ 312/553-1055). If you've got the energy to hunt through racks of not-so-great stuff, you can sometimes find good designer-label deals.

State Street has a no-frills aura compared to Michigan Avenue—but it stays busy thanks to the thousands of office workers who stroll around during their lunch hour or after work. On weekends, the street is considerably more subdued.

River North

Since the 1960s, when the Chicago Imagists (painters Ed Paschke, Jim Nutt, and Roger Brown among them) attracted international attention with their shows at the Hyde Park Art Center, the city has been a fertile breeding ground for emerging artists and innovative art dealers. Today the primary art gallery district is concentrated in the River North neighborhood—the area west of the Magnificent Mile and north of the Chicago River—where century-old redbrick warehouses have been converted into lofty exhibition spaces. More recently, a new generation of gallery owners has set up shop in the West Loop neighborhood, where you'll tend to find more cutting-edge work. (For suggestions on the best places to visit, see "Art Galleries" under "Shopping A to Z," below.)

The River North gallery season officially gets underway on the first Friday after Labor Day in September. Besides fall, another great time to visit the district is from mid-July through August, when the Chicago Art Dealers Association presents **Vision,** an annual lineup of programs tailored to the public. The *Chicago Reader,* a free weekly newspaper available at many stores, taverns, and cafes on the North Side, publishes a very comprehensive listing of current gallery exhibitions, as does the quarterly *Chicago Gallery News* (www.chicagogallerynews. com), which is available free at the city's visitor information centers. Another good resource is the Chicago Art Dealers Association (✆ 312/649-0065; www.chicago artdealers.org); the group's website has descriptions of all member galleries.

Along with its status as Chicago's primary art gallery district, River North has attracted many interesting home-design shops, with many concentrated on Wells Street from Kinzie Street to Chicago Avenue. The best include **Manifesto,** 755 N. Wells St., at Chicago Avenue (✆ 312/664-0733; www.manifestofurniture. com), which offers custom-designed furniture, as well as imports from Italy and elsewhere in Europe; edgy **Orange Skin** (p. 282), a great place to pick up one-of-a-kind modern decorative accents; and **Lightology,** 215 W. Chicago Ave., at Wells St. (✆ 312/944-1000; www.lightology.com), a massive lighting store that carries a mind-boggling array of funky lamps, chandeliers, and glowing orbs from more than 400 manufacturers. (Even if you have no intention of flying home with a stack of lamps in your luggage, it's still a fun place for the design-minded to browse.)

Looming above the Chicago River at the southern end of River North is the **Merchandise Mart,** the world's largest commercial building. The massive complex was built in 1930 by Marshall Field & Company and was bought in 1945 by Joseph P. Kennedy (JFK's dad). The Mart houses mostly interior design showrooms, which are open only to professional designers. Public tours of the whole complex are offered once a week, usually on Fridays ($12 adults; © **312/527-7762;** www.merchandisemart.com for dates and reservations).

Armitage Avenue

Hovering between the North Side neighborhoods of Old Town and Lincoln Park, Armitage Avenue has emerged as a shopping destination in its own right, thanks to an influx of wealthy young professionals who have settled into historic town homes on the neighboring tree-lined streets. I'd suggest starting at the Armitage El stop on the Brown Line, working your way east to Halsted Street, and then wandering a few blocks north to Webster Street. As you stroll around, you'll get a good sense of the area's strong community spirit, with neighbors greeting each other and catching up on the street corners.

The shops and boutiques here are geared toward sophisticated, well-heeled, predominantly female shoppers (sorry, guys). You'll find trendy clothing boutiques, including that of Chicago-area native **Cynthia Rowley,** 808 W. Armitage Ave. (©**773/528-6160;** www.cynthiarowley.com); eclectic home-decor stores; beauty emporiums; and one of my favorite impossible-to-classify gift shops, **Art Effect** (p. 281). The upscale pet accessories shop **Barker & Meowsky,** 1003 W. Armitage Ave. (©**773/868-0200;** www.barkerandmeowsky.com), has everything you need to spoil furry family members, including catnip cigars, doggy "sushi," and designer-inspired outfits.

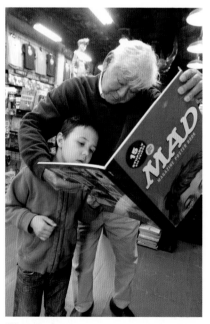

Despite the area's upscale feel, you can snag bargains at some top-notch discount and consignment shops, including **Lori's Designer Shoes, McShane's Exchange, Fox's,** and **The Second Child** (see "Vintage Fashion/Resale Shops" under "Shopping A to Z").

Lincoln Park & Lakeview

Radiating from the intersection of Belmont Avenue and Clark Street is a string of shops catering to rebellious kids on tour from their homes in the 'burbs. (The Dunkin' Donuts on the corner is often referred to as "Punkin' Donuts" in their honor.) One constant in the ever-changing youth culture has

Chicago Comics.

Wicker Park/Bucktown Shopping

W. Webster Ave.
W. Webster Ave.
N. Elston Ave.
N. Ashland Ave.
Chicago River
N. Branch

W. Charleston St.
John F. Kennedy Expressway

W. Dickens Ave. ② W. Dickens Ave.

N. Campbell Ave.
N. Western Ave.
N. Oakley Ave.
N. Hoyne Ave.

W. McLean Ave.

W. Armitage Ave.
W. Armitage Ave.

W. Homer St.

BUCKTOWN

① Western Ⓜ

W. Cortland St. ③
W. Cortland St.

Wilmot Ave.
N. Milwaukee Ave.
N. Leavitt St.
N. Damen Ave.
N. Winchester Ave.
N. Wolcott Ave.

W. Moffat St.

N. Winnebago Ave.

W. Churchill St. ⑤

W. Bloomingdale Ave.
W. Bloomingdale Ave.

W. St. Paul Ave.
W. Willow St. ⑥

⑦
W. St. Paul Ave.
⑨ ⑧

W. Wabansia Ave.
④
W. Wabansia Ave.

N. Hermitage Ave.
N. Paulina Ave.
N. Marshfield Ave.
N. Ashland Ave.

94
90

N. Oakley Ave.

⑩ ⑪

W. Concord Pl.

Flat Iron
Building

W. Honore St.
N. Wood St.

W. North Ave. 64 64 W. North Ave. 64

Damen Ⓜ W. Pierce Ave.

N. Campbell Ave.
N. Artesian Ave.

N. Elk Grove Ave.
W. Le Moyne St.

W. Pierce Ave.
W. Le Moyne St.

W. Julian St.

Claremont
Oakley
Bell
N. Leavitt St.

N. Milwaukee Ave.

W. Beach Ave.

**WICKER
PARK**

W. Hirsch St.

W. Blackhawk St.

WICKER PARK

N. Ashland
N. Bosworth

W. Schiller St.

W. Evergreen Ave.

*CLEMENTE
PARK*

N. Damen Ave.
N. Hoyne Ave.

W. Potomac Ave.
W. Ellen St.
N. Marion Ct.
N. Honore St.
N. Wood St.

W. Crystal St.

W. Division St.
W. Division St.
Ⓜ Division

N. Western Ave.

W. Haddon St.
⑫ W. Haddon St.
W. Haddon St.

W. Thomas St.
W. Thomas St.

N. Winchester Ave.
N. Wolcott Ave.
N. Honore St.

W. Cortez St.
W. Cortez St.

W. Augusta Blvd.
W. Augusta Blvd.

N. Oakley Blvd.
N. Leavitt St.
N. Hoyne Ave.
N. Damen Ave.

W. Walton St.

Ⓜ **Subway/El stop**

W. Iowa St.
W. Iowa St.

W. Rice St.

| 0 | | 1/4 mi |
| 0 | 0.25 km | |

W. Chicago Ave.

0 — 3 mi
0 — 3 km

94 41
90
Wrigley
Field

Lake
Michigan

Map area

CHICAGO
THE
LOOP

290

U.S. Cellular
Field

55
90
94

✈ Midway

been the **Alley,** 3228 N. Clark St., at Belmont Avenue (✆ **773/883-1800;** thealley.com), an "alternative shopping complex" selling everything from plaster gargoyles to racks of leather jackets. It has separate shops specializing in condoms, cigars, and bondage wear. **Tragically Hip,** a storefront women's boutique, 931 W. Belmont Ave. (✆ **773/549-1500**), next to the Belmont El train stop, has outlasted many other similar purveyors of cutting-edge women's apparel.

You can get plugged into what the kids are reading at **Chicago Comics,** 3244 N. Clark St. (✆ **773/528-1983;** www.chicagocomics.com), considered one of the best comics shops in the country. Besides the usual superhero titles, you'll find lots of European and Japanese comics, along with underground books and zines.

Southport Avenue

West of Lakeview, a few blocks from Wrigley Field, this commercial strip houses a mix of restaurants, cool (but not *too* cool) clothing boutiques, and cafes appealing to the upscale urban families who live in the surrounding area. It's worth a look if you want to hang out in a neighborhood that's a little more laid-back than the Gold Coast or Wicker Park, and the surrounding tree-lined residential streets are a pleasant place to stroll. Start at the Southport El stop on the Brown Line, and work your way north to Grace Street. (Round-trip, the walk will take you about a half-hour—but allow more if you're doing some serious shopping or want to stop for lunch.) Along the way you'll pass the historic **Music Box Theatre,** at 3733 N. Southport Ave. (✆ **773/871-6604;** www.musicboxtheatre.com), north of Addison Street, which shows independent films from around the world. **Krista K,** 3458 N. Southport Ave. (✆ **773/248-1967;** www.kristak.com), caters to hip young women with plenty of disposable income by stocking up-and-coming designers that aren't widely available, while **Cerato** (p. 276) champions made-in-Chicago fashion.

Wicker Park/Bucktown

The gentrification of the Wicker Park/Bucktown area was followed by not only a rash of restaurants and bars, but also retailers with an artsy bent that reflect the neighborhood's bohemian spirit. Mixed in with old neighborhood businesses, such as discount furniture stores and religious icon purveyors, is a proliferation of antique furniture shops, edgy clothing boutiques, and eclectic galleries and gift

---

Taking a Break in Wicker Park

When you're ready to rest your weary self, settle down at a local coffeehouse and soak in Wicker Park's artsy vibe. **Earwax Café,** 1564 N. Milwaukee Ave. (p. 127; ✆ 773/772-4019), attracts the jaded and pierced set with a no-frills, slightly edgy atmosphere. At **Gallery Café,** 1760 W. North Ave., 4 blocks east of Milwaukee Ave. (✆ 773/252-8228), the atmosphere isn't quite as memorable, but the laid-back hangout roasts its own coffee and offers a full menu of breakfast and lunch dishes. Both cafes are near the bustling intersection of North, Milwaukee, and Damen avenues—the heart of Wicker Park—and draw a steady stream of locals. It's here you'll realize that Wicker Park is really just a small town—with cooler hair and funkier shoes.

emporiums. Despite the hefty price tags in many of these shops, the neighborhood still feels gritty—so come here if you want to feel like you've gotten a real urban fix.

To browse the best of the neighborhood, start at the Damen El stop on the Blue Line, and walk north along Damen Avenue to Armitage Avenue to scope out the trendiest shops. If you've got time, some stores are also scattered along Milwaukee Avenue south of North Avenue.

The friendly modern-day Marco Polos at **Pagoda Red,** 1714 N. Damen Ave., second floor (© **773/235-1188;** www.pagodared.com), import beautiful (and expensive) antique furniture and art objects from Asia. Design-conscious shoppers head to **Stitch** (p. 282) for one-of-a-kind, stylish gifts—the kind of thing you won't find at the mall back home. Damen Avenue is also known for its concentration of independent women's clothing boutiques, which range from body-conscious, urban looks at **p45** (p. 277) to flirty dresses and skirts at **Tangerine** (p. 278).

West Division Street

Once home to just a few pioneering restaurants, Division Street is quickly being transformed from a desolate urban landscape to a hot shopping destination. It's a work in progress (you'll still find some boarded-up buildings among the cool boutiques), but for now this is what Wicker Park used to be: a place where rents are still cheap enough for eager young entrepreneurs. Begin your walk at the Division El stop on the Blue Line, and head west along Division Street; most stores are concentrated between Milwaukee Avenue and Damen Avenue (a round-trip walk will take about a half-hour). Along the way, you'll stroll past eclectic clothing and home boutiques, including the hip kids' shop **Grow** (p. 287), where eco-conscious urban parents stock up on organic-cotton baby clothes and sustainable-wood furniture.

SHOPPING A TO Z

Chicago has shops selling just about anything you could want or need, be it functional or ornamental, whimsical or exotic. Although the following list only scratches the surface, it gives you an idea of the range of merchandise available. You'll find more shops in many of these categories, such as clothing and home accessories, covered in the earlier sections of this chapter.

Antiques

If you think half the fun of antiquing is sorting through piles of junk to discover hidden treasures, you'll probably enjoy browsing the series of independently owned antiques stores along Belmont Avenue west of Southport Avenue. (Since it's a haul from the El, I'd recommend shopping here only if you have a car.) Chicago's best-organized and best-stocked antique shops are scattered throughout the city, but if you're willing to venture beyond the usual tourist neighborhoods, you'll be well rewarded.

Architectural Artifacts, Inc. ★★ 🎁 Chicago has a handful of salvage specialists who cater to the design trades and retail customers seeking an unusual architectural piece for their homes, and this is the best of them. Although it's a fair distance from downtown, it's easy enough to reach by public transportation (about a 30-min. ride from the Loop on the Brown Line). Its brightly lit, well-organized, cavernous showroom features everything from original mantels and garden ornaments to vintage bathroom hardware and American and French Art Deco lighting fixtures. The store also has a museum on the lower level to display portions of historically significant buildings. 4325 N. Ravenswood Ave. (east of Damen Ave. and south of Montrose Ave.). ✆ **773/348-0622.** www.architecturalartifacts. com. Subway/El: Brown Line to Montrose.

Broadway Antique Market ★ Visiting Hollywood prop stylists and local interior designers flock here to find 20th-century antiques in near-perfect condition. In this two-level, 20,000-square-foot vintage mega-mart, you'll spot both pricey pieces (for example, an Arne Jacobsen egg chair) and affordable collectibles for less than $100 (Roseville pottery, Art Deco barware, Peter Max scarves). 6130 N. Broadway Ave. (½ mile north of Hollywood Ave. and Lake Shore Dr.). ✆ **773/743-5444.** www. bamchicago.com. Subway/El: Red Line to Granville.

Jay Robert's Antique Warehouse This mammoth River North space is within walking distance of downtown hotels, but you'll need comfortable shoes to explore all 25,000 square feet. The selection is wildly eclectic: fine furniture that includes fireplaces, stained glass, statues, tapestries, and an impressive selection of antique clocks in a variety of styles ranging from elaborate Victorian to sophisticated Art Deco. 149 W. Kinzie St. (at LaSalle St.). ✆ **312/222-0167.** www.jay roberts.com. Subway/El: Brown Line to Merchandise Mart.

Modern Times This shop specializes in the major designers of home furnishings from the 1930s to the 1960s—the sort of pieces that style-conscious shoppers buy to furnish their newly renovated lofts. You'll also find lighting fixtures of all types, tabletop accessories, and some jewelry. *Note:* The store is open only Friday through Sunday from noon to 6pm, although you can request an appointment to visit on other days if you call ahead. 2100 W. Grand Ave. (at Damen Ave.). ✆ **312/243-5706.** www.moderntimeschicago.com. Subway/El: Blue Line to Division, then about ½-mile walk; or take a cab.

Salvage One ★ Like Architectural Artifacts, Inc. (above), this sprawling space stocks everything and the kitchen sink—literally: There's an entire room filled with vintage sinks. You'll find hundreds of one-of-a-kind pieces for the home handyperson, including doors, mantels, tubs, stained glass, and antique chandeliers. Don't worry about fitting your new purchase in your suitcase for the trip home: The store regularly ships items cross-country and even internationally. Salvage One is open only on Friday through Sunday. 1840 W. Hubbard St. (at Damen Ave.). ✆ **312/733-0098.** www.salvageone.com. Bus: 65 (Grand Ave.).

Art Galleries

Most of the city's major art galleries are concentrated in two neighborhoods. The city's original gallery district is in River North, within easy walking distance of most downtown hotels. More recently, galleries have been opening in the converted loft buildings of the West Loop, which is best reached by taxi.

Alan Koppel Gallery This expansive gallery showcases modern and contemporary works of art, as well as French and Italian modernist furniture from the '20s through the '60s (in a separate viewing area). Koppel also specializes in works by major 20th-century photographers, so if you're hankering for something by Diane Arbus, Man Ray, or Walker Evans, this is the place to look. 210 W. Chicago Ave. (at Wells St.). ✆ **312/640-0730.** www.alankoppel.com. Subway/El: Brown or Red line to Chicago.

Ann Nathan Gallery ★★ Ann Nathan, who started out as a collector, shows exciting—and sometimes outrageous—pieces in clay, wood, and metal, along with "functional art" (pieces that blur the line between furniture and sculpture). Perhaps as a contrast to her more unusual pieces, she also represents a number of figurative and realist painters. Nathan's loftlike space in the center of the River North district is one of the most beautiful galleries in the city. 212 W. Superior St. (at Wells St.). ℂ **312/664-6622.** www.annnathangallery.com. Subway/El: Brown or Red line to Chicago.

Carl Hammer Gallery A former schoolteacher and one of the most venerated dealers in Chicago, Carl Hammer touts his wares as "contemporary art and selected historical masterworks by American and European self-taught artists"—but it's the "self-taught" part that warrants emphasis. Hammer helped pioneer the field known as "outsider art," which has since become a white-hot commodity in the international art world, and he carries works by a number of the movement's best-known figures, such as Henry Darger. 740 N. Wells St. (at Superior St.). ℂ **312/266-8512.** www.hammergallery.com. Subway/El: Brown or Red line to Chicago.

Catherine Edelman Gallery One of Chicago's leading galleries in contemporary photography, Catherine Edelman represents a range of mostly American artists; she is also a proud booster of up-and-coming Chicago photographers. Across the street, **Stephen Daiter Gallery,** 230 W. Superior St. (ℂ **312/787-3350**), also specializes in photography, with a strong selection of vintage 20th-century work. 300 W. Superior St. (at Franklin St.). ℂ **312/266-2350.** www.edelmangallery.com. Subway/El: Brown or Red line to Chicago.

Donald Young Gallery ★ Renowned on the contemporary art scene since the late 1970s, Donald Young is one of Chicago's most high-profile art dealers. His Michigan Avenue gallery is a haven for critically acclaimed artists working in video, sculpture, photography, painting, and installation, including Anne Chu, Gary Hill, Martin Puryear, Bruce Nauman, Cristina Iglesias, Robert Mangold, and Charles Ray. 224 S. Michigan Ave. (btw. Adams St. and Jackson Blvd.). ℂ **312/322-3600.** www.donaldyoung.com. Subway/El: Red Line to Jackson.

Artistic Center of the Heartland

Chicago may have thrived as a business center and transportation hub, but it's also a gathering spot for artists from throughout the Midwest. In part, that's due to the presence of the **School of the Art Institute of Chicago,** considered one of the best fine arts colleges in the country. The school produces a steady stream of arts-minded graduates, many of whom stay in town to work at local art galleries or fashion boutiques. Notable Art Institute alumni include painters Georgia O'Keefe and Grant Wood; iconic '70s fashion designer Halston; sculptors Claes Oldenburg, Jeff Koons, and Richard Hunt; alternative cartoonist and illustrator Chris Ware; and humorists Sarah Vowell and David Sedaris. Another downtown academic institution, **Columbia College Chicago,** also fosters an environment of creativity: The largest private arts and media college in the country, it offers undergraduate and graduate programs in film, arts management, creative writing, journalism, dance, and photography.

Douglas Dawson Gallery ★ Offering a unique perspective to the Chicago art scene, Douglas Dawson specializes in ancient and historic ethnographic art—everything from tribal textiles to furniture, although a principal focus is African ceramics. The gallery's spectacular loft space in the West Loop looks like a museum. 400 N. Morgan St. (at Kinzie St.). © **312/226-7975.** www.douglasdawson.com. Bus: 65 (Grand).

G. R. N'Namdi Gallery George N'Namdi founded his gallery, which specializes in African-American artists, 2 decades ago in the Detroit area. His son Jumaane operates this location (there's also another in New York). Artists they've helped bring to the attention of museums and art collectors include James Vanderzee, Al Loving, Edward Clark, and Robert Colescott. 110 N. Peoria St. (at Washington St.). © **312/563-9240.** www.grnnamdigallery.com. Bus: 20 (Madison).

Kavi Gupta Gallery Owner Kavi Gupta is widely credited with kicking off the West Loop art scene when he developed this property as a home for new galleries. Gupta specializes in contemporary art by national and international emerging artists, so you never quite know what you're going to see here. Also worth checking out in the same building are the **Carrie Secrist Gallery** (© 312/491-0917; www.secristgallery.com) and **Thomas McCormick Gallery** (© 312/226-6800; www.thomasmccormick.com). 835 W. Washington St. (at Green St.). © **312/432-0708.** www.kavigupta.com. Bus: 20 (Madison).

Ken Saunders Gallery Chicago is home to two world-class galleries dealing in contemporary glass-art sculpture, conveniently located within steps of one another along Superior Street in River North. Ken Saunders Gallery houses the city's largest showcase of glass art and features world-famous artists, past and present (William Morris, Mark Fowler, and Hiroshi Yamano), as well as newcomers. Also worth a look for art-glass lovers is the nearby **Echt Gallery,** 222 W. Superior St. (© 312/440-0288; www.echtgallery.com). 230 W. Superior St. (btw. Franklin and Wells sts.). © **312/573-1400.** www.kensaundersgallery.com. Subway/El: Brown or Red line to Chicago.

Maya Polsky Gallery Gallery owner Maya Polsky deals in international contemporary art and also represents some leading local artists, but she's best known for showcasing the contemporary and post-revolutionary art of Russia, including the work of such masters as Valery Koshliakov and Sergei Sherstiuk. She also represents the estate of the Chicago Imagist painter Ed Paschke. 215 W. Superior St. (at Wells St.). © **312/440-0055.** www.mayapolskygallery.com. Subway/El: Brown or Red line to Chicago.

Rhona Hoffman Gallery The New York–born Rhona Hoffman maintains a high profile on the international contemporary art scene. She launched her gallery in 1983 and, from the start, sought national and international artists, typically young and cutting-edge artists who weren't represented elsewhere in Chicago. Today she is the purveyor of such blue-chip players as Sol LeWitt and Jeff Koons, as well as younger up-and-comers. 118 N. Peoria St. (btw. Randolph and Washington sts.). © **312/455-1990.** www.rhoffmangallery.com. Bus: 20 (Madison).

Richard Gray Gallery ★ Richard Gray—whose gallery opened in 1963—is widely considered the dean of art dealers in Chicago. (He's served as president of the Art Dealers Association of America and been a longtime board member of the Art Institute of Chicago.) The gallery specializes in paintings, sculpture, and drawings by leading artists from the major movements in 20th-century American and European art. (He also has a second location in New York.) Gray and his son, Paul, who now runs the Chicago gallery, have shown the work of such luminaries as Pablo Picasso, Jean Dubuffet, Willem de Kooning, Alexander Calder, Claes Oldenberg, Joan Miró, and Henri Matisse. John Hancock Center, 875 N. Michigan Ave., Ste. 2503 (btw. Delaware and Chestnut sts.). © 312/642-8877. www.richardgraygallery.com. Subway/El: Red Line to Chicago.

Zolla/Lieberman Gallery ★★ Bob Zolla and Roberta Lieberman kicked off the River North revival when they opened their gallery here in 1976; it's now considered the grande dame of the area. Today Zolla/Lieberman, directed by Roberta's son, William Lieberman, represents a wide range of artists, including sculptor Deborah Butterfield, installation artist Vernon Fisher, and still life painter David Kroll. 325 W. Huron St. (at Orleans St.). © 312/944-1990. www.zolla liebermangallery.com. Subway/El: Brown Line to Chicago.

Books

Abraham Lincoln Book Shop ★ This bookstore boasts one of the country's most outstanding collections of Lincolniana, from rare and antique books about the 16th president to collectible signatures, letters, and other documents illuminating the lives of other U.S. presidents and historical figures. The shop carries new historical and academic works, too. 357 W. Chicago Ave. (btw. Orleans and Sedgwick sts.). © 312/944-3085. www.alincolnbookshop.com. Subway/El: Brown Line to Chicago.

Barnes & Noble This two-level Gold Coast store comes complete with a cafe, in case you get the munchies while perusing the miles of books. There's another store in Lincoln Park, at 659 W. Diversey Ave., 1 block west of Clark Street

The Abraham Lincoln Book Shop houses one of the country's most extensive collections of Lincolniana.

(℃ 773/871-9004), and one at 1441 W. Webster Ave., at Clybourn Avenue (℃ 773/871-3610). 1130 N. State St. (at Elm St.). ℃ **312/280-8155.** Subway/El: Red Line to Clark/Division.

Borders Located in the heart of the Loop, Border's is like a minidepartment store, with a wide range of books, an excellent collection of magazines, and an upstairs cafe. 150 N. State St. (at Randolph St.). ℃ **312/606-0750.** Subway/El: Red Line to Randolph.

Powell's Bookstore Used books (especially from scholarly and small Chicago presses), dog-eared paperbacks, and hardcover classics fill the shelves at this sprawling book lover's haven in Lakeview. Allow ample time to browse, because you never know what you'll find at this eclectic spot. Powell's also has an outlet in Hyde Park, at 1501 E. 57th St. (℃ 773/955-7780). 2850 N. Lincoln Ave. (btw. Diversey Pkwy. and George St.). ℃ **773/248-1444.** www.powellschicago.com. Subway/El: Brown Line to Diversey.

Seminary Co-op Bookstore A classic campus bookstore located near the University of Chicago, this is one of the premier academic bookstores in the country. Yes, you can browse the extensive philosophy and theology sections or pick up an obscure work from a small press, but you'll find thought-provoking new fiction as well. 5757 S. University Ave. (btw. 57th and 58th sts.). ℃ **773/752-4381.** www.semcoop.com. Bus: 69 (Jeffrey Express).

Unabridged Books This quintessential neighborhood bookseller in the area known as Boys Town has strong sections in gay and lesbian literature, travel, film, and sci-fi; there's also a well-stocked children's area. Handwritten recommendations by the book-loving staff are posted throughout the store. 3251 N. Broadway Ave. (btw. Belmont Ave. and Addison St.). ℃ **773/883-9119.** www.unabridgedbookstore. com. Subway/El: Red Line to Addison.

Women & Children First ☺ This feminist and children's bookstore—located in the far North Side neighborhood of Andersonville—holds the best selection in the city of titles for, by, and about women. But the shop is far from a male-free zone; the owners promote great independent fiction by authors of both genders, making this a good place to discover books that have been overlooked by the bestseller lists. There's a section devoted to lesbian and gay books, and the store has a busy schedule of appearances by well-known and local authors. 5233 N. Clark St. (btw. Foster and Bryn Mawr aves.). ℃ **773/769-9299.** www.womenandchildrenfirst.com. Subway/El: Red Line to Berwyn.

Candy, Chocolates & Pastries

Bittersweet ★★ Run by Judy Contino, one of the city's top pastry chefs and bakers, this Lakeview cafe and shop is sought out by brides-to-be and trained palates who have a yen for gourmet cakes, cookies, tarts, and ladyfingers. Stop by at lunchtime for fresh soups, sandwiches, and quiches. The rich chocolate mousse cake, a specialty of the house, is out of this world. 1114 W. Belmont Ave. (btw. Seminary and Clifton aves.). ℃ **773/929-1100.** www.bittersweetpastry.com. Subway/ El: Red Line to Belmont.

Ghirardelli Chocolate Shop & Soda Fountain This Midwest outpost of the famed San Francisco chocolatier, just a half-block off the Mag Mile, gets swamped in the summer, so good thing they've got their soda fountain assembly line down to a science. Besides the incredible hot-fudge sundaes, there's a veritable mudslide of chocolate bars, hot-cocoa drink mixes, and chocolate-covered espresso beans to tempt your sweet tooth. Hit with a late-night craving? They're open until midnight on Friday and Saturday nights. 830 N. Michigan Ave. (btw. Michigan Ave. and Rush St.). © **312/337-9330.** Subway/El: Red Line to Chicago.

Margie's Candies ✇ This family-run candy and ice-cream shop hasn't changed much since it opened in 1921. It still offers some of the city's finest handmade fudge, whether it comes in a box or melted over a banana split served in an old-school clamshell dish. The store is known for its turtles—chocolate-covered pecan and caramel clusters—and might be the only place in the city still selling rock candy on wooden sticks. Although it's out of the way for most visitors, near a busy commercial intersection with little else to recommend it, it's worth a stop for dessert lovers if you're in the Wicker Park area. 1960 N. Western Ave. (just south of Armitage Ave.). © **773/384-1035.** www.margiescandies.nv.switchboard.com. Subway/El: Blue Line to Western.

Sarah's Pastries and Candies ★ It may be on tony Oak Street, but this friendly cafe, run by Chicago native Sarah Levy, is anything but stuffy. It makes a perfect stop for a pick-me-up during a day of Michigan Avenue shopping: Homemade creations include truffles, toffee, specialty cupcakes, flavored short-bread, and decadently rich fudge brownies. The shop also offers fresh pastries and coffee for on-the-go breakfasts, as well as a small selection of sandwiches at lunchtime. 70 E. Oak St. (btw. Michigan Ave. and Rush St.). © **312/664-6223.** www.sarahs candies.com. Subway/El: Red Line to Chicago.

Vosges Haut-Chocolat ★ 🎁 Chocolatier Katrina Markoff's exotic gourmet truffles—with fabulous names such as absinthe, mint julep, wink of the rabbit, woolloomooloo, and ambrosia—are made from premium Belgian chocolate and infused with rare spices, seasonings, and flowers from around the world. Vosges's

Exotic truffles at Vosges Haut-Chocolat.

other signature treat—a chocolate and bacon candy bar—sounds bizarre but has developed a cult following. The gleaming white, streamlined store, which looks more like a modern art gallery than a chocolate shop, includes a bar where you're welcome to sit and sip a cup of cocoa. Vosges also has a small store on trendy Armitage Avenue (951 W. Armitage Ave.; ℂ **773/296-9866**). 520 N. Michigan Ave. (in the Westfield North Bridge shopping center). ℂ **312/644-9450.** www.vosgeschocolate. com. Subway/El: Red Line to Grand.

Clothing Boutiques

In the not-so-distant past, local fashion addicts had to head for the coasts when they wanted to shop for cutting-edge designer duds. Those days are over. While over-the-top outrageousness doesn't sell here—this is still the practical Midwest—stylish Chicagoans now turn to local independent boutiques when they want to stay on top of the latest trends without looking like fashion victims. Here are some of the best:

Apartment Number 9 Chicago men aren't renowned for their sense of style; most get by just fine with a wardrobe of baseball hats and sports team T-shirts. But a few stores cater to hip young dudes, and this is the most stylish of the bunch. The clothing selection is trendy but not outrageous, with a good selection from menswear designers such as John Varvatos, Nicole Farhi, and Paul Smith, among other up-and-coming names. Best of all, you don't need to be on top of the trends to shop here: The friendly staff knows how to steer skittish male customers toward what works best. 1804 N. Damen Ave. (at Willow St.). ℂ **773/395-2999.** www. apartmentnumber9.com. Subway/El: Blue Line to Damen.

Cerato ★ 👗 Chicago has long celebrated its local writers and musicians—and now local fashion designers are getting their due. In recent years, initiatives such as the Chicago Fashion Incubator have provided financial and marketing support for designers, encouraging them to set up shop here rather than heading for New York. Cerato, a friendly women's clothing boutique in the Southport neighborhood, stocks Chicago designers almost exclusively, giving new talent a chance to shine. While the location is a detour from downtown, it's worth the trek for fashionistas in search of one-of-a-kind looks—or anyone who likes the idea of supporting local artists. 3451 N. Southport Ave. (btw. Newport and Cornelia sts.). ℂ **773/248-8604.** www.ceratoboutique.com. Subway/El: Brown Line to Southport.

🎁 Shopping with the Pros

Want to stay on top of the trends but have limited time to scout out hip boutiques? A guided tour of Chicago's coolest clothing shops is a great way to fit some concentrated shopping into a busy schedule. *An added bonus:* You'll hit the insider places only the locals know about and sometimes get exclusive discounts along the way. **Shop Walk Chicago** (ℂ **773/255-7866;** www. chicagoshopwalk.com), run by local image consultant Danielle Lutz, offers a number of different neighborhood tours (let them know the kinds of clothes you like, and they'll suggest where to go); there's also a "Made in Chicago" tour that focuses on local designers. Tours range from $50 to $90 per person for 4 hours of shopping. The company arranges custom tours on request, and for an additional fee, they'll arrange a pick-up from your hotel.

Chasalla More low-key than many of its Oak Street neighbors, this cozy, minimalist boutique is the place younger, label-conscious shoppers come to browse through men's and women's clothing from designers' more affordable labels, including D&G and Just Cavalli. 70 E. Oak St. (btw. Rush St. and Michigan Ave.). © **312/640-1940.** www.chasallafashion.com. Subway/El: Red Line to Chicago.

Clever Alice This Bucktown shop attracts a clientele of stylish women in search of creative-yet-polished looks. While the clothes here are body-conscious (including a good selection of European lines you won't find anywhere else in town), the staff takes the time to help shoppers find pieces that fit and flatter. The store's eponymous clothing line features softly draped shirts and dresses. 1920 N. Damen Ave. (at Courtland St.). © **773/276-2444.** www.cleveralice.com. Subway/El: Blue Line to Damen.

Ikram ★★★ As a behind-the-scenes fashion advisor to Michelle Obama, owner Ikram Goldman has helped craft the First Lady's stylish image. But Goldman has long been the go-to person for many of Chicago's most powerful and wealthiest women, the fashion expert they trust to match them with the perfect couture gown. Her shop has the subdued look and aura of a fine-art gallery, where the racks are filled with whichever designers *Vogue* has declared "hot" for the season. Tucked among the high-priced pieces are jewelry, stationery, and decorative accessories that give the place a personal touch. 873 Rush St. (btw. Delaware and Chestnut sts.). © **312/587-1000.** www.ikram.com. Subway/El: Red Line to Chicago.

p45 ★ You'll find a number of cool boutiques aimed at the younger crowd clustered along Damen Avenue in Bucktown, but this is the most cutting-edge, with a vibe that's funky rather than girly. A gold mine of urbane women's fashion, the spare space is filled with a unique mix of hip national labels (3.1 Philip Lim, Michelle Mason, Susana Monaco) and local designers you've never heard of. If you're looking for something no one else at home will be wearing, this is the place to shop. 1643 N. Damen Ave. (btw. North and Wabansia aves.). © **773/862-4523.** www.p45. com. Subway/El: Blue Line to Damen.

Robin Richman You'll feel like you're poking through a big, antiques-filled closet as you browse around this airy Bucktown storefront. The walls are adorned with balls of string, vintage diaries, and artful handmade wire hangers. Richman carries an assortment of men's and women's separates, many from independent European labels with a loose, unstructured aesthetic and unusual textural qualities. The store also has a great funky jewelry selection, but the big draw here is the exquisite sweaters made by Richman herself. 2108 N. Damen Ave. (at Dickens St.). © **773/278-6150.** www.robinrichman.com. Subway/El: Blue Line to Damen, and then a long walk (10 blocks) or a short cab ride.

Scoop NYC A hot spot for trendy young things with plenty of spending money, this loftlike space in Bucktown was the first Midwest outpost of the popular New York clothing boutique Scoop NYC. You'll find a mix of major fashion names (Marc Jacobs bags, Jimmy Choo shoes), along with the requisite selection of designer denim, flirty dresses, and seemingly simple T-shirts that will make you do a double-take when you check out the price tags. (The store stocks men's and kids' clothing, too.) Even if you're not planning on blowing your paycheck on a pair of artfully distressed jeans, it's fun to browse for a quick overview of the hot looks of the season, and the in-store cafe is a good place to people-watch while sipping a latte. 1702 N. Milwaukee Ave. (at Wabansia Ave.). © **773/227-9930.** www.scoopnyc.com. Subway/El: Blue Line to Damen.

Tangerine This cozy Bucktown spot specializes in colorful, feminine looks from designers such as Tocca, Nanette Lepore, and Trina Turk. You'll pay a fair amount for these cute looks—most pieces start at $100 and up—but the sales staff has an upbeat attitude to match the clothes. 1719 N. Damen Ave. (at Wabansia Ave.). ℂ **773/772-0505.** Subway/El: Blue Line to Damen.

The T-Shirt Deli ★★ 🎁 For a new twist on custom clothing, stop by this low-key Bucktown storefront, where you can order up your own personalized T-shirt creation. Browse through the entertaining books of vintage iron-on patches, and you'll find everything from '80s icons such as Mr. T to '70s-style "Foxy Lady" logos. Choose a design (or create your own message), and your shirt will be printed up while you wait. When it's done, the shirt is packaged in a paper bag with a side of potato chips—just like a real deli. You can order kids' sizes and baby onesies, too, if you're looking for a fun, one-of-a-kind gift for a little one. 1739 N. Damen Ave. (btw. Willow St. and St. Paul Ave.). ℂ **773/276-6266.** www.tshirtdeli.com. Subway/El: Blue Line to Damen.

Collectibles

Quake Collectibles Off the beaten tourist path in the Lincoln Square neighborhood (northwest of downtown), this temple to all things kitschy includes an impressive vintage lunch box collection, hordes of action figures, and ample stacks of old fan magazines a la *Teen Beat,* with Shaun Cassidy tossing his feathered tresses. Shopping in this overstuffed spot is like hunting through the ultimate memorabilia lover's basement, so allow plenty of time to browse. 4628 N. Lincoln Ave. (north of Wilson Ave.). ℂ **773/878-4288.** www.quakechicago.com. Subway/El: Brown Line to Western.

Quimby's The ultimate edgy newsstand, Quimby's stocks every kind of obscure periodical, from cutting-edge graphic novels to zines "published" in some teenager's basement. Their book selection is also decadently different from your local Barnes & Noble; categories include "Conspiracy," "Politics & Revolution," and "Lowbrow Art." The store also schedules readings and special events with an alternative slant. 1854 W. North Ave. (just east of Damen Ave.). ℂ **773/342-0910.** www.quimbys.com. Subway/El: Blue Line to Damen.

Uncle Fun ★★ 🎁 Whenever I'm looking for a quirky Christmas stocking stuffer or the perfect gag gift, I know Uncle Fun will come through for me. (1950s-era toy robots for a sci-fi-geek friend? Check. And how about some 3-D Jesus postcards for a Catholic school grad? Check.) Bins and cubbyholes are stuffed full of the standard joke toys (rubber-chicken key chains and chattering wind-up teeth), but you'll also find every conceivable modern pop-culture artifact, from Jackson Five buttons to Speed Racer's Mach-Five model car. 1338 W. Belmont Ave. (1 block east of Southport Ave.). ℂ **773/477-8223.** www.unclefunchicago.com. Subway/El: Red or Brown line to Belmont.

Department Stores

Barneys New York This Midwest satellite has the same look and feel as the New York original: minimalist-chic decor; high-priced, cutting-edge fashion; and a fair amount of attitude from the sales staff if you walk through the door in no-name shorts and sneakers. That said, the store has a stellar—if high-priced—shoe selection, along with a fun-to-browse accessories section on the ground floor (cosmetics are relegated to the basement). The top-floor cafe, **Fred's,** is a favorite hangout for the younger ladies-who-lunch crowd. In Lincoln Park, not far from the Armitage Avenue shopping district, you'll find **Barneys Co-Op,** 2209–11 N. Halsted St., at Webster Street (℡ 773/248-0426), which features collections from younger, up-and-coming designers—and lots of specialty denim. 15 E. Oak St. (at Rush St.). ℡ **312/587-1700.** www.barneys.com. Subway/El: Red Line to Chicago.

Bloomingdale's Though not as large as the New York flagship, Chicago's Bloomingdale's fills several floors of the 900 North Michigan Shops, and its selection appeals to stylish shoppers looking for just a bit of urban edge. The shoe department has a good range (with serious markdowns during semiannual sales), and a special section is devoted to souvenir Bloomingdale's logo merchandise. 900 N. Michigan Ave. (at Walton St.). ℡ **312/440-4460.** www.bloomingdales.com. Subway/El: Red Line to Chicago.

Macy's ★★★ When Macy's took over Marshall Field's—Chicago's best-known hometown department store—there was much local hand-wringing about what the buyout meant for Field's grand State Street headquarters. Although Field's iconic green awnings and shopping bags have been replaced by Macy's more dreary black, the good news is that the store itself remains impressive—a testament to the days when shopping downtown was an eagerly anticipated event rather than a chore. A number of exclusive "mini-boutiques" are scattered throughout the overwhelming space, including the **28 Shop,** which stocks the latest from hot young designers; beauty stations where you can get a manicure and pick up exclusive products; and a gourmet food department developed by celebrity chef Charlie Trotter.

If you're interested in the history of the store itself, you can download an audio tour from the website **www.visitmacyschicago.com** before your trip. You can also print out discount coupons to use while you're here.

The Water Tower store, 835 N. Michigan Ave. (℡ 312/335-7700), is a scaled-down but respectable version of the State Street store. 111 N. State St. (at Randolph St.). ℡ **312/781-1000.** www.macys.com. Subway/El: Red Line to Washington.

Neiman Marcus Yes, you'll pay top dollar for designer names here—the store does, after all, need to live up to its Needless Markup moniker—but Neiman's has a broader price range than many of its critics care to admit. It also has some mighty good sales, if you time your visit right. The four-story store sells cosmetics, shoes, furs, fine and fashion jewelry, and clothing. The top floor has a gourmet food department, as well as an attractive home accessories section. Neiman's also has two restaurants: The Freshmarket is a casual sandwich cafe while The Zodiac serves lunch in fine-dining style, with some tables looking out over Michigan Avenue. 737 N. Michigan Ave. (btw. Superior St. and Chicago Ave.). ℡ **312/642-5900.** www.neimanmarcus.com. Subway/El: Red Line to Chicago.

Nordstrom Nordstrom's spacious, airy design and trendy touches (wheatgrass growing by the escalators, funky music playing on the stereo system) gives it the feel of an upscale boutique rather than an overcrowded department store. The company's famed shoe department is large but not overwhelming; more impressive is the cosmetics department, where you'll find a wide array of smaller labels and an "open sell" environment (meaning you're encouraged to try on makeup without a salesperson hovering over you). In keeping with the store's famed focus on service, a concierge can check your coat, call a cab, or make restaurant reservations for you. 520 N. Michigan Ave., inside Westfield North Bridge mall, 55 E. Grand Ave. (at Rush St.). ℡ **312/379-4300.** www.nordstrom.com. Subway/El: Red Line to Grand.

Saks Fifth Avenue Saks Fifth Avenue might be best known for its designer collections—from classic Oscar de la Renta and Valentino looks to newer names such as Derek Lam and Proenza Schouler—but the store also does a decent job of buying more casual and less expensive merchandise. Still, the mood here can be somewhat chilly, and the high-fashion clothes on display are geared toward the super-skinny. The men's department is located in a separate building across Michigan Avenue. Don't forget to visit the cosmetics department, where Saks is known, in particular, for its large selection of fragrances and specialty skin-care lines. 700 N. Michigan Ave. (at Superior St.). ℭ **312/944-6500.** www.saksfifthavenue.com. Subway/El: Red Line to Chicago.

Gourmet Food

Chicago French Market ★ It's a little hard to track down—tucked behind the bustling NorthWestern commuter train station, on the western edge of the Loop—but this homey indoor marketplace is well worth a visit if you're staying downtown. A few dozen vendors offer a range of prepared foods and fresh produce, much of it organic or from local purveyors, and specialty kiosks serve up Mexican, Vietnamese, and Italian meals. It's a good spot to pick up healthy snacks for your hotel room or grab a quick lunch to go (there's also a modest seating area). But not all the offerings are nutritiously virtuous: Befitting a French market, there are also some mouthwatering pastry selections and a traditional crepe stand. 131 N. Clinton St. (btw. Washington and Randolph sts.). ℭ **312/575-0306.** www.frenchmarketchicago.com. Subway/El: Brown Line to Washington.

Fox & Obel ★★ The city's top gourmet market is a foodie paradise, from the wide selection of specialty cheeses to the mouthwatering display of desserts. Browsing the shelves is like taking a minitour through the best specialty foods from around the world (and I dare you to walk through the bakery section without buying a loaf of freshly baked bread). An easy walk to Navy Pier and the lakefront, it's a great place to pick up a picnic lunch or a bottle of wine and some chocolates to enjoy late-night in your hotel room. There's also an in-store cafe if you want to take a break while strolling around the Michigan Avenue area. 401 E. Illinois St. (at McClurg Court). ℭ **312/410-7301.** www.foxandobel.com. Subway/El: Red Line to Grand, and then 65 Grand bus.

Goddess & Grocer This upscale version of a neighborhood deli stocks everything you need for a mouthwatering lunch or dinner on the go—from creative sandwiches to chicken and pasta dishes to freshly baked cookies and brownies. The prepared foods are a few notches above the standard takeout spot (wild Alaskan salmon, wild mushroom risotto), and the staff can put together meals for any occasion, from a catered business lunch to a romantic evening picnic at Millennium Park. The same owners run another, smaller outpost in Bucktown, 1646 N. Damen Ave, at North Avenue (ℭ **773/342-3200**). 25 E. Delaware St. (at Rush St.). ℭ **312/896-2600.** www.goddessandgrocer.com. Subway/El: Red Line to Chicago.

Pastoral Convenient to Millennium Park and the lakefront, this European-style wine and cheese shop is a great place to pick up a gourmet treat to enjoy during a Grant Park summer concert. Taste-test the huge array of artisanal cheeses, or choose from one of their premade picnic selections. Pastoral also offers a creative lineup of sandwiches (such as the ham-and-blue-cheese combo topped with fig preserves), as well as fresh-baked bread and baguettes. Pastoral has another location in the Lakeview neighborhood, at 2945 N. Broadway, a few blocks north of Diversey Parkway (ℭ **773/472-4781**). 53 E. Lake St. (at Wabash

Ave.). ✆ **312/658-1250.** www.pastoralartisan.com. Subway/El: Brown, Green, Orange, or Purple Line to Randolph, or Red Line to Washington.

The Spice House ★ 🎁 Okay, so the Spice House isn't exactly a food store, but this aromatic, beautifully designed specialty shop is a must-see for serious home chefs and anyone else hoping to add some oomph to their cooking. Spices and herbs from around the world are displayed in racks of glass jars, creating a modern take on the classic general store. The friendly staff members are happy to provide tips on how to use everything, and most packages come with recipes. Looking for a Chicago-themed gift? Pick up one of the "Ethnic Chicago" sets, which include custom-designed spice mixes inspired by different Chicago neighborhoods and landmarks (the "Lake Shore Drive" mix, for example, is a combination of chives, shallots, scallions, and garlic powder recommended for seafood). 1512 N. Wells St. (btw. North Ave. and Schiller St.). ✆ **312/274-0378.** www.thespicehouse.com. Subway/El: Brown Line to Sedgwick.

Home Decor & Gifts

Art Effect ★★ Classifying this wonderfully eclectic Armitage Avenue shop is no easy task. (The owners refer to it as a "modern-day general store.") It's got everything from aromatherapy oils and kitchen mixing bowls designed by cookbook author Nigella Lawson to handcrafted jewelry and gag gifts, not to mention a whole room devoted to hippie-chic women's clothing and jewelry. The merchandise has a definite female slant, with a vibe that's young and irreverent rather than fussy. The wide, unpredictable selection makes this one of my favorite browsing spots in town. 934 W. Armitage Ave. (at Bissell St.). ✆ **773/929-3600.** www.arteffectchicago.com. Subway/El: Brown Line to Armitage.

Flight 001 Wish you were traveling in the golden age of jumbo jets and stylish stewardesses? This streamlined travel shop—whose curved walls recall the interior of an airplane—carries sleekly hip luggage, city maps, retro-inspired toiletry bags, and upscale travel-sized amenities. The Red Eye Pack, packaged in an FAA-approved plastic bag, includes an eye mask, earplugs, lip balm, a moisturizing towelette, and other long-haul flight necessities—the perfect gift for frequent fliers. 1133 N. State St. (at Elm St.). ✆ **312/944-1001.** www.flight001.com. Subway/El: Red Line to Clark/Division.

Orange Skin ★ It may look like an ultracool loft catering only to trendier-than-thou style experts, but don't be intimidated: Orange Skin is one of my favorite places to check out what's new in the world of modern interior design, and the staff is friendlier than you might expect. From colored clear-plastic dining chairs to bowls made of welded steel wires and ottomans that look like beach balls, the store's selections are funky, eye-catching, and always creative. Visit the shop's lower level for smaller tabletop items and kitchen accessories that make good one-of-a-kind gifts. 223 W. Erie St. (at Franklin St.). ✆ **312/335-1033.** www.orangeskin. com. Subway/El: Brown Line to Chicago.

P.O.S.H. Love pieces with a past but can't afford fine antiques? This fun shop sells discontinued china patterns from a more elegant time gone by; recent selections included dishes used for first-class service on American Airlines and a tea service once used in an English country inn. There's also a section of "flea market finds," which includes everything from collectible souvenir plates to vintage-fabric accent pillows. If you're looking for souvenirs, they also produce a custom line of Chicago skyline dinnerware. 613 N. State St. (btw. Ontario and Ohio sts.). ✆ **312/280-1602.** www.poshchicago.com. Subway/El: Red Line to Grand.

Stitch ★ 👜 A favorite gift-shopping spot for savvy local fashion experts, Stitch stocks an almost unclassifiable mix of merchandise, including candles, luggage, flatware, serving dishes, funky-kitschy artwork, and bed linens. Unlike the stereotypical, overly cutesy "gift shoppe," the selections share a streamlined, contemporary aesthetic; whatever you buy at Stitch is pretty much guaranteed to pass the cool test. 1723 N. Damen Ave. (at Wabansia St.). ✆ **773/782-1570.** www.stitch chicago.com. Subway/El: Blue Line to Damen.

Music

Dusty Groove America In 1996, using a rickety old PC, Rick Wojcik and John Schauer founded an online record store at **www.dustygroove.com**. Since then, the operation has expanded in both cyberspace and the real world. Dusty Groove covers a lot of ground, selling soul, funk, jazz, Brazilian, lounge, Latin, and hip-hop music on new and used vinyl and CDs. For the most part, selections are either rare, imported, or both. 1120 N. Ashland Ave. (1 block south of Division St.). ✆ **773/342-5800.** www.dustygroove.com. Subway/El: Blue Line to Division.

Jazz Record Mart ★★ This is possibly the best jazz record store in the country, with a selection that ranges from recent recordings to vintage collectible albums. For novices, the "Killers Rack" displays albums that the store's owners consider essential to any jazz collection. Besides jazz, there are bins filled with blues, Latin, and "New Music." The albums are filed alphabetically and by category (vocals, big band, and so on), and there are a couple of turntables to help you spend wisely. Jazz Record Mart also features a stage and seating for 50, where local and national artists coming through town entertain with in-store performances. 27 E. Illinois St. (btw. Wabash Ave. and State St.). ✆ **312/222-1467.** www. jazzrecordmart.com. Subway/El: Red Line to Grand.

New Sound Gospel Chicago is the birthplace of gospel music, and now, thanks to artists such as Kirk Franklin, it's also become big business. All the major labels have gospel music divisions, and this store on the city's far South Side is the best place in town to browse the full range of what's available. Not sure where to start? Ask the store's expert staff for advice—here you'll find everything from gospel's biggest stars to groups with names such as Gospel Gangstaz. 10723 S. Halsted St. (at

107th St.). ✆ **773/785-8001.** www.newsoundgospel.com. Subway/El: Red Line to 95th/Dan Ryan, then 108 Halsted bus to 107th St.

Reckless Records The best all-round local record store for music that the cool kids listen to, Reckless Records wins brownie points for its friendly and helpful staff. You'll find new and used CDs and albums in a variety of genres (psyche-delic and progressive rock, punk, soul, and jazz) here, along with magazines and a small collection of DVDs. There are also locations in Lincoln Park at 3126 N. Broadway Ave. (✆ **773/404-5080**), and Wicker Park at 1532 N. Milwaukee Ave. (✆ **773/235-3727**). 26 E. Madison St. (btw. State and Wabash sts.). ✆ **312/795-0878.** www.reckless.com. Subway/El: Red Line to Monroe or Brown Line to Madison.

Paper & Stationery

All She Wrote One of the many owner-operated specialty shops along Armitage Avenue, All She Wrote stocks a fun mix of cards and notepaper, all with a lighthearted, whimsical feel. There's also a section devoted to baby gifts. 825 W. Armitage Ave. (1 block west of Halsted St.). ✆ **773/529-0100.** www.allshewrote.com. Subway/El: Red Line to North/Clybourn.

Paper Boy ★ 🎁 Run by the same owners as the novelty shop Uncle Fun (see "Collectibles," above), this Lakeview stationery shop has one of the most offbeat and artsy selections of greeting cards in the city—with messages ranging from sweet to R-rated. You can also browse an eclectic assortment of knickknacks, wind-up toys, fridge magnets, and other impulse-buy items. 1351 W. Belmont Ave. (at Southport Ave.). ✆ **773/388-8811.** www.unclefunchicago.com/pboy.html. Subway/El: Brown Line to Southport.

Paper Source ★★★ The acknowledged leader of stationery stores in Chicago, Paper Source has now expanded throughout the country (with locations from Boston to Beverly Hills), but this shop in River North is the chain's home base. Paper Source's claim to fame is its collection of artistic handmade papers, which come in a staggering variety of colors and textures. You'll also find one-of-a-kind greeting cards, photo albums, a dazzling array of stationery, and a large collec-tion of rubber stamps for personalizing your own creations at home. There's also a location in the trendy Armitage shopping district at 919 W. Armitage Ave. (✆ **773/525-7300**). 232 W. Chicago Ave. (at Franklin St.). ✆ **312/337-0798.** www.paper-source.com. Subway/El: Red or Brown line to Chicago.

The Watermark Chicago socialites come here to order their engraved invita-tions, but you don't need to wait for a special occasion to visit: This stationery store also carries a fine selection of unique handmade greeting cards. Yes, they'll set you back considerably more than Hallmark, but just think of them as minia-ture works of art. 109 E. Oak St. (1 block from Michigan Ave.). ✆ **312/337-5353.** Subway/El: Red Line to Clark/Division.

Salons & Spas

Art + Science This Lincoln Park spot, just steps from the Armitage Avenue shopping strip, may look a little intimidating from the outside, but the ambi-ence inside is welcoming, no matter what your look. Stylists can get as creative as you want, but most clients here are young professional women who want the same basic cut as everyone else. There's also another location in Wicker Park at 1552 N. Milwaukee Ave. (✆ **773/227-4247**). 1971 N. Halsted St. (at Armitage Ave.). ✆ **312/787-4247.** www.artandsciencesalon.com. Subway/El: Brown Line to Armitage.

Charles Ifergan Charles Ifergan is one of the city's best-known, longtime hair-stylists, catering to an affluent Gold Coast crowd. Rates, which vary according to the seniority of the stylist, are relatively high, but the staff here are all pros (with many trained by Mr. Ifergan himself). 106 E. Oak St. (btw. Michigan Ave. and Rush St.). © **312/642-4484.** www.charlesifergan.com. Subway/El: Red Line to Chicago.

Kiva Day Spa ★ Kiva is the city's reigning "super spa," and is named for the round ceremonial space used by Native Americans seeking to quiet, cleanse, and relax the spirit. The two-floor, 6,000-square-foot space offers spa, salon, nutrition, and apothecary services, and a nutritional-juice-and-snack bar in a setting that evokes its namesake inspiration. Water Tower Place, entrance at 196 E. Pearson St. (at Mies van der Rohe Way). © **312/840-8120.** www.halcyondayssalonsandspas.com. Subway/El: Red Line to Chicago.

Salon Buzz This hip hair parlor, operated by wizardly stylist Andreas Zafiriadis (who has wielded his scissors in Paris, Greece, New York, and California), is popular with women in creative professions. But it's far from a girls-only hangout: Among the regulars are a number of local professional athletes. 1 E. Delaware Place (at State St.). © **312/943-5454.** Subway/El: Red Line to Chicago.

Spa Space ★★ 🎁 Located in the up-and-coming West Loop, this trendy spa offers the latest skin-care treatments in a stylishly modern building that feels like a boutique hotel. The gender-neutral decor and specialized menu of guy-friendly treatments (including a massage designed for golfers) brings in a far larger male clientele than other local spots. 161 N. Canal St. (at Randolph St.). © **312/943-5454.** www.spaspace.com. Subway/El: Green Line to Clinton.

Tiffani Kim Institute Occupying a modern three-story building in the heart of River North's art gallery district, the Tiffani Kim Institute is a virtual minimall of beauty treatments. Here you can get a haircut, schedule a massage or facial, or book a cosmetic surgery procedure. Wellness treatments include a detox seaweed body wrap; Asian ear candling; acupuncture and Chinese herbal medicine; and the "Serenity Stone Massage," a Tiffani Kim specialty in which smooth stones are warmed in a thermal unit to 135°F (57°C) and then used as tools in a Swedish-style massage. 310 W. Superior St. (btw. Franklin and Orleans sts.). © **312/943-8777.** www.tiffanikiminstitute.com. Subway/El: Red or Brown line to Chicago.

Truefitt & Hill ★ 🎁 Women have their pick of hair and beauty salons, but men don't often come across a place like Truefitt & Hill, the local outpost of a British barbershop listed in the *Guinness Book of World Records* as the oldest barbershop in the world. Prices are steeper than your average barber shop (about $50 for a cut), but the old-world atmosphere is dead-on, from the gregarious, bow-tied barbers to the antique leather chairs. Services include old-school lather shaves, manicures, massages, and even shoeshines. 900 N. Michigan Ave. shopping center (btw. Walton St. and Delaware Place), 6th floor. © **312/337-2525.** www.truefittandhill.com. Subway/El: Red Line to Chicago.

Urban Oasis 🎁 After a long day of sightseeing, try a soothing massage in this spa's subdued, Zen-like atmosphere. The ritual begins with a steam or rain shower in a private changing room, followed by the spa treatment you elect—various forms of massage (including a couples' massage, in which you learn to do it yourself), an aromatherapy wrap, or an exfoliating treatment. Fresh fruit, juices, or herbal teas are offered on completion. Urban Oasis also has another location in a burgeoning retail district a few blocks south of the Armitage Avenue shopping strip, at 939 W. North Ave. (✆ **773/640-0001**). 12 W. Maple St., 3rd floor (btw. Dearborn and State sts.). ✆ **312/587-3500.** www.urbanoasismassage.com. Subway/El: Red Line to Clark/Division.

Shoes & Bags

Alternatives Yes, many of the shoes you see in the window may be black, but this locally owned shop offers on-trend—and wearable—footwear for both men and women. While the prices aren't cheap, they're more affordable than in the other designer shoe boutiques in town. There's also a location on the 5th floor of the 900 N. Michigan Ave. Shops (✆ **312/266-1545**). 108 N. State St. (at Randolph St.). ✆ **312/419-2150.** www.altshoes.com. Subway/El: Red Line to Randolph.

Diego Rocha This Brazilian-born, Chicago-based handbag designer makes sophisticated clutches and carryalls that you won't see slung over the arm of every other person back home. Specialty leathers are a favorite here (particularly python), and if money is no object, you can even order a custom creation. For a more affordable splurge, slip on one of Rocha's leather cuff bracelets for an instant infusion of cool. 1050 N. State St. (at Division St.). ✆ **312/255-1884.** www.diego rocha.net. Subway/El: Red Line to Division.

1154 Lill Studio ★ 📷 Purse-a-holics and wannabe designers will find fashion heaven at this custom handbag shop. Pick a style (which includes everything from evening purses to diaper bags), and then browse the huge selection of fabrics to create your own custom interior and exterior. Your finished creation can be picked up in a few weeks or shipped to your home. Not feeling particularly creative? You can also pick from a selection of premade bags. Personal handbag parties can be arranged for groups of five or more (call in advance to set one up). 904 W. Armitage Ave. (at Fremont St.). ✆ **773/477-LILL** [5455]. www.1154lill.com. Subway/El: Brown Line to Armitage.

Lori's Designer Shoes ★★ 🔶 Lori's looks like a less organized version of Payless Shoes, with shoeboxes stacked haphazardly on the floor and women surrounded by piles of heels and boots, but the designer names on most of those shoes prove that this is not your typical discount store. A mecca for anyone obsessed with status shoes, Lori's stocks all the latest hot styles, at prices that average 10% to 30% below department store rates. 824 W. Armitage Ave. (btw. Sheffield Ave. and Halsted St.). ✆ **773/281-5655.** www.lorisdesignershoes.com. Subway/El: Brown Line to Armitage.

Pump 📷 Located in the up-and-coming Division Street shopping corridor, Pump may be off the usual tourist route, but it's a worthy stop for footwear fanatics in search of something unique. This independently owned shoe boutique stocks fun, eye-catching heels, boots, and flats from lesser-known labels, many of them European. But what really sets it apart is the friendly, personal service. 1659 W. Division St. (at Paulina St.). ✆ **773/384-6750.** www.pumpshoeschicago.com. Subway/El: Blue Line to Division.

Stuart Weitzman Head to Stuart Weitzman for shoes that make a dramatic impression—on your feet and on your wallet. Strappy high-heeled sandals from this shoe seller to the stars make regular appearances on the red carpet at the Academy Awards and other A-list celebrity events. You'll find lots of special-occasion heels here, as well as knee-high boots that look far too lovely to subject to the slush of a Chicago winter. Even if you're not planning on splurging, the artistic window displays are worth a peek. 900 N. Michigan Ave. shopping center (btw. Walton St. and Delaware Place), 1st floor. ✆ **312/943-5760.** www.stuartweitzman.com. Subway/El: Red Line to Chicago.

Tod's Characterized by detailed workmanship and top-quality materials, this upscale Italian footwear line is known for its moccasin-style driving shoes, but the shop also stocks high-heeled sandals, ballerina-style flats, mules in various colors, plus their glamorous trademark handbags. Just remember, the ritzy Oak Street location is a tip-off that such luxury doesn't come cheap. 121 E. Oak St. (btw. Michigan Ave. and Rush St.). ✆ **312/943-0070.** www.tods.com. Subway/El: Red Line to Chicago.

Souvenirs & Maps

Chicago Architecture Foundation ★★★ Stop here for the coolest design-conscious gifts in town. This bright, sleek shop is part of the Chicago Architecture Foundation, so everything in stock—including photography books, tour guides, stationery, and kids' toys—has a definite sense of style. Whether you're in the market for a $900 reproduction of a vase from Frank Lloyd Wright's Robie House or more affordable black-and-white photos of the city skyline, it's well worth a visit. 224 S. Michigan Ave. (at Jackson St.). ✆ **312/922-3432,** ext. 241. www.architecture.org. Subway/El: Red Line to Jackson.

Chicago Tribune Store Yes, you'll find plenty of newspaper-logo T-shirts here, but this shop on the ground floor of the *Tribune*'s offices also has a great collection of books by *Tribune*-affiliated authors and a decent range of Chicago-themed collectibles. You can also order reproductions of *Tribune* front pages from memorable dates in history or color prints of photos from the newspaper's archives. 435 N. Michigan Ave. (at Hubbard St.). ✆ **312/222-3080.** www.chicagotribunestore.com. Subway/El: Red Line to Grand.

City of Chicago Store Located in the Water Works Visitor Center right off Michigan Avenue, this is a convenient stop for Chicago-related souvenirs and gifts. Amid the usual T-shirts and mugs, you'll also find some truly one-of-a-kind pieces, including retired municipal equipment (although the parking meters I've seen for sale here might be a little hard to stuff in your suitcase). 163 E. Pearson St. (at Michigan Ave.). ✆ **312/742-8811.** Subway/El: Red Line to Chicago.

Sporting Goods

Fleet Feet Sports ★ 👜 If you're serious about running, jog over to this Old Town shop, where the knowledgeable staff members—all runners themselves—take the time to find the shoes that work best for you. (They'll even check out the wear patterns on your old shoes to diagnose trouble spots.) You can also stock up on stylish athletic gear and accessories such as heart rate monitors and watches. 1620 N. Wells St. (at North Ave.). ✆ **312/587-3338.** www.fleetfeetchicago.com. Subway/El: Brown Line to Sedgwick.

Niketown 👜 When Niketown first opened, it was truly something new: a store that felt more like a funky sports museum than a place hawking running shoes. These days, however, Niketown is no longer unique to Chicago (it's sprung up in cities from Atlanta to Honolulu), and the store's celebration of athletic prowess can't cover up the fact that the ultimate goal is to sell expensive shoes. But the crowds keep streaming in to snatch up products pitched by Niketown's patron saints Michael Jordan, Tiger Woods, and Lance Armstrong. 669 N. Michigan Ave. (btw. Huron and Erie sts.). ✆ **312/642-6363.** http://niketown.nike.com. Subway/El: Red Line to Grand.

Sports Authority The largest sporting-goods store in the city, Sports Authority offers seven floors of merchandise, from running apparel and soccer balls to serious camping gear. Sports fans will be in heaven in the first- and fifth-floor team merchandise departments, where Cubs, Bulls, Sox, and Blackhawks jerseys abound. Cement handprints of local sports celebs dot the outside of the building; step inside to check out the prints from Michael Jordan and White Sox slugger Frank Thomas. 620 N. LaSalle St. (at Ontario St.). ✆ **312/337-6151.** www.sportsauthority. com. Subway/El: Red Line to Grand.

Toys & Children's Clothing

Fantasy Costumes 🎭 Not exactly a toy store, this sprawling costume shop (covering an entire city block) is nonetheless devoted to make-believe and is just as fun for grownups as kids. The store stocks more than a million items, including hundreds of styles of masks (priced $1–$200) and all the accessories and makeup needed to complete any costume. There's also a full-service wig salon, should you feel the need for a head-to-toe transformation. 4065 N. Milwaukee Ave. (west of Cicero Ave.). ✆ **773/777-0222.** www.fantasycostumes.com. Subway/El: Blue Line to Irving Park.

Grow For a look at the future of baby style, head to this trendy boutique in the rapidly gentrifying West Division Street neighborhood. The bright, open space showcases streamlined, ultramodern kids' furniture (such as a modular bunk bed set and bubble-shaped high chairs that would look right at home on *The Jetsons*), as well as clothing and crib bedding made from organic fabrics. Sure, many of the environmentally friendly products on display here are out of the average parent's price range, but families that have grown weary of plastic kiddie gadgets will have fun browsing around. 1943 W. Division St. (at Damen Ave.). ✆ **773/489-0009.** www.grow-kids.com. Subway/El: Blue Line to Division.

Little Strummer ★ This compact store in the Armitage Avenue shopping district is located inside the Old Town School of Folk Music, a local institution that's been offering kids' music classes for decades. The shop stocks every kind of mini-instrument imaginable, from accordions and guitars to wind chimes and music boxes. There's also a good selection of music-related games and kid-friendly CDs. 909 W. Armitage Ave. (at Halsted St.). ✆ **773/751-3410.** Subway/El: Brown Line to Armitage.

Madison & Friends Clothing for kids that's both cute and fashion-conscious is the specialty here—what else would you expect from a boutique on style-obsessed Oak Street? From baby-sized leather bomber jackets to yoga pants for active toddlers, you'll find a wide array of trendy items, some at prices that make you think you're buying a grown-up outfit. A separate back room caters to older kids and teens—including a staggering array of designer-label jeans. 43 E. Oak St. (btw. Rush St. and Michigan Ave.). ✆ **312/642-6403.** www.madisonandfriends.com. Subway/El: Red Line to Chicago.

Psycho Baby A hangout for cool moms and their equally cool offspring, this Bucktown shop stocks baby and kids' clothes that are refreshingly free of either pastel animals or cartoon characters. (If you've been hankering for a toddler-sized pair of skull-and-crossbones sneakers or a punk-rock onesie, this is the place to come.) The creative selection and happy vibe make it fun for browsing, and there are toys scattered around to entertain the kids while you shop. If you need to pick up a gift for a little one, the store also carries a selection of creative toys. 1630 N. Damen Ave. (1 block north of North Ave.). © **773/772-2815.** www.psychobabyonline.com. Subway/El: Blue Line to Damen.

Vintage Fashion/Resale Shops

Beatnix This massive, over-the-top Boys' Town vintage store crams together pretty much every dress-up option in one overstuffed space, from fluorescent-colored wigs to tacky '70s tuxes to used wedding gowns (the more outrageous, the better). The store is especially popular in the weeks before Halloween, but given its penchant for campy looks, this is also a popular stop year-round for local drag queens in search of that special something. 3400 N. Halsted St. (at Roscoe St.). © **773/281-6933.** Subway/El: Red Line to Addison.

Fox's This no-frills shop near Armitage Avenue offers designer clothing at a steep discount. Most clothing labels are cut out, so you might not know exactly which A-list name you're buying, but Fox's stays up-to-date with the fashion pulse. *A note for the modest:* Be prepared to strip in front of your fellow shoppers in the bare-bones, open dressing room. 2150 N. Halsted St. (at Dickens St.). © **773/281-0700.** Subway/El: Brown Line to Armitage.

McShane's Exchange ★★ 🎁 This consignment shop, just a few blocks from Fox's (see above), has a selection that's more discriminating than your standard thrift store, and for designer and name-brand bargains, it can't be beat. The store expands back through a series of cramped rooms, with clothes organized by color, making it easy to scope out the perfect black dress or white blouse. The longer a piece stays in stock, the lower the price drops, which means Calvin Klein coats, Prada sweaters, and Armani jackets can all be snagged for under $100. McShane's has another Lincoln Park location with a similar but smaller selection, at 1141 W. Webster St. (© **773/525-0211**). 815 W. Armitage Ave. (at Halsted St.). © **773/525-0282.** www.mcshanesexchange.com. Subway/El: Brown Line to Armitage.

The Second Child ☺ This self-described "upscale children's resale boutique" may not look all that upscale—it's basically one long, dark room on the second floor of an Armitage Avenue town house—but take a look at the labels on these kids' clothes (Ralph Lauren, Lilly Pulitzer, and the like), and you'll see that they come from very fashionable closets. Clothes are accepted for sale only if they're in very good condition, so you won't have to sort through piles of well-worn outfits to get to the good stuff. There's also a nice—if limited—selection of maternity clothes, toys, and books. 954 W. Armitage Ave. (btw. Bissell St. and Sheffield Ave.). © **773/883-0880.** www.2ndchild.com. Subway/El: Brown Line to Armitage.

Wine & Liquor

Binny's Beverage Depot 🍷 This River North warehouse offers an enormous selection of wine, beer, and spirits, some at discounted prices. No matter what your taste—from French burgundies to obscure American craft beers to pricey imported scotch—you'll find something here that fits the bill. Binny's also has locations in Lincoln Park, at 1720 N. Marcey St. (© **312/664-4394**), and Lakeview, at 3000 N. Clark St. (© **773/935-9400**). 213 W. Grand Ave. (at Wells St.). © **312/332-0012.** www.binnys.com. Subway/El: Red Line to Grand.

House of Glunz ★★ 🎁 Not only is this Chicago's oldest wine shop, but it's also the oldest in the Midwest, with an inventory of 1,500 wines dating back to 1811. The shop periodically cracks open a few of its vintage wines for special wine-tasting events, but not all the selections here are rare or expensive. There's an extensive selection of modern wines from California and Europe, and the knowledgeable owners are happy to steer you to the right bottles for your budget. 1206 N. Wells St. (at Division St.). ✆ **312/642-3000.** www.thehouseofglunz.com. Subway/El: Brown Line to Sedgwick.

Just Grapes True to its name, this wine-centric West Loop shop stocks an impressive array of vintages from around the world. The bright, welcoming space encourages browsing, and there's even an automated tasting station, where you can try up to 24 different wines with the push of a button (you'll pay from 50 cents to $5 per sample). Managing partner Don Sritong draws on his experience as a corporate sommelier to make wine education accessible and fun; as the store's motto declares, "The best wine for you is the one you like best." 560 W. Washington Blvd. (at Clinton St.). ✆ **312/627-9463.** www.justgrapes.net. Subway/El: Brown Line to Washington.

8

CHICAGO AFTER DARK

9

C hicago's bustling energy isn't confined to daylight hours. The city offers loads of after-hours entertainment, including Broadway musicals, world-class classical music, and a theater scene that rivals New York's. Late-night hangouts run the gamut from sleek lounges to classic neighborhood taverns—and most are refreshingly attitude-free.

The international talent on stage at both the Chicago Symphony Orchestra and the Lyric Opera of Chicago is appealing to culture vultures, while theater buffs can choose between high-profile companies such as Steppenwolf and the scrappy groups that spring up in storefronts around the city. The theater scene here was built by performers who valued gritty realism and a communal work ethic, and that down-to-earth energy is still very much present. Music and nightclub haunts are scattered throughout the city, but Chicago's thriving music scene is concentrated in Lincoln Park, Lakeview, and Wicker Park, where clubs are devoted to everything from jazz and blues to alternative rock and reggae.

While the city has its share of see-and-be-seen nightspots, Chicagoans in general are not obsessed with getting into the latest hot club; for the most part, chilling out with buddies at a neighborhood bar is the evening activity of choice. To join the locals, you only have to pick a residential area and wander—it won't be long before you'll come across a tavern filled with neighborhood regulars and friendly bartenders.

For up-to-date entertainment listings, check the local newspapers and magazines, particularly the Friday editions of the *Chicago Tribune* and the *Chicago Sun-Times;* the weekly magazine *Time Out Chicago,* which has excellent comprehensive listings; and the *Chicago Reader* or *New City,* two free weekly tabloids with extensive listings. The *Tribune's* entertainment-oriented website, **www.chicago.metromix.com**; the *Reader's* website, **www.chicagoreader.com**; and *Time Out Chicago's* website, **http://timeoutchicago.com**, are also excellent sources of information, with lots of opinionated reviews.

THE PERFORMING ARTS

Chicago is a regular stop on the big-name entertainment circuit, whether it's musicals such as *Wicked* or pop music acts. High-profile shows that went on to great success in New York, including Monty Python's *Spamalot* and Mel Brooks's stage version of *The Producers,* had their first runs here before moving on to Broadway.

Thanks to extensive renovation of historic theaters, performers have a choice of impressive venues to strut their stuff. The **Auditorium Theatre,** 50 E. Congress Pkwy., between Michigan and Wabash avenues (ⓒ **312/922-2110;** www.auditoriumtheatre.org), may be the most beautiful theater in Chicago—and it's also a certified national landmark. Built in 1889 by Louis Sullivan and Dankmar Adler, this grand hall schedules mostly musicals and dance performances. Even

9

CHICAGO AFTER DARK

The Performing Arts

FACING PAGE: Patrons of Celtic Crossing, a favorite local spot, enjoy a few beers.

291

if you don't catch a show here, you can stop by for a tour. (For more details, see p. 167.)

The city's other great historic theaters are concentrated in the North Loop. The **Ford Center for the Performing Arts/Oriental Theater,** 24 W. Randolph St., and the **Cadillac Palace Theater,** 151 W. Randolph St., book major touring shows and are well worth a visit for arts buffs. The Oriental's fantastical Asian look includes elaborate carvings almost everywhere you look; dragons, elephants, and griffins peer down at the audience from the gilded ceiling. The Palace features a profusion of Italian marble surfaces and columns, gold-leaf accents a la Versailles, huge decorative mirrors, and crystal chandeliers. (If you'd like to get a look at these historic theaters for a fraction of the standard ticket price, guided tours of both start at 11am Sat and cost $10 per person; meet in the Oriental lobby.) The **Bank of America Theatre** (formerly the Schubert Theatre), 18 W. Monroe St., was built in 1906 as a home for vaudeville shows; today it books mostly well-known musicals and sometimes comedy performers. For show schedules at all three theaters, call ℂ **312/977-1700,** or visit www. broadwayinchicago.com.

The **Chicago Theatre,** 175 N. State St., at Lake Street (ℂ **312/443-1130;** www.thechicagotheatre.com), is a 1920s music palace reborn as an all-purpose entertainment venue, playing host to pop acts, magicians, stand-up comedians, and more. (Both the Chicago Theatre and the Bank of America Theatre, above, are quite large, so be forewarned that the cheaper seats are in nosebleed territory.) **Arie Crown Theater,** in the McCormick Place convention center at 23rd Street and Lake Shore Drive (ℂ **312/791-6190;** www.ariecrown.com), books musicals and pop acts, but compared to the venues listed above, the massive hall feels somewhat impersonal.

Symphony Center, 220 S. Michigan Ave., between Adams Street and Jackson Boulevard (ℂ **312/294-3000**), is the building that encompasses Orchestra Hall, home of the Chicago Symphony Orchestra (CSO). The building holds a six-story sky-lit arcade, recital spaces, and the fine-dining restaurant **Rhapsody** (p. 98). While the CSO is the main attraction, the Symphony Center schedules a series of piano recitals, classical and chamber music concerts, a family matinee series, and the occasional jazz or pop artist.

Chicago has a few other major venues for traveling shows, but they are not as convenient for visitors. The **Rosemont Theatre,** 5400 River Rd. in Rosemont, near O'Hare Airport (ℂ **847/671-5100;** www.rosemonttheatre. com), is a top suburban stop for family-friendly musicals and concerts. The **North Shore Center for the Performing Arts in Skokie,** 9501 Skokie Blvd., in the northern suburb of Skokie (ℂ **847/673-6300;** www.north shorecenter.org), is home to the well-respected Northlight Theater troupe, the Skokie Valley Symphony Orchestra, and a series of nationally known touring acts, including comics, dance troupes, and children's programs.

Finding a Better Seat

Most of Chicago's grand old theaters have balconies that go way, way up toward the ceiling—and if you're stuck in the cheap seats, you'll be straining to see what's happening onstage. While theaters are very strict about checking tickets when you arrive, the ushers relax during intermission, so scope out empty seats during the first act, and then move down to better (and much pricier) spots for the rest of the show.

Monroe Harbor

Angels and Kings
(Hard Rock Hotel) **10**

Bar Louie **15**

Buddy Guy's Legends **16**

Cadillac Palace Theater **6**

Encore (Hotel Allegro) **5**

Ford Center for the
Performing Arts/
Oriental Theater **8**

Goodman Theatre **7**

Harris Theater for
Music and Dance **11**

Kitty O'Shea's
(Hilton Chicago) **14**

Lyric Opera **3**

Lumen **2**

Miller's Pub **13**

Monk's Pub **4**

Roof (The Wit Hotel) **9**

Symphony Center **12**

The Tasting Room **1**

Classical Music

Not surprisingly, the world-class talent of the Chicago Symphony Orchestra—considered one of the best in the country—dominates the classical music calendar. However, many orchestra members play in smaller ensembles around town on a semi-regular basis; a few independent musical groups have also built loyal followings with eclectic programming.

To find out what's playing when you're in town, check out the **Chicago Classical Music** website (www.chicagoclassicalmusic.org), maintained by a consortium of the city's leading music groups.

Chicago Symphony Orchestra ★★ The Chicago Symphony Orchestra is considered among the best in the world; a legacy of the late maestro Sir Georg Solti, who captured a record-breaking 31 Grammy awards for his CSO recordings and showcased the orchestra at other major musical capitals during frequent overseas tours. Current musical director Riccardo Muti has further entrenched its international reputation. The symphony's schedule includes regular visits from internationally known guest artists, and although the repertoire has been expanded to include more modern works, crowd-pleasing favorites by Beethoven or Brahms are performed regularly as well.

Like many other orchestras around the country, the CSO has diversified its programming to attract younger audiences. The "Symphony Center Presents" series has included some of the top jazz, world beat, Latin, and cabaret artists in the world. Although concerts sell out when there's a high-profile performer, good seats sometimes become available on the day of the show, turned in by subscribers who can't make it. Call Symphony Center, or stop by the box office to check availability.

Summertime visitors have an opportunity to hear a CSO performance at the delightful **Ravinia Festival** ★★ (© **847/266-5100**), an outdoor venue in

The Chicago Symphony Orchestra is considered among the best in the world.

suburban Highland Park, led by music director James Conlon. (For more information, see p. 217.)

The highly regarded **Civic Orchestra of Chicago,** the CSO's training orchestra since 1919, presents free programs at Orchestra Hall. The **Chicago Symphony Chorus** also performs there. Orchestra Hall in Symphony Center, 220 S. Michigan Ave. ✆ **312/294-3000.** www.cso.org. Tickets $25–$120. Subway/El: Red Line to Jackson.

Grant Park Symphony and Chorus 🎣 One of the city's best cultural bargains, this music festival offers a series of free outdoor classical music concerts from June through August. The symphony, along with internationally known musicians and singers, performs in the gorgeous Frank Gehry–designed Pritzker Music Pavilion in Millennium Park. Featuring Gehry's signature sinuous lines, the pavilion is surrounded by dramatic ribbons of curved steel. The Grant Park Symphony not only looks better than ever, but it sounds great, too—thanks to a state-of-the-art sound system. Concerts are held Wednesday, Friday, and Saturday, with most performances beginning at 6:30pm (7:30pm on Sat). Seats in the front of the pavilion are reserved for subscribers, but the back rows are available on a first-come, first-served basis. There's also plenty of lawn seating, so bring a blanket and enjoy a picnic dinner with a view of the skyline as a backdrop. Pritzker Music Pavilion, Michigan Ave. and Randolph St. ✆ **312/742-7638.** www.grantparkmusicfestival.com. Subway/El: Red Line to Washington/State; or Brown, Orange, or Green line to Randolph/Wabash.

ADDITIONAL OFFERINGS

The oldest all-volunteer civic chorus in the country, **Apollo Chorus of Chicago** (✆ **312/427-5620;** www.apollochorus.org), was founded in 1872, 1 year after the Great Chicago Fire. Today, it's best known for its annual holiday-season performances of Handel's *Messiah* at Orchestra Hall. The group also presents at least two other concerts during the year at various downtown venues.

The **Chicago Chamber Musicians** (**CCM;** ✆ **312/819-5800;** www.chicagochambermusic.org), a 15-member ensemble drawn from performers from the CSO and Northwestern and DePaul universities, presents chamber music concerts at various locales around the city. The season runs September through May, and you can always find the CCM performing free noontime concerts on the first Monday of the month (except Sept and Mar) on the second floor of the Chicago Cultural Center in the Loop. The **Chicago String Quartet** is affiliated with the group.

The **Chicago Sinfonietta** (✆ **312/236-3681;** www.chicagosinfonietta. org), with its racially diverse 45-member orchestra and a wide-ranging repertoire, seeks to broaden the audience for classical music. Concerts combine works by masters such as Beethoven and Mendelssohn with music from Latin America, Asia, and others. Playing about 10 times a year at Orchestra Hall and other venues, the group often takes a multimedia approach to its multicultural mission, collaborating with dance troupes, visual artists, museums, rock bands, and gospel choirs.

Music of the Baroque (✆ **312/551-1414;** www.baroque.org) is a small orchestra and chorus that pulls members from both the CSO and the Lyric Opera orchestra, and features professional singers from across the country. The ensemble performs the music of the 16th, 17th, and 18th centuries, in appropriately Gothic church settings in various neighborhoods. The group has made several recordings and has introduced lesser-known works by composers such as Mozart and Monteverdi to Chicago audiences.

Opera

Chicago Opera Theater The "other" opera company in town, Chicago Opera Theater, doesn't get all the big names, but it offers an alternative to the more traditional Lyric by focusing on often-neglected or new works. (To make them accessible to a wider audience, English supertitles are used during performances.) It also helps that tickets are less expensive and more plentiful than the Lyric Opera's. The company performs three operas each spring (Mar–May), which usually run the gamut from classical tragedies by Handel to 20th-century satirical works. No matter what the bill, the talent and production values are top-notch. On certain evenings during the season, ticket holders are invited to a pre-performance lecture and Q&A session with the director, conductor, or other members of the artistic staff. Harris Theater for Music and Dance, 205 E. Randolph Dr. ✆ **312/704-8414.** www.chicagooperatheater.org. Tickets $35–$120 adults, half-price for students. Subway/El: Red Line to Washington/State.

Lyric Opera of Chicago ★★ One of the top American opera companies, the Lyric attracts the very best singers in the world for its lavish productions. Opening night in September remains the quasi-official kickoff of the Chicago social season, but don't be scared off by the snooty factor; audiences here are relatively casual, and you don't need a tux (or even a suit) to fit in. Talented musicians and performers satisfy opera devotees, while newcomers are often swept away by all the grandeur (English supertitles make it easy to follow the action). Another plus for both opera newbies and veterans: An hour before each performance, audience members are invited to hear a lecture about that night's show. (It's free, but you'll have to show your ticket to get in.)

The Civic Opera House is the home of the Lyric Opera of Chicago.

The Lyric Opera performs in the handsome, massive 3,563-seat Art Deco **Civic Opera House,** the second-largest opera house in the country, built in 1929. If you're sitting in one of the upper balconies, you'll definitely want to bring binoculars. (If you're nice, the regulars sitting nearby may lend you theirs.) There's only one problem with catching a show at the Lyric: The season, which runs through early March, usually sells out months in advance, although single tickets are sometimes available on shorter notice. Your other option is to call the day of a performance, when you can sometimes buy tickets that subscribers have turned in.

If you're in town in February or March, you can check out the theater by taking a tour (offered only during those months; call ✆ **312/827-5626**). The opera has an adjunct, the Lyric Opera Center for American Artists, which in spring and summer performs in smaller venues around town. Civic Opera House, Madison St. and Wacker Dr. ✆ **312/332-2244.** www.lyricopera.org. Tickets $35–$185. Subway/El: Brown Line to Washington.

Dance

Chicago's dance scene is lively, but unfortunately it doesn't attract the same crowds as theater or music performances. Some resident dance troupes have international reputations, but they spend much of their time touring to support themselves. Dance performances in Chicago tend to occur in spurts throughout the year, with visiting companies such as the American Ballet Theatre and the Dance Theater of Harlem stopping in Chicago for limited engagements. Depending on the timing of your visit, you may have a choice of dance performances—or there may be none at all.

Dance lovers should schedule their visit for November, when the annual **"Dance Chicago"** festival (✆ **773/989-0698;** www.dancechicago.com) is held at various locations around town. Featuring performances and workshops

A performance at the Harris Theater for Music and Dance.

from the city's best-known dance companies and countless smaller groups, it's a great chance to check out the range of local dance talent. Another phenomenon that has enlivened the local scene is the scintillating **Chicago Human Rhythm Project** (✆ 773/281-1825; www.chicagotap.com), a non-profit group that brings together tap and percussive dancers from around the world for a series of workshops and performances in the summer and fall.

To find out what's going on at other times of the year, visit the website for the non-profit group **See Chicago Dance** (www.seechicagodance.com), which gives a comprehensive roundup of local performances. Another good reason to check out the site: You can often find links to discounted tickets.

The major Chicago dance troupes listed below perform at the **Harris Theater for Music and Dance,** 205 E. Randolph St. (✆ 312/334-7777; www.harristheaterchicago.org), in Millennium Park. The 1,500-seat theater feels fairly stark and impersonal—the gray concrete lobby could be mistaken for a parking garage—but the sightlines are great, thanks to the stadium-style seating.

The Dance Center–Columbia College Chicago 🏛 Columbia College, a liberal arts institution specializing in the arts and media, has nurtured a new generation of creative talent. Its Dance Center—the hub of Chicago's modern-dance milieu—features an intimate "black box" 275-seat performance space with stadium seating and good sightlines. The center schedules at least a dozen performances a year by both international and national touring groups and homegrown choreographers. 1306 S. Michigan Ave. ✆ **312/369-8330.** www.colum.edu/dance_center. Tickets $15–$30. Bus: 151. Subway/El: Red Line to Roosevelt.

Hubbard Street Dance Chicago ★ If you're going to see just one dance performance while you're in town, make it a Hubbard Street one. Chicago's best-known dance troupe mixes jazz, modern, ballet, and theater dance into an exhilarating experience. Sometimes whimsical, sometimes romantic, the crowd-pleasing ensemble incorporates a range of dance traditions, from Kevin O'Day to Twyla Tharp (who has choreographed pieces exclusively for Hubbard Street). Although the troupe spends most of the year touring, it has regular week-long Chicago engagements in the fall, winter, and spring. In the summer, the dancers often perform at Ravinia, the Chicago Symphony Orchestra's lovely outdoor pavilion in suburban Highland Park (p. 217). Office: 1147 W. Jackson Blvd. ✆ **312/850-9744.** www.hubbardstreetdance.com. Tickets $25–$90.

Joffrey Ballet of Chicago ★ While this major classical company concentrates on touring, the Joffrey schedules about 6 weeks of performances a year in its hometown. Its repertoire extends from the ballets of founder Robert Joffrey, George Balanchine, and Jerome Robbins to the cutting-edge works of Alonzo King and Chicago choreographer Randy Duncan. The company is usually in town in the spring (Apr or May), the fall (Sept or Oct), and December, when it stages a popular rendition of the holiday favorite *The Nutcracker.*

A bonus for dance lovers: The Joffrey offers free tours of its beautiful, light-filled administrative and rehearsal building in the Loop. Tours are given at noon on the 2nd and 4thWednesdays of each month; call ✆ **312/386-8921** to reserve a spot. Even if you can't make a tour, you can often catch a glimpse of dancers warming up through the floor-to-ceiling windows overlooking Randolph Street. Office: 10 E. Randolph St. ✆ **312/739-0120.** www.joffrey.com. Tickets $25–$130.

CHICAGO AFTER DARK | The Performing Arts

Muntu Dance Theatre of Chicago The tribal costumes, drumming, and energetic moves of this widely touring group, which focuses on both traditional and contemporary African and African-American dance, are always a hit with audiences. The company performs throughout the area at local libraries and community events, but also presents a few shows each year at the Harris Theater for Music and Dance. Office: 6800 S. Wentworth Ave. ℂ **773/241-6080.** www.muntu.com. Tickets $25–$50.

River North Dance Company Chicago can be a brutal testing ground for start-up dance companies, which have to struggle to find performance space and grab publicity. But the odds didn't buckle the well-oiled knees of the River North Dance Company. This talented jazz dance ensemble performs programs of short, Broadway-style numbers by established and emerging choreographers. They perform periodically at the Harris Theater for Music and Dance, but you never know where they'll pop up next; check their website or call for information on upcoming shows. Office: 1016 N. Dearborn St. ℂ **312/944-2888.** www.rivernorthchicago. com. Tickets $25–$30.

Theater

Ever since the Steppenwolf Theatre Company burst onto the national radar in the late '70s and early '80s with in-your-face productions of Sam Shepard's *True West* and Lanford Wilson's *Balm in Gilead,* Chicago has been known as a theater town. As Broadway produced bloated, big-budget musicals with plenty of special effects but little soul, Chicago theater troupes gained respect for their risk-taking and no-holds-barred emotional style. Some of Broadway's most acclaimed dramas in recent years (the Goodman Theatre's revival of *Death of a Salesman* and Steppenwolf's *August: Osage County,* to name a couple) hatched on Chicago stages. With more than 200 theaters, Chicago might have dozens of productions playing on any given weekend—and seeing a show here is on my must-do list for all visitors.

The city's theaters have produced a number of legendary comedic actors, including comic-turned-director Mike Nichols *(The Graduate, Postcards from the Edge, Primary Colors),* as well as fine dramatic actors and playwrights. David Mamet, one of America's greatest playwrights and an acclaimed film director and screenwriter, grew up in Chicago's South Shore steel-mill neighborhood and honed his craft with the former St. Nicholas Players, which included actor William H. Macy *(Fargo, Boogie Nights).*

The thespian soil here must be fertile. Tinseltown and TV have lured away such talents as John Malkovich, Joan Allen, Dennis Franz, Gary Sinise, George Wendt, and John Cusack. But even as emerging talents leave for bigger paychecks, a new pool of fresh faces is always waiting to take over. This constant renewal keeps the city's theatrical scene invigorated with new ideas and energy. Many of the smaller theater companies place great emphasis on communal work: Everyone takes part in putting on a production, from writing the script to building the sets. These companies perform in tiny, none-too-impressive venues, but their enthusiasm and commitment are inspiring. Who knows? The group you see performing in some storefront theater today could be the Steppenwolf of tomorrow.

The listings below highlight the troupes that consistently present high-quality work, but they represent only a fraction of Chicago's theater scene. For a complete listing of productions that are playing while you're in town, check the comprehensive listings in the two free weeklies, the *Reader* (which reviews just about every show in town) and *New City;* the weekly *Time Out Chicago* magazine; or the Friday sections of the two daily newspapers. The website of the **League of Chicago Theatres** (www.chicagoplays.com) also lists all theater productions playing in the area.

GETTING TICKETS

You can buy tickets for most shows directly from each theater's website. Individual box offices also take credit card orders by phone, and many of the smaller theaters will reserve seats for you with a simple request under your name left on the answering machine. For hard-to-get tickets, try **Gold Coast Tickets** (✆ **800/889-9100;** www.goldcoasttickets.com).

American Theater Company This troupe's mission? To produce stories that ask the question, "What does it mean to be an American?" With that broad mandate, the company generally focuses on serious American dramas (Mamet's *American Buffalo,* for instance, and works by Sam Shepherd and Thornton Wilder), but comical and even musical fare shows up on the schedule from time to time. Recent literary adaptations have included *Catch-22* and *Working,* based on the book by veteran Chicago writer Studs Terkel. 1909 W. Byron St. (2 blocks south of Irving Park Rd. at Lincoln Ave.). ✆ **773/409-4125.** www.atcweb.org. Tickets $25–$40. Subway/El: Brown Line to Irving Park.

Briar Street Theatre ☺ The Briar Street Theatre has been the "Blue Man Theater" since the fall of 1997. The avant-garde New York City performance phenomenon known as **Blue Man Group** has transformed the 625-seat theater, beginning with the lobby, which is now a jumble of tubes, wires, and things approximating computer innards. The show—which mixes percussion, performance

---

🏷 HALF-PRICE theater TICKETS

For half-price tickets on the day of the show, drop by one of the **Hot Tix** ticket centers (✆ **312/977-1755;** www.hottix.org), located in the Loop at 72 E. Randolph St. (btw. Wabash and Michigan aves.), and the Water Works Visitor Center, 163 E. Pearson St. The website lists what's on sale for that day beginning at 10am. You can buy tickets to most shows online, but you'll have to pay Ticketmaster's irritating "convenience" charge. Branches are open Tuesday through Saturday 10am to 6pm, Sunday 11am to 4pm; on Friday you can also purchase tickets for weekend performances. Hot Tix also offers advance-purchase tickets at full price.

In addition, a few theaters offer last-minute discounts on leftover seats. **Steppenwolf Theatre Company** often has $20 tickets available beginning at 11am on the day of a performance; stop by Audience Services at the theater. Also, half-price tickets become available 1 hr. before the show; call or stop by the box office, or visit www.steppenwolf.org. At the **Goodman Theatre,** if a show doesn't sell out, half-price tickets for that evening's performance are available starting at 10am at the box office; you can also buy them on the theater's website (see below).

art, mime, and rock 'n' roll—has become an immensely popular permanent fixture on the Chicago theater scene. (**Note to those with sensitive ears:** It can also get pretty loud.) The three strangely endearing performers, whose faces and heads are covered in latex and blue paint, know how to get the audience involved. Your first decision: Do you want the "splatter" or the "nonsplatter" seats? (The former necessitates the donning of a plastic sheet.) Although the show is a great pick for older children, it's not recommended for kids 5 and under. 3133 N. Halsted St. (at Briar St.). ✆ **773/348-4000.** www.blueman.com. Tickets $49–$64. Subway/El: Red or Brown line to Belmont.

Chicago Shakespeare Theatre ★ This group's home on Navy Pier is a visually stunning, state-of-the-art jewel. The centerpiece of the glass-box complex, which rises seven stories, is a 525-seat courtyard-style theater patterned loosely after the Swan Theater in Stratford-upon-Avon. The complex also houses a 180-seat studio theater, an English-style pub, and lobbies with commanding views of Lake Michigan and the Chicago skyline. But what keeps subscribers coming back is the talented company of actors, including some of the finest Shakespeare performers in the country.

The main theater presents three Shakespeare plays a year; founder and artistic director Barbara Gaines usually directs one show. Chicago Shakespeare also books special short-run performances and events, such as a production of *Hamlet* by acclaimed British director Peter Brook. Shakespeare Theatre subscribers are loyal, so snagging tickets on weekends can be a challenge; reserve in advance, if possible. If you have a choice of seats, avoid the upper balcony; the tall chairs are uncomfortable, and you have to lean way over the railing to see all the action onstage—definitely not recommended for anyone with a fear of heights. 800 E. Grand Ave. ✆ **312/595-5600.** www.chicagoshakes.com. Tickets $50–$70. Subway/El: Red Line to Grand, and then bus no. 29 to Navy Pier. Discounted parking in attached garage.

Court Theatre 📖 Given its affiliation with the University of Chicago, it should come as no surprise that this theater knows its way around the classics, from Molière to Ibsen. The productions here, however, are far from stuffy academic exercises: The vibrant, energetic takes on well-known works draw some of the finest actors in the city. In recent years, Court's seasons have included at least one musical (Tony Kushner's *Caroline, or Change* and *Raisin,* based on Lorraine Hansberry's *A Raisin in the Sun*), as well as plays by modern masters such as August Wilson and Tom Stoppard. It's a bit of trek to get here from downtown (I'd recommend a cab at night), but no matter what show is playing when you're in town, it's well worth the trip for theater lovers. 5535 S. Ellis Ave. (at 55th St.). ✆ **773/753-4472.** www.courttheatre.org. Tickets $38–$54. Metra train: 57th St.

ETA Creative Arts Foundation Since 1971, this theater has been staging original or seldom-seen dramatic works by African-American writers from Chicago and beyond. Along with **Black Ensemble Theater** (which performs at the Uptown Center Hull House, 4520 N. Beacon St.; ✆ **773/769-4451;** www.blackensembletheater.org), this is one of the best African-American theater troupes in the city. The company stages six plays a year in its 200-seat theater, including works geared toward children that are performed on Saturday afternoons. 7558 S. Chicago Ave. (at 76th St.). ✆ **773/752-3955.** www.etacreativearts.org. Tickets $30. Subway/El: Red Line to 69th St., transfer to bus no. 30.

Factory Theater This irreverent young troupe offers the quintessential low-budget Chicago theater experience. The group specializes in original works written by the ensemble, many of which aim at a young, nontheatrical crowd. (You're encouraged to bring your own beer and drink it during the late-night shows.) The company's biggest hit was the raunchy trailer-park potboiler *White Trash Wedding and a Funeral,* and other recent productions (such as the Renaissance-Fair–inspired *RenFair: A Fistful of Ducats*) continue the cheeky fun. But the Factory also makes room for serious dramatic works written by members of its ensemble. 3504 N. Elston Ave. ✆ **312/409-3247.** www.thefactorytheater.com. Tickets $15–$20. Subway/El: Red Line to Addison, then bus no. 152 (Addison St.).

Goodman Theatre ★★ The Goodman, under artistic director Robert Falls, is the top dog of the Chicago theater scene, producing both original shows and familiar standards. (Some of its high-profile productions, including acclaimed revivals of Arthur Miller's *Death of a Salesman* and *Desire Under the Elms,* both starring Brian Dennehy, have gone on to Broadway.) Productions at the Goodman are always solid; you may not see anything revolutionary, but you'll get some of the best actors in the city and top-notch production values.

The Goodman's custom-designed home in the North Loop is a rehab of the historic Harris and Selwyn theaters, a pair of rococo former movie houses. The renovation retained none of the historic bric-a-brac, and the new structure has a modern, minimalist feel. (The side of the building glows with different colors in the evenings.) The centerpiece is the 830-seat limestone-and-glass Albert Ivar Goodman Theatre. Connected to the main theater is a cylindrical, glass-walled building that houses retail operations, the 400-seat Owen Theatre, and the restaurant **Petterino's** (p. 97).

Every December, the Goodman stages a production of *A Christmas Carol,* which draws families from throughout the Chicago area and beyond. If you're in town then, it's great fun, but buy your tickets in advance, because many performances sell out. 170 N. Dearborn St. ✆ **312/443-3800.** www.goodmantheatre.org. Tickets $28–$70. Subway/El: Red Line to Washington/State or Lake/State; Brown or Orange line to Clark/Lake.

The House Theatre 👥 If you're looking for the up-and-coming stars of Chicago theater, keep your eyes on the House. This group of young actors takes on big themes (Harry Houdini and his obsession with death, the space-age tales of Ray Bradbury) and turns them into nonstop spectacles of drama, music, and comedy. Despite budget constraints, the sets and special effects are impressive—as are the troupe's energy, imagination, and humor. Come see them while their tickets remain ultra-affordable. Office: 4611 N. Ravenswood Ave. ✆ **773/769-3832.** www. thehousetheatre.com. Tickets $25. Performances: The Chopin Theatre, 1543 W. Division St. Subway/El: Blue Line to Division.

Lookingglass Theatre Company ★ One of the most visually oriented companies in town, Lookingglass produces original shows and unusual literary adaptations in a highly physical, imaginative style. These shows emphasize the look of a show as much as the acting, whether it's having performers wade through a giant shallow pool or take to the air on trapeze. The company, founded more than a decade ago by graduates of Northwestern University (including *Friend* David Schwimmer), stages several shows each year. Recent offerings included *Metamorphoses,* a sublime and humorous modern recasting of Ovid's myths that became a hit in New York, and *Lookingglass Alice,* an acrobatic retelling of *Alice in Wonderland.* Ensemble member Mary Zimmerman—who directed *Metamorphoses*—has built a national reputation for her creative interpretations of literature, so if she's directing a show while you're in town, don't miss it. Schwimmer also appears here occasionally, as either an actor or a director. Another plus for visitors is the theater's North Michigan Avenue location, which is a walk from many downtown hotels. 821 N. Michigan Ave. (at Chicago Ave.). ℰ **312/337-0665.** www.lookingglasstheatre.org. Tickets $30–$55. Subway/El: Red Line to Chicago.

Neo-Futurists 🎭 A fixture on Chicago's late-night theater scene, the Neo-Futurists have been doing their hit *Too Much Light Makes the Baby Go Blind* since 1988. (It's now the longest-running show in Chicago.) The setting—a cramped room above a funeral home—isn't much, but the gimmick is irresistible: Every night the performers stage a new collection of "30 plays in 60 minutes." The "plays" vary from a 3-minute comedy sketch to a lightning-quick wordless tableau; the mood veers from laugh-out-loud silly to emotionally touching. The show starts at 11:30pm on weekends; get there about an hour ahead, because seats are first come, first served, and they do sell out. The late-night curtain attracts a younger crowd, but I've taken 60-something relatives who have had a great time. (Unlike many improv comedy troupes, the Neo-Futurists don't rely on raunchy or gross-out humor.) Admission is random: Theatergoers pay $9 plus the roll of a six-sided die. If you want to feel that you've experienced edgy, low-budget theater—but still want to be entertained—this is the place to go. 5153 N. Ashland Ave. (at Foster Ave.). ℰ **773/275-5255.** www.neofuturists.org. Tickets $10–$15. Subway/El: Red Line to Berwyn.

Redmoon Theater 🎭 Redmoon Theater might well be the most intriguing and visionary theater company in Chicago. Founded in 1990, the company produces "spectacle theater" involving masks, objects, and an international range of puppetry styles in indoor and outdoor venues around town. Utterly hypnotic, highly acrobatic and visceral, and using minimal narration, Redmoon's adaptations of Melville's *Moby Dick,* Mary Shelley's *Frankenstein,* Victor Hugo's *The Hunchback of Notre Dame,* and *Rachel's Love,* an original work based on Jewish folktales, were revelations that earned the company an ardent and burgeoning following. Every September, Redmoon presents an annual "spectacle," transforming a public park into a site for performance art, larger-than-life puppet shows, and dramatic visual effects. Office: 1438 W. Kinzie St. ℰ **312/850-8440.** www.redmoon.org. Tickets $20–$30.

Steppenwolf Theatre Company ★★ Once a pioneer of bare-bones guerilla theater, Steppenwolf has moved firmly into the mainstream with a state-of-the-art theater and production budgets that rival those in any big city. The company has garnered many national awards and has launched the careers of several respected and well-known actors, including John Malkovich, Gary Sinise, Joan Allen, John Mahoney (of *Frasier*), and Laurie Metcalf (of *Roseanne*). Famous for pioneering the edgy, "rock-'n'-roll" style of Chicago acting in the 1970s and '80s—characterized by such incendiary tours de force as Sam Shepard's *True West* and Lanford Wilson's *Balm in Gilead*—Steppenwolf was reinvigorated with the triumph of *August: Osage County,* a harrowing but hilarious drama that got raves when it moved to New York and won multiple Tony Awards in 2008. While shows here can be hit or miss, the acting is never less than powerful; Steppenwolf's ensemble of performers is the best in the city.

Under artistic director Martha Lavey, Steppenwolf has drawn upon its star power, bringing back big names to perform or direct from time to time. But don't come here expecting to see John Malkovich or Joan Allen on stage; most of the big-name actors are too busy with their movie careers. Smaller theater troupes often perform at Steppenwolf's smaller studio theater, which stages more experimental fare. 1650 N. Halsted St. (at North Ave.). © **312/335-1650.** www.steppenwolf.org. Tickets $25–$65. Subway/El: Red Line to North/Clybourn.

Theater on the Lake 🐟 What a great way to see two of the city's signature strengths: a sublime skyline view from the water's edge and an evening of off-Loop Chicago theater. The Prairie School–style building, built in 1920 as a sanitarium for babies and children suffering from tuberculosis, has hosted theatrical productions along the lake for half a century, but in recent years, the park district has hit upon a perfect programming gimmick. Each week a different independent theater company gets to strut its stuff, usually restaging a play they performed earlier in the year. Performances run from June into August on Wednesday to Sunday evenings, and some shows do sell out, so it pays to reserve in advance. At intermission, you can walk out the back door and look south to the city lights. If it's a cool night, bring a sweater, because the screened-in theater is open to the night air (allowing the noise of traffic on Lake Shore Dr. to intrude somewhat). And a warning for those hot summer nights: The building is not air-conditioned. Fullerton Ave. and Lake Shore Dr. © **312/742-7994.** www.chicagoparkdistrict.com. Tickets $18. Bus: 151 (Sheridan).

Theater Wit Befitting its name, this up-and-coming troupe specializes in lighthearted productions filled with clever banter; it's best known for an annual December production of David Sedaris's *The Santaland Diaries.* But true to its motto, "Smart Art," Theater Wit also challenges audiences to think while being entertained. While it started as a vagabond company that performed in various venues around town, its move to a permanent home in Lincoln Park has revitalized the group and raised its profile considerably. 1229 W. Belmont Ave. (at Racine Ave.). © **773/975-8150.** www.theaterwit.org. Tickets $20–$40. Subway/El: Red or Brown line to Belmont.

Trap Door Theatre Trap Door is emblematic of the streetwise, no-holds-barred brand of off-Loop theater. A risk-taking, emotionally high-voltage company that has somehow stayed afloat (despite performing in a converted garage hidden behind a Bucktown restaurant), Trap Door concentrates on plays with a social or political bent. Many tend to be original works or decidedly noncommercial, provocative pieces by rarely produced cerebral artists, many of them European. (A few years ago, the show *AmeriKafka,* inspired by writer Franz Kafka and his visit to a performance by a Yiddish theater troupe, even featured a brief X-rated puppet show.) Prepare to be challenged: Theater doesn't get any more up close and personal than this. 1655 W. Cortland St. (1 block west of Ashland Ave.). © **773/384-0494.** www.trapdoor theatre.com. Tickets $20. Subway/El: Blue Line to Division.

> ### 📎 Theater for All
>
> **Visitors with disabilities will find that some local theaters go the extra mile to make their performances accessible. The Steppenwolf, Goodman, and Lookingglass theaters offer sign-language interpretation for deaf patrons and audio-described performances for visually impaired audiences. Victory Gardens Theater schedules special performances throughout the year customized for audiences with different disabilities. The theater even offers deaf patrons special glasses that project captions of dialogue onto the frame of the glasses.**

Victory Gardens Theater Victory Gardens is one of the few pioneers of independent theater that has survived since the 1970s. The company was rewarded for its unswerving commitment to developing playwrights with a Tony Award for regional theater in 2001—a real coup for a relatively small theater. The five or six productions presented each season are always new works, many developed through a series of workshops. The plays tend to be accessible stories about real people and real situations—nothing too experimental. Even though most shows don't feature nationally known actors, the casts are always first rate, and the plays usually leave you with something to think about (or passionately discuss) on the way home.

Victory Gardens stages shows at its main stage inside the former Biograph movie theater (known in Chicago lore as the place where the FBI gunned down bank robber John Dillinger in 1934). Smaller independent companies such as Shattered Globe and Remy Bumppo play on four smaller stages at the Victory Gardens Greenhouse Theater, 2257 N. Lincoln Ave., a few blocks south. 2433 N. Lincoln Ave. (1 block north of Fullerton Ave.). ℭ **773/871-3000.** www.victorygardens.org. Tickets $30–$48. Subway/El: Red or Brown line to Fullerton.

COMEDY & IMPROV

In the mid-1970s, the nation was introduced to Chicago's brand of comedy through the skit-comedy show *Saturday Night Live*. Back then, John Belushi and Bill Murray were among the latest brood to hatch from the number-one incubator of Chicago-style humor, Second City. Generations of American comics, from Mike Nichols and Robert Klein to Mike Myers and Tina Fey, have honed their skills in Chicago before making it big in film and TV. Chicago continues to nurture young comics, affording them the chance to learn the tricks of improvisational comedy at Second City, the ImprovOlympic, and numerous other comedy and improv outlets.

A performance on Second City's storied main stage.

ComedySportz ☺ Most improv-comedy shows aren't exactly family-friendly, but ComedySportz does away with the barlike atmosphere and R-rated topics to deliver shows that are funny for the whole family. Chicago's only all-ages professional improv troupe sets two groups of five comedians against each other to compete for audience applause. "It isn't *about* sports—it *is* a sport," is the tagline here. Shows are held Thursdays at 8pm, Fridays at 8 and 10pm, and Saturdays at 6, 8, and 10pm; kids 10 and older are welcome at the early evening shows. 929 W. Belmont Ave. ✆ **773/549-8080.** www.comedysportzchicago.com. Tickets $22. Subway/El: Red or Brown line to Belmont.

iO 🎁 The iO improv troupe was founded in 1981 by the late, great, and inexplicably unsung Del Close, an improv pioneer who branched off from his more mainstream counterparts at Second City to pursue an unorthodox methodology (the letters "iO" stand for "ImprovOlympic," the group's original name). A legendary iconoclast, the colorful Close developed a long-form improv technique known as "The Harold." It eschewed the traditional sketch format in favor of more conceptual comedy scenes: The audience suggests a theme for the evening, and then a series of skits, monologues, and songs is built around it.

iO offers a nightclub setting for a variety of unscripted nightly performances, from free-form pieces to shows loosely based on concepts such as *Star Trek* or dating. Like all improv, it's a gamble: It could be a big laugh, or the amateur performers could go down in flames. Monday is an off night for most other clubs in town, and iO takes advantage with a show called the Armando Diaz Experience, an all-star improv night that teams up some of the best improvisers in Chicago, from Second City and elsewhere. Besides Mike Myers, successful alums include Tim Meadows, Andy Dick, Amy Poehler, and the late Chris Farley. 3541 N. Clark St. (at Addison St.). ✆ **773/880-0199.** http://chicago.ioimprov.com. Tickets $5–$20. Subway/El: Red Line to Addison.

Second City For nearly 50 years, Second City has been the top comedy club in Chicago and the most famous of its kind in the country. Photos of famous graduates line the lobby walls and include Elaine May, John Belushi, Stephen Colbert, Steve Carell, and Tina Fey.

Today's Second City is a veritable factory of improv, with shows on two stages (the storied main stage and the smaller Second City ETC) and a hugely popular training school. The main-stage ensembles change frequently, and the shows can swing wildly back and forth on the hilarity meter. Check the theater reviews in the *Reader,* a free local weekly, for an opinion on the current offering. To sample the Second City experience, catch the free postshow improv session (it gets going around 10:30pm); no ticket is necessary if you skip the main show (except Fri). 1616 N. Wells St. (in the Pipers Alley complex at North Ave.). ✆ **877/778-4707** or 312/337-3992. www.secondcity.com. Tickets $8–$25. Subway/El: Brown Line to Sedgwick.

Zanie's Comedy Club Just down the street from Second City in Old Town is Zanie's, one of the only traditional comedy clubs left in Chicago. Zanie's often draws its headliners straight off *The Late Show with David Letterman* and *The Tonight Show,* and it's a regular stop for nationally known comedians. (Recent headliners have included Craig Ferguson and Chelsea Handler.) Stand-up routines are the usual fare, played to packed, appreciative houses. Patrons must be 21 or older. 1548 N. Wells St. (btw. North Ave. and Schiller St.). ✆ **312/337-4027.** www.chicago.zanies.com. Tickets $20–$25, plus 2-item food or drink minimum. Subway/El: Brown Line to Sedgwick.

The Magnificent Mile, the Gold Coast, & River North After Dark

M Subway/El stop

GOLD COAST

STREETER-VILLE

MAGNIFICENT MILE

RIVER NORTH

The Loop

Lake Michigan

Navy Pier

Chicago River

N. Branch Chicago River

N. Lake Shore Dr.

AN ESCAPE FROM THE multiplex

Chicago has a fine selection of movie theaters, but even the so-called art houses show mostly the same films that you'd be able to catch back home (or eventually on cable). But three local movie houses cater to cinema buffs with original programming. The **Gene Siskel Film Center,** 164 N. State St. (✆ **312/846-2600;** www.siskelfilmcenter.org; subway/El: Red Line to Washington or Brown Line to Randolph), named after the well-known *Chicago Tribune* film critic who died in 1999, is part of the School of the Art Institute of Chicago.

The center schedules a selection of films in two theaters, including lectures and discussions with filmmakers. The Film Center often shows foreign films that are not released commercially in the U.S.

The **Music Box Theatre,** 3733 N. Southport Ave. (✆ **773/871-6604;** www.musicboxtheatre.com; subway/El: Brown Line to Southport), is a movie palace on a human scale. Opened in 1929, it was meant to re-create the feeling of an Italian courtyard; a faux-marble loggia and towers cover the walls and electric "stars" sparkle in the painted sky overhead. The Music Box books a selection of foreign and independent American films—everything from Polish filmmaker Krzysztof

Kieslowski's epic *Decalogue* to a sing-along version of *The Sound of Music* to the Vincent Price cult classic *House of Wax.* The vintage seats may not be the most comfortable, but the Music Box's funky, shabby feel is part of its charm.

Facets MultiMedia, 1517 W. Fullerton Ave. (✆ **773/281-4114;** www.facets. org; subway/El: Red or Brown line to Fullerton), a nonprofit group that screens independent film and video from around the world, is for the die-hard cinematic thrill-seeker. The group mounts an annual Children's Film Festival (Oct–Nov) and the Chicago Latino Film Festival (Apr–May), and rents its impressive collection of classic, hard-to-find films on video and DVD by mail.

THE MUSIC SCENE
Jazz

In the first great wave of black migration from the South just after World War I, jazz journeyed from the Storyville section of New Orleans to Chicago. Jelly Roll Morton and Louis Armstrong made Chicago a jazz hot spot in the 1920s, and their music lives on in a whole new generation of talent. Chicago jazz is known for its collaborative spirit and a certain degree of risk-taking—which you can experience at a number of lively clubs.

Andy's Jazz Club Casual and comfortable, Andy's, a full restaurant and bar, is popular with both the hard-core and the neophyte jazz enthusiast. The club has one of the busiest schedules in town, with sets starting at 5 and 9pm every day of the week. (If you're catching the late show, the kitchen stays open until midnight.) Families are welcome on Sundays, when the club is open to all ages, as long as they're seated in the dining room area. 11 E. Hubbard St. (btw. State St. and Wabash Ave.). ✆ **312/642-6805.** www.andysjazzclub.com. Cover $5–$15. Subway/El: Red Line to Grand.

Back Room One of the vestiges of the celebrated old Rush Street, the center of Chicago's jazz and cabaret scene in the swinging '60s' and '70s, the Back Room still packs a well-dressed crowd into an intimate candlelit spot at the back of a long gangway. The tuxedoed doorman offers patrons a seat on the main floor or in the balcony overlooking the stage. Shows cater to night owls, starting at 9:15pm, 10:45pm, and 12:15am Sundays through Fridays, with an additional 1:45am show on Saturday nights. Rather than booking traditional jazz quartets and trios, Back Room features acts that mix jazz with Motown, R&B, and funk. 1007 N. Rush St. (btw. Oak St. and Bellevue Place). ✆ **312/751-2433.** www.back roomchicago.com. Cover $20–$25 plus 2-drink minimum. Subway/El: Red Line to Chicago.

Deep Blue Organ Trio playing at the Green Mill jazz club.

Green Mill ★ 👥 Green Mill, in the heart of Uptown, is "Old Chicago" down to its rafters. It became a popular watering hole during the 1920s and 1930s, when regulars included Al Capone, Sophie Tucker (the Last of the Red Hot Mamas), and Al Jolson, and today it retains its speakeasy flavor. On Sunday night, the Green Mill plays host to the **Uptown Poetry Slam,** when poets vie for the open mic to roast and ridicule each other's work. Most nights, however, jazz is on the menu, beginning around 9pm and winding down just before closing at 4am (5am Sat). Regular performers include sax phenom Frank Catalano, who performs standards and some of his own compositions, and chanteuse Patricia Barber. (They're both worth seeing.) The Green Mill is a Chicago treasure and not to be missed. Get there early to claim one of the plush velvet booths. 4802 N. Broadway Ave. (at Lawrence Ave.). ✆ **773/878-5552.** www.greenmilljazz.com. Cover $6–$12. Subway/El: Red Line to Lawrence.

Blues

If there's any music that epitomizes Chicago, it's the blues. As African-Americans migrated northward in the years following World War II, they brought their musical traditions with them, including the mournful, guitar-and-harmonica-based sound known as Delta blues. In Chicago, the addition of electric guitar gave the traditional blues a jolt of new life, and local musicians such as Howlin' Wolf, Muddy Waters, and Willie Dixon influenced generations of rockers that followed. Today, blues clubs remain a staple of the cultural scene, but one that attracts mostly niche audiences. Some spots cater to out-of-towners looking for an "authentic" blues experience, while others keep a relatively low profile, surviving thanks to the loyalty of die-hard blues aficionados.

Lincoln Park & Wrigleyville After Dark

M Subway/El stop

Gifted guitarist Buddy Guy runs one of the most popular blues clubs in town, Buddy Guy's Legends.

Blue Chicago Blue Chicago pays homage to female blues belters with a strong lineup of the best women vocalists around. The 1940s-style brick-walled room, decorated with original artwork of Chicago blues vignettes, has an elongated oval bar in the middle and additional stool seating along the walls. The club is open every day, with music beginning at 9pm. 536 N. Clark St. (btw. Grand Ave. and Ohio St.). © **312/661-0100.** www.bluechicago.com. Cover $8–$10. Subway/El: Red Line to Grand.

B.L.U.E.S. On the Halsted strip, look for B.L.U.E.S.—the name says it all. This is a small joint for the serious aficionado—if you've got claustrophobia, this isn't the place for you. On the upside, the cozy space makes every performance personal; you won't miss a single move of the musicians standing onstage only yards away. Shows start at 9:30pm nightly. 2519 N. Halsted St. (btw. Wrightwood and Fullerton aves.). © **773/528-1012.** www.chicagobluesbar.com. Cover $5–$10. Subway/El: Red or Brown line to Fullerton.

Buddy Guy's Legends ★★ 🎁 A legend himself, gifted guitarist Buddy Guy runs one of the most popular and comfortable clubs in town. Blues paraphernalia, from a Koko Taylor dress to a Muddy Waters tour jacket, decorate the walls of this two-story club near the South Loop. Buddy himself plays a series of shows every January, and some of the biggest names in bluesy rock guitar—Eric Clapton, Keith Richards—have been known to stop in when they're in town. The second floor has pool tables and a smaller stage that features occasional acoustic shows; the kitchen also serves excellent Louisiana-style soul food and barbecue. 700 S. Wabash Ave. (btw. Balbo Dr. and Eighth St.). © **312/427-0333.** www.buddyguys.com. Cover $10–$20. Subway/El: Red Line to Harrison.

Kingston Mines ★ Chicago's premier blues bar is where musicians congregate after their own gigs to jam and socialize. Celebs have been known to drop by when they're in town shooting movies, but most nights the crowd includes a big contingent of conventioneers looking for a rockin' night on the town. But don't worry about the tourist factor—everyone's here to have a good time, and the energy is infectious. The nightly show begins at 9:30pm, with bands on two stages, and goes until 4am (5am Sat). The late-night kitchen serves up burgers and ribs. 2548 N. Halsted St. (btw. Wrightwood and Fullerton aves.). ☎ **773/477-4646.** www.kingstonmines.com. Cover $10–$15. Subway/El: Red or Brown line to Fullerton.

Rosa's Lounge ★ Rosa's is strictly a neighborhood hangout, but it has all the atmosphere required to fuel its heartfelt lamentations. Mama Rosa and her son, Tony Mangiullo, run a homey, lovable spot that, despite its somewhat distant location, is decidedly one of the best joints in town for spirited, authentic Chicago blues. (Because of its off-the-beaten-track location on the northwest side of the city, it attracts local fans rather than tourists.) Rosa's also sponsors a blues cruise on Lake Michigan every summer. Shows start at 9:30pm on Tuesday, and Thursday through Saturday. Closed Sunday, Monday, and Wednesday. 3420 W. Armitage Ave. (at Kimball Ave.). ☎ **773/342-0452.** www.rosaslounge.com. Cover $7–$15. Subway/El: Blue Line to Logan Sq., and then a short cab ride.

Underground Wonder Bar One of the most eclectic live-music spots in town, this intimate, below-street-level club is almost impossible to categorize. Yes, it books blues acts, but also jazz trios, folk singers, and R&B vocalists. Things really heat up when owner Lonie Walker and her Big Bad Ass Company Band take the stage at 11pm on Friday and Saturday nights, playing a raucous blues-rock. Try to stick around until the wee hours, which is when the fun really begins— musicians stop by after gigs at other clubs to improvise a final set. 10 E. Walton St. (at State St.). ☎ **312/266-7761.** www.undergroundwonderbar.com. Cover $8–$15. Subway/El: Red Line to Chicago.

Rock (Basically)

In the early 1990s, Chicago's burgeoning alternative rock scene produced such national names as the Smashing Pumpkins, Liz Phair, Veruca Salt, Urge Overkill, and Material Issue. Although the city's moment of pop hipness quickly faded (as did most of the aforementioned artists), the live music scene has continued to thrive. Although local groups still occasionally hit it big (Wilco, Fall Out Boy), most Chicago bands concentrate on keeping it real, happy to perform at small local clubs and not obsessing (at least openly) about getting a record contract. The city is also a regular stop for touring bands, from big stadium acts to smaller up-and-coming groups. Scan the *Reader, New City,* or *Time Out Chicago* to see who's playing where.

The biggest rock acts tend to play at the local indoor stadiums: the **United Center** (☎ **312/455-4500;** www.unitedcenter.com), home of the Bulls and Blackhawks,

Chicago Rocks

Come summertime, Chicago's indie-music credibility gets a major boost from two high-profile concert festivals. Every August, **Lollapalooza** (www.lollapalooza.com) takes over a prime section of Grant Park for 3 days of performances by big-name artists and rising stars. The lakefront views are great, but the number of acts and people can get overwhelming—and the weather is usually steamy. Hipster music snobs prefer the **Pitchfork Music Festival** (www.pitchforkmusicfestival.com) in July, which brings edgy young bands to play a series of shows at Union Park in the West Loop. Most are groups that mainstream rock fans haven't heard of, which is just the way hard-core Pitchfork devotees like it.

and **Allstate Arena** (✆ 847/635-6601; www.allstatearena.com), in Rosemont near O'Hare Airport. These venues are about what you expect: The overpriced seats nearest the stage are fine, but you'd better bring binoculars if you're stuck in the more affordable upper decks. During the summer, you'll also find the big names at the outdoor **First Midwest Bank Amphitheatre** (✆ 708/614-1616; www.livenation.com/venue/getVenue/venueId/785), inconveniently located in the suburb of Tinley Park, about an hour outside the city, and cursed with pretty bad acoustics.

The good news: You can catch midlevel rock acts at local venues with a lot more character. The **Riviera Theatre,** 4746 N. Racine Ave. (✆ 773/275-6800; www.jamusa.com/Venues/Riviera/Concerts.aspx), is a relic of the Uptown neighborhood's swinging days in the 1920s, '30s, and '40s. A former movie palace, it retains the original ornate ceiling, balcony, and lighting fixtures, but it has definitely gotten grimy with age. (Head upstairs to the balcony seats if you'd rather avoid the crowd that rushes toward the stage during shows.) The **Aragon Ballroom,** a few blocks away, at 1106 W. Lawrence Ave. (✆ 773/561-9500; www.aragon.com; subway/El: Red Line to Lawrence), was once an elegant big-band dance hall; the worn Moorish-castle decor and twinkling-star ceiling now give the place a seedy charm despite its less-than-ideal acoustics. A former vaudeville house is now the **Vic Theatre,** 3145 N. Sheffield Ave. (✆ 773/472-0366; www.victheatre.com; subway/El: Red or Brown line to Fullerton), a midsize venue that features up-and-coming acts. (Get there early to snag one of the lower balcony rows.)

More sedate audiences love the **Park West,** 322 W. Armitage Ave. (✆ 773/929-5959; www.jamusa.com/Venues/ParkWest/Concerts.aspx; subway/El: Brown Line to Armitage, or bus no. 22 [Clark St.]), both for its excellent sound system and its cabaret-style seating (no mosh pit here). For tickets to most shows at all these venues, you're stuck going through the service-fee-grabbing **Ticketmaster** (✆ 312/559-1212).

Here are some bars and clubs that book live music most nights of the week:

Abbey Pub Irish brogues abound at this barnlike gathering place for indie rock, folk pop, and other hard-to-classify acts. It's tucked away in a residential neighborhood—far from the usual tourist haunts—so you're pretty much guaranteed to be surrounded by locals. Besides Guinness and other Emerald Isle beers on tap, there's a full menu. Traditional Irish music sessions are held Sunday night. 3420 W. Grace St. (at Elston Ave.). ✆ **773/478-4408.** www.abbeypub.com. Cover $8–$25. Subway/El: Brown Line to Irving Park, and then a 10-min. cab ride.

Cubby Bear Across from Wrigley Field, Cubby Bear is a showcase for new rock bands and an occasional offbeat act (one recent example: Dread Zeppelin, a reggae- and Elvis-influenced Led Zeppelin cover band). The Cubby Bear draws in a scrub-faced postcollegiate crowd and gets especially packed after Cubs games during the summer. Concerts are staged on weekends and many Thursday nights. Otherwise, there are always billiards, darts, and other distractions. 1059 W. Addison St. (at Clark St.). ✆ **773/327-1662.** www.cubbybear.com. Cover $5–$10 on band nights, more for special shows. Subway/El: Red Line to Addison.

Double Door 🎁 This music venue has capitalized on the Wicker Park/Bucktown neighborhood's ascendance as a breeding ground for rock and alternative sounds, attracting buzz bands and promising unknowns to its stage. Owned by the proprietors of **Metro** (see below), the no-frills club can get steamy, but it has some of the better acoustics and sightlines in the city. When you need to escape the noise, there's a lounge-type area with pool tables in the basement. 1572 N. Milwaukee Ave. (at North Ave.). ✆ **773/489-3160.** www.doubledoor.com. Tickets $5–$25. Subway/El: Blue Line to Damen.

Elbo Room 🎸 Upstairs, Elbo Room looks like any other low-key Lincoln Park watering hole, but in the basement you'll find a delightfully schizophrenic live music venue; in any given week, the lineup could include rockabilly, hip-hop, soul, funk, and more. The subterranean setting is cozy and brings the bands up close and personal, but when the place gets packed, you might not see much of the onstage action. 2871 N. Lincoln Ave. (at George St.). ✆ **773/549-5549.** www.elbo roomchicago.com. Cover $7–$10. Subway/El: Brown Line to Diversey.

The Empty Bottle This alternative-rock club in the Ukrainian Village neighborhood—south of Wicker Park—is a haven for young arty scenesters drawn here for camaraderie, obscure bands, and cheap beer. Offerings are diverse, with live music every night, ranging from experimental jazz-pop and electronica to "hard country honky tonk" (specifically, the country-infused Hoyle Brothers, who play an early set every Fri with no cover). 1035 N. Western Ave. (btw. Division St. and Augusta Blvd.). ✆ **773/276-3600.** www.emptybottle.com. Cover $3–$12. Subway/El: Blue Line to Western, and then bus no. 49.

House of Blues The largest location in a national chain of music venues, the House of Blues could more appropriately be called the House of Pop. Although it's decorated with Mississippi Delta folk art, the bands that play here tend to be rock groups, '80s novelty acts, and the occasional hip-hop or reggae performer. This is a great place to see a show—concerts are in a theater that re-creates a gilded European opera house (minus the seats), and the stage views are pretty good no matter where you stand. A restaurant also serves lunch and dinner with hometown blues accompaniment. The popular **Sunday gospel brunch,** offering a Southern-style buffet, brings a different Chicago gospel choir to the stage each week; the three weekly "services" often sell out, so get tickets in advance. 329 N. Dearborn St. (at Kinzie St.). ✆ **312/923-2000** for general information, or 312/923-2020 for concert information. www.houseofblues.com. Tickets usually $15–$50. Subway/El: Red Line to Grand.

Joe's Bar Part sports bar, part music venue, Joe's Bar is a vast, warehouse-size space with the spirit of a quirky neighborhood tavern. There's live music Fridays and Saturdays, with local and national bands playing everything from rock to country to covers of 1980's one-hit wonders. Gimmicks abound, such as "Doggy Happy Hour" on Wednesdays in the summer, featuring treats and water for dogs and drink specials for their owners. Joe's can get crowded, but the scenery—lots of attractive people in their 20s—makes up for it. *Another bonus:* Because there are so many bar areas, you won't have to wait long to get a drink. 940 W. Weed St. (at North Ave.). ✆ **312/337-3486.** www.joesbar.com. Live music cover $5–$30. Subway/El: Red Line to North/Clybourn.

Lincoln Hall ★ The focus is firmly on the music at this welcoming Lincoln Park venue, thanks to the clear sightlines and an excellent sound system. Bookings are fairly eclectic, but concentrate on independent pop-folk acts, singer-songwriters, and other groups off the teeny-bopper radar (there's even seating in the balcony for concert-goers who prefer not to join the main floor crush). Lincoln Hall proves that rock-'n-roll clubs don't have to be gritty to succeed—even the

The Music Scene

bathrooms are clean. There's a full bar and above-average food service available before shows. 2424 N. Lincoln Ave. (at Fullerton Ave.). ✆ **773/525-2501.** www.lincoln hallchicago.com. Cover $12–$25. Subway/El: Red Line to Fullerton.

Martyrs' 🎁 Dedicated to the memories of such late great rock performers as Jimi Hendrix and Janis Joplin (who are immortalized on the mural facing the stage), Martyrs' presents a variety of local bands and the occasional performance by national touring acts. On the second Wednesday of the month, catch the popular Tributasaurus, a note-perfect rock tribute band that "becomes" a different rock legend every month. The low tables, high ceiling, and huge windows make Martyrs' one of the best places to catch a rock-'n'-roll show. 3855 N. Lincoln Ave. (btw. Berenice Ave. and Irving Park Rd.). ✆ **773/404-9494.** www.martyrslive.com. Cover $7–$20. Subway/El: Brown Line to Addison.

Metro ★ Metro is located in an old auditorium and is Chicago's premier venue for live alternative and rock acts on the verge of breaking into the big time. There's not much in the way of atmosphere—it's basically a big black room with a stage—but the place has an impressive history. Everybody who is anybody played here when they were starting out, including REM, Pearl Jam, and local heroes the Smashing Pumpkins. The subterranean Smart Bar—at the same location—is a dance club open 7 nights a week. (You sometimes can get in free if you've seen a concert that night at Metro.) Some shows are all-ages, but most require concertgoers to be at least 21. Tickets are sold in person through the adjoining **Metro Store** (sans service charges), or by phone through Ticketmaster. 3730 N. Clark St. (at Racine Ave.). ✆ **773/549-0203** or 312/559-1212 for Ticketmaster orders. www. metrochicago.com. Tickets $10–$25. Subway/El: Red Line to Sheridan.

Phyllis' Musical Inn Typical of the borderline dive-y neighborhood bars that used to be scattered around Wicker Park—before rampant gentrification brought hip lounges and overpriced martinis—Phyllis' is a small, generally uncrowded hangout that books live rock music (sometimes jazz and blues) on weekends. Depending on the night, you could be surrounded by a crowd of hipsters or find yourself chatting with a far-from-busy bartender. Either way, Phyllis' will whisk you back to the days of blue-collar Chicago. 1800 W. Division St. (at Wood St.). ✆ **773/486-9862.** Cover $3–$5. Subway/El: Blue Line to Division.

Country, Folk & Ethnic Music

Known as a musician-friendly town, Chicago attracts artists from a wide range of genres. While the big-name country music stars tend to play at stadium-sized arenas, "alt country" groups are a staple of the local music scene, mixing traditional American tunes with more experimental sounds. One highlight of the city's eclectic offerings is The Old Town School of Folk Music, a flourishing center that regularly hosts well-known singer-songwriters, bluegrass groups, Celtic fiddlers, and other traditional music from around the world.

Exedus II Like its flashier neighbor, the **Wild Hare** (see below), Exedus offers reggae. The specialty here is Jamaican dancehall, performed live or by DJs. Although this small storefront tavern gets crowded, the music's good and the attitude of the international crowd is laid-back. In general, it's more authentic than the competition, which tends to draw more of the frat-party element. Closed Tuesday. 3477 N. Clark St. (at Cornelia Ave.). ✆ **773/348-3998.** www.exeduslounge.com. Cover usually under $10. Subway/El: Red Line to Addison.

The Old Town School of Folk Music, a training center that offers a broad spectrum of music classes, has hosted greats like Pete Seeger and Alison Krauss.

The Hideout 🔱 This friendly tavern's OLD STYLE BEER sign shines like a beacon, guiding roots-music fans through the grimy industrial neighborhood that surrounds it. The owners' beer-can collection and some "celebrity" memorabilia are on display in the front room. In back, local musicians play country, rock, and bluesy tunes on a small stage backed by an impressive stuffed sailfish. It's no-frills, all right, but the Hideout also books some of the best lineups of folk and "alt country" bands in the city, including Jeff Tweedy (of Wilco), Kelly Hogan, and the New Duncan Imperials. 1354 W. Wabansia Ave. (btw. Elston Ave. and Throop St.). ✆ **773/227-4433.** www.hideoutchicago.com. Cover usually $5–$10. Subway/El: Blue Line to Damen.

Old Town School of Folk Music ★ 🎁 Country, folk, bluegrass, Latin, Celtic—the Old Town School of Folk Music covers a spectrum of indigenous musical forms. Best known as a training center offering a slate of music classes, the school also plays host to everyone from the legendary Pete Seeger to bluegrass phenom Alison Krauss. The school's home, in a former 1930s library, is the world's largest facility dedicated to the preservation and presentation of traditional and contemporary folk music. The Old Town School also houses an art gallery showcasing exhibitions of works by local, national, and international artists; a music store offering an exquisite selection of instruments, sheet music, and hard-to-find recordings; and a cafe. In midsummer it sponsors the popular Folk and Roots outdoor music festival. The school maintains another retail store and offers music classes at its prior location, 909 W. Armitage Ave. 4544 N. Lincoln Ave. (btw. Wilson and Montrose aves.). ✆ **773/728-6000.** www.oldtownschool.org. Tickets $10–$35. Subway/El: Brown Line to Western.

Schubas Tavern 🎁 Country and folk singer-songwriters have found a home in this divine little concert hall in a former Schlitz tavern. It's a friendly and intimate place with impeccable sound. There's music 7 nights a week, and Schubas occasionally books big-name performers such as John Hiatt and Train. But it's known for consistently booking the biggest stars of tomorrow—like Feist, John Mayer, Sarah McLachlin, Dave Matthews—while they're on their way up. You'll also find a bar up front and an attached restaurant, Harmony Grill, where you can grab a pretty good burger and fries after the show. 3159 N. Southport Ave. (at Belmont Ave.). ✆ **773/525-2508.** www.schubas.com. Tickets $10–$25. Subway/El: Red or Brown line to Belmont.

Cabarets & Piano Bars

Chicago's relatively low-key cabaret scene is concentrated in River North and tends to attract a relaxed—but well dressed—clientele.

The Baton Show Lounge This River North lounge hosts the city's longest-running revue of female impersonators, which has been showcasing fabulous "gals" in outrageous getups for more than 40 years. Shows are Wednesday through Sunday at 8:30 and 10:30pm, and 12:30am. This is a very popular spot for bachelorette outings, so be prepared for groups of rowdy women; the club recommends advance reservations on weekends. 436 N. Clark St. (btw. Hubbard and Illinois sts.). ✆ **312/644-5269.** www.thebatonshowlounge.com. Cover $10–$15 plus 2-drink minimum. Subway/El: Red Line to Grand.

Coq d'Or Whether you're huddled close around the piano or hanging back on the red Naugahyde banquettes, this old-time, clubby haunt in The Drake Hotel offers an intimate evening of song stylings. (It's one of the few downtown hotel lounges that still offers live music.) The Coq d'Or claims to be the second bar in Chicago to serve drinks after the repeal of Prohibition in 1933—and the place hasn't changed much since then. In The Drake Hotel, 140 E. Walton St. (at Michigan Ave.). ✆ **312/787-2200.** No cover or drink minimum. Subway/El: Red Line to Chicago/State.

Davenport's Piano Bar & Cabaret 🎁 The youthful hipster haunt of Wicker Park isn't the first place you'd expect to find a tried-and-true piano bar and cabaret venue, but Davenport's does its best to revive a fading art form. Owner Bill Davenport and his partners transformed a single-story storefront into an intimate, chic gem that provides a much-needed showcase for Chicago-bred talent, with a sprinkling of visiting performers from New York and L.A. The piano bar in front is flashier than the subdued cabaret in back, featuring a singing waitstaff, blue velvet banquettes, funky lighting fixtures, and a hand-painted mural-topped bar. The cabaret's sound equipment is first rate. 1383 N. Milwaukee Ave. (just south of North Ave.). ✆ **773/278-1830.** www.davenportspianobar.com. Cover $15–$20 plus 2-drink minimum. Subway/El: Blue Line to Damen.

The Baton Show Lounge has been hosting "gals" in outrageous costumes for more than 40 years.

Jilly's Named for Frank Sinatra's former manager, Jilly's has a retro feel that's timeless, not dated. Music and a lively buzz from the patrons spill into the street during warm weather, and pianists and trios play the dark room decorated with photos of the Rat Pack, Steve and Eydie, and the like. The crowd includes everyone from wealthy Gold Coast residents to young singles catching up after work. 1007 N. Rush St. (at Oak St.). ✆ **312/664-1001.** www.jillyschicago.com. Subway/El: Red Line to Chicago.

Redhead Piano Bar The Redhead attracts a well-heeled, sharp-dressed Gold Coast clientele with its classic, old-time lounge vibe. The walls are covered with yesteryear memorabilia—movie-star glamour shots, playbills, and old sheet music—and the drink list focuses on single-malt scotch and other premium liquors rather than flavored martinis. (The crowd teeming around the piano is a throwback as well.) Suggested attire is "business casual," so don't show up wearing shorts and gym shoes. 16 W. Ontario St. ✆ **312/640-1000.** www.redheadpianobar.com. No cover or drink minimum. Subway/El: Red Line to Grand.

Zebra Lounge 🍸 The most quirky piano bar in town, Zebra Lounge has a loyal following despite (or maybe because of) the campy decor. Just as you would expect, black-and-white stripes are the unifying element at this dark, shoebox-size Gold Coast spot, furnished with black vinyl booths, a small mirrored bar, and zebra kitsch galore. Bar lore has it that the Zebra Lounge opened December 5, 1933—the day Prohibition ended. Since then, it has passed through numerous owners, but the name, a tribute to a long-forgotten tavern in New York, has remained. For the past quarter-century, it has been a raucous piano bar, attracting a multigenerational crowd of regulars. The place is relatively mellow early in the evening, though it can get packed late into the night on weekends. 1220 N. State Pkwy. (btw. Division and Goethe sts.). ✆ **312/642-5140.** No cover or drink minimum. Subway/El: Red Line to Clark/Division.

THE CLUB SCENE

Chicago is the hallowed ground where house music was hatched in the 1980s, so it's no surprise to find that it's also home to several vast, industrial-style dance clubs with pounding music and an under-30 crowd. Some spots specialize in a single type of music, while others offer an ever-changing mix of rhythms and beats that follow the latest DJ-driven trend. Many clubs attract a different clientele on each day of the week (Sun night, for example, is gay-friendly at many of the clubs listed below), so check the club's website to get an idea of each night's vibe. Given the fickle nature of clubgoers, some places listed below might have disappeared by the time you read this, but there is an impressive list of longtime survivors—clubs that have lasted more than a decade but continue to draw crowds.

Berlin One of the more enduring dance floors in Chicago, Berlin is primarily gay during the week but draws dance hounds of all stripes on weekends and for special theme nights (from disco on Wed, to special events featuring the music of Björk or Prince). It has a reputation for outrageousness and creativity, making it prime ground for people-watching. The space isn't much—basically a square room with a bar along one side—but the no-frills dance floor is packed late into the evening. The owners are no dummies: The cover charge applies only on Friday and Saturday after 11pm, which is about an hour or two earlier than you ought to show up. (For more, see "The Gay & Lesbian Scene," p. 336.) 954 W. Belmont Ave. (at Sheffield Ave.). ℂ **773/348-4975.** www.berlinchicago.com. Cover $5. Subway/El: Red or Brown line to Belmont.

Funky Buddha Lounge A bit off the beaten path, west of the River North gallery district, this club blends in with its industrial surroundings—even the whimsical Buddha sculpture on the heavy steel front door is a rusted husk. Inside is a different scene altogether: low red lighting, seductive dens with black-leather and faux leopard-skin sofas, lots of candles, and antique light fixtures salvaged from an old church. The DJs are among the best in the city, flooding the nice-size dance floor with everything from hip-hop, bhangra, and funk to African, soul, and underground house. The crowd is just as diverse as the music—everything from yuppies and after-dinner hipsters to die-hard clubhoppers and barely legal wannabes. Hugely popular Thursday nights pack in the young, mostly white club kids; Friday and Saturday feature a cool, urban crowd decked out in funky gear. The bus runs to this area, but take a cab at night. 728 W. Grand Ave. ℂ **312/666-1695.** www.funkybuddha.com. Cover free Thurs, $10 Fri, $20 Sat. Bus: 65 (Grand Ave.).

Rednofive Taking its name from the ubiquitous dye used in food products, Rednofive is no fake, thanks to its sleek design and tight lineup of local DJs spinning a sonic deluge of progressive and abstract house music, hip-hop, and pop, sometimes accompanied by a percussionist on drums. The glittering space—with antique crystal chandeliers and red velvet banquettes—attracts a well-dressed crowd; you probably won't make it past the doorman in shorts and sneakers. That said, the club prides itself on keeping the crowd diverse, so you don't have to be draped in the latest designer label to get inside. The bi-level space offers booth seating—with an elevated VIP area—but devoted dance fans will throw down just about anywhere. 440 N. Halsted St. (at Hubbard St.). ℂ **312/733-6699.** www.rednofive.com. Cover $10–$20. Subway/El: Green Line to Clinton.

Smart Bar A long-established name on the dance circuit, Smart Bar, tucked in the basement below the rock club **Metro** (p. 316), spins the latest musical forms, from underground house and punk to ethereal and gothic. The scene starts late, and the dancing denizens vary widely, depending on which bands are playing upstairs (concertgoers get free admission to the Smart Bar). The no-frills club, which has stayed in business (amazingly) since 1982, attracts a diverse and edgy crowd, and that's part of the appeal. This is an established Chicago spot where clubbers can come as they are, and you'll see a range of fashion. Smart Bar stays open until 5am on weekends. 3730 N. Clark St. (at Racine Ave.). ℂ **773/549-4140.** www.smartbarchicago.com. Cover $10–$15 on weekends (free with some shows at Metro). Subway/El: Red Line to Addison.

Sound-Bar DJs are the stars at this multilevel, high-tech dance club, which prides itself on booking top international nightlife names. The look is industrial chic, with silver banquettes, frosted-glass walls, and stainless-steel accents; holographic images and laser lights flash across the massive central dance floor. The crowd tends to be young and club-savvy on weeknights, with a little more diversity on weekends. (Dress well if you want to make it past the bouncers.) While there's a fair amount of posing, overall this crowd comes for the music, which includes electronic dance, trance, and house. If you want a primer on Chicago house, this is a good place to start. 226 W. Ontario St. (at Franklin St.). ℂ **312/787-4480.** www.sound-bar.com. Cover $20. Subway/El: Red Line to Grand, or Brown Line to Merchandise Mart.

Spy Bar This River North spot mixes an urban lounge look with house and progressive techno beats. The exposed brick, wood beams, and relatively compact size give the feel of a cool loft party—a really popular party, as you're likely to get up close and personal with other dancers on the weekend. There's limited bottle-service seating, but Spy Bar is mostly one big dance floor, where things really heat up during Saturday night's house music sets. 646 N. Franklin St. (at Ontario St.). ☎ **312/337-2191.** www.spybarchicago.com. Cover $20. Subway/El: Red Line to Grand.

Transit Carved out of a warehouse space beneath the elevated train tracks in the West Loop, Transit is a no-nonsense dance club that doesn't trick itself out with a wacky theme. Its 10,000 square feet feature a sleek, boldly colored geometric interior with modern, minimalist furniture. The post-industrial metal staircases surrounding the large dance-floor area lead to a VIP room, and an upper-level space where DJs spin Latin dance and reggaeton. The bone-rattling, state-of-the-art sound system blasting progressive dance, remixed hip-hop, and R&B draws die-hard dance fans. Transit is open Fridays and Saturdays; come wearing your best club attire. 1431 W. Lake St. ☎ **312/491-8600.** www.transitnightclub chicago.com. Cover $10. Subway/El: Green Line to Ashland.

Underground With its faux-grungy, bunkeresque look, this subterranean River North club might not look like a hot spot, but it draws Chicago's well-connected party elite and visiting Hollywood A-listers. The walls are adorned with a war room–like lighted map of the world, triangular nuclear fallout symbols are everywhere, and modelesque servers work the compact room in skimpy military-inspired get-ups. Two bars make getting a drink manageable, even when the club is crowded, and the sound system is sufficiently loud but never overbearing. The limited food menu of small bites is better than you might expect, but most regulars don't come here to eat—by the end of the night, half of the club is dancing on the banquettes. 56 W. Illinois St. (between Dearborn and Clark sts). ☎ **312/644-7600.** www.theundergroundchicago.com. Thurs-Fri 9pm-4am; Sat 9pm-5am; Sun 10pm-4am. Cover $20. Subway/El: Red Line to Grand.

Vision The spot known as Vision has been through several name and decor changes, but it keeps plugging away, taking advantage of a tourist-friendly location not far from Michigan Avenue. Stretching over four levels, Vision caters to the current club trend of providing different environments in different spaces. The dance floor—thumping with house, trance, progressive, and hip-hop—fills the first floor; upper floors offer plenty of nooks and crannies for groups to sit and chat. Vision prides itself on offering some of the best turntable talent in the city—the club's owners even bring in internationally known DJs for occasional residencies. The club is open on Fridays and Saturdays only. 640 N. Dearborn St. (at Ontario St.). ☎ **312/266-1944.** www.visionnightclub.com. Cover $10–$20. Subway/El: Red Line to Grand/State.

THE BAR & CAFE SCENE

If you want to soak up the atmosphere of an authentic neighborhood tavern or sports bar, it's best to venture beyond downtown. Lincoln Park, Wrigleyville, and Bucktown/Wicker Park have well-established nightlife zones that abound with bars that range from bright and upscale to borderline-dingy but full of character. You'll also find numerous dives and no-frills "corner taps" in the blue-collar neighborhoods.

LATE-NIGHT bites

Chicago's not much of a late-night dining town; most restaurants shut down by 10 or 11pm, leaving night owls with the munchies out of luck. But if you know where to go, you can still get a decent meal past midnight. Here are a few spots that serve real food until real late:

In the Loop, your best—and practically only—choice is **Miller's Pub** (p. 323), 134 S. Wabash Ave. (☎ 312/645-5377), which offers hearty American comfort food until 2am daily. Many late-night visitors to this historic watering hole and restaurant are out-of-towners staying at neighboring hotels.

In the South Loop, food is available until 4am at **Bar Louie** (p. 323), 47 W. Polk St. ☎ 312/347-0000). The menu is a step above mozzarella sticks and other standard bar food: Focaccia sandwiches, vegetarian wraps, and salads are among the highlights.

After a night out, Wicker Park and Bucktown residents stop by **Northside Café** (p. 144), 1635 N. Damen Ave. (☎ 773/384-3555), for sandwiches and salads served until 2am (3am Sat). In nice weather, the front patio is the place to be for prime people-watching.

The bright, welcoming atmosphere at **Clarke's Pancake House**

(pictured below), 2441 N. Lincoln Ave. (☎ 773/472-3505), is a dose of fresh air after an evening spent in dark Lincoln Park bars. Yes, there are pancakes on the menu, as well as plenty of other creative breakfast choices, including mixed skillets of veggies, meat, and potatoes. If you need to satisfy a *really* late-night craving, Clarke's is open 24 hours.

When the Lincoln Park bars shut down at 2am, the action moves to the **Wieners Circle,** 2622 N. Clark St. (☎ 773/477-7444). This hot dog stand is strictly no-frills: You shout your order across the drunken crowd, get sassed by the counter staff, then try to snag a spot on one of the picnic tables out front (the only seating provided). Open until 4am during the week and 6am on weekends, the Wieners Circle is the center of predawn life in Lincoln Park—and some people swear that the greasy cheese-topped fries are the perfect hangover prevention.

As for nightlife downtown, virtually every hotel in Chicago has some kind of bar. Many are little more than undistinguished groupings of tables and chairs in the lobby, but others have become trendy clublike hotspots. If you're looking for an old-school, cocktail-lounge vibe, the piano bar at The Drake Hotel, **Coq d'Or** (p. 318), is a standout. Some of the other top hotel lounges are highlighted in the box "Hotel Hopping," p. 324.

Bars

THE LOOP & VICINITY

Bar Louie A slightly more upscale take on the neighborhood bar concept, Bar Louie has built its reputation on better-than-average bar food and a creative selection of beers and cocktails. (The concept was so successful here that it's since expanded to cities across the country.) Bar Louie isn't doing anything revolutionary, but its friendly service and approachable atmosphere make it a popular spot for locals who want a casual night out. Professionals gather here after work in the Printer's Row neighborhood of the South Loop; their restaurant and club equivalents stop by between 1 and 3am. 47 W. Polk St. (at Federal St.). ✆ **312/347-0000.** www.restaurants-america.com/barlouie. Subway/El: Red Line to Harrison.

Lumen The gimmick at this former meat-packing facility in the West Loop is light, particularly the overhead LED display, which changes color throughout the night. The 5,000-square-foot space features concrete, stainless steel, and bamboo in its design, along with the aforementioned light spectacle, which is coordinated with its powerful sound system. There's no VIP list, which gives it an everyman kind of feel and means minimal line-waiting out front. 839 W. Fulton Market, at Halsted St. ✆ **312/733-2222.** www.lumen-chicago.com. Subway/El: Green Line to Clinton.

Miller's Pub ★ A true Loop landmark, Miller's has been serving up after-work cocktails to downtown office workers since 1935; it's one of the few places in the area that offers bar service until the early morning hours. There's also a full dinner menu. Autographed photos of movie stars and sports figures cover the walls; while some might be unrecognizable to younger patrons, they testify to the pub's long-standing tradition of friendly hospitality. 134 S. Wabash Ave. (btw. Jackson Blvd. and Adams St.). ✆ **312/645-5377.** www.millerspub.com. Subway/El: Red Line to Jackson.

Monk's Pub 👪 A no-nonsense hangout for downtown workers, this is the kind of joint you'd walk by without even knowing it's there. But once inside, you'll discover a one-of-a-kind, German–Old English hodgepodge of a place, where shelves stocked with vintage books line one wall and wooden barrels are tucked in the rafters overhead. In business since 1969, Monk's has a decent lineup of beer on tap, as well as a full lunch and dinner menu. (A burger is your best bet—they've got more than 10 varieties.) 205 W. Lake St. (btw. Randolph St. and the Chicago River). ✆ **312/357-6665.** www.mmonks.com. Subway/El: Brown Line to Clark/Lake.

The Tasting Room Step into this sophisticated wine bar, with its exposed-brick walls, high ceilings, and contemporary stainless-steel accents, and you'll feel like you've walked into a stylish friend's downtown loft. (Adding to the insider feeling is the remote far West Loop location, where few other tourists venture.) Located upstairs from Randolph Wine Cellars, a well-stocked wine shop, the Tasting Room caters to wine lovers with a variety of themed flights, as well as cheese and charcuterie plates. But even better than the vintages are the views, thanks to the large windows that look out over the Loop. 1415 W. Randolph St.,

Forget the stereotypical bland hotel bar filled with drunken conventioneers. In downtown Chicago, some of the most distinctive watering holes are in hotel lobbies. In the Loop, **Encore** in the Hotel Allegro, 171 W. Randolph St. (☎ **312/236-0123**), is a popular happy hour spot, with a black-and-white color scheme and urban lounge feel. For late-night drinks in a low-lit, intimate space, head to **Angels and Kings,** the bar in the Hard Rock Hotel, 230 N. Michigan Ave. (☎ **312/345-1000**). The look is glam rock, and the music (live acts or a DJ) is always good. If you prefer to stick to tradition, **Kitty O'Shea's,** 720 S. Michigan Ave. (☎ **312/294-6860**), is an authentically appointed Irish pub inside the Hilton Chicago—a genuine Irish bartender will even pour your Guinness. Farther north, in the blocks surrounding the Magnificent Mile, you'll find style-conscious spots such as **Le Bar,** in the Sofitel Chicago Water Tower, 20 E. Chestnut St. (☎ **312/324-4000**), a popular after-work hangout with a

sophisticated vibe. At **Whiskey Sky,** on the top floor of the W Chicago-Lakeshore Hotel, 644 N. Lakeshore Dr. (☎ **312/943-9200**), there's not much seating and the decor is minimal, but the views—of both the surrounding skyline and the gorgeous staff—are terrific. **Vertigo Sky Lounge,** atop the Dana Hotel and Spa, 660 N. State St. (☎ **312/202-6060**), is a dark, clublike space with live DJs, but expansive floor-to-ceiling windows make you feel like you're floating amid the high-rises. An added bonus is the outdoor deck, a great spot to take in the views when the weather's nice. But for sheer drama, the current hotel-bar champ is **Roof,** atop The Wit Hotel, 201 N. State St. (☎ **312/467-0200**). The sprawling space includes a Miami Beach–style terrace with fire pits for chilly nights and a large indoor seating area (with cozy fireplaces) so that even winter visitors can enjoy the views. If you dare, you can even book a table with a see-through glass floor that juts out from the roof's edge.

at Loomis St. ☎ **312/942-1313.** www.thetastingroomchicago.com. Subway/El: Green Line to Ashland, but I'd recommend a cab at night.

NEAR THE MAGNIFICENT MILE

Billy Goat Tavern 🔥 Hidden below the Wrigley Building is this storied Chicago hole-in-the-wall, a longtime hangout for newspaper reporters over the years, evidenced by the yellowed clippings and memorabilia papering the walls. The "cheezborger, cheezborger" served at the grill inspired the famous *Saturday Night Live* sketch. Despite all the press, the Goat has endured the hype without sacrificing a thing (including its vintage decor, which pretty much epitomizes the term *dive bar*). 430 N. Michigan Ave. ☎ **312/222-1525.** www.billygoattavern.com. Subway/El: Red Line to Grand/State.

Elm Street Liquors In a neighborhood often teeming with tourists, this lounge for locals exudes an urban but laid-back style with its anything-goes attitude. Dressing to impress here means an old-school T-shirt and Chuck Taylors (leave the striped button-down at home, boys). The music is familiar, and the drinks are forward-thinking, boasting cocktails made with champagne and beer rather than the ubiquitous flavored martinis found at almost every other nightspot in Chicago. 12 W. Elm St. (at State St.). ☎ **312/337-3200.** www.elmstreetliquors.com. Subway/El: Red Line to Clark/Division.

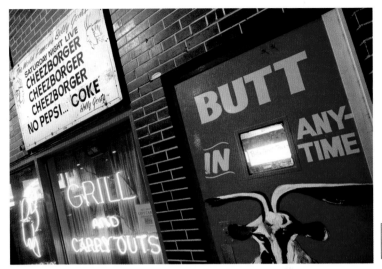
Billy Goat Tavern, a local watering hole and inspiration for a famous *Saturday Night Live* skit.

Signature Lounge For the price of a trip to the John Hancock tower observatory (two floors below), you can drink in the view and a cocktail at this lofty lounge. Yes, the drinks may be somewhat overpriced and you'll probably be surrounded by other tourists, but the views are fabulous (especially at sunset), making this an only-in-Chicago experience. You can also order from a limited menu of appetizers and desserts. This makes an especially appealing after-dinner stop; it's open until 12:30am Sunday through Thursday and until 1:30am on the weekends. 96th floor, John Hancock Center, 875 N. Michigan Ave. ℂ **312/787-7230.** www.signature room.com. Subway/El: Red Line to Chicago.

RIVER NORTH & VICINITY

Brehon Pub Big front windows, a high tin ceiling, and a great antique back bar lend charm to this little neighborhood bar in (often) tourist-packed River North. Brehon regulars hang out weeknights after work and even at lunchtime, when the tavern serves sandwiches and soup. In the 1970s, the *Sun-Times* newspaper set up this spot as a phony bar and used it to expose city corruption (see "The Great Bar Sting" box). 731 N. Wells St. (at Superior St.). ℂ **312/642-1071.** www.brehonpub. com. Subway/El: Red or Brown line to Chicago.

Butterfly Social Club At last, a lounge that Al Gore can appreciate. This eco-chic sister property to the **Funky Buddha** nightclub (p. 320) incorporates recy-cled and natural materials into its design, such as "trees" made from mud, sand, clay, and straw. Sip your drink (made with organic juice, of course) and curl up in one of the tree house–like nooks, or groove to the upbeat world music thump-ing through speakers made of recycled wood. 722 W. Grand Ave. (btw. Union Ave. and Halsted St.). ℂ **312/666-1695.** www.funkybuddha.com. Bus: 65 (Grand Ave.).

Celtic Crossings Drop in on a Saturday evening for the bar's weekly live Irish music concert, and you're sure to hear an authentic brogue. There's also a decent jukebox stocked with Irish and American favorites, delicious pints of Guinness (the best in Chicago, claim many Irish expats), tons of quaint bric-a-brac, and a

The Clark Street Ale House boasts more than 95 varieties of beer.

cozy fireplace. 751 N. Clark St. (btw. Superior St. and Chicago Ave.). ℂ **312/337-1005.** www. celticcrossingschicago.com. Subway/El: Red or Brown line to Chicago.

Clark Street Ale House 🎁 A handsome, convivial tavern and a popular after-work spot for white- and blue-collar types alike, Clark Street Ale House features a large open space filled with high tables and a long cherrywood bar along one wall. Better than the atmosphere are the 95 varieties of beer, a large majority of them from American microbreweries. The bar also offers a wide selection of scotches and cognacs. 742 N. Clark St. ℂ **312/642-9253.** www.clarkstreetalehouse.com. Subway/El: Red or Brown line to Chicago.

Fado This sprawling, multilevel theme-park facsimile of an Irish pub lures the masses on weekends, despite grumblings that this chain pub lacks authentic Irish soul. Bursting with woodwork, stone, and double-barreled Guinness taps (all of it imported from Ireland), Fado has several themed rooms, each designed to evoke a particular Irish pub style—country cottage and Victorian Dublin, for instance. The pub fare is above par. 100 W. Grand Ave. ℂ **312/836-0066.** www.fado irishpub.com/Chicago. Subway/El: Red Line to Grand.

J Bar Yes, this lounge is just off the lobby of the James Hotel, but it's no con-ventioneer hangout. The low-slung leather couches, seating cubes, and flickering votive candles give it the look of an upscale urban club, and its laid-back vibe has made it a gathering place for stylish locals in their 20s and 30s. The drinks also have a sense of style. (The house martini blends blue raspberry vodka and elderflower cordial and is served in a glass coated with a raspberry-candy shell.) *One drawback:* You have to call and reserve a table if you want to be guaranteed a place to sit into the late-night hours. 610 N. Rush St. (at E. Ontario St.). ℂ **312/660-7200.** www.jameshotels.com/Chicago.aspx. Subway/El: Red Line to Grand.

LaSalle Power Co. With a little something for everyone, this three-level night-spot opened in 2009 but has the semi-grungy vibe of a place that's been around far longer. The ground floor is the main bar area, where the cocktails lean toward the classics rather than original concoctions. Upstairs you'll find a diner-style restaurant where you can chow down on everything from burgers to waffles, while the top floor is a live-music club, which books mostly indie bands. With its black tables, booths, and red-lit ceilings, LaSalle Power Co. re-creates the look of a lost-in-time rock club, but the crowd is more clean-cut-Midwest than edgy-alternative. 500 N. LaSalle Blvd. (at Illinois St.). ✆ **312/661-1122.** www.lasallepowerco.com. Subway/El: Red Line to Grand.

Martini Ranch Staying in a Magnificent Mile hotel and looking for a late-night libation? Martini Ranch serves 40 different versions of its namesake cocktail until 4am during the week, attracting bar and nightlife insiders—and a fair share of insomniacs. The Western theme is subtle (paintings of Roy Rogers and other cowpoke art) and the seating is minimal (come early to snag one of the four red booths), but fans swear by the chocolate martini, and the pop-rock soundtrack keeps the energy level high. If the crowded bar scene is too much, chill out at the pool table in the back room, or settle down at one of the tables in the heated beer garden. 311 W. Chicago Ave. (at Orleans St.). ✆ **312/335-9500.** www.martiniranchchicago.com. Subway/El: Red or Brown line to Chicago.

Pops for Champagne 🛉 The Pops champagne bar is one of the prettiest rooms in the city, and its River North location makes it a convenient walk from most downtown hotels. The list of more than 125 varieties of bubbly includes a good selection by the glass—as well as staggeringly expensive impress-your-date bottles. A jazz trio plays Sunday through Thursday nights, starting at 9pm. 601 N. State St. (at Ohio St.). ✆ **312/266-7677.** www.popsforchampagne.com. Subway/El: Red Line to Grand.

Rockit Bar & Grill This roadhouse-chic restaurant and late-night hangout was designed by Oprah's sidekick, Nate Berkus (see restaurant listing on p. 126). The buzzing upstairs bar area is where clean-cut professionals in their 20s and 30s go to flirt or catch up with friends—there are some pool tables, but posing attractively seems to be the main recreational activity here. Expect to be among the nose-pressers cooling your heels outside if you don't arrive early enough. 22 W. Hubbard St. (btw. State and Dearborn sts.). ✆ **312/645-6000.** www.rockitbarandgrill.com. Subway/El: Red Line to Grand.

10pin A modern interpretation of the classic bowling alley, this lounge is tucked away under the Marina Towers complex on the Chicago River. Everything feels bright and new (even the rental shoes), and there's a full menu of designer beers and upscale snacks (gourmet pizzas, smoked salmon, specialty martinis). A giant video screen overlooks the 24 bowling lanes, and a top-notch sound system gives the place a nightclubby vibe. You don't *have* to bowl—the bar area is a casual, welcoming place to hang out—but I'd certainly recommend giving it a try. 330 N. State St. (btw. Kinzie St. and the Chicago River). ✆ **312/644-0300.** www.10pinchicago.com. Subway/El: Red Line to Grand or Brown Line to Merchandise Mart.

RUSH & DIVISION STREETS

Around Rush Street are what a bygone era called singles bars—although the only singles that tend to head here now are suburbanites, out-of-towners, and barely legal partiers. Rush Street's glory days may be long gone, but there are still a few vestiges of the old times on nearby Division Street, which overflows with party-hearty spots that attract a loud, frat-party element. They include **Shenanigan's House of Beer,** 16 W. Division St. (✆ 312/642-2344); **Butch McGuire's,** 20 W. Division St. (✆ 312/337-9080); the **Lodge,** 21 W. Division St. (✆ 312/642-4406); and **Mother's,** 26 W. Division St. (✆ 312/642-7251). Many of these bars offer discounts for women, as loud pitchmen in front of each establishment will be happy to tell any attractive ladies who pass by.

OLD TOWN

The center of nightlife in Old Town is **Wells Street,** home to Second City and Zanies Comedy Club, as well as a string of reliable restaurants and bars, many of which have been in business for decades. You're not going to find many trendy spots in Old Town; the nightlife here tends toward neighborhood pubs and casual restaurants, filled mostly with a late-20s and 30-something crowd.

Corcoran's Owned by the same family for more than 30 years, this is one of Old Town's favorite local hangouts, and it makes a good stop before or after a show at Second City, which is located right across the street. The cozy, wood-lined interior and hearty pub food (bangers and mash, shepherd's pie, fish and chips) will put you right at ease. In nice weather, check out the beer garden in back, which offers a tranquil retreat from the city traffic. 1615 N. Wells St. (at North Ave.). ✆ **312/440-0885.** www.vaughanhospitality.com. Subway/El: Brown Line to Sedgwick.

Goose Island Brewing Company 🎁 The city's best-known brewpub is somewhat hidden on the western fringes of Old Town, but it's well worth the trip for beer lovers. The attractive, high-ceilinged space—with exposed-brick walls and a large central bar—is a welcoming place to linger while sampling Goose's ever-changing lineup of drinks. Their basic lager, Honker's Ale, is the most popular, but you can also order porters, stouts, and pilsners; try a tasting sampler if you can't make up your mind. The attached restaurant serves comfort food dishes that are quite a few notches up from standard bar food (p. 137). Goose Island also has an outpost in Wrigleyville, at 3535 N. Clark St. (✆ 773/832-9040). 1800 N. Clybourn Ave. ✆ **312/915-0071.** www.gooseisland.com. Subway/El: Brown Line to Armitage.

Old Town Ale House This was one of Old Town's legendary saloons until the ironic college kids discovered it. A dingy neighborhood hangout since the late 1950s, with a fading mural that captures the likenesses of a class of regulars from the early 1970s, the place has been cleaned up somewhat, but its divey vibe remains. The old-timers may have moved on and made way for a mainly 20s clientele, but the jukebox is still filled with a selection of crooner tunes and instrumental jazz. 219 W. North Ave. (at Wells St.). © **312/944-7020.** www.oldtownalehouse. net. Subway/El: Brown Line to Sedgwick.

Spoon The closest Old Town has to a trendy nightspot, this bar and restaurant pulls in an attractive, professional crowd on weekend evenings. The modern, loft-like space would be right at home in the River North neighborhood, but it's a novelty in tradition-bound Old Town. Although Spoon attracts loud groups of singles on weekends, weeknights are a little less frenzied, and locals are able to sip their Mucho Mango martinis in peace. 1240 N. Wells St. (at Division St.). © **312/642-5522.** www.spoonchicago.com. Subway/El: Red Line to Clark/Division.

Stanley's Kitchen & Tap Staying true to the neighborhood bar formula, Stanley's has built its long-standing reputation on providing a comfortable atmosphere and good food for its loyal patrons. Stanley's has a Southern-roadhouse–inspired vibe and home-style cooking, and is a great place to catch a game (and don't forget the free mashed potatoes offered every night at midnight). Sunday nights are live-band karaoke, which often attracts musicians passing through town and a host of athletes such as the Chicago Blackhawks hockey team. If you need to recover from a big night out, Stanley's also has a popular Sunday buffet, with a Bloody Mary bar. 1970 N. Lincoln Ave. (at Armitage Ave.). © **312/642-0007.** www. stanleyskitchenandtap.com. Bus: 22 (Clark St.).

LINCOLN PARK

Lincoln Park, with its high concentration of apartment-dwelling singles, is one of the busiest nightlife destinations in Chicago. Prime real estate is at a premium in this residential neighborhood, so you won't find many warehouse-size dance clubs here; most of the action is at pubs and bars. Concentrations of in-spots run along Halsted Street and Lincoln Avenue.

The Duke of Perth This traditional Scottish pub serves one of the city's best selections of single-malt whiskey, along with cross-cultural specialties such as the Scotch Egg Burger (topped with a fried egg and roasted red pepper). You can also dig in to more traditional pub food, such as the baskets of fish and chips (on Wed and Fri, get all you can eat for $9.50). The outdoor beer garden is especially inviting on warm summer nights. 2913 N. Clark St. (at Wellington Ave.). © **773/477-1741.** www.dukeofperth.com. Subway/El: Brown Line to Diversey.

Duke's Bar and Grill 🎁 Sophisticated yet unpretentious, Duke's looks like a cross between a mountain lodge and an urban cocktail lounge, with broad-plank wood walls and cream-colored leather banquettes. It's attractive enough to feel like a step up from a neighborhood bar, but the vibe never gets snooty. If you're hungry, try one of the burgers: There are always at least 20 varieties on the menu. It's a good bet you'll be surrounded by locals who think of Duke's as their own special discovery. 2616 N. Clark St. © **773/248-0250.** www.dukeschicago.com. Bus: 22 (Clark).

Galway Arms The large heated front patio, which is open from St. Patrick's Day through late fall, sets this Irish bar apart from all the other pubs in town. Indoors, the quaint, cozy dining rooms with fireplaces attract a slightly more up-scale crowd than other neighboring watering holes. Every Sunday night, the pub hosts a traditional Irish music session, where a rotating group of musicians jams from 8pm on. 2442 N. Clark St. (at Arlington). © **773/472-5555.** www.galwayarms.com. Subway/El: Red or Brown line to Fullerton.

Glascott's Groggery A favorite meeting spot for young Lincoln Park professionals, Glascott's has been in the same family since it opened in 1937. It attracts an eclectic mix of neighborhood regulars of all ages: groups of guys stopping in after their weekly basketball game, couples coming in after dinner to catch up with their friends, and singles discretely checking each other out. 2158 N. Halsted St. (at Webster Ave.). © **773/281-1205.** www.glascotts.com. Subway/El: Brown Line to Armitage.

Tilli's A favorite gathering spot for good-looking 20- and 30-somethings, Tilli's is an upscale version of the neighborhood bar. In nice weather, the entire front opens to the street; when it's chilly, try to snag a table near the brick fireplace in the main dining room. You can snack on appetizers or order dinner, but the main attraction is the front room, where everyone people-watches around the bar. 1952 N. Halsted St. (at Armitage Ave.). © **773/325-0044.** www.tillischicago.com. Subway/El: Brown Line to Armitage.

Webster's Wine Bar It's a bit off the beaten track—on the western fringe of Lincoln Park—but the low-lit, sophisticated decor makes Webster's a good alternative to the usual beer blast. The waitstaff can help you choose from a list of dozens of wines by the bottle or glass, or you can hone your taste buds with a flight of several wines. There's also a tapas-style menu for noshing. Step back into the library area to recline on the couch. 1480 W. Webster Ave. (btw. Clybourn and Ashland aves.). © **773/868-0608.** www.websterwinebar.com. Subway/El: Red or Brown line to Fullerton, and then a short cab ride.

WRIGLEYVILLE, LAKEVIEW & THE NORTH SIDE

Real estate in Wrigleyville and Lakeview is a tad less expensive than in Lincoln Park, so the nightlife scene here skews a little younger. You'll find a mostly post-collegiate crowd partying on Clark Street across from Wrigley Field (especially after games in the summer). But head away from the ball field, and you'll discover some more exotic choices.

Chicago Brauhaus Lincoln Square—a few miles northwest of Wrigley Field—used to be the heart of Chicago's German community. Although not much of that tradition remains, a few Old World–style delis and European shops (including a terrific old-fashioned apothecary) dot Lincoln Avenue from Wilson to Lawrence avenues. For a dose of Oktoberfest at any time of year, stop into the Brauhaus. German bands perform on weekends, when the older crowd puts the young-sters to shame on the dance floor. The Erdinger, Spaten, and BBK flow freely, and the kitchen serves up big plates of 'wurst, schnitzel, and sauerkraut. 4732 N. Lincoln Ave. (btw. Leland and Lawrence aves.). © **773/784-4444.** www.chicagobrauhaus. com. Subway/El: Brown Line to Western.

404 Wine Bar One of the most inviting bars in the city, 404 Wine Bar makes you feel as if you've been invited to a party in a private home (it adjoins Jack's, a standard sports-and-beer spot; make sure you go in the entrance on the left side of the building). Tables and soft leather couches fill a series of cozy, low-lit rooms; the laid-back vibe attracts groups of friends and couples rather than on-the-prowl singles. The wine list features more than 100 labels from around the world, all fairly reasonably priced. Order by the bottle, glass, or flight. (The selection changes every 2 weeks.) In the summer, tables are set up in an outdoor courtyard; in the winter, fireplaces fill the rooms with a warm glow. 2852 N. Southport Ave. (at George St.). © **773/404-5886.** www.404winebarchicago.com. Subway/El: Brown Line to Wellington.

Ginger Man Tavern Ginger Man definitely plays against type in a row of predictable sports bars across the street from Wrigley Field. On game days, the earthy bar has been known to crank classical music in an attempt to calm drunken fans—or at least shoo them away. Pool tables (free on Sun) are always busy with slightly bohemian neighborhood 20-something

The cozy, low-lit rooms at 404 Wine Bar are perfect for sipping a wide variety of wines.

things, who have more than 80 beers to choose from. 3740 N. Clark St. (at Racine Ave.). © **773/549-2050.** Subway/El: Red Line to Addison.

Irish Oak Owned and staffed by folks from the Old Sod, this is one of the city's nicest Irish bars. It may be little more than 10 years old, but the handsome woodwork, copper canopy over the bar, and eclectic collection of antiques give the tavern a timeless feel. There are plenty of whiskeys, stouts, and ales to sip, and the kitchen offers shepherd's pie and other Irish fare. Overall, the mood is laid-back and mellow—except when the post–Cubs game crowds invade. Things also liven up on Friday and Saturday nights, when local bands perform. 3511 N. Clark St. (btw. Cornelia Ave. and Addison St.). © **773/935-6669.** www.irishoak.com. Subway/El: Red Line to Addison.

Sheffield's Beer and Wine Garden A popular neighborhood gathering spot for years, the main claim to fame at Sheffield's is the large beer garden, where you can order off an extensive menu of BBQ dishes. The bar boasts a selection of more than 30 draft beers, including a number of specialty craft beers and one featured beer of the month. Sheffield's can get jammed with a young, loud crowd, but the attitude is welcoming—there always seems to be room to squeeze in one more person. 3258 N. Sheffield Ave. (btw. Belmont Ave. and Roscoe St.). © **773/281-4989.** www.sheffieldschicago.com. Subway/El: Red or Brown line to Belmont.

WICKER PARK & BUCKTOWN

The closest Chicago has to an alternative scene is Wicker Park and Bucktown, where both slackers and adventurous suburbanites populate bars dotting the streets leading out from the intersection of North, Damen, and Milwaukee avenues. Don't dress up if you want to blend in: A casually bohemian getup and low-key attitude are all you need. While you can reach most of these places relatively easily by public transportation, I recommend taking a cab at night—the surrounding neighborhoods are what I'd call "transitional."

Betty's Blue Star Lounge Just south of Wicker Park in Ukrainian Village, what was once an unpretentious neighborhood tavern has been transformed into a pseudo-trendy late-night destination. The action is in the back room, equipped with a stellar sound system and lots of mirrors. This wannabe club enforces a dress code on the weekends (no sneakers or shorts), as well as an annoying $10 cover. But it's one of the only places in the area with live DJs and a dance floor, so if you're looking to get your groove on, you may well end up here. Betty's has a 5am license on Saturday; the early morning people-watching can be priceless. 1600 W. Grand Ave. ✆ **312/243-8778.** www.bettysbluestarlounge.com. Bus: 65 (Grand Ave.), but I'd recommend a cab at night.

The Bucktown Pub ✍ The owners' collection of groovy 1960s and '70s rock-'n'-roll posters and cartoon art is phenomenal. However, most Bucktown patrons are more interested in nursing their pints of imported and domestic microbrews than in gawking at the walls. Other Wicker Park/Bucktown bars try to come off as low-key; this is the real thing, where attitude is firmly discouraged at the door and dogs are welcome until 8pm. The psychedelic- and glam-rock–filled jukebox keeps toes tapping, and competition on the skittle-bowling machine can get quite fierce. Credit cards not accepted. 1658 W. Cortland St. (at Paulina St.). ✆ **773/394-9898.** www.bucktownpub.com. Subway/El: Blue Line to Damen.

The California Clipper Located in Humboldt Park (southwest of Wicker Park), the Clipper is a bit removed from the main drag, but this beautifully restored 1940s tavern is well worth seeking out, with its gorgeous Art Deco bar and red walls bathed in dim light. Friday and Saturday nights feature live music, mostly rockabilly and "country swing." And the Clipper is proud to have no TVs. 1002 N. California Ave. ✆ **773/384-2547.** www.californiaclipper.com. Subway/El: Blue Line to Division, then a short cab ride.

Cortland's Garage This cozy spot in Bucktown is unpretentious and cleanly designed, with a retractable glass garage door in front, and exposed brick walls and leather-clad bench seating inside. Nine high-definition TVs broadcast sports games, some with the sound turned up, while DJs spin records Friday and Saturday nights from 10pm until close. 1645 W. Cortland St. (btw. Ashland and Hermitage aves.). ✆ **773/862-7877.** www.cortlandsgarage.com. Subway/El: Blue Line to Damen.

Danny's Tavern Located off the beaten Milwaukee/Damen path, Danny's has become the neighborhood hangout of choice for Bucktown's original angry young men and women, the ones who complain that an influx of yuppies is ruining the area. Just finding Danny's takes insider knowledge: The only sign out front flashes SCHLITZ in neon red. Inside, votive candles on the tables provide dim lighting; head to the back room to grab a seat on the leather couches and chairs. Once there, you can revel in the fact that you're hanging with the cool kids—just don't let them know you're a tourist. And bring cash—Danny's doesn't accept credit cards. 1951 W. Dickens Ave. (at Damen Ave.). ✆ **773/489-6457.** Subway/El: Blue Line to Damen.

EvilOlive That's right, it's a palindrome, and the palindromes don't end with the name of this 4am bar (5am on Sat); they're also scribbled on the wall ("If I had a hi-fi") and printed on the drink menu (try a "Dr. Awkward"). Hand-stuffed olives

Wicker Park/Bucktown After Dark

W. Webster Ave.

N. Elston Ave.

N. Ashland Ave.

N. Branch Chicago River

W. Dickens Ave.

W. Dickens Ave.

W. McLean Ave.

W. Armitage Ave.

W. Armitage Ave.

N. Hoyne Ave.

John F. Kennedy Expressway

W. Homer St.

BUCKTOWN

N. Campbell Ave.

N. Western Ave.

N. Oakley Ave.

W. Cortland St.

W. Cortland St.

W. Moffat St.

Western Ⓜ

Wilmot Ave.

N. Milwaukee Ave.

W. Churchill St.

N. Leavitt St.

N. Damen Ave.

N. Winchester Ave.

N. Wolcott Ave.

W. Bloomingdale Ave.

N. Winnebago Ave.

W. Bloomingdale Ave.

W. St. Paul Ave.

W. Willow St.

W. St. Paul Ave.

N. Hermitage Ave.

N. Paulina St.

N. Marshfield Ave.

N. Ashland Ave.

94

90

W. Wabansia Ave.

W. Wabansia Ave.

N. Oakley Ave.

N. Wood St.

W. Concord Pl.

64

N. Campbell Ave.

N. Artesian Ave.

N. Leavitt St.

Claremont

Oakley

N. Bell Ave.

W. North Ave.

64

Flat Iron Building

W. North Ave.

64

Damen Ⓜ

W. Pierce Ave.

W. Pierce Ave.

N. Elk Grove Ave.

W. Le Moyne St.

W. Le Moyne St.

W. Le Moyne St.

W. Julian St.

WICKER PARK

W. Schiller St.

N. Milwaukee Ave.

W. Beach Ave.

W. Blackhawk St.

N. Bosworth Ave.

WICKER PARK

W. Evergreen Ave.

N. Hoyne Ave.

Damen Ave.

W. Potomac Ave.

W. Ellen St.

N. Marion Ct.

N. Honore St.

N. Wood St.

W. Crystal St.

CLEMENTE PARK

Division Ⓜ

W. Division St.

W. Division St.

W. Haddon St.

W. Haddon St.

W. Haddon St.

N. Western Ave.

N. Oakley Blvd.

W. Thomas St.

W. Thomas St.

W. Cortez St.

W. Cortez St.

N. Winchester Ave.

N. Wolcott Ave.

N. Honore St.

N. Ashland Ave.

W. Augusta Blvd.

W. Augusta Blvd.

N. Hoyne Ave.

N. Damen Ave.

⑪

W. Walton St.

Ⓜ Subway/El stop

0   1/4 mi
0   0.25 km

N. Leavitt St.

W. Iowa St.

W. Iowa St.

W. Rice St.

94

41

90

Wrigley Field

Map area

CHICAGO

THE LOOP

290

U.S. Cellular Field

55

90

41

✈ Midway

Lake Michigan

0   3 mi
0   3 km

Betty's Blue Star Lounge **12**

The Bucktown Pub **5**

The California Clipper **11**

Cortland's Garage **4**

Danny's Tavern **2**

Davenport's Piano Bar & Cabaret **8**

Double Door **7**

EvilOlive **10**

The Map Room **1**

Marie's Riptide Lounge **8**

Phyllis' Musical Inn **9**

The Violet Hour **6**

333

are a specialty here, too, both in drinks and on plates. The place has an upscale rock club feel, with oversize booths, a pool table, a photo booth, and projected movies. A DJ spins rock and hip-hop well into the wee hours. 15551 W. Division St. (at Ashland Ave.). ✆ **773/235-9100.** www.evil-olive.com. Subway/El: Blue Line to Division.

The Map Room ★ 👜 Hundreds of travel books and guides line the shelves of this globe-trotter's tavern. Peruse that tome on Fuji or Antarctica while sipping a pint of one of the 25-odd draft beers. The Map Room's equally impressive selection of bottled brews (more than 200) makes this place popular with beer geeks as well as the tattered-passport crew. Tuesday is "International Night," featuring the food, music, and spirits of a certain country, accompanied by a slide show and tales from a recent visitor. 1949 N. Hoyne Ave. (at Armitage Ave.). ✆ **773/252-7636.** www.maproom.com. Subway/El: Blue Line to Damen.

Marie's Riptide Lounge Nothing here looks as though it has been updated since the 1960s (owner Marie is long past retirement age), but personal touches and the retro cool of the place have made it a hip stop on the late-night circuit. A jukebox stocked with campy oldies, a curious low-tech duck-hunting "video" game, and the occasional blast of black light make Marie's a hoot. The owner takes great pains to decorate the interior of the little bar for each holiday season. (The wintertime "snow-covered" bar is not to be missed.) 1745 W. Armitage Ave. (at Hermitage Ave.). ✆ **773/278-7317.** Subway/El: Blue Line to Damen.

The Violet Hour This bar has a retro ambience that's unique in the Chicago nightlife scene, especially in verging-on-gritty Wicker Park. The interior feels like an English or French country manor, with blue walls and white crown molding; glittering chandeliers; extra-high wingback chairs; and dramatic floor-length curtains. The door policy maintains the civilized mood: Customers aren't admitted until there's room for them to sit (and, no, they don't take reservations, so you might be waiting a while on weekends). The specialties here are cocktails served up by expert "mixologists" (don't call them bartenders!), such as the Juliet & Romeo, a mix of gin, mint, cucumber, and rose water. ***One annoyance:*** The bar is too cool to put a sign out front; you'll find it on the corner of Damen Avenue and Pierce Street, marked only by a series of abstract, multicolored murals. 1520 N. Damen Ave. (at Pierce St.). ✆ **773/252-1500.** www.theviolet700.com. Subway/El: Blue Line to Damen.

Cafes

Café Jumping Bean A great little cafe in the heart of Pilsen, just southwest of the Loop, the Jumping Bean is ideal for taking in this vibrant Mexican-American neighborhood. It serves the usual espresso drinks, muffins, and pastries, but it also offers decent salads, cheesecakes, natural vegetable and fruit juices, and—best of all—a tantalizing selection of *liquados,* Mexican drinks made with milk, sugar, ice, and fresh fruit (try the mango). The artistic doings outside, characterized by colorful outdoor murals, spill over into the cafe, which features rotating exhibitions of paintings and hand-painted tables by local artists. The place even schedules live flamenco music and poetry readings in Spanish. Everyone is welcome, from families with little kids to the loft-dwelling artists who've lately infiltrated Pilsen. 1439 W. 18th St. (2 blocks east of Ashland Ave.). ✆ **312/455-0019.** www.cafejumpingbean.org. Subway/El: Blue Line to 18th St.

Intelligentsia A down-to-earth San Francisco married couple set up this coffee-roasting operation in the heart of Lakeview, and their brew has become one

Café Jumping Bean embodies the vibrant Mexican-American Pilsen neighborhood.

of the most popular in town. (You'll see it on the menus of some of the city's top restaurants.) A French roaster dominates the cafe, and the owners also make their own herbal and black teas. Warm drinks are served in handsome cups nearly too big to get your hands around, and tea sippers receive their own pots and brew timers. Sit at the window or, in fair weather, at a table on the sidewalk. 3123 N. Broadway Ave. (btw. Belmont Ave. and Diversey Pkwy.). © **773/348-8058.** www.intelligentsia coffee.com. Subway/El: Red Line to Addison.

Julius Meinl ★ Austria's premier coffee roaster chose Chicago—and, mysteriously, a location near Wrigley Field—for its first U.S. outpost. The result is a mix of Austrian style (upholstered banquettes, white marble tables, newspapers hanging on wicker frames) and American cheeriness (lots of natural light, smiling waitstaff, smoke-free air). The excellent coffee and hot chocolate are served European style on small silver platters with a glass of water on the side, but it's the desserts that keep the regulars coming back. Try the apple strudel or millennium torte (glazed with apricot jam and chocolate ganache), and for a moment you'll swear you're in Vienna. 3601 N. Southport Ave. (at Addison St.). © **773/868-1857.** www.meinl.com/northamerica/home.html. Subway/El: Brown Line to Southport.

Third Coast ★ Just steps from the raucous frat-boy atmosphere of Division Street is this laid-back, classic, independent coffeehouse. The below-ground space is no-frills but comfortable, attracting a mix of office workers, students, and neighborhood regulars. The full menu is available late, and the drinks run the gamut from lattes to cocktails. There's often some kind of folk music on weekends. 1260 N. Dearborn St. (north of Division St.). ✆ **312/649-0730.** www.3rdcoastcafe.com. Subway/El: Red Line to Clark/Division.

Uncommon Ground ★★ When you're looking for refuge from Cubs game days and party nights in Wrigleyville, Uncommon Ground offers a dose of laid-back, vaguely bohemian civility. Just off busy Clark Street, the cafe has a fireplace in winter (when the cafe's bowl—yes, bowl—of hot chocolate is a sight for cold eyes) and a spacious sidewalk operation in more temperate months. Breakfast is served all day, plus there's a full lunch and dinner menu. Music figures strongly, with live performances from singer-songwriters on weekends. Open until 2am daily. There's also another location, in Rogers Park on the far North Side of the city, at 1401 W. Devon Ave. (✆ **773/465-9801**). 1214 W. Grace St. (at Clark St.). ✆ **773/929-3680.** www.uncommonground.com. Subway/El: Red Line to Addison.

THE GAY & LESBIAN SCENE

Most of Chicago's gay bars are conveniently clustered on a stretch of North Halsted Street in Lakeview (in what's known as Boys Town), making it easy to sample many of them in a breezy walk. Men's bars predominate—few places in town cater exclusively to lesbians—but a few gay bars get a mix of men and women. A helpful free resource is the weekly entertainment guide *Nightspots*. The bars and clubs recommended below don't charge a cover unless otherwise noted.

Berlin Step into this frenetic Lakeview danceteria, and you're immediately swept into the mood. The disco tunes pulse, the clubby crowd chatters, and the lighting bathes everyone in a cool reddish glow. Special nights are dedicated to disco, amateur drag, and 1980s new wave; male dancers perform some nights. Don't bother showing up before midnight; the club stays open until 4am Friday and 5am Saturday. 954 W. Belmont Ave. (east of Sheffield Ave.). ✆ **773/348-4975.** www.berlinchicago.com. Cover after midnight Fri–Sat $5. Subway/El: Red or Brown line to Belmont.

Big Chicks 👬 One of the more bohemian bars in the city, Big Chicks is a magnet for the artsy goateed set (perhaps a bit weary of the bars on Halsted St.), lesbians, a smattering of straights, and random locals from the surrounding rough-hewn neighborhood. (The bar's motto is "Never a Cover, Never an Attitude.") They come for owner Michelle Fire's superb art collection, the midnight shots, and the free buffet on Sunday afternoon. There is also dancing on weekends. The same owner also runs the restaurant next door, **Tweet,** 5020 N. Sheridan Rd. (✆ **773/728-5576**), which offers a menu of mostly organic American comfort food; it has become a popular gay-friendly weekend brunch spot. 5024 N. Sheridan Rd. (btw. Argyle St. and Foster Ave.). ✆ **773/728-5511.** www.bigchicks.com. Subway/El: Red Line to Berwyn.

Circuit It has all the necessary nightclub elements: flashing lights, a killer sound system, the biggest dance floor in Boys Town, and plenty of eye candy. Open till 4am on weekends, Circuit attracts a hard-partying, minimally dressed crowd after all the other local bars have closed. Friday is "girls' night." 3641 N. Halsted St. (at Addison St.). ✆ **773/325-2233.** www.circuitclub.com. $5–$10 cover. Subway/El: Red Line to Addison.

The Closet The Closet is an unpretentious neighborhood spot with a loud and constant loop of music videos (and sports, when the game matters) that draws mostly lesbian regulars, although gay men and straights also show up. The space is not much bigger than a closet, which makes it easy to get up close and personal with other partiers. There's also a small dance floor that's usually packed on weekends. Open until 4am every night, 5am on Saturday. 3325 N. Broadway Ave. (at Buckingham St.). ✆ **773/477-8533.** Subway/El: Red or Brown line to Belmont.

Cocktail This corner spot is a friendly hangout in the afternoons and early evenings, when it's easy to converse and watch the passing parade from big picture windows (on Sun afternoons, regulars even stop by with their dogs in tow). Things get a little more frenzied after 10pm, Thursday through Sunday, when the club's lineup of go-go dancers hits the floor. 3359 N. Halsted St. (at Roscoe St.). ✆ **773/477-1420.** www.cocktailbarchicago.com. Subway/El: Red or Brown line to Belmont.

Crew Crew is a gay-friendly sports bar, where local softball leagues stop by for a drink after the game. Up to eight pro games play on multiple TVs, and there's a full menu of sandwiches, salads, and shareable appetizer plates. Located in the residential neighborhood of Uptown, a few miles north of the main Halsted Street strip, Crew attracts a crowd that's more interested in hanging out than hooking up. The same owners also own a pub next door, **Wild Pug,** 4810 N. Broadway Ave. (✆ **773/784-4811**), which has DJs and dancing on the weekends. 4804 N. Broadway Ave. (at Lawrence St.). ✆ **773/784-CREW** [2739]. www.worldsgreatestbar.com. Subway/El: Red Line to Lawrence.

Downtown With almost all gay-friendly hangouts concentrated on the North Side of the city, this friendly River North bar is the only one convenient to downtown condos and hotels, making it a draw for out-of-town visitors, Loop office workers, and high-rise dwellers. The look is low-key, as is the clientele—except when the occasional cabaret performer adds a dose of drama. 440 N. State St. (at Illinois St.). ✆ **312/464-1400.** www.downtownbarandlounge.com. Subway/El: Red Line to Grand.

Roscoe's Tavern 🏳️ The picture windows facing Halsted Street make Roscoe's, a gay neighborhood bar in business since 1987, an especially welcoming place. It has a large antiques-filled front bar, an outdoor patio, a pool table, and a large dance floor. The 20- and 30-something crowd is friendly and laid-back—except on weekends, when the dance floor is hopping. The cafe serves sandwiches and salads. 3356 N. Halsted St. (at Roscoe St.). ✆ **773/281-3355.** www.roscoes.com. Cover after 10pm Sat $4. Subway/El: Red or Brown line to Belmont.

Scarlet The name of this lounge is an homage to the semi-underground gay community of the 1920s, when members wore a piece of scarlet-colored clothing to signal their affiliation to others. Today, though you can wear whatever you want here, the attractively designed space might inspire you to take your wardrobe up a notch. From the glowing red-orange lights behind the bar to the red glass chandelier in the men's room, Scarlet has a more upscale vibe than most other places in Boys Town—and attracts an upscale clientele to match. 3320 N. Halsted St. (at Aldine Ave.). ✆ **773/348-1053.** www.scarletbarchicago.com. Subway/El: Red or Brown line to Belmont.

Sidetrack 🎁 If you make it to Roscoe's (see above), you'll no doubt end up at Sidetrack. The popular bars are across the street from each other, and there's a constant flow of feet between the two. Sidetrack is a sleek video bar where TV monitors are never out of your field of vision, nor are the preppy professional patrons. Don't miss Show Tunes Night on Sunday, Monday, and Friday, when the whole place sings along to Broadway and MGM musical favorites. 3349 N. Halsted St. (at Roscoe St.). ✆ **773/477-9189.** www.sidetrackchicago.com. Subway/El: Red or Brown line to Belmont.

Spin This dance club attracts one of Halsted Street's most colorful crowds, a mix of pretty boys, nerds, tough guys, and the occasional drag queen. The video bar in front houses pool tables and plays a steady stream of dance-friendly music videos. The club thumps with house music. Spin keeps regulars coming back with daily theme parties, featuring everything from Friday-night shower contests to cheap drinks. 800 W. Belmont Ave. (at Halsted St.). ✆ **773/327-7711.** www.spin-nightclub.com. Cover $5 Sat. Subway/El: Red or Brown line to Belmont.

The Gay & Lesbian Scene

CHICAGO AFTER DARK

PLANNING YOUR TRIP TO CHICAGO

10

A s with any trip, a little advance preparation will pay off once you arrive in Chicago. This chapter provides a variety of planning tools, including information on how to get here, local visitor resources, and tips on getting around. As a major American city, Chicago has a variety of public transportation options, from trains and buses to taxis and bike rentals, so finding your way between the sights is relatively easy once you've got your bearings.

GETTING THERE
By Plane

Chicago's **O'Hare International Airport** (✆ 773/686-2200; www.flychicago.com; online airport code ORD) has long battled Atlanta's Hartsfield-Jackson Airport for the title of the world's busiest airport. O'Hare is about 15 miles northwest of downtown Chicago. Depending on traffic, the drive to or from the city center can take anywhere from 30 minutes to more than an hour during the busy morning and afternoon rush hours.

O'Hare has information booths in all five terminals; most are on the baggage level. The multilingual employees, who wear red jackets, can assist travelers with everything from arranging ground transportation to getting information about local hotels. The booths, labeled "Airport Information," are open daily from 9am to 8pm.

Every major U.S. airline and most large international airlines fly in to O'Hare. You'll find the widest range of choices on United Airlines (which is headquartered in Chicago) and American Airlines (which has a hub at O'Hare). To find out which other airlines travel to Chicago, please see "Airline Websites."

At the opposite end of the city, on the southwest side, is Chicago's other major airport, **Midway International Airport** (✆ 773/838-0600; www.flychicago.com; online airport code MDW). Although it's smaller than O'Hare and handles fewer airlines, Midway is closer to the Loop and attracts more discount airlines, so you may be able to get a cheaper fare flying into here. (Always check fares to both airports if you want to find the best deal.) A cab ride from Midway to the Loop usually takes between 20 and 30 minutes. You can find the latest information on both airports at the city's Department of Aviation website: www.flychicago.com.

GETTING INTO TOWN FROM O'HARE & MIDWAY

Taxis are plentiful at both O'Hare and Midway, but you can get downtown relatively easily by public transportation as well. A cab ride into the city will cost about $35 from O'Hare and $25 from Midway. *One warning:* Rush-hour traffic can be horrendous, especially around O'Hare, and the longer you sit in the traffic, the higher the fare will be.

PREVIOUS PAGE: **No trip to Chicago is complete without a ride on the El.**

PLANNING YOUR TRIP | Getting There

If you're not carting a lot of luggage and want to save money, I highly recommend taking public transportation, which is convenient from both airports. For $2.25, you can take the El (elevated train) straight into downtown.

O'Hare is on the Blue Line; a trip to downtown takes about 40 minutes. (If you're staying on or near Michigan Ave., you'll want to switch to the Red Line, which will add another 10 or 15 min. to your trip.) Trains leave every 6 to 10 minutes during the day and early evening, and every half-hour at night.

Getting downtown from Midway is much faster; the ride on the Orange Line takes 20 to 30 minutes. (The Orange Line stops operating each night at about 11:30pm and resumes service by 5am.) Trains leave the station every 6 to 15 minutes. The train station is a fair walk from the terminal—without the benefit of O'Hare's moving sidewalks—so be prepared if you have heavy bags.

Though you can see all the major sights in the city without a car, both airports have outposts for every major car-rental company.

GO Airprt Express (© **888/2-THEVAN** [284-3826]; www.airport express.com) serves most first-class hotels in Chicago with its green-and-white vans; ticket counters are at both airports near baggage claim (outside Customs at the international terminal at O'Hare). For transportation to the airport, reserve a spot through one of the hotels (check with the bell captain). The cost is $28 one-way ($50 round-trip) to or from O'Hare, and $22 one-way ($37 round-trip) to or from Midway. Group rates for two or more people traveling together are less expensive than sharing a cab, and children ages 6 to 12 ride for $15 each. The shuttles operate from 4am to 11:30pm.

For limo service from O'Hare or Midway, call **Carey Limousine of Chicago** (© **773/763-0009;** www.carey.com) or **Chicago Limousine Services** (© **312/726-1035**). Depending on the number of passengers and whether you opt for a sedan or a stretch limo, the service will cost about $100 to $150 from Midway and $150 to $200 from O'Hare, excluding gratuity and tax.

> ## O'Hare, Oh My
>
> Chicago's O'Hare International Airport competes with Atlanta's Hartsfield-Jackson International Airport as the busiest airport in the world. Approximately 970,000 planes take off and land at O'Hare each year, generating about 500,000 jobs for the region. O'Hare is completely self-supporting, requiring no local taxpayer dollars to keep it going.

> ## Insider Tours—Free!
>
> Want a personalized view of the city— aside from your trusted Frommer's guidebook? A program called **Chicago Greeter** matches tourists with local Chicagoans who serve as volunteer guides. Visitors can request a specific neighborhood or theme (everything from Polish heritage sites to Chicago movie locations), and a greeter gives them a free 2- to 4-hour tour. (Greeters won't escort groups of more than six people.) Specific requests should be made at least a week in advance, but "InstaGreeters" are also available on a first-come, first-served basis at the Chicago Cultural Center, 77 E. Randolph St., from Friday through Sunday. For details, call © **312/744-8000** or visit **www.chicagogreeter.com**, where you can browse a list of specific tour topics.

By Car

Interstate highways from all major points on the compass serve Chicago. I-80 and I-90 approach from the east, crossing the northern sector of Illinois, with I-90 splitting off and emptying into Chicago on the Skyway and the Dan Ryan Expressway. From here, I-90 runs through Wisconsin, following a northern route to Seattle. I-55 snakes up the Mississippi Valley from the vicinity of New Orleans and enters Chicago from the west along the Stevenson Expressway; in the opposite direction, it provides an outlet to the Southwest. I-57 originates in southern Illinois and forms part of the interstate linkage to Florida and the South, connecting within Chicago on the west leg of the Dan Ryan. I-94 links Detroit with Chicago, arriving on the Calumet Expressway and leaving the city on the Kennedy Expressway en route to the Northwest.

Here are approximate driving distances in miles to Chicago: From **Milwaukee,** 92; from **St. Louis,** 297; from **Detroit,** 286; from **Denver,** 1,011; from **Atlanta,** 716; from **Washington, D.C.,** 715; from **New York City,** 821; and from **Los Angeles,** 2,034.

For information on car rentals and gasoline (petrol) in Chicago, see "Getting Around by Car," later in this section.

By Train

Chicago's central train station is **Union Station,** 210 S. Canal St., between Adams and Jackson streets (✆ **312/655-2385**). A hub for both national train routes operated by Amtrak and local commuter lines that run to the Chicago suburbs, it's located just across the river from the Loop. Although Union Station is relatively convenient to downtown, you'll most likely want to take a taxi or bus to your hotel if you have luggage. Bus nos. 1, 60, 125, 151, and 156 all stop at the station on their routes through downtown. The nearest El stop is at Adams and Wells streets (Brown Line), a 4-block walk.

For train tickets to Chicago from other cities in the U.S., consult your travel agent or call **Amtrak** (✆ **800/USA-RAIL** [872-7245] in the U.S. or Canada; ✆ **001/215-856-7953** outside the U.S.; www.amtrak.com). Ask the reservations agent to send you Amtrak's travel planner, with useful information on train accommodations and package tours.

International visitors can buy a **USA Rail Pass,** good for 15, 30, or 45 days of unlimited travel. The pass is available online or through many overseas travel agents. See Amtrak's website for the cost of travel within the western, eastern, or northwestern United States. Reservations are generally required and should be made as early as possible. Regional rail passes are also available.

By Bus

Bus travel is often the most economical form of public transit for short hops between U.S. cities. **Greyhound** (✆ **800/231-2222;** www.greyhound.com) is the sole nationwide bus line. International visitors can obtain information about the **Greyhound North American Discovery Pass** from foreign travel agents or through www.discoverypass.com. The ticket allows for unlimited travel and stopovers in the U.S. and Canada. Chicago's Greyhound station is at 630 W. Harrison St. (✆ **312/408-5821**), just southwest of downtown.

If you're planning on traveling elsewhere in the Midwest, **Megabus** (✆ **877/GO2-MEGA** [462-6342]; www.megabus.com) offers low-cost trips to cities such as Milwaukee, Minneapolis, and St. Louis. The well-kept double-decker buses—which come equipped with free Wi-Fi—are a popular option for students. Buses leave from the city's main train station, Union Station.

GETTING AROUND
By Train (the El)

The **Chicago Transit Authority,** better known as the **CTA** (🕿**836-7000** or TTY 836-4949 from any area code in the city and suburbs; **www.transit chicago.com**), operates an extensive system of trains throughout the city of Chicago; both the below-ground subway lines and aboveground elevated trains are know collectively as the El. The system is generally safe and reliable, although I'd avoid long rides through unfamiliar neighborhoods late at night.

Fares are $2.25 per ride, regardless of how far you go. For an additional 25¢, you can transfer to the bus or take a different El ride within 2 hours. Children 6 and under ride free, and those between the ages of 7 and 11 pay $1. Seniors can also receive the reduced fare if they have the appropriate reduced-fare permit (call 🕿 **312/836-7000** for details on how to obtain one, although this is probably not a realistic option for a short-term visitor).

The CTA uses credit card–size fare cards that automatically deduct the exact fare each time you take a ride. The reusable cards can be purchased with a preset value already stored, or riders can obtain cards at vending machines located at all CTA train stations and charge them with whatever amount they choose (a minimum of $2.25 and up to $100). If within 2 hours of your first ride you transfer to a bus or the El, the turnstiles at the El stations and the fare boxes on buses will automatically deduct from your card just the cost of a transfer (25¢). If you make a second transfer within 2 hours, it's free. The same card can be recharged continuously.

The CTA operates seven major train lines, identified by color: The **Red Line,** which runs north-south, is most likely the only one you'll need, since it runs parallel to the lakefront and past many tourist attractions. The **Green Line** runs west–south; the **Blue Line** runs through Wicker Park/Bucktown west–northwest to O'Hare Airport; the **Pink Line** branches off from the Blue Line and serves the southwest side of the city; the **Brown Line** runs in a northern

---

📎 **Ticket to Ride**

Visitors who plan on taking a lot of train or bus trips should consider buying a **Visitor Pass,** which works like a fare card and allows individual users unlimited rides on the El and CTA buses over a 24-hour period. The cards cost $5.75 and are sold at airports, hotels, museums, transportation hubs, and Chicago Office of Tourism visitor information centers (you can also buy them in advance online at www.transitchicago.

com or by calling 🕿 **888/YOUR-CTA** [968-7282]). You can also buy 3- and 7-day passes. While the passes save you the trouble of feeding the fare machines yourself, they're economical only if you plan to make at least three distinct trips at least 2 or more hours apart (remember that you get two additional transfers within 2 hr. for an additional 25¢ on a regular fare).

zigzag route; and the **Orange Line** runs southwest, serving Midway airport. The **Purple Line,** which runs on the same Loop elevated tracks as the Orange and Green lines, serves north-suburban Evanston and runs only during rush hour.

I highly recommend taking at least one El ride while you're here—you'll get a whole different perspective on the city (not to mention fascinating views inside downtown office buildings and North Side homes as you zip past their windows). While the Red Line is the most efficient for traveling between the Magnificent Mile and points south, your only views along this underground stretch will be of dingy stations. For sightseers, I recommend taking the aboveground Brown Line, which runs around the downtown Loop and then north through residential neighborhoods. You can ride all the way to the end of the line at Kimball (about a 45-min. ride from downtown), or hop off at Belmont to wander the Lakeview neighborhood. Avoid this scenic ride during rush hour (before about 9am and 3:30–6:30pm), when your only view will be of tired commuters.

Study your CTA map carefully (there's one printed on the inside back cover of this guide) before boarding any train. Most trains run every 5 to 20 minutes, decreasing in frequency in the off-peak and overnight hours. The Orange Line train does not operate from about 11:30pm to 5am, the Brown Line operates only north of Belmont after about 9:30pm, the Blue Line's Cermak branch doesn't run overnight and on weekends, and the Purple Line operates only during the morning and afternoon rush hours on weekdays. (The Red Line runs 24 hr.)

By Bus

The best way to get around neighborhoods along the lakefront—where the trains don't run—is by public bus. Look for the **blue-and-white signs to locate bus stops,** which are spaced about 2 blocks apart. Each bus route is identified by a number and the name of the main street it runs along; the bus that follows Grand Avenue, for example, is the no. 65 Grand.

Buses accept the same fare cards used for the El, but you can't buy a card onboard. That means you have to stop by a train station to buy a card in advance, or pay $2.25 cash when you board. The bus drivers cannot make change, so make sure that you've got the right amount in coins and dollar bills before hopping on.

A few buses that are particularly handy for visitors are the **no. 146 Marine/ Michigan,** an express bus from Belmont Avenue on the North Side that cruises down North Lake Shore Drive (and through Lincoln Park during nonpeak times) to North Michigan Avenue, State Street, and the Grant Park museum campus; the **no. 151 Sheridan,** which passes through Lincoln Park en route to inner Lake Shore Drive and then travels along Michigan Avenue as far south as Adams Street, where it turns west into the Loop (and stops at Union Station); and the **no. 156 LaSalle,** which goes through Lincoln Park and then into the Loop's financial district on LaSalle Street.

PACE buses (✆ 836-7000 from any Chicago area code or 847/364-7223; Mon–Fri 8am–5pm; www.pacebus.com) cover the suburban zones that surround Chicago. They run every 20 to 30 minutes during rush hour, operating until midevening Monday through Friday and early evening on weekends. Suburban bus routes are marked with nos. 208 and above, and vehicles may be flagged down at intersections where stops aren't marked.

By Commuter Train

The **Metra** commuter railroad (✆ 312/322-6777 or TTY 312/322-6774; Mon–Fri 8am–5pm; at other times, call the **Transit Information Center** at ✆ 312/836-7000 or TTY 312/836-4949; www.metrarail.com) serves the six-county suburban area around Chicago with 12 train lines. Several terminals are located downtown, including **Union Station** at Adams and Canal streets, **LaSalle Street Station** at LaSalle and Van Buren streets, the **Ogilvie Transportation Center** at Madison and Canal streets, and **Randolph Street Station** at Randolph Street and Michigan Avenue.

To view the leafy streets of Chicago's northern suburbs, take the **Union Pacific North Line,** which departs from the Ogilvie Transportation Center, and get off at one of the following scenic towns: Kenilworth, Winnetka, Glencoe, Highland Park, or Lake Forest.

The **Metra Electric** (once known as the Illinois Central–Gulf Railroad, or the IC), running close to Lake Michigan on a track that occupies some of the most valuable real estate in Chicago, will take you to Hyde Park. (See "Exploring Hyde Park" in chapter 6.) You can catch the Metra Electric in the Loop at the Randolph Street Station and at the Van Buren Street Station at Van Buren Street and Michigan Avenue. (Both of these stations are underground, so they're not immediately obvious to visitors.)

Commuter trains have graduated fare schedules based on the distance you ride. On weekends, on holidays, and during the summer, Metra offers a family discount that allows up to three children 11 and under to ride free when accompanying a paid adult. The commuter railroad also offers a $5 weekend pass for unlimited rides on Saturday and Sunday.

By Taxi

Taxis are a convenient way to get around the Loop and to reach restaurants and theaters beyond downtown, in residential neighborhoods such as Old Town, Lincoln Park, Bucktown, and Wicker Park.

Taxis are easy to hail in the Loop, on the Magnificent Mile and the Gold Coast, in River North, and in Lincoln Park, but if you go far beyond these key areas, you might need to call. Cab companies include **Flash Cab** (*© 773/561-4444*), **Yellow Cab** (*© 312/TAXI-CAB* [829-4222]), and **Checker Cab** (*© 312/CHECKER* [243-2537]).

The meter in Chicago cabs currently starts at $2.25 for the first mile and costs $1.80 for each additional mile, with a $1 surcharge for the first additional rider and 50¢ for each person after that. You will also have to pay an additional $1 fuel surcharge whenever gas prices are above $3 per gallon.

By Car

One of the great things about visiting Chicago is that you don't need to rent a car to get around: Most of the main tourist attractions are within walking distance of downtown hotels or public transportation. If you do drive here, Chicago is laid out so logically that it's relatively easy for visitors to find their way around. Although

SKY TRAIN: chicago's el

Watch any Hollywood film or TV series set in Chicago, and chances are, they'll feature at least one scene set against our screeching elevated train system, more commonly known as the **"El"** (witness *The Fugitive, ER,* and others). The trains symbolize Chicago's gritty, "city-that-works" attitude, but they actually began as cutting-edge technology.

After the Great Fire of 1871, Chicago made a remarkable recovery; within 20 years, the downtown district was swarming with people, streetcars, and horses (but no stoplights). To help relieve congestion, the city took to the sky, building a system of elevated trains 15 feet above all the madness. The first El trains were steam powered, but by the end of the century, all the lines—run by separate companies—used electricity. In 1895, the three El companies collaborated to build a set of tracks into and around the central business district that all the lines would then share. By 1897, the "Loop" was up and running.

Chicago's El wasn't the nation's first. That honor belongs to New York City, which started running its elevated trains in 1867, 25 years before Chicago. But the New York El has almost disappeared, moving underground and turning into a subway early last century. With 289 miles of track, Chicago has the biggest El and the second-largest public transportation system in the country.

rush-hour traffic jams are just as frustrating as they are in other large cities, traffic runs fairly smoothly at most times of the day. Chicagoans have learned to be prepared for unexpected delays; it seems that at least one major highway and several downtown streets are under repair throughout the spring and summer months. (Some say we have two seasons: winter and construction.)

Great diagonal corridors—such as Lincoln Avenue, Clark Street, and Milwaukee Avenue—slice through the grid pattern at key points in the city and shorten many a trip that would otherwise be tedious on the checkerboard surface of the Chicago streets. On scenic **Lake Shore Drive** (also known as Outer Dr.), you can travel the length of the city (and beyond), never far from the great lake that is Chicago's most awesome natural feature. If you're driving here, make sure you take one spin along what we call LSD; the stretch between the Museum Campus and North Avenue is especially stunning.

DRIVING RULES Unless otherwise posted, a right turn on red is allowed after stopping and signaling. As in any big city with its share of frustrating rush-hour traffic, be prepared for aggressive drivers and the occasional taxi to cut in front of you or make sudden, unexpected turns without signaling. Chicago drivers almost universally speed up at the sight of a yellow light; you'll most likely hear some honking if you don't make that mad dash before the light turns red.

GASOLINE (PETROL) Over the past few years, the price of gas in Chicago has fluctuated between $3 and $4 per gallon. Taxes are already included in the printed price. One U.S. gallon equals 3.8 liters or .85 imperial gallons. In general, you pay more within the Chicago city limits than you will in the suburbs (the city adds an extra tax into the price), so if you're planning a day trip, it pays to fill up once you're out of town.

PARKING As in most large cities, parking is at a premium in Chicago, so be prepared to pay up. Throughout downtown, street parking is limited to 2 hours (if you can find a spot); you must purchase a receipt from a designated pay box and display it on your dashboard.

Read signs carefully, because parking regulations are vigorously enforced throughout the city. Many streets around Michigan Avenue forbid parking during rush hour—and I know from bitter firsthand experience that your car will be towed immediately. If you're visiting in the winter, make note of curbside warnings regarding snow plowing. Many neighborhoods also have adopted resident-only parking that prohibits others from parking on their streets after 6pm each day (even all day in a few areas, such as Old Town). The neighborhood around Wrigley Field is off-limits during Cubs night games, so look for yellow sidewalk signs alerting drivers about the dozen-and-a-half times the Cubs play under lights. You can park in permit zones if you're visiting a friend who can provide you with a pass to stick on your windshield.

A safe bet is valet parking, which most restaurants provide for $8 to $12. Downtown you might also opt for a public garage, but you'll have to pay premium prices. Several garages connected with malls or other major attractions offer discounted parking with a validated ticket.

If you'll be spending an entire day downtown, the best parking deal in the Loop is the city-run **Millennium Park** garage (© **312/742-7644**), which charges $19 for up to 3 hours and $21 for up to 8 hours (enter on Columbus Dr., 1 block east of Michigan Ave., between Monroe and Randolph sts.). A little farther south are two municipal lots underneath **Grant Park,** with one entrance at Michigan Avenue and Van Buren Street and the other at Michigan Avenue and Madison Street (© **312/616-0600**). Parking costs $14 for the first hour and $27 for 2 to 8 hours. Other downtown lots (where prices are comparable or even higher) include **Midcontinental Plaza Garage,** 55 E. Monroe St. (© **312/986-6821**), and **Navy Pier Parking,** 600 E. Grand Ave. (© **312/595-7437**). There's also a large lot next to the **McCormick Place Convention Center,** 2301 S. Lake Shore Dr. (© **312/791-7000**).

CAR RENTAL All the major car-rental companies have offices at O'Hare and Midway, as well as locations downtown.

If you're visiting from abroad and plan to rent a car in the United States, keep in mind that foreign driver's licenses are usually recognized in the U.S., but you may want to consider obtaining an international driver's license. International visitors also should note that insurance and taxes are almost never included in quoted rental car rates in the U.S. Be sure to ask your rental agency about additional fees for these. They can add a significant cost to your car rental.

By Bicycle

The city of Chicago has earned kudos for its efforts to improve conditions for bicycling (designated bike lanes have been installed on stretches of Wells St., Roosevelt Rd., Elston Ave., and Halsted St.), but it can still be a tough prospect to compete with cars and their drivers, who aren't always so willing to share the road.

The **Active Transportation Alliance** (© **312/427-3325;** www.active trans.org), a nonprofit advocacy group, has been at the forefront of efforts to make the city more bike-friendly. Their website lists upcoming bike-focused events, including the annual "Bike the Drive," when Lake Shore Drive is closed to cars.

Bike Chicago rents all sorts of bikes, including tandems and four-seater "quadcycles," as well as in-line skates, from three locations: North Avenue Beach, Millennium Park, and Navy Pier (© **888/BIKE-WAY** [245-3929]; www.bikechicago.com). Bike rentals start at $10 an hour or $30 a day. Helmets, pads, and locks are provided free of charge. The shops are open daily from 9am to 7pm, weather permitting.

[FastFACTS] CHICAGO

Area Codes The 312 area code applies to the central downtown business district and the surrounding neighborhoods, including River North, North Michigan Avenue, and the Gold Coast. The code for the rest of the city is 773. Suburban area codes are 847 (north), 708 (west and southwest), and 630 (far west). You must dial 1 plus the area code for all telephone numbers, even if you are making a call within the same area code.

Business Hours Shops generally keep regular American business hours, 10am to 6pm Monday through Saturday. Many stores in downtown Chicago stay open later at least 1 evening a week. Certain businesses, such as bookstores, are almost always open during the evening hours all week. Most shops are also open on Sundays, usually from 11am to 6pm. Malls are generally open until 7pm and on Sunday as well. Banking hours in Chicago are normally from 9am (8am in some cases) to 5pm Monday through Friday, with select banks remaining open later on specified afternoons and evenings.

Car Rental See "Getting There by Car," earlier in this chapter.

Cellphones See "Mobile Phones," later in this section.

Crime See "Safety," later in this section.

Doctors Most hotels in Chicago keep a list of local doctors who are available to tend to guests; in case of health problems, your best bet is to contact your hotel's concierge or manager. **Northwestern Memorial Hospital,** 251 E. Huron St., a well-regarded downtown hospital, also has a physician referral service (✆ **877/926-4664**), if you need to find a specialist. Also see "Hospitals," later in this section.

Drinking Laws The legal age for purchase and consumption of alcoholic beverages is 21; proof of age is required and often requested at bars, nightclubs, and restaurants, so it's always a good idea to bring ID when you go out. Do not carry open containers of alcohol in your car or any public area that isn't zoned for alcohol consumption. The police can fine you on the spot. Don't even think about driving while intoxicated.

In Chicago, beer, wine, and other alcoholic beverages are sold at liquor stores and supermarkets. Bars may sell alcohol until 2am, although some nightclubs have special licenses that allow alcohol sales until 4am.

Driving Rules See "Getting Around," earlier in this chapter.

Electricity Like Canada, the United States uses 110 to 120 volts AC (60 cycles), compared to 220 to 240 volts AC (50 cycles) in most of Europe, Australia, and New Zealand. Downward converters that change 220 to 240 volts to 110 to 120 volts are difficult to find in the United States, so bring one with you.

Embassies & Consulates All embassies are in the nation's capital, Washington, D.C. Some consulates are in major U.S. cities, and most nations have a mission to the United Nations in New York City. If your country isn't listed below, call for directory information in Washington, D.C. (✆ **202/555-1212**) or check **www.embassy.org/embassies**.

The embassy of **Australia** is at 1601 Massachusetts Ave. NW, Washington, DC 20036 (✆ **202/797-3000;** www.usa.embassy.gov.au). Consulates are in New York, Honolulu, Houston, Los Angeles, and San Francisco.

The embassy of **Canada** is at 501 Pennsylvania Ave. NW, Washington, DC 20001 (✆ **202/682-1740;** www.canadainternational.gc.ca/washington). Other Canadian consulates are in Buffalo (New York), Detroit, Los Angeles, New York, and Seattle.

The embassy of **Ireland** is at 2234 Massachusetts Ave. NW, Washington, DC 20008 (✆ **202/462-3939;** www.embassyofireland.org). Irish consulates are in Boston, Chicago, New York, San Francisco, and other cities. See website for complete listing.

The embassy of **New Zealand** is at 37 Observatory Circle NW, Washington, DC 20008 (✆ **202/328-4800;** www.nzembassy.com). New Zealand consulates are in Los Angeles, Salt Lake City, San Francisco, and Seattle.

The embassy of the **United Kingdom** is at 3100 Massachusetts Ave. NW, Washington, DC 20008 (✆ **202/588-6500;** http://ukinusa.fco.gov.uk). Other British consulates are in Atlanta, Boston, Chicago, Cleveland, Houston, Los Angeles, New York, San Francisco, and Seattle.

Emergencies For fire or police emergencies, call ✆ **911.** This is a free call. If it is a medical emergency, a city ambulance will take the patient to the nearest hospital emergency room. The nonemergency phone number for the Chicago Police Department is ✆ **311.**

Family Travel Chicago is full of sightseeing opportunities and special activities geared toward children. To locate those accommodations, restaurants, and attractions that are particularly kid-friendly, refer to the "Kids" icon throughout this guide. Chapter 4 includes a list of the best hotel deals for families, and chapter 5 lists kid-friendly restaurants. Also see "Kid Stuff" in chapter 6 for information on family-oriented attractions. The guidebook *Frommer's Chicago with Kids* (Wiley Publishing, Inc.) highlights the many family-friendly activities available in the city.

Gasoline Please see "Getting Around by Car," earlier in this chapter.

Hospitals The best hospital emergency room in downtown Chicago is at **Northwestern Memorial Hospital,** 251 E. Huron St. (✆ **312/926-2000;** www.nmh.org), a state-of-the-art medical center right off North Michigan Avenue. The emergency department (✆ **312/926-5188** or 312/944-2358 for TDD access) is located at 251 E. Erie St., near Fairbanks Court. For an ambulance, dial ✆ **911,** which is a free call.

Insurance For information on traveler's insurance, trip cancelation insurance, and medical insurance while traveling, please visit www.frommers.com/planning.

Internet & Wi-Fi If you are traveling without your own computer, almost every hotel in Chicago has a business center with Internet access for guests (although you may have to pay extra to use it). The **Harold Washington Public Library** (p. 169) has computers available to the public for free. You can also pay per hour to use computers at **FedEx Offices;** centrally located stores include one at Illinois Center, 111 W. Wacker Dr., near Michigan Avenue and Chicago River (✆ **312/938-0650**), and inside the John Hancock Center, 875 N. Michigan Ave. (✆ **312/664-5966**).

In Lincoln Park, you'll find **Screenz,** 2717 N. Clark St., 1 block south of Diversey Ave. (✆ **773/912-1565;** www.screenz.com), a computing center where you can check e-mail, burn CDs, and print out your digital photos. The only downside is that it's not within walking distance of downtown hotels. To find other cybercafes in the city, try **www.cybercafe.com.** Both O'Hare and Midway airports have **Internet kiosks** that provide basic Web access for a per-minute fee.

If you plan to bring your own computer, both airports, most hotels, and many cafes and restaurants throughout the Chicago area have gone Wi-Fi, becoming "hotspots" that offer free high-speed access or charge a small fee for usage. In the Loop, **Millennium Park; Daley Plaza** (along Washington St. btw. Dearborn and Clark sts.); the **Chicago Cultural Center,** 78 E. Washington St.; and the **Harold Washington Library Center,** 400 S. State St., all have free wireless access. Elsewhere in downtown Chicago, Starbucks, the sandwich chain Cosí, and McDonald's have numerous locations that offer Wi-Fi access for customers. Wireless hotspots in Lincoln Park include **Panera Bread,** 616 W. Diversey Pkwy. (✆ **773/528-4556**), and **Argo Tea,** 958 W. Armitage Ave. (✆ **773/388-1880**).

To find more public Wi-Fi hotspots in Chicago, go to **www.jiwire.com**; its Hotspot Finder holds the world's largest directory of public wireless hotspots.

Legal Aid While driving, if you are pulled over for a minor infraction (such as speeding), never attempt to pay the fine directly to a police officer; this could be construed as attempted bribery, a much more serious crime. Pay fines by mail, or directly into the hands of the clerk of the court. If accused of a more serious offense, say and do nothing before consulting a lawyer. In the U.S., the burden is on the state to prove a person's guilt beyond a reasonable doubt, and everyone has the right to remain silent, whether he or she is suspected of a crime or actually arrested. Once arrested, a person can make one telephone call to a party of his or her choice. The international visitor should call his or her embassy or consulate.

LGBT Travelers While it's not quite San Francisco, Chicago is a very gay-friendly city. The neighborhood commonly referred to as "Boys Town" (roughly from Belmont Ave. north to Irving Park Ave., and from Halsted St. east to the lakefront) is the center of gay nightlife—and plenty of daytime action, too. **Gay and Lesbian Pride Week** (📞 **773/348-8243;** www.chicagopridecalendar.org), highlighted by a raucous parade on the North Side, is a major event each June. To browse listings of gay-friendly events when you're in town, visit the **Chicago Pride** website (http://chicago.gopride.com) before your visit.

The **Center on Halsted,** 3656 N. Halsted St. (📞 **773/472-6469;** www.centeron halsted.org), is a gay social service agency and community center that's become an informal gathering place for Boys Town residents. Inside you'll find an organic grocery store, cafe, and plenty of couches for hanging out and taking advantage of the center's free Wi-Fi. You might also want to stop by **Unabridged Books,** 3251 N. Broadway (📞 **773/883-9119**), an excellent independent bookseller with a large lesbian and gay selection. Here, and elsewhere in the Lakeview neighborhood, you can pick up several gay publications, including the weekly *Windy City Times* (www.windycitytimes.com), which covers local news and entertainment.

Mail At press time, domestic postage rates were 28¢ for a postcard and 44¢ for a letter. For international mail, a first-class letter of up to 1 ounce costs 98¢ (75¢ to Canada and 79¢ to Mexico); a first-class postcard costs the same as a letter. For more information go to **www.usps.com**.

If you aren't sure what your address will be in the United States, mail can be sent to you, in your name, c/o General Delivery at the main post office of the city or region where you expect to be. (Call 📞 **800/275-8777** for information on the nearest post office.) The addressee must pick up mail in person and must produce proof of identity (driver's license, passport, etc.). Most post offices will hold mail for up to 1 month, and are open Monday to Friday from 8am to 6pm, and Saturday from 9am to 3pm.

Medical Requirements Unless you're arriving from an area known to be suffering from an epidemic (particularly cholera or yellow fever), inoculations or vaccinations are not required for entry into the United States.

Mobile Phones As with all large American cities, Chicago is covered by the major national cellphone networks, including AT&T, Sprint, Nextel, and T-Mobile. If you're traveling from elsewhere in the U.S., your phone should work here—although you may be hit with roaming charges that make your per-minute costs higher than usual.

Although you can rent a cellphone through companies such as **InTouch USA** (📞 **800/872-7626;** www.intouchglobal.com) or most rental car locations, it's simpler and relatively affordable to buy a prepaid cellphone. Companies such as Virgin Mobile and Cricket sell basic, bare-bones phones for as little as $15, and you can pay as you go for calls, without signing up for a monthly plan. You can find prepaid phones at many of the large downtown drugstores, including **Walgreens,** 757 N. Michigan Ave. (✆ **312/664-8686**), and **CVS,** 137 S. State St. (✆ **312/609-1215**).

If you're not from the U.S., you'll be appalled at the poor reach of the **GSM (Global System for Mobile Communications) wireless network,** which is used by much of the rest of the world. Your phone should work in Chicago, but it definitely won't in many rural areas. To see where GSM phones work in the U.S., check out www.t-mobile.com/coverage. And you may or may not be able to send SMS (text messaging) home.

Money & Costs Frommer's lists exact prices in the local currency. The currency conversions quoted above were correct at press time. However, rates fluctuate, so before departing consult a currency exchange website such as **www.oanda.com/currency/converter** to check up-to-the-minute rates.

THE VALUE OF THE DOLLAR VS. OTHER POPULAR CURRENCIES

US$	Aus$	Can$	Euro (€)	NZ$	UK£
1	A$1	C$1	€.73	NZ$1.27	£.63

While not as expensive as New York or London, Chicago's hotel and restaurant prices are near the high end compared to other American cities. It's hard to find a hotel room for less than $200 a night in the summer (prime tourist season), and entrees at the city's best restaurants can set you back around $30.

Credit cards are accepted just about everywhere, aside from a few hole-in-the-wall restaurants. You should have no trouble using traveler's checks at most hotels and downtown restaurants (places that are used to accommodating international visitors), but they may not be accepted at smaller businesses in the city's residential neighborhoods.

ATMs are easy to find throughout the city, especially downtown and near tourist attractions. (Most Chicagoans refer to them as "cash stations".) Most ATMs belong to one of two networks: **Cirrus** (✆ **800/424-7787;** www.mastercard.com) or **PLUS** (✆ **800/843-7587;** www.visa.com). Go to your bank card's website to find convenient ATM locations before you leave, and be sure you know your daily withdrawal limit before you depart.

Beware of hidden credit-card fees while traveling. Check with your credit or debit card issuer to see what fees, if any, will be charged for overseas transactions. Recent reform legislation in the U.S., for example, has curbed some exploitative lending practices. But many banks have responded by increasing fees in other areas, including fees for customers who use credit and debit cards while out of the country—even if those charges were made in U.S. dollars. Fees can amount to 3% or more of the purchase price. Check with your bank before departing to avoid any surprise charges on your statement.

WHAT THINGS COST IN CHICAGO	US$
Taxi from O'Hare Airport to downtown	35.00
Taxi from Midway Airport to downtown	25.00
Double room, expensive	300.00–500.00
Double room, moderate	200.00–250.00
Double room, inexpensive	100.00–150.00
Three-course dinner for one without wine, moderate	30.00–50.00
Bottle of beer	3.00–8.00
Cup of coffee	1.50–3.00
1 gallon/1 liter of gasoline	3.50
Admission to most museums	10.00–20.00

For help with currency conversions, tip calculations, and more, download Frommer's convenient Travel Tools app for your mobile device. Go to www.frommers.com/go/mobile and click on the Travel Tools icon.

Multicultural Travelers Chicago is a cosmopolitan city with a population that's about 36% African American, 30% white, and 26% Latino. (Chicago has the second-largest Mexican population in the U.S., after Los Angeles.) Visitors of all racial and ethnic groups shouldn't expect to encounter any discrimination; Chicagoans are used to welcoming tourists and businesspeople from around the world.

Still, Chicago is extremely divided residentially along racial lines. The South Side is overwhelmingly African American, the North Side is mostly white, and Latino residents tend to settle in neighborhoods such as Pilsen, just southwest of downtown.

African-American travelers can explore the city's rich black heritage with a specialized tour (see "Neighborhood Tours," p. 230). Visitors with an interest in Latin-American art might want to stop by the vibrant National Museum of Mexican Art and explore the surrounding neighborhood of Pilsen (p. 206).

Newspapers & Magazines The *Chicago Tribune* (✆ **312/222-3232;** www.chicago tribune.com) and the *Chicago Sun-Times* (✆ **312/321-3000;** www.suntimes.com) are the city's two major daily newspapers. The *Tribune* focuses on sober, just-the-facts reporting; the *Sun-Times* is a scrappier, attitude-filled tabloid. Both have cultural listings, including movies, theaters, and live music, not to mention reviews of the latest restaurants that have opened since this guidebook went to press. The Friday edition of both papers contains a special pullout section with more detailed, up-to-date information on special events happening over the weekend.

The weekly magazine *Time Out Chicago* (✆ **312/924-9555;** www.timeoutchicago.com) lists just about everything going on around town during the week, from art openings to theater performances; if you want to squeeze in as much culture as you can while you're here, I highly recommend picking up a copy. The *Chicago Reader* (✆ **312/828-0350;** www.chicagoreader.com) is a free weekly that appears each Thursday, with all the current entertainment and cultural listings. *Chicago* magazine (www.chicagomag.com) is a monthly with an especially good restaurant review section.

The *Chicago Defender* (www.chicagodefender.com) covers local and national news of interest to the African-American community. The Spanish-language *La Raza* (www.laraza.com) reports on stories from a Latino point of view. The *Windy City Times* (www.windycitytimes.com) publish both news and feature articles about gay and lesbian issues.

Packing In general, you should be prepared for rapid weather shifts while you're in town, especially in the spring and fall. Unless you'll be here in July or August, bring at least one jacket and warm sweater in case of a sudden cold front. The winds off the lake, in particular, can be frosty well into the spring. Your best bet is to bring a selection of long- and short-sleeved shirts that can be layered to adapt to changing temperatures (it's not unusual to start out the morning shivering only to be sweating by afternoon). If you're brave enough to venture to Chicago in the winter, make room for hats, gloves, scarves, and boots: You'll need them.

Chicago is a casual town, so standard tourist-wear is acceptable at all the city's museums and most of the restaurants and theaters. A few traditional fine-dining restaurants have a jacket requirement for men, but otherwise male travelers probably won't need to pack a suit. (Dress codes are noted where appropriate in the restaurant listings in chapter 5.)

For more helpful information on packing for your trip, download our convenient Travel Tools app for your mobile device. Go to www.frommers.com/go/mobile and click on the Travel Tools icon.

Passports Virtually every air traveler entering the U.S. is required to show a passport. All persons, including U.S. citizens, traveling by air between the United States and Canada, Mexico, Central and South America, the Caribbean, and Bermuda are required to present a valid passport. *Note:* U.S. and Canadian citizens entering the U.S. at land and sea ports of entry from within the western hemisphere must now also present a passport or other documents compliant with the Western Hemisphere Travel Initiative (WHTI; see www.getyouhome.gov for details). Children 15 and under may continue entering with only a U.S. birth certificate, or other proof of U.S. citizenship.

Passport Offices Australia Australian Passport Information Service (✆ **131-232,** or visit www.passports.gov.au).

Canada Passport Office, Department of Foreign Affairs and International Trade, Ottawa, ON K1A 0G3 (✆ **800/567-6868;** www.ppt.gc.ca).

Ireland Passport Office, Setanta Centre, Molesworth Street, Dublin 2 (✆ **01/671-1633;** www.foreignaffairs.gov.ie).

New Zealand Passports Office, Department of Internal Affairs, 47 Boulcott St., Wellington, 6011 (✆ **0800/225-050** in New Zealand or 04/474-8100; www.passports.govt.nz).

United Kingdom Visit your nearest passport office, major post office, or travel agency or contact the **Identity and Passport Service (IPS),** 89 Eccleston Sq., London, SW1V 1PN (✆ **0300/222-0000;** www.ips.gov.uk).

United States To find your regional passport office, check the U.S. State Department website (http://travel.state.gov/passport) or call the **National Passport Information Center** (✆ **877/487-2778**) for automated information.

Petrol Please see "Getting Around by Car," earlier in this chapter.

Police For emergencies, call ✆ **911.** This is a free call (no coins required). For non-emergencies, call ✆ **311.**

Safety Although Chicago has one of the highest murder rates in the United States, the vast majority of those crimes are tied to drug dealing or gang activity and take place in areas visitors are unlikely to be walking around. In all my years of living here, I've yet to hear of a violent crime specifically targeted at a tourist.

That said, Chicago has the same problems with theft and muggings as any other major American city, so use your common sense and stay cautious and alert. After dark, stick to well-lit streets along the Magnificent Mile, River North, Gold Coast, and Lincoln Park, which are all high-traffic areas late into the night.

Late at night, avoid wandering dark residential streets on the fringes of Hyde Park and Pilsen, which border areas where gangs are active. You can also ask your hotel concierge or an agent at the tourist visitor center about the safety of a particular area.

The El is generally quite safe, even at night, although some of the downtown stations can feel eerily deserted late in the evening. Buses are a safe option, too, especially nos. 146 and 151, which pick up along North Michigan Avenue and State Street and connect to the North Side via Lincoln Park.

Blue-and-white police cars are a common sight, and officers also patrol by bicycle downtown and along the lakefront and by horseback at special events and parades. There are police stations in busy nightlife areas, such as the 18th District station at Chicago Avenue and LaSalle Street in River North, and the 24th District station (known as Town Hall) at Addison and Halsted streets.

Senior Travel Traveling as a senior can definitely save you money in Chicago; people 60 and older qualify for reduced admission to most major cultural attractions and lower-priced theater tickets. At major museums such as the Art Institute and Field Museum of Natural History, the senior rate is about 30% less than the general admission price.

Smoking Smoking is banned in all public buildings in Chicago, including offices, restaurants, and bars. Hotels are still allowed to have smoking rooms available, though, so request one if you plan on lighting up.

Student Travel The best resource for students in Chicago is **STA Travel** (www.statravel.com), one of the biggest student-travel agencies in the world, which can set you up with an ID card and get you discounts on plane tickets and rail travel. There is an STA office in the suburb of Evanston, near Northwestern University, at 900 Church St. (✆ **847/475-5070**).

Chicago also has several hostels offering students and other travelers inexpensive, no-frills lodging. The best is **Hosteling International Chicago,** 24 E. Congress Pkwy., in the Loop (✆ **312/360-0300;** fax 312/360-0313; www.hichicago.org). It features many amenities (including a free buffet breakfast) and can help set up activities throughout the city. Another hostel open year-round is the more basic **Chicago Getaway Hostel,** 616 W. Arlington Place, Chicago, IL 60614 (✆ **773/929-5380;** fax 773/665-5485; www.getawayhostel.com), in Lincoln Park.

Taxes The United States has no value-added tax (VAT) or other indirect tax at the national level. Every state, county, and city may levy its own local tax on all purchases, including hotel and restaurant checks and airline tickets. These taxes will not appear on price tags.

When visiting Chicago, be prepared to pay up: The city's 9.75% sales tax is among the highest in the country, and the hotel room tax is a steep 14.9%.

Telephones Many convenience groceries and packaging services sell **prepaid calling cards** in denominations up to $50. Many public pay phones at airports now accept American Express, MasterCard, and Visa. **Local calls** made from most pay phones cost either 25¢ or 35¢. Most long-distance and international calls can be dialed directly from any phone. **To make calls within the United States and to Canada,** dial 1 followed by the area code and the seven-digit number. **For other international calls,** dial 011 followed by the country code, city code, and the number you are calling.

Calls to area codes **800, 888, 877,** and **866** are toll-free. However, calls to area codes **700** and **900** (chat lines, bulletin boards, "dating" services, and so on) can be expensive—charges of 95¢ to $3 or more per minute. Some numbers have minimum charges that can run $15 or more.

For **reversed-charge or collect calls,** and for person-to-person calls, dial the number 0 then the area code and number; an operator will come on the line, and you should specify whether you are calling collect, person-to-person, or both. If your operator-assisted call is international, ask for the overseas operator.

For **directory assistance** ("Information"), dial 411 for local numbers and national numbers in the U.S. and Canada. For dedicated long-distance information, dial 1, then the appropriate area code plus 555-1212.

Time The continental United States is divided into **four time zones:** Eastern Standard Time (EST), Central Standard Time (CST), Mountain Standard Time (MST), and Pacific Standard Time (PST); Chicago is in the Central time zone. Alaska and Hawaii have their own zones. For example, when it's 9am in Los Angeles (PST), it's 7am in Honolulu (HST),10am in Denver (MST), 11am in Chicago (CST), noon in New York City (EST), 5pm in London (GMT), and 2am the next day in Sydney.

Daylight saving time (summer time) is in effect from 1am on the second Sunday in March to 1am on the first Sunday in November, except in Arizona, Hawaii, the U.S. Virgin Islands, and Puerto Rico. Daylight saving time moves the clock 1 hour ahead of standard time.

For help with time translations, and more, download our convenient Travel Tools app for your mobile device. Go to www.frommers.com/go/mobile and click on the Travel Tools icon.

Tipping In hotels, tip **bellhops** at least $1 per bag ($2–$3 if you have a lot of luggage) and tip the **chamber staff** $1 to $2 per day (more if you've left a big mess for him or her to clean up). Tip the **doorman** or **concierge** only if he or she has provided you with some specific service (for example, calling a cab for you or obtaining difficult-to-get theater tickets). Tip the **valet-parking attendant** $1 every time you get your car.

In restaurants, bars, and nightclubs, tip **service staff** and **bartenders** 15% to 20% of the check, tip **checkroom attendants** $1 per garment, and tip **valet-parking attendants** $1 per vehicle.

As for other service personnel, tip **cab drivers** 15% of the fare; tip **skycaps** at airports at least $1 per bag ($2–$3 if you have a lot of luggage); and tip **hairdressers** and **barbers** 15% to 20%.

For help with tip calculations, currency conversions, and more, download our convenient Travel Tools app for your mobile device. Go to www.frommers.com/go/mobile and click on the Travel Tools icon.

Toilets You won't find public toilets or "restrooms" on the streets in most U.S. cities but they can be found in hotel lobbies, bars, restaurants, museums, department stores, railway and bus stations, and service stations. Large hotels and fast-food restaurants are often the best bet for clean facilities. Restaurants and bars in resorts or heavily visited areas may reserve their restrooms for patrons.

Travelers with Disabilities Almost all public establishments in Chicago, including restaurants, hotels, and museums, provide accessible entrances and other facilities for those with disabilities. All city buses are equipped to accommodate wheelchairs, but not all El stations are accessible (some can be reached only via stairs). Contact the **Chicago Transit Authority (CTA)** at ℂ **312/836-7000** for a list of accessible stations. For more information on facilities for people with disabilities, contact the **Mayor's Office for People with Disabilities,** 121 N. LaSalle St., Room 1104, Chicago, IL 60602 (ℂ **312/744-7050** for voice, or 312/744-4964 for TTY; www.cityofchicago.org/disabilities). The office is staffed from 8:30am to 4:30pm Monday through Friday.

Horizons for the Blind, 2 N. Williams St., Crystal Lake, IL 60014 (ℂ **815/444-8800**), is a social service agency that provides information about local hotels equipped with Braille signage and cultural attractions that offer Braille signage and special tours. The **Illinois Relay Center** enables hearing- and speech-impaired TTY callers to call individuals or businesses without TTYs 24 hours a day. Calls are confidential and billed at regular phone rates. Call TTY at ℂ **800/526-0844** or voice 800/526-0857. The city of Chicago operates a 24-hour information service for hearing-impaired callers with TTY equipment; call ℂ **312/744-8599.**

Visas The U.S. State Department has a **Visa Waiver Program (VWP)** allowing citizens of the following countries to enter the United States without a visa for stays of up to 90 days: Andorra, Australia, Austria, Belgium, Brunei, Czech Republic, Denmark, Estonia, Finland, France, Germany, Greece, Hungary, Iceland, Ireland, Italy, Japan, Latvia, Liechtenstein, Lithuania, Luxembourg, Malta, Monaco, the Netherlands, New Zealand, Norway, Portugal, San Marino, Singapore, Slovakia, Slovenia, South Korea, Spain, Sweden, Switzerland, and the United Kingdom. (**Note:** This list was accurate at press time; for the most up-to-date list of countries in the VWP, consult http://travel.state.gov/visa.)

Even though a visa isn't necessary, in an effort to help U.S. officials check travelers against terror watch lists before they arrive at U.S. borders, visitors from VWP countries must register online through the Electronic System for Travel Authorization (ESTA) before boarding a plane or a boat to the U.S. Travelers must complete an electronic application providing basic personal and travel eligibility information. The Department of Homeland Security recommends filling out the form at least 3 days before traveling. Authorizations will be valid for up to 2 years or until the traveler's passport expires, whichever comes first. Currently, there is a US$14 fee for the online application. Existing ESTA registrations remain valid through their expiration dates. **Note:** Any passport issued on or after October 26, 2006, by a VWP country must be an **e-Passport** for VWP travelers to be eligible to enter the U.S. without a visa. Citizens of these nations also need to present a round-trip air or cruise ticket upon arrival. E-Passports contain computer chips capable of storing biometric information, such as the required digital photograph of the holder. If your passport doesn't have this feature, you can still travel without a visa if the valid passport was issued before October 26, 2005, and includes a machine-readable zone; or if the valid passport was issued between October 26, 2005, and October 25, 2006, and includes a digital photograph. For more information, go to **http://travel.state.gov/visa**. Canadian citizens may enter the United States without visas, but will need to show passports and proof of residence.

Citizens of all other countries must have (1) a valid passport that expires at least 6 months later than the scheduled end of their visit to the U.S.; and (2) a tourist visa.

For information about U.S. visas go to **http://travel.state.gov** and click on "Visas." Or go to one of the following websites:

Australian citizens can obtain up-to-date visa information from the **U.S. Embassy Canberra,** Moonah Place, Yarralumla, ACT 2600 (✆ **02/6214-5600**) or by checking the U.S. Diplomatic Mission's website at **http://canberra.usembassy.gov/visas.html**.

British subjects can obtain up-to-date visa information by calling the **U.S. Embassy Visa Information Line** (✆ **09042-450-100** from within the U.K. at €1.20 per minute; or ✆ **866/382-3589** from within the U.S. at a flat rate of $16, payable by credit card only) or by visiting the "Visas to the U.S." section of the American Embassy London's website at **http://london.usembassy.gov/visas.html**.

Irish citizens can obtain up-to-date visa information through the **U.S. Embassy Dublin,** 42 Elgin Rd., Ballsbridge, Dublin 4 (✆ **1580-47-VISA** [8472] from within the Republic of Ireland at €2.40 per minute; **http://dublin.usembassy.gov**).

Citizens of **New Zealand** can obtain up-to-date visa information by contacting the **U.S. Embassy New Zealand,** 29 Fitzherbert Terrace, Thorndon, Wellington (✆ **644/462-6000; http://newzealand.usembassy.gov**).

Visitor Information Before your trip, check in with the **Chicago Convention & Tourism Bureau** (✆ **877/CHICAGO** [244-2246]; www.choosechicago.com) to find out about upcoming events and travel packages. (They'll also mail you a packet of materials, if you want.) Click the "Maps" link on the right side of the home page for links to maps of Chicago neighborhoods. The **Illinois Bureau of Tourism** (✆ **800/2CONNECT** [226-6632], or 800/406-6418 TTY; www.enjoyillinois.com) will also send you information about Chicago and other Illinois destinations.

Once you're here, you may want to stop by one of the city's two official visitors' centers. The **Chicago Cultural Center,** 77 E. Randolph St. (at Michigan Ave.), once the city's public library, is a beautiful landmark building that's worth a look as you're passing through the Loop. Its visitors' center is open Monday through Friday from 8am to 6pm, Saturday from 9am to 6pm, and Sunday from 10am to 6pm; it's closed on holidays.

The **Chicago Water Works Visitor Center** is in the old pumping station at Michigan and Chicago avenues in the heart of the city's shopping district. The entrance is on the Pearson Street side of the building, across from the Water Tower Place mall. It's open daily from 7:30am to 7pm. This location has the added draw of housing a location of **Hot Tix,** which offers both half-price day-of-performance and full-price tickets to many theater productions around the city, as well as a gift shop.

For more travel planning information, see chapter 1 for a list of the best Chicago websites.

Wi-Fi See "Internet & Wi-Fi," earlier in this section.

INDEX

Accommodations

PHOTO CREDITS

p. i: © Vincent DeWitt; p. iii: © Vincent DeWitt; p. 1: © Vincent DeWitt; p. 2: © Vincent DeWitt; p. 3: © Vincent DeWitt; p. 4: © Vincent DeWitt; p. 5: © Courtesy Park Hyatt; p. 6, left: © Courtesy Charlie Trotter's; p. 6, right: © Vincent DeWitt; p. 7: © Vincent DeWitt; p. 8: © Vincent DeWitt; p. 9: © Vincent DeWitt; p. 10, left: © Vincent DeWitt; p. 10, right: © Vincent DeWitt; p. 11: © Vincent DeWitt; p. 12, top: © Chuck Eckert / age fotostock; p. 12, bottom: © Vincent DeWitt; p. 13: © Vincent DeWitt; p. 14: © Vincent DeWitt; p. 15: © Vincent DeWitt; p. 16: © Jed Jacobsohn/Getty Images; p. 18: © Brian Kersey/UPI/Newscom; p. 22: © Niday Picture Library / Alamy; p. 23: © The Art Archive / Alamy; p. 24: © Julian Wasser/Time & Life Pictures/Getty Images; p. 27, top: © Vincent DeWitt; p. 27, bottom: © Vincent DeWitt; p. 30: © Vincent DeWitt; p. 32: © Everett Collection Inc / Alamy; p. 34, left: © Ric Carter / Alamy; p. 34, right: © AB5 WENN Photos/Newscom; p. 35: © Vincent DeWitt; p. 45: © Vincent DeWitt; p. 46: © Vincent DeWitt; p. 47: © Vincent DeWitt; p. 50: © Vincent DeWitt; p. 53: © Vincent DeWitt; p. 56, top: © Vincent DeWitt; p. 56, bottom: © Michele Falzone / Alamy; p. 57: © Vincent DeWitt; p. 58, left: © Vincent DeWitt; p. 58, right: © Vincent DeWitt; p. 60: © Vincent DeWitt; p. 61: © Vincent DeWitt; p. 62: © Vincent DeWitt; p. 63: © Vincent DeWitt; p. 91: © Vincent DeWitt; p. 101: © Vincent DeWitt; p. 113: © Vincent DeWitt; p. 117: © Vincent DeWitt; p. 150: © Vincent DeWitt; p. 154: © Vincent DeWitt; p. 155: © Vincent DeWitt; p. 156: © Vincent DeWitt; p. 157: © Vincent DeWitt; p. 158, top: © Vincent DeWitt; p. 158, bottom: © Vincent DeWitt; p. 160, top: © Vincent DeWitt; p. 160, bottom left: © Vincent DeWitt; p. 160, bottom right: © Vincent DeWitt; p. 161: © Vincent DeWitt; p. 162, top: © Vincent DeWitt; p. 162, bottom: © Vincent DeWitt; p. 163, top: © Vincent DeWitt; p. 163, bottom: © Vincent DeWitt; p. 164: © Vincent DeWitt; p. 165: © Vincent DeWitt; p. 166: © Vincent DeWitt; p. 167: © James Caulfield from *Louis Sullivan: Creating a New American Architecture,* Courtesy Auditorium Theatre of Roosevelt University; p. 170: © Vincent DeWitt; p. 171, left: © Vincent DeWitt; p. 171, right: © Vincent DeWitt; p. 172: © Vincent DeWitt; p. 174, top: © Vincent DeWitt; p. 174, bottom: © Vincent DeWitt; p. 176: © Vincent DeWitt; p. 177: © Vincent DeWitt; p. 178: © Vincent DeWitt; p. 180: © Vincent DeWitt; p. 181, top: © Vincent DeWitt; p. 181, bottom: © Chuck Place / Alamy; p. 182: © Vincent DeWitt; p. 183: © Vincent DeWitt; p. 184: © Vincent DeWitt; p. 185: © Vincent DeWitt; p. 186: © Vincent DeWitt; p. 187: © Vincent DeWitt; p. 188: © Vincent DeWitt; p. 190: © Vincent DeWitt; p. 192: © Vincent DeWitt; p. 193: © Vincent DeWitt; p. 194: © Vincent DeWitt; p. 195: © Vincent DeWitt; p. 197: © Vincent DeWitt; p. 198: © Vincent DeWitt; p. 199, top: © Vincent DeWitt; p. 199, bottom: © Vincent DeWitt; p. 200: © Vincent DeWitt; p. 201: © Vincent DeWitt; p. 202, top: © Vincent DeWitt; p. 202, bottom: © Vincent DeWitt; p. 203, top: © Vincent DeWitt; p. 203, bottom: © Vincent DeWitt; p. 204: © Vincent DeWitt; p. 206: © Vincent DeWitt; p. 207: © Vincent DeWitt; p. 211: © Vincent DeWitt; p. 212: © Vincent DeWitt; p. 214: © Vincent DeWitt; p. 215, left: © Vincent DeWitt; p. 215, right: © Vincent DeWitt; p. 216: © Vincent DeWitt; p. 217: © Vincent DeWitt; p. 218: © Chuck Eckert / Alamy; p. 220: © Vincent DeWitt; p. 221: © Vincent DeWitt; p. 222: © Vincent DeWitt; p. 224: © Vincent DeWitt; p. 225: © Vincent DeWitt; p. 226: © Vincent DeWitt; p. 228: © Vincent DeWitt; p. 232, top: © Vincent DeWitt; p. 232, bottom: © Vincent DeWitt; p. 233: © Vincent DeWitt; p. 235: © Vincent DeWitt; p. 236: © Vincent DeWitt; p. 240: © Vincent DeWitt; p. 242: © Vincent DeWitt; p. 245: © Vincent DeWitt; p. 247, top: © Vincent DeWitt; p. 247, bottom: © Vincent DeWitt; p. 249: © Vincent DeWitt; p. 250: © Vincent DeWitt; p. 252: © Vincent DeWitt; p. 256: © Vincent DeWitt; p. 258: © Vincent DeWitt; p. 263: © Vincent DeWitt; p. 266: © Vincent DeWitt; p. 273: © Vincent DeWitt; p. 275: © Vincent DeWitt; p. 290: © Vincent DeWitt; p. 294: © Todd Rosenberg/AFP/Getty Images/Newscom; p. 296: © Vincent DeWitt; p. 297:

PHOTO CREDITS

NOTES